# Region, State and Capitalism in Mexico

Nineteenth and Twentieth Centuries

Wil Pansters
Arij Ouweneel (eds.)

# Region, State and Capitalism in Mexico

## Nineteenth and Twentieth Centuries



CEDLA

*A CEDLA Publication*
Centrum voor Studie en Documentatie van Latijns Amerika
Centro de Estudios y Documentación Latinoamericanos
Centro de Estudos e Documentação Latino-Americanos
Centre for Latin American Research and Documentation

Keizersgracht 395-397
1016 EK Amsterdam
The Netherlands / Países Bajos



ISBN 90 70280 61 2


CIP-GEGEVENS KONINKLIJKE BIBLIOTHEEK, DEN HAAG

Region

Region, state and capitalism in Mexico : nineteenth and twentieth centuries / ed. by Wil Pansters and Arij Ouweneel. - Amsterdam : Center for Latin American Research and Documentation (CEDLA). - Ill. - (CEDLA Latin America studies ; 54)
ISBN 90-70280-61-2
SISO am-mexi 337 UDC 32(72)"18/19" NUGI 641
Trefw.: Mexico ; politieke geschiedenis ; 19e eeuw / Mexico ; politieke geschiedenis ; 20e eeuw.

## Table of Contents

## Editors' Acknowledgements

*Whereas historians usually delimit the periods of their research neatly, this volume seeks to examine the parallels between economic and political development in Mexico during the nineteenth and twentieth centuries. Although the topics, regions and periods dealt with in this book are diverse, the closely interrelated themes of capitalist development and political centralization are in varying degrees present in all of the chapters.*

*The authors -historians, sociologists and anthropologists- discussed their work during the annual Workshop of the Interuniversity Centre for Latin American Research and Documentation (CEDLA) held in Amsterdam, June 12 and 13, 1987. We especially want to thank Lorraine Nencel for her great help in organizing the workshop.*

*The publication was made possible through the generous support of CEDLA, Amsterdam, and the Center for Caribbean and Latin American Studies (CARLAS), of the State University of Utrecht. CEDLA sponsored the translation of Romana Falcón's essay; CARLAS sponsored the typing of several other essays and the editing of Wil Pansters' essay. Invaluable linguistic assistance was provided by Simon Miller (who must have lost hours), Jean Carrière, Sheila Gogol, Peter Mason, Frans Schryer, Guy Thomson, and Paul Garner, although all errors remain our responsibility. Finally, we would like to thank Paula Duivenvoorde, Petra Nesselaar, and Virginie Rozemeijer for typing the several versions of the manuscript for this book.*

*Utrecht and Amsterdam, August 11, 1989*

*Wil Pansters and Arij Ouweneel*

# MEXICAN REGIONS

[The numbers refer to the chapters of this book]

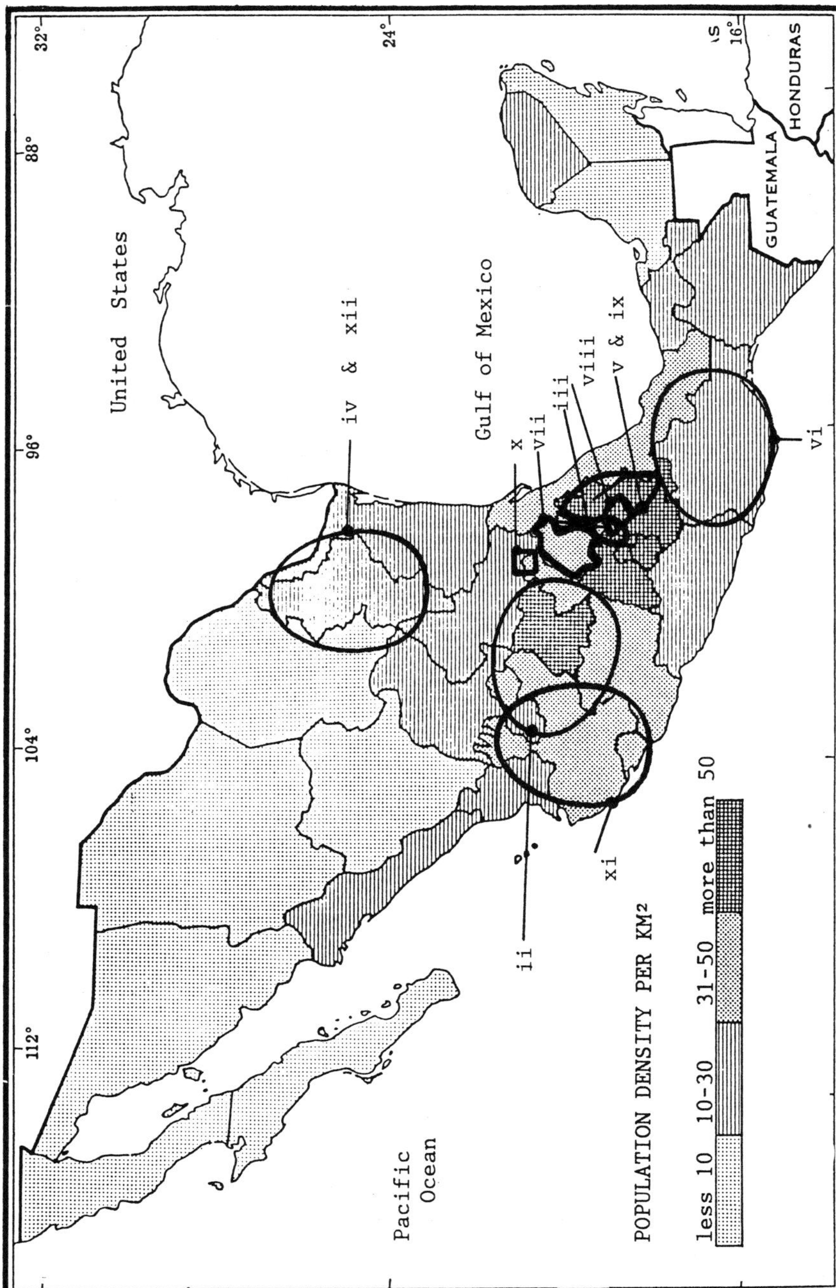

# THE UNITED STATES OF THE MEXICAN REPUBLIC

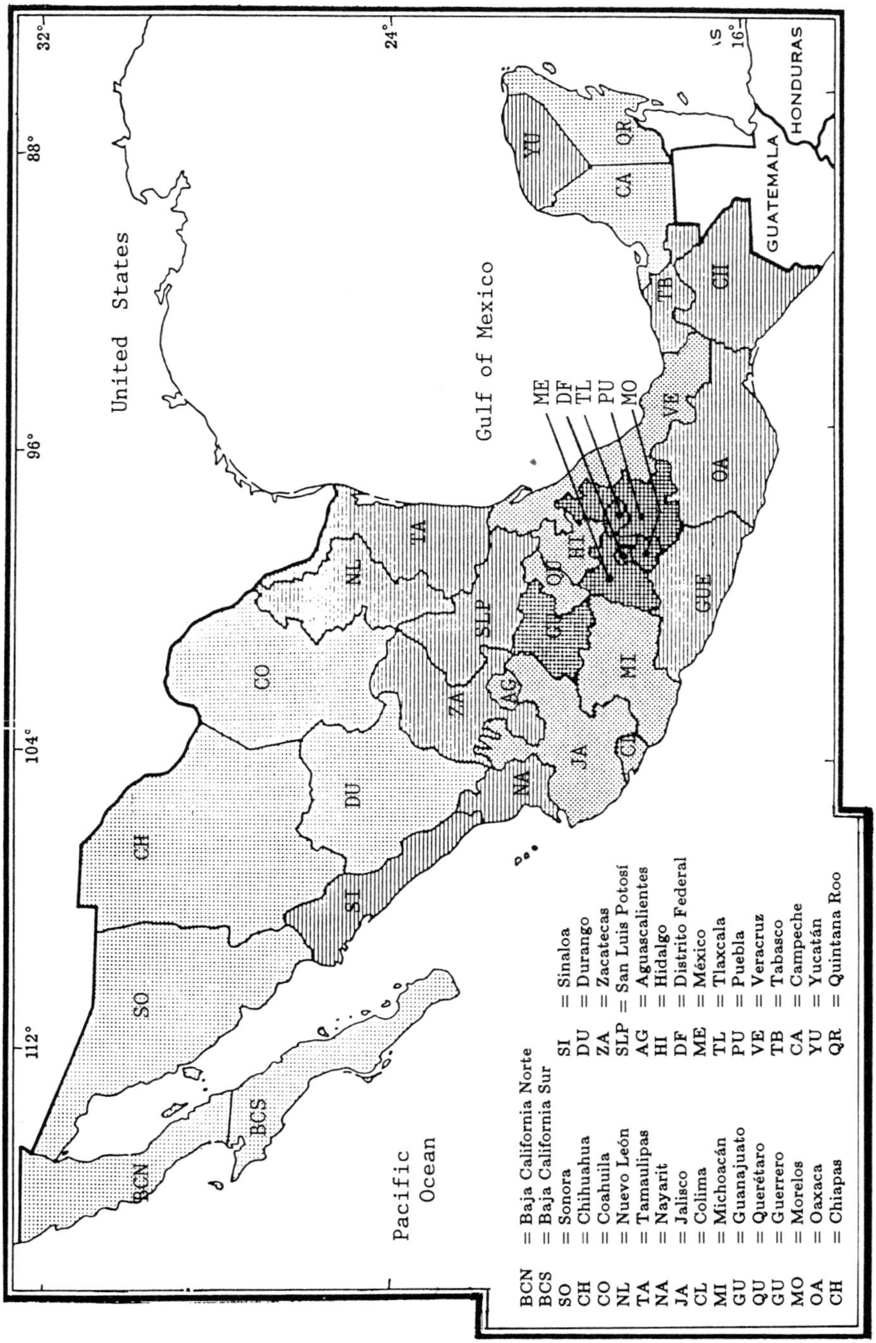

CHAPTER ONE

# Capitalist Development and Political Centralization Before and After the Revolution: An Introduction

ARIJ OUWENEEL AND WIL PANSTERS*

*"I have honoured the republican and democratic principles and I respect them; but in certain specific cases I do not apply them."*

- Ulises Heureaux, 1882 -

## I

Historian Moisés González Navarro must have received the book of François Guerra on the origins of the Mexican Revolution of 1910 with a certain excitement. At last, a modern synthesis of this rebellion! However, after reading it, the historian and leftist political scientist was very much disappointed and wrote a review, entitled: *Un nuevo refuerzo francés a la derecha mexicana.* He was not the only historian to reject Guerra's book; indeed, Alan Knight, himself author of an epic on the Revolution, was even hostile in his review. It is clear that we have to conclude that almost eighty years after its outburst the Mexican Revolution still causes hot polemical debate. It seems that writing on that important period in the country's history is to communicate with the present in Mexico.[1] Social scientists act as if they are actively involved in revolutionary

* - *Ouweneel is Historian, CEDLA, Keizersgracht 397, 1016 EK Amsterdam, The Netherlands;*
- *Pansters is Political Scientist, Center for Caribbean and Latin American Studies, University of Utrecht, Heidelberglaan 2, P. O. Box 80.140, 3508 TC Utrecht, The Netherlands.*

1. Moisés González Navarro, "La guerra y la paz, o un nuevo refuerzo francés a la derecha mexicana," in *Secuencia*, (1987, Jan./Apr.), 57-69. Alan Knight, *The Mexican Revolution. [I. Porfirians, Liberals and Peasants; II. Counter-Revolution and Reconstruction]* (2 Vols. Cambridge, 1986). François-Xavier Guerra, *Le Mexique. De L'Ancien Régime à la Revolution* (Paris, 1985). Guerra attempts to analyze the Díaz regime (1876-1910) within the context of Modern Mexican history. One of the major results of Guerra's study of official papers, debates of the Senate and Chamber of Deputies and the like is the firm critique of Moisés González Navarro's (!) three volumes of statistics of the *Porfiriato*; especially appendix V contains warnings on terminology and statistics [confirmed, by the way, by Jean Meyer in his "Haciendas y ranchos, peones y campesinos en el porfiriato. Algunas falacias estadísticas" in *Historia Mexicana* (hereafter *HMex*), 35 (1986/139), 477-510; as well as by Frank Schenk, "Grondbezit in Mexico, een schets van het district Sultepec in de laat-negentiende eeuw," in *Leidschrift* 3:8 (1987), 71-96]. Knight's critique focuses, correctly by the way, on Guerra's rather cursory attention to English-language sources and archival data. See Alan Knight's review in the *Hispanic American Historical Review* (hereafter *HAHR*), 68 (1988), 139-143, and subsequent debate with Guerra in *HAHR* 69 (1989), 381-388; as well as Brian Hamnett's review in *Boletín de Estudios Latinoamericanos y del Caribe*, 42 (1987), 119-122; and Paul J. Vanderwood, "Resurveying the Mexican Revolution: Three Provocative New Syntheses and Their Shortfalls," in *Mexican Studies/Estudios Mexicanos* (hereafter *MS/EM*), 5:1 (1989), pp. 145-163.

struggles themselves and take positions that do not seem to be very different from the ones in the last days of Porfirio Díaz (1876-1910). It is commonly assumed that in the interaction between theory and practice theories influence the purposive actions of people. For past and present commentators the period is seen as one of action, and theoretical controversy on the Revolution seems to be controversy on the future of Mexico.

The current consensus seems to be that the Díaz epoch marked the full-scale adoption of 'modernization' as a socio-economic goal which provided the basis for post-revolutionary governments, especially after 1940, to accelerate the industrialization and urbanization of Mexico.[2] François Guerra agrees with such an interpretation and views the Revolution as the culmination of a minority liberalism imposed upon the country by means of Díaz' dictatorship. It was the outcome, then, of a basic polarization between the rival values of tradition and modernity; between, on the one hand, family, clan, *pueblos*, *haciendas* and Church, and on the other hand, the modernizing elites in their Bourbon, liberal, neoliberal and revolutionary outfit, grouped in masonic clubs and working class movements. It is not surprising that this author seems to be strongly influenced by the tradition of French historical discourse: he romanticizes banditry and *pueblos* based on 'solidarity', constructs an awkward vision of peonage and ignores valuable English-language sources pointing at hard socioeconomic logic rooted in the struggle for subsistence. Hence, here the revolutionary actors are presented as acting upon a prior *mentalité* and less as the result of material conditions.

According to Guerra the *Porfiriato* was not the last remnant of an agonizing *ancien régime* but rather the culmination of a minority liberalism imposed upon the largely traditional country. The strength of Porfirio Díaz lied in his ability to mediate between the two worlds and to build a compromising network of personal loyalties that incorporated the central modernizing elites and the local traditional elites. The contradictions in the system are easy to detect. While individualism was acclaimed, people were actually ruled by traditional bonds (*caciquismo*), and while political liberalism was recorded in the constitution of 1857, the country drifted towards dictatorship. When, during the late 1890s, power shifted increasingly towards the liberal minorities in Mexico City, represented by a group called the *científicos*, the compromise between Díaz and local, traditional powerholders broke apart. This division within the ranks of the elites was accentuated during the difficult years of social and economic instability that plagued Mexico after 1900. According Guerra, the result was a *refeudalización* of power, very similar to what happened after 1810. Only after years of widespread and heterogeneous conflicts did the reconstruction of a new legitimate political system make a start, in a manner very similar to the first years of Don Porfirio's rule.[3]

Two themes can be deduced from the work of Guerra:

- the difficult articulation between two 'worlds', two different political cultures and ways of social organization;
- the importance of *caciquismo* as the crucial articulatory institution.

Traditional society is seen as stagnant and precapitalist, even 'feudal', while 'modern society' is dynamic and industrial. Behind the notions of modernity and tradition one can easily identify the tensions between the increasingly centralising federal state and the local power structures. This means that one should analyze *caciquismo* in terms of its mediating role between the federal state and the local population.

Alan Knight presents a somewhat different picture of the Revolution. According to him, it started only because Díaz had failed to make effective arrangements for his owm succession. There was no vanguard party taking the lead and expressing a coherent ideology and the Revolution owed almost nothing to external influences. The revo-

2. See Thomas Benjamin and Marcial Ocasio-Meléndez, "Organizing the Memory of Modern Mexico: Porfirian Historiography in Perspective, 1880s-1980s," in *HAHR*, 64 (1984), 323-364.

3. Interview with Guerra in *NEXOS*, 134 (1989), 44.

lutionary process was characterized throughout by an astonishing degree of duplicity, cynicism and an uninhibited recourse to violence, in short, a protracted fight between rival *caudillos*.[4] A Great Rebellion?, Knight wonders. A Revolution!, he answers, at least during the decade after 1910.[5] It was a real Revolution, not only because of the impressive change in leadership whom it elevated to power, but also because it was achieved by recourse to arms on the part of unsophisticated countrymen seeking to remedy what they saw as economic and political oppression. As Runciman correctly praises him, Knight is never disposed to underestimate the deeper reasons for which different groups and categories of Mexicans fought. It did not make much difference that most of these simply followed local *caciques* and not so much a 'revolutionary cause', or, that the Revolution served to settle many personal scores. It was certainly no clash between 'traditional' and 'modern'. The main thing was, according to Knight, that the main villains of the Díaz epoch would not return: the encroaching *hacendado* and the thuggish *jefe político*.

Knight was given a chance to further explain his argument with Guerra in a recent issue of the *Hispanic American Historical Review*. He correctly argues that the economic data Guerra presents, though useful, do not contribute to a rounded socioeconomic interpretation, and disputes Guerra's forthright political interpretation, which seems to aim to refute the old notion of a popular social revolution. Such a refutation is in agreement with the new current of *imaginairism* that sweeps the historical community of France these days; and, indeed, Guerra follows warmheartedly Fûret's mainly political and philosophical interpretation of the French Revolution of 1789. Most historians would agree with Knight's remark that the English and American revolutions involved ideas and patterns which were also globally influential and innovative; and reading Dealy's articles we could add that in the Latin American case the influence of the American revolution perhaps had a much broader impact. The Mexican liberals projected an economic modernization of their country, inspired by global examples of economic development. Adopting an economic interpretation, Knight concludes, the Mexican Revolution went beyond the French, which did not possess such a comparable conscious economic project. The movement against the *ancien régime* in France was directed against a monarchical and aristocratic old regime that was based on remaining feudal structures, whereas the revolutionary movement in late nineteenth and early twentieth century Mexico was directed against a neoliberal dictatorship. The words *ancien régime* can be used here only metaphorically, not for analogical purposes.[6]

Further evidence for Knight's thesis was provided by Tutino's masterly written, and sometimes provocative, book *From Insurrection to Revolution*.[7] Tutino's vision underscores many recently published studies on popular protest: the large-scale rural revolts in Mexico between 1810 and 1940 are seen as products of agrarian grievances occurring in conjunction with popular perceptions of elite or state responsibility for worsening conditions during periods of intra-elite conflict and state breakdown. Although Tutino

4. Knight, *The Mexican Revolution*. See also W. G. Runciman, "Viva Alan Knight," in *London Review of Books*, 9:18 (October 1987), 3, 5.

5. Alan Knight, "The Mexican Revolution: Bourgeois? Nationalist? Or just a 'Great Rebellion'?," in *Bulletin of Latin American Research* (hereafter *BLAR*), 4:2 (1985), pp 1-37.

6. "Communication," in *HAHR* 69 (1989), 381-388 includes a letter from Guerra dated November 7, 1988, answering Knight's review, and a rejoinder by Knight, dated December 16, 1988. Glen C. Dealy shows the enormous influence of the American Constitution in Latin America around 1821-1826 in his "Prolegomena on the Spanish American Political Tradition," in *HAHR*, 48 (1968), 37-58, not cited by Guerra. Compare some interesting articles, that could be used in further analyzing Mexican politics from this point of view, for example, Glen C. Dealy, "The Tradition of Monistic Democracy in Latin America," in *Journal of the History of Ideas* (hereafter *JHId*), 34:4 (1974), 625-646; and, Louisa S. Hoberman, "Hispanic American Political Theory as a Distinct Tradition," in *JHId*, 41:2 (1980), 199-218.

7. John M. Tutino, *From Insurrection to Revolution in Mexico: Social Bases of Agrarian Violence, 1750-1940* (Princeton, 1987).

refers to Scott's formulation, he echoes E. P. Thompson's magnificent *moral economy* thesis.[8] Like other authors, Tutino places, in a basically structuralist and materialist orientation, considerable emphasis on security and autonomy in rural economic and social relationships. The balance that was to be the result of this was extremely disturbed by the agrarian crises of the late nineteenth century and the ensuing political conflicts, which deeply divided the powerholders and permitted rural rebellions to fuel decades of Revolution. The 'pact' between Díaz and the leaders of villages and small towns was broken. The period from 1880 to 1910 brought indeed political stability and commercial expansion, Guerra's 'modernization', but renewed agrarian 'social compression' as well: it brought together population growth and the privatization of village lands which accelerated the rapid loss of autonomy and the forced shift to dependent insecurity across much of Mexico.

But to ascribe the rural rebellions after 1910 simply to agrarian discontent distorts the picture. What took place was mass mobilization under the control of *caudillos*, whose backgrounds and aspirations were frequently at odds with those of their rural followers. In Sonora local chieftains put together a professional army devoid of ties to the agrarian question, in San Luis Potosí the local leader's strong alliance with the national state limited the scope of land reform there, in Guerrero similar local leaders rebelled against the political and economic monopoly of the central state of the *ancien régime*; in other states no significant peasant uprisings occurred and leaders had to *organize* the revolution from above; and besides this, half of the country's dirt farmers, many of them on *haciendas*, sat out the conflict. It was the local leaders, the provincial *caudillos*, who sprang up with Francisco I. Madero.

Both Knight and Guerra might be criticized for neglecting worldwide economic transformation and the role of international capitalism, although Knight in his *HAHR*-letter does acknowledge the influence of global examples of economic development in the liberals' ideology. As John Hart successfully argues, behind the emergence of, for example, the bourgeoisie lies foreign interest: Mexico had become an economic appendage the economy of, above all, the United States of America.[9] Hart's line of argument, which is deliberately Marxist but mainly built on careful primary research in U.S.-Mexican Claims Commission archives, details the penetration on the Mexican patrimony by North American big business. His sweeping and convincing story shows the reader every step of the growth of the railways, the growth of landed interest in North American hands and the domination of the country's financial system. This process alienated segments of society like the *caciques* in the rural areas and the *pequeña burguesía* in most part of the country. The Revolution appears primarily as a movement of national liberation. The importance of the changing shape of international capitalism in the explanation of the Revolution is underscored by an extensive analogical chapter on 'similar' revolutions in other parts of the world, mainly China, Russia and Iran. Hart concludes that if international capitalism with its internal effects stood at the cradle of the Revolution, foreign political and military pressure also proved decisive for its outcome. Massive arms shipments in combination with official United States commitment

8. E. P. Thompson, "The Moral Economy of the English Crowd in the Eighteenth Century," in *Past and Present*, 50 (1971), 71-136; also Harvey J. Kaye, *The British Marxist Historians. An Introductory Analysis* (Cambridge and Oxford, 1984), 167-220. James C. Scott, *The Moral Economy of the Peasant. Rebellion and Subsistence in Southeast Asia* (New Haven and London, 1976). Other titels of interest are: Erick D. Langer, "Labor Strikes and Reciprocity on Chuquisaca Haciendas," in *HAHR*, 65 (1985), 255-278; Arij Ouweneel, *Onderbroken groei in Anáhuac. De ecologische achtergrond van ontwikkeling en armoede in Centraal-Mexico (1730-1810)* (Amsterdam, 1989); Berry Bock, "De sociale positie van de landarbeiders van San Bartolomé de los Tepetates" (Doctoraalscriptie Vrije Universiteit Amsterdam, 1989).

9. John M. Hart, *Revolutionary Mexico: The Coming and Process of the Mexican Revolution* (Berkeley, 1987), esp. 105-162.

to president Carranza eventually secured a victory over more radical groups like the *villistas* and *zapatistas*.

On this issue Knight, Guerra and Tutino would most certainly disagree. Knight dismisses the idea of the Revolution as a nationalistic uprising. Ordinary people sought to turn the tide of capitalist commercialization and whether or not that process was controlled by foreigners seemed of secondary importance. Some support for Hart, however, is provided by Hans Werner Tobler. This author sees the Revolution also as a result of the two-sided process of political and economic modernization during the *Porfiriato* and the crises that came along with it after 1900. Like Hart, he emphasizes the influence of foreign governments and economic pressure groups. But he disagrees entirely with Hart, Knight and Tutino on the events between 1910 and 1920, which are labelled by the anglo-saxon authors as a genuinely popular and, for Knight at least, even a social revolution. Tobler, however, states that despite the broad participation of the masses and the violence of the events, this period does not deserve to be defined as one of social revolution. What the events brought about was the destruction of the old army and the removal of the oligarchy. In other words, the period witnessed a decisive *political transformation*, which proved to be the condition for the great economic and social (*gesellschaftliche*) reforms in the second half of the 1930s. This, finally, gave the Revolution its social character. To label it a social revolution, one has to extend the analysis from 1910 to 1940, including the *cardenista* era of 1934-1940.[10]

The works we have reviewed above differ on periodization, methodology and on the ideological position of the authors. Nevertheless, some general observations can be made. The first one relates to the growing tendency among authors to discuss the Revolution in a longterm perspective. The second observation concerns the breakdown of the Revolution into its regional and local components. Without any doubt, these tendencies have contributed to a re-evaluation of the Revolution as a major historical event. It was a connection of two different periods. Even though Knight has recently gone into war against such a revisionist interpretation, regional and long-term perspectives have shed a new light on the causes and development of the events in Mexico at the beginning of our century.

Long-term regional analysis is not only useful to dissect and refine a heterogeneous process, its causes and consequences, but it also automatically forces the reader to reflect upon the difficult and deepseated tensions between the Mexico's capital city and the regional compounds of the country; between regional and federal power, politics and economics. Historians agree that it is hardly possible to detect a nationally homogeneous historical process. Regional analysts must not limit themselves to differentiating or specifying the historical development after 1821, because the modern history of Mexico *is*, in fact, the history of a process of the building a national state and national economy on the basis of regional power groups. It appears more feasible to identify and explain a set of different regional developments, which would ultimately be linked with the contemporary national state. But this should be done from two points of view: one from the nineteenth century and one from the twentieth, comparing both prelude and aftermath of the Revolution.

10. Hans Werner Tobler, *Die mexikanische Revolution. Gesellschaftlicher Wandel und politischer Umbruch, 1876-1940* (Frankfurt, 1984), 17, 139-140, 367; and, "Die mexikanische Revolution in vergleichender Perspektive. Einige Faktoren revolutionären Wandels in Mexiko, Russland und China im 20. Jahrhundert," in *Ibero-Amerikanisches Archiv*, 14:4 (1988), 453-472.

## II

In a well known essay, James Lockhart sets out to describe the characteristics of a framework of regional analysis.[11] He adopts a rough classification of the Mexican regions as South (Yucatán, Oaxaca, Chiapas), Center (the area from coast to coast according a line from Veracruz to Acapulco), and North (the area not included in the others, consisting of Michoacán, Guanajuato, Querétaro, Jalisco and the large northern states). One wonders if this is correct: has Querétaro, for instance, a state hardly out of sight of Mexico City, more in common with, say, Coahuila than with the state of Mexico? Nevertheless, the intention of this classification was to point to three types of situations common in Spanish America:

- thinly populated areas, with hardly any mobile indigenous population; what is left is a *relatively* strong Spanish penetration, usually interested in cash crops, cattle industry or mining activities (the Mexican North);
- densely populated areas, consisting of both a sedentary indigenous population, as a strong Spanish population (the Mexican Center);
- thinly populated areas, consisting of a mainly sedentary indigenous population, and relatively slow, weak Spanish immigration (the Mexican South).

As Lockhart correctly points out, much of the reason for the spatial distribution of the Europeans goes back to the colonial heritage. The distribution of deposits of silver in the North attracted a lot of Spanish immigrants, although only a minor percentage of all Spanish immigrants really arrived there. The Center was Mexico's largest, most populous, and wealthiest imperial agglomerate. The South was thinly populated, with the exception of the small areas of densely populated highlands of Oaxaca and Chiapas (then a part of Guatemala). There were not many Spaniards congregated so far from the capital of New Spain, and it was hot and unhealthy for them.

But the scheme existed in preconquest times as well. The North was *Chichimeca*-territory, non-sedentary Indians raiding constantly to the Center. The Center and South were the home of relatively well developed sedentary Indians. For the colonial period four regional economies could be identified, using several types of data, from monument-building and the network of overland communications to economic diversification and population density.[12] These four regions were Central-Mexico, Michoacán, Guadalajara and Oaxaca. Van Oss and Slicher spoke of concentric circles, characterized by high levels of population concentration, intensive agriculture, intensive religious and architectural activity, a large variety of professions, etc. As one moved out towards the periphery, population levels declined as did the other criteria. The far north and Yucatán were excluded from both authors' work for lack of data, but can nevertheless be included in the model: the north would seem to be a thinly populated, peripheral area including some minor *oases* like Zacatecas, Saltillo, Parral or Torreón; and Yucatán was only densely populated around Mérida in the northwestern part of the peninsula.

From the articulation of these regional units would emerge the contemporary national state, and with it a centralized political and governmental apparatus, a decidedly national economy, and social classes capable of exercising control on a national scale. But

---

11. James Lockhart, "Introduction," in *Provinces of Early Mexico. Variants of Spanish American Regional Evolution*, Ida Altman and James Lockhart, eds. (Los Angeles, 1976), 3-28.

12. Adriaan C. van Oss, "Architectural Activity, Demography and Economic Diversification: Regional Economies of Colonial Mexico," in *Jahrbuch für Geschichte von Staat, Wirtschaft und Gesellschaft Lateinamerikas* (hereafter *JbLA*), 16 (1979), 53-145; Bernard Slicher van Bath, "Economic Diversification in Spanish America around 1600: Centres, Intermediate Zones and Peripheries," in *JbLA*, 16 (1979), 97-146, "Dos modelos referidos a la relación entre población y economía en Nueva España y Perú durante la época colonial," in *Empresarios, indios y estado. Perfil de la economía mexicana (Siglo XVIII)*, Arij Ouweneel and Cristina Torales Pacheco, comps. (Amsterdam, 1988), 15-44, see especially maps 2, 3 and 4 on pp. 29-31.

this was a painful process, which had hardly begun around 1800. Van Young even calls the economy of the late eighteenth century a *disarticulated economy*, which was the result of the loss of the momentum of the colonial economy during the earlier and middle decades of the eighteenth century.[13] He suggests that under the conditions of inflation and pauperization around 1800, with transport costs remaining relatively high, the relationship between income, consumption, and markets had been set, so that the antecedent regionalization of the Mexican economy became a given. A strong spatial segmentation of the colonial economy was the result and the waning of central power after 1821 accelerated this process even further.

In the nineteenth century, so it seems, Mexican economic and political centralization began from scratch. The country was parceled into regions, which can be analyzed focussing on four fundamental issues:[14]

- the emergence and development of regional power groups, mostly bourgeois, assuming the form of separate social classes during the Díaz era;
- the persistence of clientelism in local politics;
- the formation of a national market due to regional expansion and national politics;
- a rebirth of capitalism (nascent capitalism was already present in the eighteenth century).

At first sight there seems to have been a return to the late colonial development. The interventionist state, the politicized economy, and the family enterprise with its patronage networks were carried over from colonial to modern times.[15] As in colonial times, bankruptcy was common in family enterprises and still speculation was preferred to long-lasting commercial bonds. However, shortly after Independence state finances were strangled, productivity declined, and economic development distorted. Business practices did not provide a consistent income for all family members. The Mexican state experienced a progressive fiscal breakdown between 1821 and 1856, causing a corresponding erosion of the power of central government. A recent study of the public debt in Mexico shows that the generalized failure of commerce, agriculture, and industry in the private sector soon after Independence encouraged the wholesale parasitization of the public sector by private moneylenders called *agiotistas*.[16]

Each region, and a myriad of smaller entities in the West or North as well, viewed the demise of the Spanish empire from its own local perspective. While many ties with the old colonial structure disintegrated, a more constructive process was also underway. Several regional societies, already existing in colonial times, had to decide whether or not to unite as a nation. And, as Tutino has argued, much of the confusion during the early years of the Mexican republic reflected both underlying struggles among local elites and the various attempts to forge them into an enduring national framework, be

13. Eric Van Young, "A modo de conclusión: el siglo paradójico," in *Empresarios, indios y estado*, 206-231.

14. We follow Mario Cerutti, "Recent Contributions and the Relevance of Regional Research for the Second Half of the Nineteenth Century in Mexico" (Paper, Amsterdam, 1987). See also John Womack, *Zapata and the Mexican Revolution* (New York, 1969); Luis González González, *Pueblo en vilo. Microhistoria de San José de Gracia* (Mexico-City, 1968); Gilbert M. Joseph, *Rediscovering the Past at Mexico's Periphery* (Tuscaloosa, Alabama, 1986).

15. Note the striking similarity between the entrepreneurs discussed by, for instance, Cristina Torales Pacheco, "Tradicionalismo y modernidad en el comercio novohispano de la segunda mitad del siglo XVIII: la Compañía de Francisco Ignacio de Yraeta," in *Empresarios, indios y estado*, 59-70; or John M. Tutino, "Creole Mexico: Spanish Elites, Haciendas, and Indian Towns, 1750-1810" (Ph. D. diss. University of Texas, Austin, 1976); and David W. Walker, *Kinship, Business, and Politics: The Martínez del Río Family in Mexico, 1823-1867* (Austin, 1986); or, indeed, William H. Beezley, *Judas at the Jockey Club and Other Episodes of Porfirian Mexico* (Lincoln, 1987).

16. Barbara Tenenbaum, *The Politics of Penury: Debts and Taxes in Mexico, 1821-1856* (Albuquerque, 1986).

it a federal or central state.[17] Of course, as has been suggested by David Walker, the post-Independence breakdown scarred the monied classes of Mexico so badly, that afterwards it was reluctant to take essential entrepreneurial risks. But this problem notwithstanding, many studies of the nineteenth century present data or facts, explicitly or implicitly, from which the tendency toward the formation and expansion of the national market can be inferred. The analysis of the *problématique* of this century, then, must be at the same time political and economic.

## III

Don Porfirio Díaz controlled the destiny of the Mexican nation for a third of a century. It was a vital period in the entire western world; an era of innovation in technology, in political and economic systems, in social values, in artistic expression. Bismarck transformed the German states into a nation, Gladstone introduced England to a new kind of liberalism, the leading powers of Europe partitioned Africa and Asia unto themselves, and Pope Leo XIII enunciated *Rerum Novarum*, proclaiming that employees should be treated more as men than as tools. Most important, however, were that the United States of America emerged as a leading world power. Spain finally lost the last remnants of her once-glorious empire. From 1875 to 1914 the national income of the United Kingdom at fixed prices more than doubled and the national income per capita increased by 60 percent and the national income per capita of those working in both Germany and the United States about doubled. Technological change, which was the primary source of economic growth, proceeded at an accelerated pace. The reciprocating steam engine, which was the prime mover of early machines for industry and transportation, began already to give way to electric and internal combustion engines. Science was at a threshold of becoming the handmaiden to industry, the chemist's laboratory replacing the machinist's workshop as the primary site of new product development. At the beginning of the Industrial Revolution, change took place primarily in a triangle with apexes in England, Belgium and Northern France, but later on it spread to Germany, Bohemia, Austria, Northern Italy, New England and the Middle Atlantic of the United States, and finally it reached Mexico, where Porfirio Díaz was by then an aged person. And everyone awaited his resignation.[18] The kaleidoscopic, often turbulent story of regional development in Mexico during Don Porfirio's reign is intriguing, though still somewhat incompletely told, and hotly debated, in both academic and political circles. We will try to sketch it out briefly, following the regional model outlined above. We will start in the northern regions of Mexico, going south, ending in Yucatán.

The northern states of Coahuila, Chihuahua, Durango, Nuevo León, Sinaloa, Sonora, and Tamaulipas played a prominent role during the Revolution. These thinly populated

17. John Tutino, "Regional Diversity and National Unity in the Era of Mexican Independence," in *Latin American Research Review* (hereafter *LARR*), 15:1 (1980), 225-230.

18. Michael C. Meyer and William L. Sherman, *The Course of Mexican History* (New York & Oxford, 1979), 431; Shepard B. Clough and Richard T. Rapp, *European Economic History. The Economic Development of Western Civilization* (3rd. ed., Tokyo and Auckland, 1975), 381-382. *Other Mexicos: Essays on Regional Mexican History, 1876-1911*, T. Benjamin and W. McNellie, eds. (Albuquerque, 1984). See also: *Caudillo and Peasant in the Mexican Revolution*, D. A. Brading, ed. (Cambridge, 1980); *Mexico: From Independence to Revolution, 1810-1910*, W. Dirk Raat, ed. (Lincoln, 1982); *Después de los latifundios*, Heriberto Moreno García, ed. (Zamora, 1982); *Formación y desarrollo de la burguesía en México: siglo XIX*, Ciro Cardoso et.al. (Mexico City, 1978); *Riot, Rebellion, and Revolution: Rural Social Conflict in Mexico*, Friedrich Katz, ed. (Princeton, 1988).

states experienced their first unprecedented population growth in the era of Porfirio Díaz and later on again in the middle decades of the twentieth century. In most of the states population was doubling between about 1860 and about 1900, sometimes even tripling.[19] Growth figures here were almost the highest of all Mexico in those days. This is the more surprising, since the region is one of the driest of Mexico, hardly useful for sustaining an agrarian economy. As such it must be considered a frontier zone in expansion, peripheral in every sense, which underwent sudden and dramatic transformation after about 1880, especially caused by the completion of rail links with central Mexico and the United States in the 1880s. This brought rapid development in mining, stock grazing, and where irrigation permitted, cotton cultivation and other agriculture. Some studies emphasize the scale of change which took place in these areas during the *Porfiriato*, accentuating the relative brevity of the period. Mark Wasserman and Charles Harris show in monographs on Chihuahua how the combined impact of military campaigns, the sporadic but severe attacks of the Apaches, and prolonged drought devastated the area's economy off and on until Don Porfirio's seizure of power. The Laguna was underdeveloped and largely uninhabited, known for little more than its location, barren desert, and erratic water supply. The Yaqui Indians in Sonora were successful in resisting the loss of land and water rights to private landholders, and although the centers of production and the working population were concentrated in mining camps, *haciendas* and ranches, there were substantial numbers of Indians who adamantly refused to volunteer for the rural proletariat.[20]

But much changed in the later decades of the century, when the northern provinces were suddenly incorporated into growing export economies. The peopling of the region resulted from migration from other overpopulated regions, a mass movement stimulated by the promises of work and higher earnings. Several great enterprises were born in the region. Wasserman concentrates a large part of his attention on the careers and accomplishments of one of the most successful entrepreneurial Porfirian families: the Terrazas-Creel clan of Chihuahua. The family emerged from relatively humble origins to a preeminence of political power and economic fortune, which rested on foreign markets for cattle and minerals. Wasserman's account is replete with the detail of how Terrazas manoeuvred within the factionalism of Chihuahua politics to transcend such internal divisions, thereby securing a real measure of political independence from the central authority in Mexico City, as well as economic autonomy from his capitalist

19. Viviane Brachet, *La población de los estados mexicanos (1824-1895)* (Mexico City, 1976).

20. The nineteenth century is certainly no longer the 'forgotten century', for many recent studies outline its basic development trends from social, economic and political points of view. On the northern peripheries: John H. Coatsworth, *Growth Against Development: The Economic Impact of Railroads in Porfirian Mexico* (DeKalb, 1981); Charles Harris III, *A Mexican Family Empire: The Latifundio of the Sánchez-Navarros, 1765-1867* (Austin, 1975); Mark Wasserman, *Capitalists, Caciques, and Revolution* (Chapel Hill, 1984); Jane Dale Lloyd, *El proceso de modernización capitalista en el noroeste de Chihuahua (1880-1910)* (Mexico City, 1987); William K. Meyers, "Politics, Vested Rights, and Economic Growth in Porfirian Mexico: The Company Tlahualilo in the Comarca Lagunera, 1885-1911," in *HAHR*, 57 (1977), 425-454; María del Carmen Velázquez, *Cuentas de sirvientes de tres haciendas y sus anexas del Fondo Piadoso de las Misiones de las Californias* (Mexico City, 1983); María Vargas-Lobsinger, *La hacienda de 'La Concha': una empresa algodonera de la Laguna, 1883-1917* (Mexico City, 1984); Manuel Plana, *Il regno del cotone in Messico: La struttura agraria de La Laguna, 1855-1910* (Milan, 1984); Fernando Rello, *State and Peasantry in Mexico: A Case Study of Rural Credit in La Laguna* (Geneva, 1987); *Monterrey, Nuevo León, El Noreste: Siete estudios históricos*, coordinated by Mario Cerutti (Monterrey, 1987); Stuart F. Voss, *On the Periphery of Nineteenth-Century Mexico: Sonora and Sinaloa, 1810-1877* (Tucson, 1982); Ramón Eduardo Ruíz, *The People of Sonora and Yankee Capitalists* (Tucson, 1988); Evelyn Hu-DeHart, *Yaqui Resistance and Survival: The Struggle for Land and Autonomy, 1821-1910* (Madison, 1984); Steven E. Sanderson, *Agrarian Populism and the Mexican State: The Struggle for Land in Sonora* (Berkeley, 1981); Manuel A. Machado, Jr., *The North Mexican Cattle Industry, 1910-1975: Ideology, Conflict, and Change* (Austin College Station, 1981); Knight, *Mexican Revolution*, I, passim.

partners across the border. It is interesting to note that at the state level every family head in the region who had enjoyed political power (such as the Maderos in Coahuila) was displaced by Don Porfirio to make way for his clients, but that the Terrazas could maintain their positions. Political power enabled the family to extend the landed property at very low cost, and helped the Terrazas to diversify and consolidate their economic empires. This is typical of Porfirian politics in which Díaz's appointees were given the opportunities to use their political offices to enrich themselves and others were paid off by being allowed to thrive economically. Such typicalities give the Porfirian state a quite 'colonial' outlook.

One of the significant consequences of development in the northeastern states was the emergence of a regional bourgeoisie in the city of Monterrey. **Mario Cerutti** argues, in his essay published in this volume, that the rise and growth of this bourgeoisie was intertwined with three processes: primitive accumulation of capital as a consequence of the growth of trade with the United States, the transfer of this capital toward capitalist production, benefiting from the conditions created by the *Porfiriato*, and the outburst of industrialization. The group started as commercial traders, but were transformed during the *Porfiriato* into a group of agrarian producers -the cotton production of La Laguna- and later on into industrial producers. Following growing international trade possibilities and the growth of the internal market, already in 1908 industry had largely displaced the agricultural sector from the vanguard position it had up to 1885. Cerutti shows that the Porfirian order had effectively accompanied this process, stimulating capitalist development, and Díaz's 'national state' was embraced by the Monterrey bourgeois without major reservations. The industrial base of this empresarial bourgeoisie allowed it to weather the turmoils of the Revolution with skill and flexibility.

In Sonora capitalist development exacerbated conflicts, created an ambitious middle-class, while organizing labor, mainly miners. New social climbers, so it appears, spawned by several decades of capitalistic growth saw their visions of further advancement shattered and so in frustration they later turned to open rebellion against the very system which had decidedly favoured them before. During the Revolution they were joined by other dissatisfied elements like unemployed miners, Indians dispossessed of their lands, and proletarians demanding better pay and working conditions. Curiously, also involved were *hacendados* angry at Díaz's policy of deporting supposedly rebellious Yaqui Indians to Yucatán who happened to be their peons. In the Laguna the railroads opened national and international markets, causing a shift to cotton production, and leading to disputes over land and water rights between the cotton producers and villagers and *rancheros* already present in the district. The vast majority of the inhabitants of the Laguna were estate dependents, mostly tenants, sharecroppers and labourers; immigrants attracted by the cotton boom; a growth from 20,000 in 1880 to 200,000 in 1910. In Chihuahua agrarian tensions escalated when estate development assaulted the rights of the *ranchero* immigrants, who had arrived there recently, backed by the local state government. Under Terrazas family rule a municipal land law was passed that legally denied the right of *ranchero* settlements. The inhabitants of these settlements saw their autonomy threatened by actions of a government led by the largest landowners in the region. The depression of 1907-1909 is depicted as a major impetus toward the revolution, for, although the lower classes had previously benefited through working on estates and by serving as transporters, unemployment now became widespread as different parts of the economy shrank simultaneously. At the same time scarcities because of crop failures after severe droughts pushed social grievances to a peak. Nationalism and hostility toward the elite increased as foreigners and the wealthy weathered the economic setback better than other groups did.[21] Concluding that, on the

21. See Tutino, *From Insurrection to Revolution*, 297-305; Wasserman, *Capitalists*, 104-112; Friedrich Katz, *The Secret War in Mexico: Europe, the United States, and the Mexican Revolution* (Chicago, 1981), 8-9, 12-14; Vargas-Lobsinger, *Hacienda*, 56-58, 86-87, 122, 130.

northern fringes of Mexico capitalism created wealth and poverty, is forcing an open door.

The region around Guadalajara, consisting of the states of Aguascalientes, Colima, Jalisco and Zacatecas had rates of population growth that were much lower than the northern states. Of the major geographic regions of New Spain at the close of the colonial period, Michoacán and Guadalajara are often cited as being among the most dynamic economically, displaying the characteristics of strong regional autarchy.[22] Van Young has done some recasting and analysis of data developed in a statistical treatise of about 1850. It reveals a large degree of homogeneity in the regional commercial network. Of the approximately twenty small towns covered in the survey, an average of about 65 percent were small retail establishments, with the service and artisan-retail types dividing up the remainder.[23] Despite increasing agricultural commercialization and rural proletarization, this region sustained a remarkably complex agrarian structure in those days, including a large group of *rancheros*. The markets here were of a very limited geographic range, the level of regional export for agricultural commodities was low and there was an overall low level of exchange with other regions. In fact, only cattle was exported.

There is so much emphasis on the *rancheros* in modern historiography that we almost forget that many *hacendados* were also living in the region of Guadalajara. As **Simon Miller**, for Guadalajara (Jalisco) and Michoacán (The Bajío), and **Ricardo Rendón**, for central highland *hacendados*, in their essays in this volume argue, these *hacendados* were 'modern' entrepreneurs, not feudal lords. Capitalist agriculture was not an easy task though, for Mexico was known for its variable soils, unreliable rainfall and enormous transport problems: its dramatic terrain was hardly open to easy communication. Nevertheless, Miller and Rendón show that *hacendados* administered profitable, bourgeois enterprises. They were not absentee *seigneurs*, but were applying themselves assiduously to the business of estate administration, willing to reduce production costs and raising levels of productivity. Miller stresses that these kinds of strategies were not merely limited to the adoption of bourgeois attitudes to production, but that they were also translated into another essential bourgeois attribute: investment.

During the nineteenth century the region saw a lot of rebellions come and go and several villages and *ranchero*-settlements, especially those in the *Altos de Jalisco* northeast of the city of Guadalajara, maintained their subordination for years. It was also a region of bandits who sometimes participated in local insurrections. Upland sections became famous as districts of *rancheros* during the nineteenth century, where landed elites, who could either let their lands to poor sharecroppers or sell off their estates in fractions, saw the decline of the *hacienda* and the triumph of *rancheros*. Estate production was turned over to many tenants and these, like the sharecroppers in the northern states, gained some autonomy at the costs of persisting insecurities. Interesting enough, as early as the 1820s the local state government proposed the abolition of peasant community landholding (the *desamortización*). Liberalism was obviously very strong in this region. Although much village land was officially privatized, the measure created enough disruptions to delay the process for decades.[24]

The region of Michoacán, the third region, consisted of the states of Guanajuato, Michoacán, Querétaro, and San Luis Potosí. The rates of population growth here were somewhat higher than in neighbouring Guadalajara, but the number of inhabitants per square kilometer was much more elevated, especially in Guanajuato. However, no industrialization comparable with that in Monterrey or Guadalajara took place. As is

22. See Van Young, "A modo de conclusión," 217-221.

23. Van Young, "A modo de conclusión," 218, also in his "Rural Life in Eighteenth-Century Mexico: The Guadalajara Region, 1675-1820" (Ph. D. diss., University of California, Berkeley, 1978), passim.

24. Tutino, *From Insurrection to Revolution*, 167-174, 193-194, 239, 316-317; Jean Meyer, *Esperando a Lozada* (Zamora, 1984); Knight, *Mexican Revolution*, I, passim.

shown by González, Brading, Miller and Tutino, in Michoacán *ranchero* societies flourished from the eighteenth century in formerly little-populated regions, which were hardly integrated in the colonial system. The integration of the *rancheros* was a typical nineteenth-century phenomenon. As in Guadalajara, the *ranchero*-communities were settled as tenants or owners on large, but poorly developed, estates and expanded through both local population growth and immigration from the nearby highlands. In this region, there is no evidence that the *Porfiriato* witnessed any concentration of landownership in the hands of landlords. Estate ownership became increasingly unstable in times of financial constraints and weak markets and elites turned over their lands in order to gain at least some income. After 1880, sharecropping was the primary means of cultivating maize on estate lands, a system which would provoke agrarian grievances as soon as elites tried to press more demands upon their tenants. Tutino rightly concludes that the result of the expansion of tenant production was a system of social relations of dependent insecurity.[25]

It will be clear that there were not many Indian villages in Michoacán. But the ones that existed since colonial times were confronted by difficulties in the second part of the nineteenth century. After 1856 local politicians had to decide whether to execute the *Ley Lerdo* or not. As is known by now, the implementation of the law was skillfully delayed by local politicians, under strong political pressure of *caciques* and other village leaders. The privatization of lands held by a village called Churumuco, for example, had to wait first until 1868, when liberal state officials began to press local leaders to implement the law, and then until 1878 because local leaders managed to delay the process for another ten years. In the end, over 200 local residents received titles to community lands, but conflicts between villagers, that had been present since 1872 when a village minority had started to support liberal state officials, were endemic right into the twentieth century. In the village of Tamazunchale, and some surrounding villages in San Luis Potosí, a long and violent uprising from 1876 to 1883 impeded privatization as well. The government of Porfirio Díaz began to discuss it only in 1894, emphasizing that privatization would not cause the loss of lands among villagers. When this advice was ignored by local officials, Díaz imposed a *desamortización* that left the lands in the hands of the villagers. After 1900, being aware of the fact that the *Ley Lerdo* had been a pretext for the expropriation of village lands all over the country, Díaz amended it to allow non-Church corporations to hold lands. On the other hand, it has long been assumed that the Indian villages had lost their lands because of the 1883 law on the *compañías deslindadores* (land surveying companies), which authorized the federal government to hire these companies to survey public lands. For these companies would be granted one-third of these lands, they are said to ride roughshod over the villages' land rights. This conclusion, which can be found in almost all main textbooks, has been sharply disputed recently by several authors. One of these, Robert Holden, was the first scholar to examine surveying companies' records. He has studied six Mexican states and concluded that despite some flagrant cases of expropriations of village lands, the villagers successfully opposed the companies' claims. They were even backed by local authorities, who forced the companies' to respect village communal landholding.[26] On the basis of this kind of research, we think it is safe to assume that

25. Tutino, *From Insurrection to Revolution*, 227-230, 239-240, 242-246; González, *Pueblo en vilo*, 64-113; David A. Brading, *Haciendas and Ranchos in the Mexican Bajío: León, 1680-1860* (Cambridge, 1978), 148-173; Simon Miller, "The Mexican Hacienda between the Insurgency and the Revolution: Maize Production and Commercial Triumph on the *Temporal*," in *Journal of Latin American Studies* (hereafter *JLAS*), 16:2 (1984), 309-336; Knight, *Mexican Revolution*, I, 97-102, 122, 131-133, 145, 161, 199, 206, 210-214, 219-221, 231, 237-239, 241, 245, 250, 259-261, 270, 281, 299-300, 349-352, 355-360, 364, 384, 402-403, 446, 461, 463, 467-469, 472.

26. Gerardo Sánchez Díaz, "La transformación de un régimen de propiedad en un pueblo: conflictos agrarios en Churumuco, 1869-1900," in *Después de los latifundios*, 63-78; Donald F. Stevens, "Agrarian Policy and Instability in Porfirian Mexico," in *The Americas*, 39:2 (1982), 153-166.

within a few decades from now the old thesis of the loss of the village lands will be strongly rejected as nothing but a myth.

The region of Central-Mexico consisted mainly of the central highlands and its *faldas*. Included are the states of Mexico, Hidalgo and Morelos (for a longtime one single state), Tlaxcala and Puebla. The states of Guerrero (formed in 1857 with provinces from Mexico, Puebla and Michoacán) and Veracruz may also be included in this regional entity. Growth rates of population were high only in coastal Veracruz and the tiny state of Tlaxcala; elsewhere population growth was moderate. It was predominantly an *Indian* region, although one could find the big cities of Mexico City and Puebla there as well. The central highlands had experienced a different development than the surrounding *faldas*. In contrast with the western and northern states, there were hardly any *rancheros* to be found in the highlands. It was Indian in the sense of its colonial heritage: the existing Indian villages, the *pueblos de indios* belonging to the *República de Indios* of the colonial period. It had been a quiet region, in which the subsistence of the poor was provided by the Spanish state, merchants and *hacendados*, and above all, of course, by the villagers themselves, who knew how to handle the Spanish economic and political system.[27]

As Tutino correctly notes, in 1848, for the *first time* since Spanish conquest, widespread agrarian uprisings developed across the communities of the central highlands directed against the landed elites and their state. In Chalco, a district just to the southeast of Mexico City and subject of an intriguing study by Tutino, the elites had faced repeated problems in financing their estate operations, but after the war with the United States they were able to seek new means of reviving this. They built new irrigation systems, they experimented with seeds to increase production, and they tried new products like dairying. These innovations provided chances for the expansion of estate revenues, but, as one could expect, they led to confrontations with the villagers in the district, where, because of population growth, good cultivable land had become increasingly scarce. A new phenomenon had occurred: elites claimed village lands. At first, by going to court the villagers responded according to the colonial heritage. But, contrary to their Spanish predecessors, the courts repeatedly backed elite claims. Several years of lengthy protests, strikes, obstructions, violent damages and open revolts were the obvious result. In 1849 the state of Mexico declared the end of community property rights, the *pueblos de indios* would cease to exist.

However, the state lacked the power to implement the *Ley Lerdo*. It was torn apart by the civil war and the French invasion. As in Michoacán, the village leaders and local *caciques* were able to postpone the process of *desamortización* for decades. A new sequence of rebellion in Chalco in 1868 brought villagers to demand the redistribution of estate holdings. An impressive army was necessary to defeat a nascent guerrilla-gang. The army was immediately sent to put down the rebellions that had followed in the Valley of Mezquital, state of Hidalgo, and several districts elsewhere on the *altiplano*. In non-rebellious communities the privatization began in the 1870s. According to Tutino in the state of Mexico, in 1870 about 65,000 claimants of village lands around Zumpango, Tenango del Valle and Tenancingo obtained titles, worth nearly 1,000,000

Also: Tutino, *From Insurrection to Revolution*, 273. Robert Holden, "The Mexican State Manages Modernization: The Survey of the Public Lands in Six States 1876-1911" (Ph.D. diss., University of Chicago, 1986). See also Friedrich Katz, "Rural Rebellions after 1810," in *Riot, Rebellion, and Revolution*, 521-560, esp. note 16 pp. 534-535.

27. Ouweneel, *Onderbroken groei in Anáhuac*, passim. On the nineteenth and twentieth-century in the region of Central-Mexico, among other studies: Tutino, *From Insurrection to Revolution*, 254-258, 264, 271-273, 312-325, 336-342, 361; Moisés González Navarro, *Anatomía del poder en México, 1848-1853* (Mexico City, 1977); Margarita Menegus Bornemann, "Ocoyoacac: Una comunidad agraria en el siglo XIX," in *Estudios Políticos*, 5:18-19 (1979), 81-112; Leticia Reina, *Las rebeliones campesinas en México, 1819-1906* (Mexico City, 1980), 61-63, 124-126, 157-177; Knight, *Mexican Revolution*, I, passim.

*pesos*. But the majority of community properties were not privatized until after 1885, or even perhaps 1894, in a period when the Díaz regime was increasingly successful in preventing rural protests by force or by negotiations with local village leaders, as happened in Michoacán. Village inhabitants increasingly lived as dependents of landed elites, facing the loss of autonomy and a rapid shift to dependent insecurity: a good reason to join agrarian revolt.

During the late nineteenth century, the village economy in the southern parts of Tlaxcala had faced rapid changes: overpopulation had made economic development possible, in which home manufacturing -even industrial labor- and subsistence agriculture coincided. This is, of course, not a reason for revolutionary upheaval -on the contrary!-, but if living conditions are rapidly deteriorating, the subsequent development of dependent relationships with the elites are reasons for upheaval. For example, there was a growing annoyance among peasants about the policies of governor Prospero Cahuantzi, who controlled the state for more than 25 years as a local *cacicazgo* and was loosing legitimacy during years of crisis. As Buve shows, unemployment during the crises of industrial development in southern Tlaxcala and Puebla, the consequences of the *desamortización*, and the decision to tax ownership of land shortly after 1900 -years of crises!- were part of this.[28]

The central highlands can not be properly understood without discussing the influence of the *faldas*, the surrounding mountainous districts in Guerrero, Morelos, southern and northern Puebla, Veracruz and northern Hidalgo. In contrast to the highlands, the *faldas* were *indígena* districts with strong *ranchero* and *cacique* influences. **Guy Thomson** traces, meticulously, the origins of *Montaña* power groups in Puebla -originating from what we would like to call the *faldas*- in contrast to *Llanura* power groups, living on the altiplano. With Díaz accession to the presidency, *Montaña* leaders, who were loyal *porfiristas* since 1862, assumed control of state politics, until during the late 1880s they were united with the *Llanura* groups -who had held state power between 1867 and 1876. His description of local politics and rivalries has a wider resonance when one thinks of the protracted conflicts between the landed interests of central Jalisco and the peasant forces in the *Altos* or the challenges similar landed groups in the central areas of Michoacán faced from rebellions in their mountain districts, as discussed above. The parties did not remain anonymous, as is shown by Wil Pansters: the *Montaña* influence on state politics would grow to a powerful *cacicazgo* of the Avila Camacho family from the same *Sierra Norte*, who assumed governorship, ruled state politics in Puebla and even accessed to the national presidency.

By 1800, the *indígena* districts in the *faldas* were not altogether Indian anymore, but a zone of immigration for Spaniards, *mestizos*, and Indians from overpopulated highlands. Censuses reveal an impressive increase in the number of *rancheros*, cattle *estancias* and small sugar mills. Thomson defines a broad spectrum of grievances among both the non-Indian and Indian population, not much different from the ones that were behind the rebellions in Papantla between 1836-1838. Economic and political development supported centralist interests, *Llanura* in Thomson's words, and by the time *Montaña* leaders took up state government in Puebla the economic and political equilibrium had shifted to the central plateau. Over the first decade of the twentieth century the *Sierra Norte* slumbered in a complacent *caciquismo*. It had, in fact, been divided into two *cacicazgos*, one controlled by the Márquez-Galindo brothers, an old liberal family of *rancheros*, and the other led by General Juan Francisco Lucas. Lucas died in 1917 and the Márquez brothers, who were seen as a threat to the development of the federal state, were assassinated a few weeks later, in an act of unprecedented violence and thoroughness. According to Thomson it was the beginning of a different

28. Raymond Buve, "Peasant Movements, *Caudillos*, and Landreform during the Revolution (1910-1917) in Tlaxcala, Mexico," in *Boletín de Estudios Latinoamericanos y del Caribe*, 18 (1975), 112-154, esp. 122-128.

kind of *caciquismo* in the *Sierra*, which would play a vital role in Puebla politics through until the twentieth century; that of Maximino Avila Camacho, a harsh and ruthless *caudillo militar*, who did not hesitate to eradicate every form of opposition to his policy.

The southern part of the country forms just another face of the *Porfiriato*. It remained badly connected with the rest of the Republic. Agricultural commercialization promoted the rise of isolated plantation economies, which were characterized by a complete dependence on international markets. In the Soconusco area of Chiapas export oriented coffee production came off the ground after Díaz had taken steps to colonize the area. Here it was German entrepreneurs, backed by commercial and financial companies in their homeland, who came to monopolize export business. The proletarianization of former villagers was the result of the rise of coffee prices and the expansion of plantation acreage at the cost of local food production.[29] The case of Yucatán is even more eloquent. The development of the region is relatively well known. Until the opening of Mexico by railways and motorcars the region of Yucatán was virtually an island. This region was a very thinly populated region. The population growth between 1860 and 1895 was quite moderate. Gilbert Joseph has noted the boom in Yucatecan historiography by Mexican and non-Mexican historians and social scientists in recent years. He emphasizes that the henequén production has received significantly more attention than any other aspect of the region's modern past. This development caused the emergence of an agro-commercial bourgeoisie, dominated by a small number of families, called the *Casta Divina*, not much different from the Terrazas-Creel clan of Chihuahua. One man, Olegario Molina, controlled vital sources of economic power, like transport and marketing, because of his excellent contacts with North American cordage manufacturers. As a consequence of the henequén boom peasants were driven off their lands and turned into labourers, working under harsh conditions. According to Joseph, a *de facto* slave society came into existence. And as Wells shows, the ultimate beneficiaries were Olegario Molina and International Harvester, leaving the rest of those involved, owners and workers alike, very much at the mercy of 'boom and bust' economic cycles.[30]

At the end of the *Porfiriato* the contours of a national state had become visible as regional powerholders clearly gave way to centralised power and railroads penetrated the vast territory, making military control more easy and effective. Don Porfirio's policies certainly enhanced political centralization and economic growth. Yet, as Guerra has argued, while Díaz marginalized regional *caciques*, he replaced them with his own men -like Rosendo Márquez and Mucio Martínez in the state of Puebla- and thus keeping the political structure essentially personalistic. Furthermore, economic expansion had quite different effects in different parts of the country. As Thomas Benjamin concludes: *"Díaz's Mexico had repressed but not supplanted its many selves."*[31]

29. Daniela Spenser, "Soconusco: The Formation of a Coffee Economy in Chiapas," in *Other Mexicos*, 123-143. On Chiapas one could consult Robert Wasserstrom, *Class and Society in Central Chiapas* (Berkeley, 1983); Fernando Alvarez, "Peasant Movements in Chiapas," in *BLAR*, 7:2 (1988), 277-298; and, Neil Harvey, "Personal Networks and Strategic Choices in the Formation of an Independent Peasant Organization: The OCEZ of Chiapas, Mexico," in *BLAR*, 7:2 (1988), 299-312.

30. On Yucatán we have used: Francisco Paoli and Enrique Montalvo, *El socialismo olvidado de Yucatán* (Mexico City, 1977); Gilbert M. Joseph, *Revolution from Without. Yucatán, Mexico and the United States, 1880-1924* (Durham, 1988), and this author's *Rediscovering*; Allen Wells, *Yucatán's Gilded Age* (Albuquerque, 1985).

31. Quote from Benjamin's introduction of *Other Mexicos*, 13.

## IV

It can be no wonder that by the time the Revolution came around it was a heterogeneous uprising, linked to the specificities of local and regional societies. The 'Many Mexicos' revolted for an equal amount of many reasons. The result was, as indicated by Guerra, a *refeudalización* of power. It was not until armies from the northern states had managed to control power and their leaders to become dominant on the national political level, that a process of national reconstruction could begin in the 1920s. The governments led by the northerners, the so-called *Sonorenses* (1920-1934), were characterized by the still precarious equilibrium between central state authority and traditional regional power groups. The *Sonorenses* intended to fortify the central state while relying on regional strongbosses, especially during times of rebellion. This makes the period between 1920 and 1934 one of transition from regional autonomies to centralized bureaucratic control. Several military and popular uprisings occurred during this period, which sometimes helped to crush regional power groups and fortified others. Finally, some economic integration returned, and with it a political, social and economic situation that looks not much different from the one during the last years of the *Porfiriato*. But again, like during the *Porfiriato*, there were enormous regional differences.

The development outlined above is well illustrated by the example of the Carreras, the Cedillos, the Santos and many others in San Luis Potosí.[32] Their roots can be found in the *Porfiriato*, when it was, again, a typical *ranchero* region; already in the 1820s over 40 percent of estate crops were raised by tenants. The economic and political integration of the state with the rest of the country and the United States was achieved by the investments in the railways. However, in 1910 still 80 percent of the inhabitants lived in the poverty stricken countryside. No wonder, agrarian struggles predominated here, but they did not only revolve around simple demands for the restitution of land. As elsewhere in Michoacán or Guadalajara, the absence of a vigorous network of centuries-old Indian villages meant that the peasants, estate residents, here demanded higher wages and better living conditions. The overwhelmingly Indian *Valle del Maíz* and the *Huasteca Potosina* were the only exceptions, and here violent conflicts on land titles between villages and local elites emerged in 1876, resulting in 1881 in calls for the division of estate lands among villagers. This rebellion was crushed in 1883.

At the center of *ranchero* movements in the Micoacán region stood the *cacique* and the elaborate network of reciprocal exchanges of power ('conservative') and resources between patron and clientele. As is shown by **Romana Falcón** in her contribution to this book, these *caciques* were both guarding their own self-interest, applying crude political methods, and acting as power-brokers between local peasant factions, mostly *ranchero*, and Mexico City. The permanence in power of the *caciques* and officials meant that political control and a considerable part of the region's wealth remained in the hands of the few. As in other states, in the end the centralizing influence of the Díaz era was also sizeable, which meant that the executive bodies consulted regularly with Don Porfirio on the choice of officeholders, as well as other matters of policy. The Revolution meant that the power structure in the state became centred on local conflicts. Falcón describes in a lively way the violence that was seen in the countryside in the period after 1910. What she calls the *Golden Age of Cacicazgo* started in the

32. *Potosina* nineteenth and twentieth-century history: Jan Bazant, *Cinco haciendas mexicanas: tres siglos de vida rural en San Luis Potosí* (Mexico City, 1975); Romana Falcón, *Revolución y caciquismo. San Luis Potosí, 1910-1938* (Mexico City, 1984); Dudley Ankerson, *Agrarian Warlord: Saturnino Cedillo and the Mexican Revolution in San Luis Potosí* (DeKalb, 1984); González Navarro, *Anatomía del poder*, 71, 140; Tutino, *From Insurrection to Revolution*, 231-233, 239, 253, 270-271, 340-341; Knight, *Mexican Revolution*, I, 95-97, 102, 106-109, 131, 159, 180, 258, 339-243, 352, 395, 446-447, 458, 467.

1920s: the weakness of the central authorities and the fear of new uprisings gave pride of place to arms as the key to power and economic development, in short, we see the rise of military *cacicazgos*.

Military *caciques* who had emerged from the revolutionary turmoil made it possible to give some kind of structure to national political life. One of the well-known and most powerful *caciques* of San Luis Potosí was Saturnino Cedillo, who finally led the last unsuccessful military coup in Mexico when he revolted against the national government in May 1938. At that moment, his peasant power base had been eroded after land distribution was taken out of his hands by the Cárdenas government. This insurrection closed the chapter on the last open conflict between centralist governments and local *cacique* powergroups. By the beginning of the 1930s the power of the central state in Mexico City had become more stable and was more able to carry out its power. It drastically came to lose its dependence on the strong military *caciques* of the interior. The *Cristero* war was over, the major political party, the *Partido Nacional Revolucionario* (*PNR*), was created and under the leadership of Plutarco Elías Calles a process of political institutionalization was set in and the state was able to stress its monopoly control of the legitimate means of coercion within society. The destruction of Cedillo's power, however, did not end all the regional islands of power, because some *cacicazgos* survived and others even sprang up and flourished. Under the new conditions of *PNR* power, another system began in San Luis Potosí under the leadership of the Santos family. The new regime was able to pacify the various popular rebel movements to small-scale *guerrillas* without solid territorial control and to restore the position of the landowners.

The history of the revolutionary process in the southwestern *faldas* of the state of Guerrero, described by Ian Jacobs, plot a similar course of conservative revolution led by rural middle-class *rancheros*. Again the same story: the decades which followed the *Ley Lerdo* did not witness much land grab by local *hacendados*, but it were the relatively prosperous middle-class *rancheros* who profited from the laws of the *Reforma*. In Guerrero the Figueroa brothers stood out. They embraced with enthusiasm Madero's *Plan de San Luis Potosí*, reaped political profit from Madero's military victory, but urged him to give legal protection to the landowners. Their political and military influence was eliminated during the De la Huerta revolt of 1923-24, because *Sonorense* president Alvaro Obregón was unwilling to tolerate this quasi-autonomous *cacicazgo* in Guerrero. Instead he supported young civilians who completely depended on the federal bureaucracy.[33]

In the *faldas* of Veracruz, to the east of the highlands, Fowler-Salamini, Falcón and others describe the regional origins of the peasant movement, how it came to power, and how eventually it was coopted into the national, corporate political structure, leaving the lands of Veracruz once again in the hands of commercial agricultural interests.[34] In Veracruz Governor Adalberto Tejeda moulded the local peasant organizations into his political and military powerbase and created an independent *guerrilla* force to confront the powerful commercial and agricultural interests in the state. The studies on Tejeda illustrate the inevitable confrontation between local *agraristas* and the national *callista* government to reverse the course of the agrarian revolution and to integrate the peasantry into political-economic structures dominated by non-peasants.

33. Ian Jacobs, *The Mexican Revolution in Guerrero* (Austin, 1983), 122.

34. Romana Falcón, *El agrarismo en Veracruz: la etapa radical, 1928-1935* (Mexico City, 1977); Heather Fowler Salamini, *Agrarian Radicalism in Veracruz, 1910-1938* (Lincoln, 1978); Carmen Blázquez Domínguez, *Veracruz liberal, 1858-1860* (Mexico City, 1986); Berta Ulloa, *Veracruz, capital de la nación, 1914-1915* (Mexico City, 1986); Romana Falcón and Soledad García, *La semilla en el surco: Adalberto Tejeda y el radicalismo en Veracruz, 1883-1960* (Mexico City, 1986); Ricardo Corzo Ramírez, José G. González Sierra, and David A. Skerritt, *...Nunca un desleal: Cándido Aguilar, 1889-1960* (Mexico City, 1986); Knight, *Mexican Revolution*, I, II, passim.

The authors note a structural similarity between the role of the revolutionary elite and that of *Porfirian* authority, a similarity between the pre-revolutionary and post-revolutionary periods.

The *Sonorenses* were forced into rather ambivalent policies due to the fact that they lacked the monopoly of coercive instruments, broad popular support and clear, institutionalized, rules for the succession in power. While striving towards the consolidation of a strong national state they sometimes had to rely on regional *cacicazgos*. Following the informative analysis of **Raymond Buve** and **Romana Falcón** in their comparative history of *Sonorense* politics, the difference between, for example, revolutionary Tlaxcala and San Luis Potosí is obvious. In Tlaxcala, a fierce peasant-based revolutionary movement, mainly led by Domingo Arenas, had been able to oust local elites as early as 1914, while in San Luis Potosí, like other states in Michoacán or Guadalajara, members of the former *Porfirista* establishment had been able to return to secure power. Buve argues, that the radical *agrarista* peasant movement in Tlaxcala was probably unique to Central-Mexico, because it was able to control regional state power shortly after the Revolution had broken out.[35]

The revolutionaries in Tlaxcala were never able to reach a long-term degree of autonomy. Already in 1914 the movement was split by a *zapatista* defection, led by Domingo Arenas, and a constitutionalist *carranzista* wing, led by Máximo Rojas. A few years later, Arenas rejoined the constitutionalist groups in the state, gaining virtual autonomous power over local society and the opportunity to implement his *agrarista* policy. Many *haciendas* were occupied by Arenas's troops for distribution among villages. Buve's short comparison between Cedillo and Arenas highlights the crucial difference between Cedillos's *cacicazgo* in San Luis Potosí and the movement of Arenas in Tlaxcala: Cedillo and the *Potosina caciques* did not change the agrarian structure -the *hacienda* workers and sharecroppers had only switched bosses, from *hacendados* to *caciques*-, while in Tlaxcala the take-over of *haciendas* was combined with land distribution. Arenas was murdered in 1917 and the constitutionalist position in the state was transferred to outsiders, who started to pacify local peasant groups by requiring their loyalty and obedience in exchange for a quick legalization of their claims on *hacienda* lands. In the early 1920s the Tlaxcalan movement was controlled by Ignacio and Rafael Mendoza, both of lower class, 'urban' origin and former allies of Rojas. In the turmoil of 1920, they brought the villagers and local *caciques* into full support of centralist power, personified by general Alvaro Obregón. The crucial characteristic of the Mendoza *cacicazgo*, its relationship with central government and a combined civilian and party institutional organisation, gave it a *PRI* face *avant la lettre*.

The position of Mendoza was not checked by competing factions and he received full-scale federal support until 1932. The delicate political situation in Puebla, discussed by Wil Pansters, may have been another reason for federal support. A system of clientelism gradually developed between *hacendados* in the northern parts of Tlaxcala and the new regime in the city of Tlaxcala; landowners received support and protection -they produced food and provided tax income- in exchange for regular gifts, contracts, participation in profits and the tax payments in advance. In local industry the state clientelism was not different. Between Calles and Mendoza a firm axis of complementary interests and support developed, which robbed the local opposition of its political bases and finally gave Mendoza the opportunity for creating his own, state-wide *cacicazgo*.

Because the cases of San Luis Potosí and Tlaxcala differed radically, Buve and Falcón are able to demonstrate the pragmatic policies of the *Sonorenses*. These were the two basic patterns for the attainment and consolidation of regionally based power groups during this important period in post-revolutionary Mexico. The Mendoza group in Tlaxcala had acquired regional predominance due to their loyal but dependent rela-

35. Buve, "Peasant Movements, *Caudillos*, and Landreform," passim.

tionship with the federal bureaucracy and state-derived sources for patronage. In stark contrast, Cedillo's power base was located outside these new institutional structures and was in fact antithetical to them. At the beginning of the 1930s both were entering a period of tense relations with the government in Mexico City. The 'fiefdom' of the Mendoza group was easily wiped out by centralist power in 1932, because it had always depended on federal support, but Cedillo could hang on for a few more years precisely because of his more autonomous position. Cedillo's desparate revolt proved that the federal state had finally succeeded in establishing its monopoly over the means of coercion and could in general dictate that the institutional structures would be the paramaters of the new rules of the game.

Although the *cardenista* period signalled the end of regional military groups, it created at the same time space for those who were willing to accept the new conditions. One of the clearest examples is the strong new regional *cacicazgo* of the Avila Camachos, that sprang up in the state of Puebla and is described by **Wil Pansters**. He traces the route Maximino Avila Camacho followed while laying the foundations for an authoritarian *cacicazgo*. Despite his overt conservatism and anti-*agrarista* policies Avila Camacho was backed by Cárdenas, because of his loyalty to the power of the central state. In fact, his brother Manuel was to succeed Cárdenas in the national presidency. The *avilacamachistas* operated within the confines of the structures of bureaucray and party. But personalist relationships did not cease to exist. This so-called *modernized cacicazgo* of Maximino Avila Camacho was based on the corporatist control of the working classes, disciplining regulations within the party structure and educational system, the common interests of the new bourgeoisie and political elites, and the subordination of key elements of civil society.

The integration of the peasantry and the working classes by pragmatic alliances between central government and local modernized *caciques* is further illustrated by the emergence of the new, state allied *cacicazgo* of General Juvencio Nochebueno in Hidalgo. **Frans Schryer** analyzes a violent peasant revolt in Huejutla, in northern Hidalgo, as late as the 1970s, that formed the peasants' reaction to the destruction of the 'modernized' *cacicazgo* of General Juvencio Nochebuena after 1960. In 1981 it culminated in the expropriation by the state of most privately owned land. Schryer is known for stressing for the first time the role of the *rancheros* in the Revolution. The *rancheros*, according to Schryer a peasant bourgeois class, arose in formerly poorly integrated, frontier districts during the *Porfiriato* and transformed the local subsistence economy into a commercially oriented one based on wage labor. He contends convincingly that this class should not be confused with either a poor family farmer or an individual smallholder who relies primarily on his own labor. On the contrary, he may have been a genuine family-sized plotholder or land leaser but actively engaged in commerce, constituting the local upper class. Because, as Schryer has argued in a book-length study,[36] in 1910 at least one-third of the rural population could have been under the control of the peasant bourgeoisie, later the main concern of the official party became the control of rural politics through manipulation and cooptation of rival factions of the peasant bourgeoisie rather than through simple manipulation of the poor peasantry in the villages or *ejidos*. This explains the party's concern with local *caciques*.

In his contribution Schryer stresses not only the political side of the modernized *cacicazgos*, but also the economic. As Schryer explains, in Huejutla the chief collaborator of Cárdenas turned out to be Nochebuena. The period that coincided with the career of this general, between 1930 and 1960, was a period of economic growth in Huejutla in which rich Indian peasants and former *hacendados* became 'modern' businessmen, a transformation that involved a process of increased concentration in land ownership.

36. See Frans J. Schryer, *The Rancheros of Pisaflores: The History of a Peasant Bourgeoisie in Twentieth-Century Mexico* (Toronto, 1980).

The new elite was able to reward their seasonal employees with access to land and short-term loans, as well as other forms of assistance and advice. Economic exploitation, Schryer notes, was thus compatible with a set of cultural values that have been referred to as the *moral economy of the poor* (or the *subsistence ethic*). But further economic developments along capitalist lines, like the rapid expansion of capitalist cattle production, brought about a breakdown of the legitimacy of the rich. After 1960 the patron-client ties were rapidly eroded, setting the stage for overt class conflicts. Nochebuena's strongboss rule was no longer required by the Mexican state, and the by then old-fashioned *rancheros* were also no longer compatible with the economic interests of new types of more educated farmers. The erosion of Nochebuena's power, of course, meant the end of the 'moral economy' in Huejutla, and violent uprisings were the result. The state could only react by expropriating lands in 1981 and by reorganizing the government bureaucracy in the districts to develop new forms of control and ideological influence over a radicalized peasant population. The 'modernized' *cacicazgos* from the 1930s to the 1960s apparently were not only part of a process of political transition, but also, or even mainly, of economic change.

The economic development of post-revolutionary Mexico dominates any analysis of the period after Cárdenas. As is indicated above, the power of the Porfirian elites in the northern estates provoked generalized envy and provided an obviously visible target for the deprived and dissident. The era of the insurrection itself (1910-1920) witnessed the theft and sale of roughly 70 percent of the northern cattle in exchange for munitions and supplies for the rebellion. During the 1920s the vast Terrazas holdings were expropriated and compensation paid. The years of president Cárdenas (1934-1940) added governmental intervention and pressure for land reform, but the cattle industry survived as cattlemen adapted to the new regime. Cárdenas finally provided the decree of unaffectability that was required for the recovery of the industry, but soon enough the interdependency of the Mexican and United States' cattle industries became apparent. Increased international trade during the period of 1946-1960 led to increased production. The government allowed large ranches to remain intact as long as they contributed two percent of their annual calf crop to the *ejidos*. Cattle exports to the United States stabilized in the 1970s at more than 500,000 head per year.

In Monterrey, frictions with the Cárdenas regime on issues of land reform, could not prevent the local industrial bourgeois from becoming one of the principal beneficiaries of Cárdenas' policy to industrialize the country. As **Menno Vellinga** shows in his essay, this is verified by the unprecedented growth of manufacturing in the city, brought about in the 1940s. The number of industries in Nuevo León rose from 438 in 1937, to 1509 in 1945, and to 2440 in 1950; the invested capital in industry increased from 153 to 530 million *pesos*; the number of workers grew from 13,000 in 1900, to 24,000 in 1930, and 40,000 in 1940. The bourgeoisie managed to build a regional economic and political bastion from which could be negotiated with the central state in policy areas pertaining to their interests. The growing influence of the state in the economy caused tensions with the Monterrey entrepreneurs, completely identified as they were with the ideology of a free market and free enterprise. Nevertheless, conjunctures of political stability, offering perspectives of virtually unbridled capital accumulation, were responded to by the entrepreneurial families and they took great effort to see to it that their interests were respected. The *Grupo Monterrey* had appeared as a regional powerbloc on the national political scene.[37]

Quite different was the situation in the western regions of the country. The *rancheros* of Jalisco and Michoacán, who lived a poor life in isolated uplands producing small surpluses for sale, remained quiet during the period of the Madero revolt, but sudden-

37. See also Alex Saragoza, *The Monterrey Elite and the Mexican State (1880-1940)* (Austin, 1988), 96-135. For a review of works on recent industrialization, see Jeffrey Bortz, "The Postwar Mexican Economy," in *MS/EM*, 3:1 (1987), 151-162.

ly, in 1926, they took up arms *against* the victors of the previous decade. It was for this reason that their movement was labelled counter-revolutionary. These people, once immigrants from the Indian Highlands of Central-Mexico, were considered *mestizos*, and relied heavily on private property, but shared the deeply religious feelings of the Indians of the *altiplano* and were devoted to their priests and churches. Also in this region, population growth made *radical solutions* most urgent; *non-radical solutions* like subdividing the lands and opening up new areas had already caused immense tensions. There emerged a landless class that lived by sharecropping and providing seasonal labour on estates, usually on estates of other *rancheros* who were often family members. Ties of kinship prevented the outbreak of massive rebellion in 1910; there were no oppressive elites like in the northern states and no need for land reforms was felt, although some redistribution was carried out. The Revolution reached Guadalajara by *Sonorense* Plutarco Elias Calles' attacks against the Church. Grievances rooted in the growing economic difficulties, the government's assaults on private property rights and the closing of churches and suspension of religious ceremonies provided the background for insurrection: the so-called *Cristero Revolt*, 1926-1929. The *Cristeros* fought to be left alone by Mexico City in the possession of their lands and the exercise of their religion. And although about 30,000 of them died for this cause, they were not defeated.[38]

The business of the *hacendados* in the region of Guadalajara, mentioned above, was interrupted but not halted by the Revolution or the *Cristero* war, and, as **Carlos Alba Vega** and **Dirk Kruijt** show, the landowning elites were transformed into an urban bourgeoisie. Industry came late in Guadalajara, as late as the early 1940s. It caused a switch from a rural-commercial accent into an urban-industrial one; the 1930s and 1940s saw the growth of the city of Guadalajara and a rapid urbanization. This resulted in the improvement of the economic infrastructure, a gradual mechanization of agriculture, and, finally, industrialization. And, as could be expected, this provoked unequal development; improving the conditions of the wealthy meant the pauperization of the poor. Emigration was one of the consequences of such a development, and in a single year 475,000 Mexicans emigrated to the United States.

The group of industrialists in Jalisco was heterogeneous in character. As pointed out above, economic and political power were linked to the Church. Not only the *rancheros* defended the Church, but also the *hacendados* and later again, the *tapatío* urban bourgeoisie. Alba and Kruijt make clear that the ideology of the business community is Catholic: respect for the social order, obedient, non-aggressive, following a tendency to accommodate and to share power. But there were other groups as well: Germans, French, Lebanese and Spaniards; all joined their own ethnic clubs, a situation not much different from colonial times when *Criollos*, *Vascos* and *Europeos* were organized in similar clubs. The presence of various groups and large enterprises, each dominating one or two sectors of the economy, the diversity of industrial chambers and the lack of leadership, or hegemony, we think, is really the same as the rivalry among factions that quarreled in the *Consulado*s before 1820. The large industrialists in Guadalajara have not managed to formulate a clear and congruent ideology that would unite them as a class. Only since the 1970s have the ethnic ties been dissolving and foreign families integrating into *tapatío* society.

As has been indicated in the previous section, history in the southern regions of Mexico does differ somewhat from the histories just told. The smallest regions, no doubt, were Oaxaca, Chiapas (since 1824 Mexican) and Tabasco. Population growth in these regions was moderate, the number of inhabitants per square kilometer were rather low. The outstanding monograph on Oaxaca in the nineteenth century by Charles Berry tells

38. Tutino, *From Insurrection to Revolution*, 342-346.

the same story of delayed *desamortización* as others have done.[39] The *Oaxaqueño* exception stands out, however: the coming of the railroads in the *Porfiriato* did *not* break the economic isolation of the region, there was no rapid expansion of demand for estate products and therefore hardly any pressure from local elites seeking peasant lands, although a small provincial oligarchy, who identified itself with Don Porfirio's regime, had been promoting and beneficiaring a limited expansion of the local economy. Although agrarian tensions existed throughout the state, these were mostly between rival villages over territorial disputes. Consequently, the villagers remained generally passive during the years of revolutionary upheaval elsewhere in Mexico. It even seems, that the *Oaxaqueño* elites were particularly devoted to the national *caudillo* in Mexico City. But the Revolution did not remain unnoticed in Oaxaca. **Paul Garner** shows how the main crisis here resulted from the *fall* of Díaz in 1910 and not from its policies before that date. The integration of Oaxaca into the new central state of Carranza, and later, Obregón and Calles proved difficult, mainly because it was presented through the barrel of a rifle.

The Revolution also reached Yucatán 'from without' in 1915, when Carranza disciple Alvarado started to introduce capitalist ways of production centered around *pequeña propiedad*. His reforms included the abolishment of forced labour, the foundation of labour unions and the distribution of *hacienda* lands, were in danger after World War I, when henequén prices fell and the relationship between Alvarado en Carranza deteriorated. Subsequentlt, Carranza became quite annoyed by the radical activities of the new regional strongboss Carrillo Puerto. But Carrillo Puerto's reform movement was hampered by the lack of a mobilized peasantry, of central government support, and the collapse of the henequén market. According to Joseph, Carrillo Puerto's movement rested heavily on local *cacicazgos* and not so much on grassroots groups; again, we find the persistence of clientelism and personalist relationships in combination with institutionalized politics. After Alvarado's fall Carrillo Puerto's activities were severely suppressed and he disappeared from the stage in 1923.

After the Revolution Yucatán experienced economic development not much different from other regions in Mexico. In the Cárdenas *sexenio* the region experienced a forceful attempt to agrarian reforms, causing, in fact, an almost complete breakdown of henequén production. The nationalization of the cordage industry in 1964 could not improve the situation. Brannon and Baklanoff demonstrate that Mexico City's intervention in the henequén market -for example the government's inept management of a worldwide fiber glut during the *sexenio* of Echeverría, or the shallow and ultimately futile reorganization during the *sexenio* of López Portillo- hampered the efforts of efficient private producers. After the victory of the rightwing *PAN* in Mérida in 1967, the Echeverría government poured enormous sums of credit into the *ejidos*, creating, however, massive corruption instead of a revitalization of the henequén industry. In sum, agrarian reform in Yucatán created an inefficient, dependent, excessively subsidized, and corrupt *ejidal* sector. As a result, nowadays the region is kicking the henequén habit by an increasing agricultural and industrial diversification. Brannon and Baklanoff conclude that development in Yucatán is a classic example of how paternalistic government intervention can retard rather than advance development. Social justice, local politics and political stability were more important than the purely economic objectives.[40]

---

39. Charles Berry, *Reform in Oaxaca, 1856-76: A Microhistory of the Liberal Revolution* (Lincoln, 1981); Ronald Waterbury, "Non-revolutionary Peasants: Oaxaca Compared to Morelos in the Mexican Revolution," in *Comparative Studies in Society and History*, 17:4 (1975), 410-442. See also Tutino, *From Insurrection to Revolution*, 253-255, 273, 288, 320-321; Knight, *Mexican Revolution*, I, passim.

40. Jeffrey Brannon and Eric N. Baklanoff, *Agrarian Reform and Public Enterprise in Mexico: The Political Economy of Yucatán's Henequen Industry* (Tuscaloosa, Alabama, 1987).

## V

What, finally, are the implications of these strong regional differences for generalizations on the national state in Mexico? The works under review discuss the construction of the national state toward the end of the nineteenth century and its consolidation during the twentieth century. In this sense the Revolution was *not* a revolution, and modern research confirms the old theory that it was just a mere step in capitalist evolution to free the country from 'feudal' or 'pre-capitalist' constraints. The development of the internal market, the formation of bourgeois groups joining to form a national dominant class, and the return of capitalist development all united to promote the construction of Don Porfirio's national state. In the end, international capitalism, embraced by this politically centralizing regime, gripped the country. Of course, according to liberal principles, this development was not orchestrated from the center. What could be done from the capital, however, was to try to built a nationwide infra-structure and abolishing regional trade barriers, which, however, caused discontent in the provinces. Central power, the political and administrative capacity of the state to control the country from Mexico City, was still weak and Díaz in fact ruled over regional power groups, built more on compromise than on force, that differed from the industrial bourgeoisie in the city of Monterrey to local *caciques* in the countryside. And after the Revolution, the revolutionary party again ruled over regional power groups, ranging from the *regiomontana* bourgeoisie to the *cacicazgo* of Avila Camacho in Puebla, while capitalist development proceeded and even accelerated.

In the meantime, the 'creator' of the national state had fallen, wiped out by regional elites who were angered by Díaz's challenge to their power, by the part of the bourgeoisie that was denied sufficient share of the profits, and by organized urban workers and peasants determined to end unjust exploitation and improve their standard of living. In several regions, capitalist development had gone very fast, causing untold misery among common people, violation of traditional rights, and political rifts. The global recession of 1907 depressed the economy even further and by then, after years of political tension and suppression, the legitimacy of the Porfirian system fell down, revealing Don Porfirio as a ruthless tyrant. Although authors like Knight and Hart stress the 'popular' character of the Revolution, Vanderwood correctly points to the fact that mass participation *followed* political breakdown and did not preceed it.[41]

If we follow Guerra, the breakdown of Don Porfirio's regime is not caused by political and economic tensions alone, but by cultural ones as well. The fall of legitimacy of his rule was brought about by disappointment and bitterness over the results of the once promising Constitution of 1857. During the *Porfiriato* liberal ideas clashed with a 'traditional society', not much different from the clashes in eighteenth-century Europe. It resembled the situation of transforming pre-industrial economies in general, as is stated elsewhere, in which the world of *moral economy* was not capable of adapting to the world of *political economy*.[42] Indeed, *political economy* could not develop without accomodating itself to the *moral economy*, but at the same time a system built on compromise with local *caciques* hindered the full expansion of the *political economy* in the liberal sense.

Several frictions were the result: the 'federal-liberal' state was centralized, 'democracy' rested increasingly upon dictatorship, 'elections' brought the same persons to power again and again, the 'development of individuality' was hampered by the compromise with collective and even corporate institutions (in 1904, even the privatization of land tenure was stopped). And eventually, during the years of crises, *moral economy*

41. Vanderwood, "Resurveying the Mexican Revolution," 151.

42. Arij Ouweneel, "Don Claudio Pesero y la administración de la hacienda de Xaltipan (Tlaxcala, 1734-1737)," in *Empresarios*, 165-185.

and *political economy*, to use the concepts of Thompson, Tutino, Ouweneel and Schryer, openly split the elites, when a *Reyista* faction, represented by General Bernardo Reyes, respecting longheld privileges, paternalist rule and the society of compromise, disagreed expressively with the *científicos*, who favoured the rapid transformation of Mexico to an industrial nation. The fatal step, if we understand Guerra well, was Don Porfirio's open support of the *científicos* in 1904. The president agreed to accept a vice-president nominated by them. He ended the policy of compromise with the *caciques*, and would built a 'true liberal democracy'. Díaz abdicated in 1910, and all kinds of pretenders later erupted in a violent uprising to assume the empty seat of his throne. And Madero was only one of them, but one who carried the heritage of Bernardo Reyes with him. Guerra's ideas urgently need more evidence and might be wrong, but we cannot fail to sympathize with them.

The option of Tutino, Hart and Knight to label the Revolution as a genuine populist revolt does not contradict Guerra's more general arguments. Once the *Porfirian* state had collapsed, local *caciques* ran for power, first regional later national. The solidarity of the peasants was with these local strongbosses, who had generally upheld the legitimacy of their status and power during the difficult years of crises, unemployment, and relative overpopulation. In fighting for power, the *caciques* served their own goals as well as those of their peasant clientele. The popular forces no doubt were *"at best, the instruments of manipulative caciques, of aspiring bourgeois or petty bourgeois leaders"*, as Knight recalls contemporary observer Frank Tannenbaum.[43] Supporting the new leaders brought them the demise of the *hacienda* after decades of expansion at the expense of their villages or independence.

The rural masses that rebelled were by far not the monolithic peasantry which prevailed in the literature until recently (and still present in Hart's book!). Although the distinctions were all but clear to note in practice it is possible to identify peasants who fought for lands to distribute among themselves on a more equitable basis and peasants who wanted to regain municipal freedom and the right to make their own decisions. The first group opted for a kind of 'farmers' road to capitalism', while the second opted for the return of the privileged communities that had existed before (in fact, old colonial system of *pueblos de indios*), and the new *cacicazgos* promised to give both groups what they wanted. In the decades that followed Díaz's fall land was redistributed, long-standing grudges were settled and local issues resolved. It is this *image of change and improvement* that constituted the legitimacy and therefore the political power of the new regime of the *Sonorenses* and their followers. Knight even insists that the *mentalidad* of Mexicans had changed: class and status differences were partially broken down and people *"thought themselves more equal."* They obviously were not.

Nevertheless, the change in *mentalidad* could have been much more important than the often cited goals of land reform. Of course, the mid-nineteenth-century issue of land reform, that entertained from the outset the twofold aim of encouraging commercial agriculture in the hands of smallholders and satisfying the claims of the peasantry to divide large estates, did return in the era of the *Sonorenses*. But after the Revolution most *haciendas*, divided into *ranchero*-tenancies or not, were able to avoid the intrusion of an *ejido*. And afterwards, it was the prosperous farmer, independent *ranchero* and the heir of the former *hacendado*, who profited most from the immense increase in urban demand for foodstuffs that occurred in the twentieth century. Brading argues that it is possible that even without agrarian reform, in any case hardly present in for example the Bajío, the intensification of agricultural production and the subsequent rise in land values would anyway have promoted the slow dissolution of the great estate.[44]

43. Knight, *Mexican Revolution*, I, xi.

44. Brading, *Haciendas and Ranchos*, 208-217.

We can afford a small epilogue. For with the role of the Institutional Revolutionary Party, *PRI*, we are back at centralization and the return of central authority from Mexico City, although the relationships both within and between *PRI* and other parties or federal and regional organizations have always been complex, often stormy and neither entirely dependent nor independent. But there are differences with the era preceding the Revolution.[45] The opposition parties started to serve a ceremonial function of pluralism within the legislative branch, because, as in the time of Díaz, presidential patronage remained the mechanism for ensuring widespread cooperation from various sectors on key matters. In its early years the party attempted to broaden its base by including more popular participation, but the *PRI* is mainly supported by public officials and farmers and the rightwing *PAN* in general by the business community. The left-wing parties used to rely heavily on alienated political leaders, academicians, and economic and social marginals. However, during the presidential campaign of 1988 a coalition of the left with dissident *PRIistas* was able to challenge the pre-dominance of the *PRI*.

There seems to be another analogy. Camp's cohort analysis shows that a crucial pattern of socialization came to be found in the high degree of influence exercised by the teachers at the National Preparatory School and the National Autonomous University of Mexico (*UNAM*), which can be intertwined with age and the post-revolutionary sense of belonging to a special epoch. Students think at a relatively early age that political involvement is necessary for upward mobility in the dominant Party. In addition to the growing centrality of the University, the extensive personal networks that links political, bureaucratic and educational elites in the country Camp identifies as a career pool for national government. According to Smith, the authoritarian nature of the system has tightened the social requirements for admission to the ruling circles in that higher education and a professional occupation have almost become a *sine qua non* for access to the elite. It brings attention to the growing influence of the *técnicos*, the economists, in the government, in general opposed by the traditional party leaders, government bureaucracy and intellectual elites. Would this not have been familiar to Don Porfirio?

Contrary to the Díaz era, the *PRI*, as Smith shows, had been an open regime, leaving space to the upward mobilization of the expanded middle classes at the expense of both upper and lower classes, national and regional. The authors here reviewed generally conclude that the state indeed has been and is contradictory, and that it functioned in both authoritarian and non-authoritarian capacities. On the one hand, the president, always from the *PRI*, formulates and carry out policies, leaving the congress to perform the ritualized task of debating at length, dutifully chronicled by the media. But on the other hand, the regime compromises with social, economic and political power groups on a national and regional level. The epigraph at the beginning of this chapter, then, expresses concisely the concepts of government of both *Porfiriato* and the still lasting *'PRIriato'*. Although Lázaro Cárdenas' son Cuauhtémoc challenged the official candidate during the 1988 elections -like Reyes did during Don Porfirio's reign-, one could still label this a regime of 'PRIpotism'. The process sketched out above is a good reason for ordering the essays in this book chronologically and not regionally.

45. Peter H. Smith, *Labyrinths of Power. Political Recruitment in Twentieth-Century Mexico* (Princeton, 1979); Roderic A. Camp, *Mexico's Leaders: Their Education and Recruitment* (Tucson, 1980), and, *The Making of a Government. Political Leaders in Modern Mexico* (Tucson, 1985); Miguel Basáñez, *La lucha por la hegemonía en México, 1968-1980* (Mexico City, 1981); Judith Adler Hellman, *Mexico in Crisis* (2nd. edition, New York, 1983); James D. Cockroft, *Class Formation, Capital Accumulation, and the State* (New York, 1983); Dale Story, *The Mexican Ruling Party: Stability and Authority* (New York, 1986); *Mexican Politics in Transition*, Judith Gentleman, ed. (Boulder, 1987); John Gledhill, "Agrarian Social Movements and Forms of Consciousness," in *BLAR*, 7:2 (1989), 257-276.

Region, State and Capitalism
CEDLA, Amsterdam, 1989

CHAPTER TWO

# Social Dislocation and Bourgeois Production on the Mexican *Hacienda*: Querétaro and Jalisco

SIMON MILLER*

## INTRODUCTION

The period 1810-1876 following the *Insurgencia* in Mexico has in the past been generally depicted as one of economic stagnation. In contrast, the years of the *Porfiriato* have been thought of as times of economic recovery and rapid growth. There are good reasons for this chronological arrangement. There can be no doubt that the two features most often associated with the *Porfiriato*, political stability and the spread of the railways, make a sharp contrast with the images of military chaos and multiple governments so characteristic of the earlier period. Furthermore, it would be foolish to disavow the importance of these two developments to the *Porfiriato*'s economic revival.

Even so, there are problems with this perspective. The most important of these is the way it has tended to give the impression that the Mexican economic renaissance owed its origins to a change of political regime. Characteristic of this is the statement made by Roger Hansen that *"the key to the economic growth of the period was undoubtedly the Porfirian political system."*[1] Clearly, the way in which the politics of the dictatorship provided for peace and an influx of foreign investment was an essential component of the economic revival, but such factors should not be regarded as sufficient conditions for growth. To reach a more balanced understanding of this growth we need to know more about the class nature of the society; and in particular we need to know how the infrastructural improvements of the *Porfiriato* were so quickly exploited and by whom.

---

* *Sociologist, Faculty of Economic and Social studies, Department of Sociology, University of Manchester, Manchester M13 9PL, England.*

*This chapter is a reprint from the* ***Bulletin of Latin American Research****, 2:1 (1982), courtesy of the Society of Latin American Studies. We are greatful for the permission of the editors.*

*Unpublished sources used, Querétaro: Notarial Archive, Archive of the Public Registry Office, Archive of the Department of Agrarian Reform, and, Private Archives of Señora de la Llata de Estrella, and of the Señores Loyola, Villasante, Soto, Cabello, Cevallos, and Amieva. To all these last mentioned I am immeasurably indebted, without their cooperation this research would have been impossible. I am also indebted to all the people connected with the public archives -their help was invaluable to me.*

1. R. Hansen, *The Politics of Mexican Development* (Baltimore, 1974), 15.

## THE SEARCH FOR A RURAL BOURGEOISIE

A recent collection of essays edited by Ciro Cardoso has set out to tackle these questions, and has in the process done much to rescue the mid-century decades from comparative obscurity. The book's claim that this period witnessed the beginnings of primitive accumulation is open to doubt, but the way in which the essays serve to draw attention to developments which occurred prior to the *Porfiriato* is useful and legitimate. Part of the book's value lies in its focus on the emergence of a bourgeoisie. Nowhere is this more pertinent than in the relation tot the rural economy. Until quite recently the conventional view of this sector was dominated by the stereotype of the *hacienda* as feudal estate and the *hacendado* as an absentee seigneur. Although much has been done in the last ten years to revise this image we are still in need of studies which concentrate on the pace and process of the metamorphosis of the rural bourgeoisie.[2]

According to Cardoso the crucial influence in this process was the Liberal *Reforma*. There are others who would dispute this account of the liberal state's attack on Church and communal property, and there are also studies of specific regions which suggest that the origins of a rural bourgeoisie preceded the *Reforma* by a number of decades.[3] Even so, there is a general consensus that the measures had the unintended effect of creating a windfall for the *hacendado* class, and to this extent Cardoso is right to designate the period as a crucial episode.

The benefits thus accruing to the *hacendados* were of two main kinds. In the first place the measures gave the *hacienda* economy a new lease of life. Previously the mayority of Mexico's *haciendas* had been subject to heavy demands from various clerical sources in the form of tithes, annuity payments, and interest accruing on large mortgages. The *Reforma* released them from this crippling burden, thereby raising levels of profitability and increasing scope for capitalization. In the second place, the *Reforma* dealt a mortal blow to the remnants of the corporate Indian village. Here the benefits to the *hacienda* were threefold, although it should be emphasized that each of these represented an accentuation of an existent trend rather than the introduction of something new. Legal measures against corporate ownership broke up the communal village lands and made them subject to individual title: the effect here was to hasten the full development in Mexico of a free market in land and to accommodate further *hacienda* encroachment on the peasant economy. This in turn had repercussions for the state of the market in agricultural produce and in labour.

Two of the problems which the *hacienda* had faced in the eighteenth century was that labour had been hard to find, and that maize prices had been held down by the volume of supply coming from the autonomous peasant or Indian sector. Subsequent population growth had eased this problem by the end of the eighteenth century, but there can be no doubt that the *Reforma*'s contribution to this same process was important: subversion of the communal village meant that more labour was available in the market and that competition in maize continued to decline. For Cardoso these devel-

2. *México en el Siglo XIX*, Ciro Cardoso, ed. (Mexico City, 1980).

3. Luis González, "Era de Juárez," in *La economía mexicana en la época de Juárez* (Mexico, 1972); Jan Bazant, *Alienation of Church Wealth in Mexico* (Cambridge, 1971). With reference to the earlier emergence of the bourgeoisie see the works of David A. Brading, "Hacienda Profits and Tenant Farming in the Mexican Bajío 1700-1860," in *Land and Labour in Latin America*, Kenneth Duncan and Ian Rutledge, eds. (Cambridge, 1977), *Haciendas and Ranchos in the Mexican Bajío* (Cambridge, 1978); Eric Van Young, *Haciendas and Markets in Eighteenth-Century Mexico* (Berkeley, 1981); Jan Bazant, *Cinco haciendas mexicanas. Tres siglos de vida rural en San Luis Potosí (1600-1910)* (Mexico City, 1975); and Enrique Florescano, *Precios del maíz y crisis agrícolas en México, 1708-1810* (Mexico City, 1969).

opments signify the establishment of a landowning bourgeoisie and the beginnings of a dispossessed rural proletariat. Whether or not these classes were crystallized out of the effects of the *Reforma* is a question which falls outside the scope of this chapter. What I am concerned with here is the precise workings of the *hacienda* at that time, and especially with the degree to which the existent patterns of management can be shown to correspond to a model of bourgeois production. The information required to satisfy such a question is extremely rare, and so I had to limit my investigation to two case studies. One concerns the *hacienda* of San Marcos which was situated in the south-west corner of the state of Jalisco, adjacent to the state of Colima and only some 100 kilometers from the Pacific. The other is the *hacienda* San Juanico, which was located on the edge of the city of Querétaro, itself some 160 kilometers to the north-west of Mexico City.

The literature on agrarian history, whether Latin American or European, is rife with advice on the hazards of seeing individual cases as typical. It is prudent to advance then with extreme caution. Even so, both *haciendas* do fall within a roughly defined region of some cultural and economic homogeneity, a crescent-shaped area stretching from Mexico City north and west to include the Bajío, Guadalajara, and the states of Michoacán and Jalisco. Given this loose coherence it does not seem too farfetched to regard the following cases as at least not exceptional within this important zone. The focus then is on the production patterns of these two *haciendas*. But before passing on to make a careful analysis of their specific arrangements we should be clear about the more general context within which they were having to operate.

## NINETEENTH-CENTURY MEXICO: ECONOMIC STAGNATION?

Explanations for the poor performance of Mexican agriculture in the years before the *Porfiriato* are more or less the same as those offered during the Colonial period. Variable soils, unreliable rainfall, backward technology, shortage of capital, damaging financial burdens, mismanagement and seigneurial consumption all received attention. But particularly noteworthy to the free-trading tourists of the early nineteenth century were the factors of transport and trade.

Mexico's dramatic terrain was hardly open to easy communication. This natural disadvantage had then been compounded by the effects of endemic banditry and restrictive excise. Von Humboldt's Mexican cornucopia was apparently sealed by government ineptitude and the hazards of the road. As a result there was general agreement amongst the business-minded tourists of the time that the newly liberated Mexico had a great future if only the assets of high yields, made famous by Von Humboldt, could be matched by free trade and cheap transport. As it was, far from managing to enter the lucrative flour trade in the sugar-dominated Caribbean, transport charges made Mexican wheat more expensive on her own coasts than imports from the United States, even after the latter had been subjected to a stiff tariff. This was the stuff of popular comment on the problems facing Mexican agriculture. Similar viewpoints can be found elsewhere. Fanny Calderón de la Barca for instance tell us of the *hacendado* who complained that the freight charges on a 200 kilometer journey to Mexico City made it uneconomic to produce wheat on his fertile and irrigated *hacienda*.

Certainly these depictions reflect a part of the reality. But it is also possible that such views were partial and did not reflect the attitudes of the most enterprising producers. The evidence too is fragmentary and variable -a survey of nineteenth-century sources on freight charges reveals estimates which range from $0.50 to $5 per 100 lbs/100 km.*

Furthermore, if the position argued by Cardoso is acceptable, even if only as a latent trend, then it must be concluded that this overall picture of economic stagnation is not the whole story. It is with this proposition in mind that I wish to present the case studies of the *haciendas* of San Juanico in Querétaro and San Marcos in Jalisco. Expressed very crudely, the central question seems to come down to the fundamental economic potential of the *hacienda*: were the factors outlined above too adverse to transcend, or could the *hacienda* with the assistance of bourgeois management turn in a profit and provide for accumulation, even in this most inauspicious of periods?

## THE *HACIENDA AZUCARERA* OF SAN MARCOS, JALISCO 1850-1865

This first case study refers to the *hacienda* of San Marcos which nestled in the southern basins of Jalisco and within the shadow of the volcano Colima. Although some of its income came from such lines as stock-breeding (in 1859 revenues from this activity amounted to around 3,000 *pesos*), the main enterprise was sugar production: refined white sugar, the cruder brown known locally as *panocha*, and distilled *aguardiente* or rum. Sugar had a long history in Mexico in general, and also in this part of Jalisco, but Mexican products had never competed with those of the Caribbean. Ward Barrett's account of the *haciendas del Valle* in Morelos shows that sugar was not the fortune-maker it is often thought to have been, and there can be no doubt that profits had been further jeopardized by the devastations of the *Insurgencia*.[4] According to John Womack, recovery in even the most favoured of sugar-producing areas, the state of Morelos, was slow in coming; significant changes in production did not apparently take place until the very end of the 1870s, changes which Womack describes as involving a transition from 'manor to factory'.[5] However, if the case of San Marcos can be taken as representative of the most progressive regimes, then it is clear that the basis for this seemingly sudden leap forward had been established some years previously.

TABLE 1. URBAN CENTRES IN DISTANCE FROM SAN MARCOS AND POPULATION SIZE

| Urban centre | Distance from San Marcos | Population |
|---|---|---|
| Colima | 30 km. | 30,000 |
| Zapotlán | 75 km. | 15,000 |
| Guadalajara | 200 km. | 73,000 |
| Guanajuato | 450 km. | 69,000 |
| Aguascalientes | 475 km. | 41,000 |
| Zacatecas | 600 km. | 22,500 |

* $ refers to *pesos*.

4. W. Barrett, *The Sugar Haciendas of the Marqueses del Valle* (Minneapolis, 1970).
5. John Womack, *Zapata and the Mexican Revolution* (Harmondsworth, 1969).

### *San Marcos: Location and Markets*

The most important areas in Mexico for sugar production were the states of Morelos and Veracruz. Comparison of yields between San Marcos and these areas shows that the latter was endowed with fertile soils and good growing conditions. The comparison with the area around Cuernavaca is especially favourable to San Marcos since the latter's production was based on a three-year cycle, whilst in Cuernavaca only the first year, or *planta*, was harvested. However, in terms of market access it was a very different story. Perhaps the market in which San Marcos had to compete was easier than that which faced the *haciendas* in Morelos and Veracruz, but much more significant was the distance from important markets. The best that could be said for San Marcos was that it was conveniently placed alongside the road linking the Pacific port of Manzanillo to the regional capital of Guadalajara. But even here there were problems: Mexican roads were generally bad, and this specific road was not improved to qualify as a main trunk road (*camino troncal*) until the very end of the 1860s. The following list of urban centres, given in order of their accessibility and population size for 1862, clearly makes the point that sugar produced in San Marcos was by no means easy to sell (see Table 1).

Given the prohibitive costs of transport referred to earlier, this list looks daunting. Such an impression is compounded by the state of mid-century lawlessness in the area: the *hacendado* of San Marcos complained bitterly about this, and specifically about two Indian risings in 1852 and 1857 and about the depredations of the notorious soldier-brigand Colonel Rojas.

### *The Administration of San Marcos: An Exception to the Rule?*

On the surface this would appear to have been an inauspicious period for the expansion of *hacienda* production; indeed, one would expect on the contrary to find that San Marcos underwent a period of economic entrenchment and withdrawal. What is interesting, and tends to confirm Cardoso's argument, is that the picture of San Marcos derived from fragmentary accounts for the period is in fact very different. Over the period 1850 to 1863 sugar production in San Marcos was sustained and even showed an overall tendency to rise. Yearly production ranged from 13,000 *arrobas* to 30,000, and 600 to 1,500 barrels of *aguardiente*. Beyond the bald statistics of production there are levels of fragmentary data which accommodate careful interpretation, such that it is possible to access the degree to which San Marcos conformed to a bourgeois enterprise, and to reveal some of the strategies adopted by the *hacendado* in his attempt to overcome the difficulties of his situation.

The *hacienda* had been part of the estate of a Colonel José Francisco Figueroa, which, on his death in 1850, had passed to his children. The eldest of these and only son, Pres. José Francisco Figueroa, then proceeded to administer the *hacienda* on behalf of himself and his four sisters. Contrary to the popular image of the *hacendado* as absentee and unenterprising, Pres. Figueroa clearly undertook responsibility for the administration of the *hacienda* himself, and spent the vast majority of his time conducting its affairs, which even included writing business letters on Christmas Day. Although there was an administrator on the *hacienda*, Pres. Figueroa more or less lived at San Marcos, and only left to deal with demands of the business in other places. In every aspect of his business regime he showed great meticulousness, regularly soliciting accounts from his employees, and consistently pursuing tardy debtors and making no exception for relatives.

### *San Marcos in 1856: Production, Marketing, and Profitability*

If we take the accounts for the year 1856 (since more detail remains for this than for other years), it is possible to reconstruct the pattern of marketing employed by the *hacienda*. The product for that year was in the region of 18,000 *arrobas*, of second and third grade quality and *panocha*, as well as some 850 barrels of *aguardiente*. Of this total, some 10 percent of the sugar and almost 30 percent of the *aguardiente* was sold on the premises of the *hacienda*; a further 45 percent of both sugar and *aguardiente* was transferred to a subsidiary agency in Zapotlán, which was administered by an employee of the business called José Dolores Perez, who then retailed the product locally; and finally the remaining 45 percent of the year's product was transported considerable distances and marketed in the main through commissioned agencies, all of which received a percentage, probably of 4 percent. Three significant inferences can be made on the basis of these data.

In the first place, the *hacendado* showed considerable enterprise in overcoming transport costs and the hazards of the roads. It is clear that he managed to market the *hacienda*'s sugar very far afield. This was accomplished through the use of commissioned agents: 13 percent of the sales made in this way took place in Colima, 63 percent travelled some 200 kilometers to Guadalajara, and the remaining 24 percent undertook the road journey to the port of Manzanillo where it was transferred to boats for the trip on to Mazatlan, a port some 650 kilometers further up the coast. Of the *aguardiente* marketed on this pattern, 112 barrels were sold in Colima, 10 in Guadalajara, whilst 80 were shipped through Manzanillo and Mazatlan to Zacatecas, and another 130 ended up in far-off Guanajuato, which Figueroa had already acknowledged to be within the marketing compass of Morelos. Secondly, since no actual transactions occurred before the point of retail sale, and since I was unable to find any obvious deductions for *alcabalas*, it is perhaps fair to speculate that this system may have been a way of reducing the burden of taxation. Thirdly, this method of marketing maximized the profit margin to be made on the sale of sugar and *aguardiente*, by cutting out the percentage normally lost to the middleman. In this way, sugar valued as a wholesale commodity in San Marcos at $2.50 per *arroba*, and registered as such, in fact yielded the business a return of $3.50 when marketed through *la Casa de Zapotlán* or one of the commissioned agents. The same system operated with the sale of *aguardiente*, which commanded a wholesale value of around $7 the barrel, but ultimately rendered the *hacienda* a sum of anything between $9 and $12, according to the regional variation in value.

### *Hacienda profitability and the freight factor*

Given the emphasis on transport costs in the popular view of the time, it is perhaps worth taking a closer look at the way in which the *hacendado* of San Marcos handled the problem of moving his produce over distances of up to 600 kilometers. The reputedly prohibitive costs of hiring muleteers had made self-sufficiency in this sector an axiom of *hacienda* management. The lesson had not ben lost on the Figueroas. The inventory of estate taken in 1851 shows that San Marcos had at its disposal no less than 196 mules equipped for transport; these were spread over six teams, each of which was supplied with supplementary beasts saddled for riders. The total number of animals involved came to 264, and was estimated to e worth 7,250 *pesos*.

Judging from the inventoried lists of brood mares, it seems unlikely that San Marcos would have been able to maintain the quantity of her mule trains on the basis of autonomous breeding; this speculation is indeed confirmed by at least one entry for the purchase of mules equipped for carriage in 1856, at a cost of over $2,300, and by the fact that the 1863 inventory shows a reduced number of them. Even so, based on the rough calculation that each mule would have been loaded with a cargo of 300 lbs, and that the maximum distance it could have thus covered in a day would have been 30 kilometers, it is possible to deduce that the *hacienda*'s mule trains were indeed sufficient to cover its transport needs -a conclusion which is strengthened by the occasional entry for the hiring out of mules to other less well stocked *hacendados*. Furthermore, it is clear from the *hacendado*'s own estimate of cost for transport at around $1.50 per *carga* of 300 lbs per 75 kilometers, that had the *hacienda* been obliged to hire *fletero* for the lack of its own mule trains, then the annual cost to the *hacienda* would have exceeded $3,500 even in a year of low production. Such a figure represents close to 50 percent of the total capital value of the *hacienda*'s mule trains, and shows how self-sufficiency in transport amounted to a very real saving.

In any event, given this combination of transport and marketing, the enterprise based on the *hacienda* of San Marcos takes on the appearance of a very profitable business, with total profits for 1856 being $35,000, or a 22½ percent return on the 1851 capital value. It is unfortunate that the accounts do not allow for a comprehensive survey of the strategies employed in relation to production, since these would be of great interest. Even so, it is possible to detect the important point that Pres. Figueroa took the view that costs could be reduced, especially in the sphere of field labour, and also to confirm that, over the years of his administration, production was substantially increased through the extension of the irrigable cane fields, and through improved extraction, brought about by the introduction of machinery worth over $30,000 imported from the United States of America in 1852. To emphasize the extent to which the level of investment in the *hacienda* had been raised by Pres. Figueroa, it is only necessary to note that there had been an increase of 90 percent in inventoried values between 1851 and 1863.

## THE *HACIENDA* OF SAN JUANICO, QUERETARO

The San Juanico *hacienda* has a long history, stretching back to the founding *cacique* of the city of Querétaro. It is also associated with another of the most celebrated families of Querétaro, since in 1846 it was bought by Don Timoteo Fernández de Juáregui, whose direct predecessors had been responsible for the construction of the famous Los Arcos. This in itself is of interest since it offers us a case study of a family akin to Mexican nobility, which we may expect *a priori* to be uninterested in the business of *hacienda* production. It is clear that don Timoteo was no yeoman farmer, but at the same time it should be noted that he did not neglect the business: from 1846 to 1856 he lived at his way in which it was administered; during this time he also took responsibility for the running of a marketing enterprise, which was held in partnership with a José Noriega Llaca of Mexico City. It is unfortunate that there is so little evidence on this business, since it was responsible for the export of produce from Querétaro to Mexico, and most interestingly, of *garbanzo* to Spain (in 1856 the partnership shipped 85 *cargas* from San Juanico through Mexico City and Veracruz).

### *San Juanico: An Example of Diversified Production*

By 1856 don Timoteo was exasperated with the poor performance of the *hacienda*, and replaced the unsatisfactory administrator with a profit-sharing contract with Bernabé Loyola, a man who was as astute as he was versatile. This partnership flourished for over 10 years, until don Bernabé was ready to branch out on his own. Under his guidance and enterprise San Juanico developed into a flourishing and diversified unit of production. The regime took full advantage of the *hacienda*'s proximity to the city of Querétaro, whilst being remarkably successful in reducing the effect of its disadvantages -bearing in mind that the area was bedevilled during these years by competing armies and expropriating generals. In this way don Bernabé initiated the production and sale of milk and -when circumstances restricted this- the production and delayed sale of cheese. A variety of other products were marketed in Querétaro, such as camote, melon, chile, and vegetables, including even lettuce. At the same time don Bernabé also developed experimental plots in cotton, tobacco, and different varieties of beans and wheat. Clearly the pattern of production on the *hacienda* had moved a long way from reliance on the revenues of rent and maize production.

This diversification has of course been anticipated and identified in the works of such people as Enrique Florescano and David Brading, their investigations show how the combined pressures of climate, low market demand, and labour shortage, had exacted an essential change in production patterns if the *hacienda* was to survive the Colonial period. Two survival strategies have been identified: the hoarding of maize until the inevitable droughts sent maize prices through the roof, and the move into the production of wheat based on irrigation. In both cases the *hacendado*'s crucial access to capital gave him the advantage over his competitor, the family-based peasant producer. The case of San Juanico shows how these strategies were further modified during the nineteenth century, when, in spite of the adverse conditions precipitated by the *Insurgencia* and subsequent social disruption, the factors of market demand and labour supply had at least shifted towards the *hacienda*. This trend is perhaps exemplified in San Juanico by the apparent decline in importance of maize hoarding and the emergence in its place of less speculative strategies, such as the production patterns mentioned above, and particularly the intensive cultivation of wheat.[6]

### *Wheat Production and Profits in San Juanico*

If we take the year 1862, it is clear that wheat production was indeed a basis for considerable revenue. Thirty-eight *cargas* were sown; it is not known on how much land, but it might be estimated to have been something in the region of 180-190 hectares. In any event the harvest was an outstanding success for San Juanico, and can therefore be taken to be representative of optimum production. Costs of the work, including seed and labour, but not accounting for the use of draught animals and implements, were a little over $1,600, and the harvest yielded something in excess of 2,000 *cargas*. These were sold at different prices until the crop had been completely sold by January 1865, and, combined with the proceeds derived from the sale of straw, the gross profits amounted to over $25,000 -a very considerable sum indeed.

However, this should not give us the impression that the strategy of wheat production for the *hacendado* was without risk. It may have been a much more secure option than maize, but it was too vulnerable to the vagaries of the Mexican environment. The system of irrigation was after all little more than a system of rainwater storage, and thus was susceptible to prolonged droughts. Furthermore, wheat was also subject to the effects of hail and frost, and also subject to a virulent blight known as *chahuitle*. If we examine the unit costs entailed in the production of the wheat crop year by year, the variation, and therefore the risks, are dramatically apparent. Thus, over the years 1856-63, the range of unit costs per *carga* of wheat produced runs from a low of $0.78 to a high of $4.15, a variation of some 532 percent. At the same time these figures show that there was always the security that profits would be made on average, since the average unit cost over this period came down to $2.14, at a time when wheat prices rarely fell below $7 per *carga*.

Clearly then, wheat was a preferable option to maize, even if the latter was cheaper to produce. Such a preference is even more rational when the whole enterprise is

6. Florescano, *Precios del maíz y crisis agrícolas*, passim, *Estructuras y problemas agrarias de México 1500-1821* (Mexico, 1971); Brading, "Hacienda Profits," passim, *Haciendas and Ranchos*.

placed within the context of marketing possibilities -and thus, of the costs and hazards of freight. Since, as has been emphasized earlier, freight loomed large as a cost factor in the ultimate outcome of the enterprise, it was essential that the *hacienda* should produce a crop which would secure, in terms of a return on weight, a relatively high revenue, and thereby go some way towards offsetting the high costs of transport. Per *carga*, wheat was always around three times as valuable as maize, and thus the figures for San Juanico show on average an annual gross profit for wheat of around $8,000, representing a return of 10 percent on the value of the *hacienda*, with no allowance made for other sources of income.

### *The Pattern of Marketing Wheat in San Juanico*

Although the evidence available on San Juanico is fragmentary it is possible to make certain inferences. In the first place, it is clear that the previous tendency for *haciendas* to mill their own wheat had given way by 1840s to a hegemony of superior water-powered mills. If the San Juanico wheat was sold locally it went to the mill of San Antonio, which was powered by the same water course as the famous textile factory of Hercules. It appears that the local hegemony enjoyed by this mill gave it some power over producers relating to the price of wheat.

At the same time the data imply that producers enjoyed better conditions of sale if they could get their product to Mexico City, but that this was regarded as an unreasonable risk whilst disorder and brigandage prevailed. Once the problems of security had been reduced, apparently by the public hanging of a bandit outside Celaya, don Bernabé opened a discussion in correspondence on the respective merits of marketing locally and in Mexico City -and in 1865 we find him hurrying his crop down the road to catch the boom value of $15.50 and anguishing over its decline to $14 whilst he failed to find muleteers.

In this way it is possible to appreciate the degree to which don Bernabé attempted to maximize his returns through the exploitation of market fluctuations: to this end he is to be found in regular contact with associates and relatives in the capital and the state of Mexico as to the respective values of wheat, maize and beans. Here again the factor of freight looms large, both in terms of cost and availability, and don Bernabé was adamant that the *hacienda* should make its own provision for mule trains. Presumably the failure of the *hacienda* to do this can only be attributed to the shortage of pasture land or the worry of military expropriation, since it is clear from the records that the transportation of a crop of 2,000 *cargas* to Mexico City would have cost the *hacienda* fully $7,000, enough to equip it with the six mule trains of San Marcos.

## CONCLUSION

The case studies of San Marcos and San Juanico provide us with valuable glimpses of the region's agrarian economy in the middle of the nineteenth century. Whilst we must be wary of regarding them as typical, it is clear from other studies that such instances of commercial orientation and solid profits are far from being exceptional.[7] What is particularly interesting about these two cases is that they demonstrate that these profits were made during times most inimical to production and marketing. Both *hacendados* were often at pains to deplore these years as anathema to expansion and good business,

7. See the works of Brading, Van Young, and Florescano mentioned in previous notes. Also, Herman W. Konrad, *A Jesuit Hacienda in Colonial Mexico* (Stanford, 1980).

and yet both belied these attitudes by succeeding in expanding production and extending the compass of their trade.

In this respect both *hacendados* exhibit characteristics of management which at least conform to models of bourgeois enterprise. Gone is the image of the absentee seigneur: both Figueroa and Loyola lived on the premises, and both applied themselves assiduously to the business of *hacienda* administration. Whilst Figueroa pursued even close relatives for unpaid debts, however small, we also find Loyola chiding his senior partner on the high level of family expenditure and firmly suggesting that holiday allowances in Europe be kept down to 5 *pesos* a day. Both also showed a willingness to reduce the costs on the *hacienda*. We have seen how Figueroa appeared to have bypassed excise duties; he also argued forcefully that his sugar production be categorized as 'industrial' and therefore subject to a lower rate of tithe. In a similar vein we find Don Bernabé attempting to avoid paying land taxes by posing as tenant of San Juanico.

But more important is the way in which both *hacendados* recognized the need to reduce production costs. We have already noted how they were both aware of the importance of being self-sufficient in transport. In addition to this, both showed an eager interest in raising levels of productivity; Figueroa was in the process of reducing field labour when he sold up, and had already introduced costly machinery to improve the *hacienda*'s refining capacity. In a similar way don Bernabé was to be found testing out different varieties of crops, showing an active interest in all kinds of agricultural machinery, even artesian wells, and also attempting to raise levels of efficiency in harvesting wheat -where he reckoned that up to 25 percent of the crop was lost. Here it should be emphasized that such strategies were not merely limited to the adoption of bourgeois attitudes to production, but that they were also translated into that other essential attribute of the bourgeois regime, investment -Figueroa in refining plant, and Loyola most significantly in irrigation.

All of this is reminiscent of the analysis and advice to be found in Raso's careful study of agriculture in Querétaro for the early 1840s.[8] In this work he noted that recovery from the *Insurgencia* had not yet been completed, and that in particular the *hacienda* economy was hounded by a shortage of ready cash. Yet, even under the difficult conditions of the time, Raso reckoned that the prospects for *hacendados* were good -but only if they followed the examples of successful local *hacendados* such as Velasco de la Torre and Pedro Villaseñor. Aspects of their successful regimes had included radical savings in the threshing of wheat through the use of a machine, but Raso attributed much of their success to skilled management and constant supervision. As a result, he was pleased to be able to observe that the practice of running *haciendas* through an employed manager seemed to be in decline by the 1840s- at the time of his survey only 15 percent of the production units in the state of Querétaro were not in the hands of owner or tenant. Given this, it is perhaps worth speculating that the *Insurgencia* had been partly responsible, and that bankruptcies induced by the devastation had opened the way for a less aristocratic type of landowner.

Certainly the inefficiencies of absenteeism had been widely remarked upon. Morin goes so far as to suggest that whatever problems faced the *hacienda* at the end of the eighteenth century, prominent amongst the reasons for these was the waste due to costly administration.[9] Reference to two cases cited by David Brading for the years after the *Insurgencia* suggest that this assessment may not be far off the mark.[10] Both El Sauz and Duarte, maizeproducing haciendas in the area of León, had been brought to their knees after years of successful exploitation under regimes of owner-management. To be sure, El Sauz had suffered severe decapitalization as a result of a disputed inheritance, and was thereby unable to maintain cultivation for lack of sufficient oxen.

8. J. A. Raso, *Notas estadísticas del departamento de Querétaro* (Mexico City, 1848).
9. Claude Morin, *Michoacán en la Nueva España del Siglo XVIII* (Mexico City, 1979).
10. Examples of this cited in Brading, *Haciendas and Ranchos*, and "Hacienda Profits," passim.

Even so, the accounts left by the contract manager show that a more alert regime might have restocked faster, and certainly would have reduced the level of manning on the *hacienda* -since the number of men employed on a permanent basis is not justified by the number of animals. The case of Duarte is even more illustrative. Here the contract manager can hardly be faulted on the efficiency of the regime since maize production was maintained throughout the trying years of the *Insurgencia*, but what is significant is that the cost of this administration actually halved the *hacienda*'s disposable income, reducing the return on capital from about 10 percent to only 5 percent.

Seen in this context the cases of San Juanico and San Marcos take on further significance. There are solid indications that the years directly preceding the *Insurgencia* witnessed the final stages in the triumph of the *hacienda*. Problems of labour supply and market demand had at last been resolved, and many haciendas were undergoing a process of rationalization and accentuated commercialization. Certainly there were others that lagged behind, but the evidence suggests that these represented the residue of a prior age. Increasingly the trend was towards more efficient production and for old customary arrangements for labour supply and land renting to be replaced by harder monetary contracts. All of this was to be interrupted by the *Insurgencia*, and these trends only made their reappearance towards the middle of the nineteenth century. What the cases of San Marcos and San Juanico show is that this re-emergence was sufficiently strong to withstand the difficulties of those years, such that *haciendas* of this ilk, benefiting from a bourgeois regime of production, were able to enter the epoch of Porfirio Díaz fully prepared to make the most of its advantages of peace and easy transport.

CHAPTER THREE

# Paternalism and Moral Economy on Two Tlaxcalan *Haciendas* in the *Llanos the Apan* (1857-1884)

RICARDO RENDON GARCINI*

*"Workers on other haciendas would only wish they were treated in the manner they are treated here on our haciendas, -as children of God-, provided with all kinds of spiritual, medical and school services. As for money, it is of little importance as it serves the purpose of fostering vices only and not well-being (...)"*

*"Our employers have feelings of affection for all their employees and are saddened by their leaving. They would want -a fact known to me- that all of us enjoy generous remunerations, but if each of the peons or employees perceived the salaries of administrators, no hacienda could subsist, besides that human nature demands that there be several social groups for its own progress (...)"*

*- Antonio Castro, administrator -*

*- October 30, 1911 -* *- May 18, 1929 -*

## INTRODUCTION

Labor relations on Mexican *haciendas* have been subject to diverse interpretations. The perspective put forward by various writers in and outside Mexico towards the end of the last century and the beginning of the present one, like that of Molina Enríquez, is discussed in the preceding chapters by Ouweneel and Pansters and by Miller. It is pointed out that writers like Molina Enríquez prompted and expressed their work more on the basis of political than on scientific arguments. Relying on these works, many other essays were subsequently developed which like Molina Enríquez condemned *the hacienda* forthrightly as an irrefutable cause of evils suffered by all agricultural workers. The liberation of the *hacienda*'s workers should explain and justify the Mexican Revolution of 1910. Nowadays, documentary evidence has made such a concept of the

* *Historian, Departamento de Historia, Universidad Iberoamericana, Prolongación Paseo de la Reforma 880, Colonia Lomas de Santa Fe, 01210 México DF; as well as Vakgroep Talen en Culturen van Latijns-Amerika, Rijksuniversiteit Leiden, Van Wijkplaats 3, Postbus 9515, 2300 RA Leiden, The Netherlands.* *This chapter is a part of a more ample work, entitled "Dos haciendas pulqueras en Tlaxcala, 1857-1884," submitted as Tesis de Maestría in 1986.* *The author is grateful for the assistance grated by different persons and diverse institutions who have made the research possible; among these is the Secretaría de Agricultura y Recursos Hidraulicos (SARH).*

origins of the Revolution questionable. A new series of studies developed in contemporary historiography has been slowly revising this orthodox interpretation of the *hacienda* system. At the same time the new historiography has demonstrated the need to analyze, at least regionally, the multiple characteristics of the Mexican *haciendas* and rejected the possibility of relying on a supposedly unique model of the *hacienda*; such an approach has commended careful analysis of the different variables, like periodization, geographic characteristics, types and levels of production, and labor supply.

One of the themes historians have begun to question is the image of the docile and compliant *hacienda* worker, or peon, over whom the *hacendado* had near absolute control. Recently E. P. Thompson's model of the 'moral economy' has been invoked to interpret the relationship between *hacendado* and laborers. The moral economy thesis places importance on material concerns as well as on the relationship between culture and economy. The paternalistic relations between the *hacendados* and their workers, i.e. the consequent response of labor services and loyalty within the traditional relationship between employer and clientele, were supposedly based upon the idea of 'subsistence insurance'.[1] Thompson argued that rural folk in eighteenth-century England had committed acts of revolt and violence against property or symbols of traditional authority because they saw the social and economic fabric of their world unravelling. It was the manifestation of a consistent traditional view of social norms and obligations, of the proper economic functions of the social groups within the society. As Stavig concluded from Thompson's essay,[2] the moral economy emphasizes the importance of a popular consensus on custom and tradition in the determination of relations between groups or individuals, such as those between *hacendados* and their laborers. These relations, rooted in unwritten but well-known norms of conduct and reciprocity, gave cultural meaning to the more formal agreements that required the laborers to render labor to the *patrón* in exchange for the provision of subsistence insurance. Although this thesis sheds light on the typical characteristics of peonage, we are dealing, however, as Nickel says, more with *"a complementary interpretative opportunity"* than with *"a satisfactory explanation in every sense."*[3]

In this chapter I will attempt to extend Miller's argument somewhat and examine the policy of the *hacendados* inside the *hacienda*. In doing so, I will discuss some of the principles of the moral economy thesis on the basis of a case study of two *pulque*-producing *haciendas* in the northwestern part of the state of Tlaxcala, the *haciendas* of Mazaquiahuac and El Rosario. More specifically I will concentrate on the labor policy

1. E. P. Thompson, "The Moral Economy of the English Crowd in the Eighteenth Century," *Past and Present*, 50 (1971), 76-136; James C. Scott, *The Moral Economy of the Peasant: Rebellion and Subsistence in Southeast Asia* (New Haven, 1976); Erick D. Langer, "Labor Strikes and Reciprocity on Chuquisaca Haciendas," in *Hispanic American Historical Review* (hereafter *HAHR*), 65 (1985), 255-277; Arij Ouweneel, "Don Claudio Pesero y la administración de la hacienda de Xaltipan (Tlaxcala, 1734-1737)" in *Empresarios, indios y estado. Perfil de la economía mexicana (Siglo XVIII)*, Arij Ouweneel and Cristina Torales Pacheco, eds. (Amsterdam, 1988), 165-185; Herbert J. Nickel, "Elemente der 'Moral Economy' in den Arbeitsverhältnissen Mexikanischer Haciendas," *Ibero-Amerikanisches Archiv*, 14:3 (1988), 357-400 (I have used an unpublished translated version: "Elementos de la economía moral en las relaciones laborales de las haciendas mexicanas").

2. Ward Stavig, "Ethnic Conflict, Moral Economy, and Population in Rural Cuzco on the Eve of the Thupa Amaro II Rebellion," *HAHR*, 68 (1988), 737-770, esp. 739-740. Also, Harvey J. Kaye, *The British Marxist Historians. An Introductory Analysis* (Cambridge and Oxford, 1984), 178, 194.

3. Nickel, "Elementos de la economía moral," 7; or in the German essay: *"Wenn dies im folgenden in Anlehnung an den* moral-economy*-Ansatz geschieht, dann soll damit nicht behauptet werden, dieser biete eine allseits befriedigende Erklärung an. Vielmehr sehe ich in ihm eine komplementäre Interpretationschance, die das politische Verhalten der Landarbeiter zu Beginn der Revolution wahrscheinlich besser zu erklären vermag als andere Ansätze."* See Nickel, "Elemente der 'Moral Economy'," 8.

of the owners of these *haciendas*, the family Solórzano-Sanz, during a period that stretches from the middle of the nineteenth century until the middle of the twentieth.[4] It is important to shed more light on certain credit allowances granted to two groups of workers and to the dynamics sustained by them throughout the mentioned period, with the aim of recreating some of the important manifestations of the paternalism existing on these *haciendas*. It will be shown that an implicit pact was forged to exchange goods and services between the *hacendado* and his workers, thereby guaranteeing the subsistence of the latter. Certain well-known information related to the organization of the work force, the different types of jobs and the wages, rations and other credit allowances granted to the workers will be omitted.

## THE *ACASILLADOS* AND OTHER PERMANENT WORKERS

On the *haciendas* were working and living several groups. One of these consisted of the permanent employees who lived on the estates, called *peones acasillados*. The debts of these labourers on the *haciendas* Mazaquiahuac and El Rosario were not large enough to bind them to the *haciendas*, nor were they passed on to the workers' children for generations, as has commonly been assumed. It even seems that indebtedness was not used as the indispensable means of retaining the labor force on these *haciendas*.[5] The *patrón* was always concerned to prevent the debts of his employees from growing to the point of their not being repayable. Such a concern was extended from the 1880s when *hacendados* with a more entrepreneurial turn of mind attempted to modify the system of peonage -which was considered damagingly anachronistic to an updated capitalistic administration- and to develop instead a system of regularly salaried workers who were entirely free from debts. He thought such a system would render him higher profits. The aim was to reduce the number of peons in favor of a greater number of laborers who would be weekly paid, so as to *"change their dependency on grants."* Moreover, the *hacendado* frequently ordered that loans be reduced to a minimum and be granted to only a small number of laborers. The practice of money lending continued, but now in a sporadic manner, principally on occasions like Christmas, Carnival or Easter. The loans were preferably granted to the least indebted peons or to the peons who were considered *good workers*. No loans were granted to *"the lazy or vice-ridden who offered no guarantees."* Nevertheless the *hacienda* owner always thought that money-lending to his laborers was a waste, a redundant custom that had to be dispensed with, as it *"hindered the progress of the hacienda."* He believed that workers ought to restrict their consumption to the necessities and give up costly goods that would increase their indebtedness.[6]

Although the new entrepreneurial ethos gave sufficient economic rationale for the abolition of this system of endebted peonage, the deeply-rooted paternalistic attitude that had developed in parallel to these debts could not so easily be changed. Such new directions were constrained by a complex edifice of culture and subsistence needs; the

4. During the whole period studied here (1857-1914) the owner of the *haciendas* was Doña Josefa Sanz González V. She never took direct charge of the administration of her property, but delegated authority as usual to persons she could trust: from 1857 to 1875 *albaceas legales* (legal executors), from 1875 to 1911 her husband José Solorzano Mata, from 1911 to 1921 and from 1927 to 1930 to one of her husbands' nephews, Antonio Castro, and during the periods of 1921-1927 and 1930-1941 to her eldest son José Solórzano Sanz. Since all of them exercised fairly uniform policies I will refer to them by the generic terms *hacendado, owner, land owner, employer, patrón, management* or *the Solórzano-Sanz*.

5. See the discussion in Ricardo Rendón, *Dos haciendas pulqueras en Tlaxcala, 1857-1884* (Tlaxcala, 1989).

6. *Universidad Iberoamericana, Archivo de Haciendas* (hereafter *UIA.AH*), 1.3.21, exp 1; 1.2.3, exp. 6; 1.3.23, exp. 12-14; 1.3.24, exp. 1-5; 1.3.26, exp. 2-6; 1.1, cajas 2, 3, 4, passim.

modernizing *hacendado* was confined by many factors such as the increase in the price of maize or other staples and basic foods, the obligation of the workers to pay for broken or missing tools or for killed or missing animals due to negligence, the socio-religious obligations like baptisms or weddings, as well as the practical need to keep a minimum of workers provided with houses in periods of scarce temporary labor; all these factors made the *hacendado* resign himself to a policy of mere reduction of the debts of his personnel, rather than of eradicating them as he wished. The Solórzano-Sanz were not the only *hacienda* owners who attempted to eradicate the indebtedness of their workers, nor the only ones who had to reverse their decision in the face of the practical impossibility of implementing the policy. Studies on the *haciendas* of Tochatlaco and Tepetates in the *Llanos de Apan*, a valley covering southeastern Hidalgo, northeastern state of Mexico and western Tlaxcala, lead to similar conclusions.[7]

Indeed, the custom was so deeply imbedded, that it could not be abolished even when groups of *hacienda* owners allied in order to end the practice. As examples of such failures there are the *Congreso Agrícola* held in Tuxtla Gutiérrez (state of Chiapas) in 1896 and that of Tulancingo (state of Hidalgo) in 1905. The *Junta de Apizaco* in Tlaxcala in 1914 called for the abolition of workers' debts on *haciendas* and in factories. Nevertheless, there is evidence affirming that after that date pending debts were still being collected from some of the workers on the *haciendas* of Mazaquiahuac and El Rosario. At any rate, the pact between clientele and employers had undergone some fissure by then and some workers indeed had been excluded from one of the subsistence resources. This certainly undermined peon loyalty to the *haciendas*. The mere reduction of loans and other credit facilities could have made the *patrón* a less generous and understanding employer in the eyes of his workers. Also a change in the criteria to grant credits could have had such an effect. The workers might feel, perhaps, that credits would not be granted indiscriminately to all workers, but instead on the basis of, for example, efficiency, age, honesty, fidelity and the moral uprightness of the workers. In this respect, indebtedness fulfilled the objective of functioning as a bonus which could vary according to the employer's wishes, while at the same time they could serve as an indicator of the status to which workers could aspire.[8]

But there was more to it, because the *haciendas* provided other types of assistance to its workers, especially to those who were permanent. This was the case, for example, with the *leva* obligation, a burdensome task for the peons demanded intensively by the National Guard during the turbulent years of war which followed the French Intervention (1861-1867). Risking serious punishment from the republican government -like fines, prison or even death, since obstructing the *leva* was considered treason- the administrator of Mazaquiahuac and El Rosario did everything possible to prevent the seizure of his peons (*"llevaran en leva"*). Of course, usually it was not convenient for

---

7. On Tepetates, Berry Bock, personal communication -his *doctoraalscriptie* (thesis) "De sociale positie van de landarbeiders van San Bartolomé de los Tepetates" is not published yet-, also the work of Nickel mentioned before. On Tochatlaco see the book by Marco Bellingeri, *Las haciendas en México. El caso de San Antonio Tochatlaco* (Mexico City, 1980).

8. Modern historians consider workers' debts as a supplement of their loans. See Ouweneel, "Don Claudio Pesero"; Friedrich Katz, "Labor Conditions on Haciendas in Porfirian Mexico: Some Trends and Tendencies," *HAHR*, 54 (1974), 1-47; Herbert J. Nickel, "The Food Supply of Hacienda Labourers in Puebla-Tlaxcala During the Porfiriato: A First Approximation," in *Haciendas in Central Mexico from the Late Colonial Times to the Revolution*, Raymond Buve, ed. (Amsterdam, 1984), 113-159; Arnold J. Bauer, "Rural Workers in Spanish America: Problems of Peonage and Oppression," in *HAHR*, 59 (1979), 34-63; Eric Van Young, "Mexican Rural History Since Chevalier: The Historiography of the Colonial Hacienda," *Latin American Research Review*, 8:3 (1983), 5-61; John Tutino, "Life and Labour on North Mexican Haciendas: The Querétaro-San Luis Potosí Region, 1775-1810," in *El trabajo y los trabajadores en la historia de México*, Elsa Cecilia Frost *et al.*, eds. (Mexico and Tucson, 1979), 339-377. A somewhat contrasting view is expressed by Alan Knight, "Mexican Peonage: What Was It and Why Was It?," *Journal of Latin American Studies*, 18 (1986), 41-74.

the *hacendado* to obstruct official government decrees, but he certainly did not want to lose a sizable number of his peons. The *leva* would disrupt the production pattern of the *haciendas*. In addition, to safeguard their economic interests, the *hacienda* owner also felt the moral obligation to protect the physical well-being of his employees. Under pressure from the government and his labourers at the same time, the *patrón* chose an intermediate course: to turn over to the *leva* some of his peons and to protect the majority (but not the ones who in the middle of the confusion of the epoch preferred to escape the *leva* duty). It must be said, however, that both *haciendas* had little to lose, because, although the number of workers decreased temporarily, the levels of production were not seriously affected. Nevertheless, the result was, that by defending them against outside danger like this, the *patrón* might have improved his image as a protective and paternalistic *patrón* before his peons.[9] The situation repeated itself during the Revolution, especially the decade of the 1910s, the *haciendas* Mazaquiahuac and El Rosario tried again to protect its resident workers, despite the fact that the situation was more confusing than during the French Intervention. The most loyal and trustworthy were armed. Others were permitted to leave the *haciendas* or to hide away in the surrounding hills. The *hacendado* also paid the ransom to revolutionary bands which had kidnapped *hacienda* residents. In the face of constant attacks by *zapatistas* or *carrancistas* the *hacendados*' orders were to save lives above all, even if the *haciendas* were plundered.[10]

Besides the credits from the *haciendas*, the workers were given *raciones*, rations of maize, beans etc. on a weekly basis. Although, as I will discuss later on, the *hacendados*' protective attitude could also be extended to temporary workers, it should be pointed out that the rations were granted fundamentally to peons who lived on the *haciendas* and other permanent workers. It should be pointed out as well that in general terms the amounts and the deliveries of the rations, as well as the prices of the maize sold on credit to the workers, were not subject to fixed norms. The *hacendado* granted these benefits according to flexible criteria that adjusted to the circumstances and the persons involved. Among the factors that could influence his decision were: the abundance or scarcity of grain in the *haciendas*' granaries, the fluctuation of the market price, the greater or lesser need of labor at the *haciendas*, the degree of tranquility in the area, and the labor measures taken by the revolutionary governments.

On a number of occasions, the *hacendado* restricted the quantities of maize that was sold on credit to prevent workers from reselling it to outsiders. Such a practice was considered to be dishonest, because the *haciendas* provided the maize to their workers below the market prices precisely to benefit them -we would say that it was done to guarantee their subsistence and to supplement their real wages, but not to gain extra income to "*squander on vices.*" This measure was applied in times of scarcity of maize as well as in times of abundance, because the *patrón* did not consider many of his workers capable of adequately administering their own reserves of maize. On Mazaquiahuac and El Rosario the basic rations of maize were never lacking, because even in times of harvest failures extra quantities were brought into the area. In cases when this was not possible the workers' wages were raised in order to be able to buy the maize somewhere else.

The family Solórzano-Sanz did not question the custom of granting rations of maize and other goods like meat, milk or *pulque* until the revolutionary government deman-

9. *UIA.AH*, 1.2.1, exp. 2; 1.2.2, exps. 5, 9, 10; 1.2.3, exp. 1.

10. On the role of *hacienda* laborers during the Revolution, see Herbert J. Nickel, "Agricultural Laborers in the Mexican Revolution (1910-40): Some Hypotheses and Facts about Participation and Restraint in the Highlands of Puebla-Tlaxcala," in *Riot, Rebellion, and Revolution. Rural Social Conflict in Mexico*, Friedrich Katz, ed. (Princeton, 1988), 376-416. On the attitude of the *hacendados*, see Ricardo Rendón, "La Revolución Armada vista por el administrador de dos Haciendas Tlaxcaltecas (1910-1920)," in *Haciendas in Central Mexico*, 273-305. Also *UIA.AH*, 1.1.7, from *libro* 28 to 35.

ded the payment of minimum wages were on a higher level than the prevailing ones. The *hacendado* considered the rations from then as part of the wage itself, paid in kind, and not an obligation the *haciendas* had to provide any longer. Once the tradition was broken by this external agent of the revolutionary government, the criteria for granting rations became more flexible, although the *haciendas* continued to grant them until the agrarian reform of the 1930s.[11]

Besides these credits and rations, some permanent workers were assigned so-called *pegujales*, or small lots of land to cultivate their own maize, beans etc. Again, this grant was not arranged according to formal rules and the *patrón* decided at will upon the extent, the location, and the workers to be chosen. In general, the workers who had their houses at the *haciendas* -another grant- also received *pegujales*, although there is some evidence that in the last years before the agrarian reforms of the 1930s small lots were also given to the *tlachiqueros* (the workers who collected the *aguamiel*, the juice of the *maguey* plant that was needed for the preparation of the *pulque*).[12] Something similar happened in the case of the permission granted to the workers to keep their own animals and cattle on the *haciendas*. Moreover, there were Christmas bonuses, retirement payments and widows' pensions.[13] Although the Christmas bonuses were in general given to all permanent workers, on many occasions this was not the case because the *haciendas* lacked sufficient resources or the *hacendado* decided to use the bonus to reward workers for their loyalty or their labour efforts in the recent past. In the eyes of the *patrón*, to conduct themselves in such a modest, loyal, and hard-working way during a long period in service of the *haciendas* was the only reason to grant them a modest pension. The old peons had deserved their subsistence pensions this way. Other pensions were granted to the widows of permanent workers who likewise had been long and faithful servants on the *haciendas*. The widows were granted a ration of maize, which was apparently in proportion to the wage paid to their late husbands, as well as to the position this peon had occupied in the labour hierarchy. Occasionally the aid was increased if the widow had small children to support.

According to Nickel, the *tienda de raya*, the store of the *hacienda*, can be seen as another expression of paternalistic assistance.[14] The *tienda de raya* has been subject of heated discussion. The traditional way of presenting the store was as another means used by the *hacendados* to exploit his workers. More recently it has been argued that the *tienda de raya* contributed to the stabilization of the real wages, because the prices at the *hacienda* store were lower than those in the market, and because there was no intention of running the store for profit. Indeed, the *tiendas de raya* of Mazaquiahuac and El Rosario were always leased out. These could not be called 'company stores' in the strict sense, because the leasers were not encharged with the distribution of rations or parts of the workers' wages that were paid in kind.

Nevertheless, at the risk of cancelling the lease, the *hacendado* required that the lease-holder would make efforts to have ample supplies of goods suitable to the needs of the workers, would sell the goods at reasonable prices, make sure to use legal weights and measures, and would control the quality of the goods. The Solórzano-Sanz family urged the lease-holder to fulfill what were called 'humanitarian objectives' -i.e. to favor the workers instead of doing harm to them- by offering facilities for competitive shopping within the *haciendas*. In difficult times, such as war or revolution, the *hacendado* insisted upon attempts to have the most indispensable staples in the store to satisfy the basic needs of the *hacienda* workers. The *hacendado* was adamantly opposed to the transformation of the *tienda de raya* to nothing but *"a mere tavern or pulque*

11. For precise information on the rations see Ricardo Rendón, "Tenencia de la tierra y organización agraria de dos centros de producción agrícola en el estado de Tlaxcala. Mazaquiahuac y El Rosario, 1875-1941" (Manuscript SARH-UIA, Mexico City, 1982); and *Dos haciendas pulqueras*.

12. *UIA.AH*, 1.1.11.44, foja 427.

13. *UIA.AH*, 1.2.2, exp. 6; 1.2.4, exp. 1.

14. See, Nickel, "Elementos de la economía moral," pp. 26 and 52.

*bar."* In fact, one of the few price increases he would permit was on *pulque*, which was often sold on a retail basis to prevent people from becoming habitual drinkers.

For a long time a good portion of the purchases made at the stores of the two Tlaxcalan *haciendas* were on a credit basis. Not only did the workers buy on credit, but also people from outside the *haciendas* -villagers, for example- did and on such a scale that they were generally indebted to a greater degree than the *hacienda* workers. There is no quantitative data vailable to suggest that the management of the two *haciendas* accepted the responsibility of redeeming workers' debt by deduciing sums from their wages. The accounts of the store were made entirely independent from those of the *haciendas*. What is known, however, is that by the 1920s the *hacendado* recommended that the storekeeper desist from selling on credit any longer, since the collection of such debts would be his responsibility and the *haciendas* would not pay the debts of their peons.[15]

The *tienda de raya* continued to function this way until the *haciendas* of Mazaquiahuac and El Rosario disappeared as large-scale agricultural estates at the end of the 1930s. All the complaints against the store that are known were those collected by the *hacendado* in order to use them demanding from the lease-holder to live up the contract. In practice this meant the provision of ample supplies at low prices. In exchange for all these demands the *hacendado* guaranteed the tenant a local monopoly by preventing other retailers from selling in the immediate surroundings of the *haciendas*. Retailers would not compete fairly with the *tienda de raya*, because they had no overhead costs nor rents to pay.

All these examples show that in the proprietors' vision there seemed to be a moral obligation to guarantee the subsistence needs of his workers and their families until their death, although in most cases the workers had to behave well and work when necessary. When death occurred, families were sometimes even helped with the funeral expenses and the cost of the masses. These types of assistance -religious, medical, housing, education- were the only benefits the Solórzano-Sanz family never denied or conditioned to any of their workers. They had introduced them to their *haciendas* even before the revolutionary governments made some of these benefits compulsory for employers.

## THE *TRABAJADORES EVENTUALES* OR CASUAL LABOURERS

The *haciendas* also made use of seasonal workers, who generally lived in local villages. The crisis unleashed by the Reform War (*Guerra de Reforma*, 1857-1860), followed by the French Intervention of 1861-1867, made it necessary for the *hacendados* to protect *hacienda* production as well as the assurance of labour by means of the implementation of additional credits and other benefits to labourers, that would guarantee not only the subsistence of their workers but their presence at the *haciendas* as well. Among these workers were, of course, the *semaneros*, weekly paid labourers, and the *tlachiqueros*, the collectors of *maguey* juice, because due to the acute shortage of currency during this time of war, the *haciendas* had serious difficulties in paying them on time. This problem could last for weeks. In order to contract these people, the *hacendado* would try to satisfy these workers' basic subsistence needs. Besides borrowing cash from neighboring *haciendas*, he would even provide maize rations to the temporary workers, although they usually were not assigned rations in addition to their wages.[16] Once this crisis was over the *hacendado* agreed to continue this practice of granting rations to the temporary workers until 1873, but not to all of them, so that it became yet another traditional right to challenge the drive to modernize later on. For this reason, in the last

15. *UIA.AH*, 1.3.20, exp. 1; 1.3.21, exp. 21.
16. *UIA.AH*, 1.3.23, exp. 12-14; 1.3.24, exp. 1-5; 1.3.26, exp. 2-6.

decade of the nineteenth century, payments to the *semaneros* are registered in silver coins without notice of payments in kind. There were not even additional sales of maize on account. But during the most difficult years after 1910, when maize was scarce and prices high, the *hacendado* was compelled to restore the system of paying parts of the wages in kind (maize).

The *hacendados* in general preferred to work with *peones acasillados*, i.e. workers who lived on the *haciendas*, and not so much with *semaneros*, because these had the image of *"leaving whenever they were needed most"* and, of course, without previous notice. Therefore, for the remainder of the period studied, the management of the *haciendas* of Mazaquiahuac and El Rosario adopted a special attitude towards the temporary workers. The *hacendado* tried to contract the least number of workers from outside and at the lowest possible salary for work during the peak times of the agricultural schedules only. He preferred labourers from nearby areas to save on transportation costs, which were traditionally covered by the *hacienda*. In times of labor shortage, when higher wages were inevitable, the employer also insisted on assigning more tasks to the same workers. The probability of *semaneros* obtaining land, in tenure or as *pegujales*, was low on Mazaquiahuac and El Rosario because this was simply refused by the *patrón*.[17]

In comparison with the permanent workers, the *semaneros*, like other casual workers, remained largely on the fringe of the *hacendados*' paternalistic protection. This explains why a wave of strikes broke out in Tlaxcala in 1911, as well as in the *haciendas* of Mazaquiahuac and El Rosario. These strikes reflected the demands of the *semaneros* to reduce their tasks, work fewer hours, and receive higher wages.[18] At first the owners of Mazaquiahuac and El Rosario refused to give in, but under pressure to harvest their crops in time they finally had to look for an agreement with the seasonal labourers. Some of the concessions were part of an overall agreement between Tlaxcalan *hacendados* and labourers in general. Due to the influence of radical *maderista* revolutionaries this insubordination was followed by unrest amongst some of the *peones acasillados* inside the *haciendas*, referred to above, to whom some concessions were also granted. This was unrest brought in 'from without'. The administrator of Mazaquiahuac and El Rosario added to this that a particular factor could have been important:[19] some *hacendados* were deeply involved in state politics and wanted to remove the *maderistas* from power, while others, like the Solórzano-Sanz, were not. On the *haciendas* of politically active *hacendados* the strikes were prolonged because of the involvement of the *maderistas*, while on Mazaquiahuac and El Rosario they ended quickly and without violent suppression.

The possibility of insubordination of a major proportion of the workers, if not all of them, had been a major concern for years. At any rate, these strikes -or the Revolution in general- accelerated rather than initiated the modification of the criteria used in the *hacendados*' paternalism. Although he was not afraid to violate the law at times, in not granting legal days of rest, withdrawing the travel costs, or not paying the boy who brought them food (*tlacualero*), from this moment on the *hacendado* observed the treatment of the *semaneros* more closely, adhering to legal obligations. The unrest within the group of *semaneros* did not vanish and in the 1930s they integrated into the

17. *UIA.AH*, 1.1.7.21, foja 490; 1.1.9.25, foja 151; 1.1.12.32, foja 235.

18. On these strikes, see R. Th. J. Buve, "Agricultores, dominación política y estructura agraria en la revolución mexicana: el caso de Tlaxcala (1910-1918)," in *Haciendas in Central Mexico*, 199-271, esp. 218-224, as well as Chapter Eight of this volume; Mario Ramírez Rancaño, "El socialismo en Tlaxcala 1926-1933," in *Secuencia*, 5 (1986), 62-80.

19. Numerous Tlaxcalan land owners organized themselves in the *Liga de Agricultores* in opposition to the government of Madero and subsequently plotted to overthrow the governor of the state, Antonio Hidalgo. One of the *hacendados*, Diego L. Kennedy, managed to become interim governor after the fall of the Porfirian government in Tlaxcala.

*agrarista* movement that would successfully demand the expropriation of the two *pulque-haciendas*.

In this respect, the *semaneros* were joined by another group of temporary workers, the *tlachiqueros*, pieceworkers who extracted the *maguey* juice. They received the lowest wages on the *haciendas*. Traditionally the *tlachiqueros* were not entitled to fixed wages or credit facilities like advances on the wages, loans, rations of food, credit at the *tienda de raya*, or bonus goods. However, on Mazaquiahuac and El Rosario the *hacendado* modified this situation when he thought that their subsistence level was in danger, or when the *haciendas* needed more *tlachiqueros* because of a bonanza in the *pulque* trade. Sometimes the *hacendado* offered the *tlachiqueros* additional work at fixed wages, like uprooting *magueyes*, including access to credit facilities and rations of *pulque*, especially when there were not sufficient *magueyes* to exploit. In such a case the additional work allowed them to keep a reasonable income. Loans were granted in periods of maize scarcity or during wartime and they kept this right sometime after the end of the fighting.[20]

The *hacendado* considered some customs in the production of *pulque* detrimental to the economy of the *haciendas*. Towards the end of the nineteenth century he tried to suspend the rights of the *tlachiqueros* to the *tlaxilole* (a free ration of *pulque*) and the right to extract *mezcal*, a product that was obtained during scraping of the *maguey* and was used as animal fodder. In 1897, in reaction to this change in working conditions, the *tlachiqueros* attempted a strike. Immediately, once work had stopped, the *hacendado* decided to reverse his decision, especially because he lacked the backing of the owners of neighbouring *hacendados*, who at first had committed themselves to adopt the same measures. The *tlachiqueros* ended their strike, but two years later the measures were succesfully imposed without any apparent complaint from the *tlachiqueros*. Perhaps crucially, on this occasion half a dozen neighboring *haciendas* had also imposed the same measures.[21]

Years later, when the Revolution changed the life on the *haciendas*, the *raciones de pulque* were once again established as a custom. Furthermore, in answer to the crisis the Revolution had caused, the *patrón* provided the *tlachiqueros raciones de maíz* and tools, which under normal conditions they bought themselves. After the major fighting was over the *hacendado* maintained the right to *tlaxilole*, but only in small amounts to prevent his workers from selling it to outsiders. Other grants that were sporadically given them were the privilege of credit at the store -by the store-keeper not by the *patrón*, that is- and pensions in kind or cash to some of their widows.

Nevertheless, the *tlachiqueros* joined the *semaneros* at the end of the 1930s in the *agrarista* movement that attacked the *haciendas*. At that time, in a last effort to pacify these workers the Solórzano-Sanz family granted some of the *tlachiqueros* small parcels of land, *pegujales*, which was a totally new measure -but granted rather late and perhaps even counterproductively, since it brought the workers closer to the land they longed for. It might have been the case that in this period the *tlachiqueros* had better credit facilities than the *semaneros*, due to the fact that their work was more important to the final product of the enterprise: *pulque*. However, the *tlachiqueros* in general remained excluded from the paternalistic system enjoyed by the permanent workers. They were trapped in an intermediate situation that might explain why the *tlachiqueros* wavered between loyalty and insubordination.

---

**20**. *UIA.AH*, 1.2.25, exp. 5; 1.2.3.1.

**21**. *UIA.AH*, 1.1.6.18, fojas 153-158; 1.1.7.20, fojas 335.

## CONCLUSION

My discussion of the *hacendados*' paternalism towards his labour force is in no way intended to imply that generosity and just remuneration reigned on the two *haciendas* out of the mere altruistic motives of their owners. The *hacendado*, José Solórzano-Sanz, stated in May 1925 in a clear bourgeois manner, that *"it is counterproductive to treat people with sweetness and gentleness, it is not convenient on the other hand to treat them unjustly or with undue harshness."* I have attempted to confirm the existence of a paternalistic regime which endeavored to guarantee the subsistence and security of both the permanent and the casual labourers. In the practical application of those principles there was ample flexibility within the limits determined in turn by the the *hacendados*' bourgeois attitude and again by the moral economy apparently established over time by traditional customs and concessions won by workers on the *haciendas*.

We are dealing with a situation in which there was apparently never a grave subsistence crisis among the workers, just as there never was a massive rebellion against the *patrón*. The insubordination that did occur was sporadic in character, never got out of control, and reflected fissures in the unwritten pact of loyalty in exchange for protection. On the *haciendas* of Mazaquiahuac and El Rosario the winds of modernization in labor organization were gentle and soft, but evident enough to provoke reactions which in turn produced moderation and revived traditions. Paternalistic relationships, although modified, survived within the *haciendas* even after the outbreak of the Revolution. Precisely the tardy disappearance of Mazaquiahuac and El Rosario in 1941 still offers opportunities for reinterpreting the labor relations and the productive organization of the *haciendas*. My essay is only a small contribution to an unfinished work.

CHAPTER FOUR

# The Formation and Consolidation of a Regional Bourgeoisie in Northeastern Mexico

## [MONTERREY: FROM REFORM TO REVOLUTION]

MARIO CERUTTI*

## INTRODUCTION

Between the spatial disintegration implicit in the break with the colonial system and the rearticulation finally achieved by the consolidation of the national state, Mexico experienced a particular historical process. Our research on Monterrey and the northeastern part of the country begins with a critical period in this process when the war against the United States (1846-1847) abruptly moved the northern border closer to Monterrey and substantially modified its role with respect to a broad area in the northern part of the country. There were many changes in this city and in its surroundings in the second half of the nineteenth century. Among the most significant of these was the emergence of a regional bourgeoisie whose rise and growth were visibly intertwined with three decisive processes:[1]

a) primitive accumulation of capital, carried out with mechanisms which virtually excluded the capitalist mode of production and which occurred in the crucial decades after the modification of the northern border;
b) from 1890 on, the massive transfer of that capital toward capitalist production benefitting from the conditions created by the *Porfiriato*, the new ties

* *Historian, Depto. de Historia, Universidad Autónoma de Nuevo León, CD Universitaria AP 3024, Monterrey, Nuevo León, México. CEDLA 1987 Visiting Research Fellow.*

1. This article is a synthesis of former work which, for the most part, Has been published in Spanish. For a more extensive treatment of these issues, and for information on the primary sources, the following titles: *Burguesía y capitalismo en Monterrey (1850-1910)* (Mexico City, 1983), *Economía de guerra y poder regional en el siglo XIX* (Monterrey, 1983), "Patricio Milmo, empresario regiomontana del siglo XIX," in *Formación y desarrollo de la burguesía en México. Siglo XIX*, Ciro Cardoso, ed. (Mexico City, 1978, "Burguesía regional, mercados y capitalismo. Apuntes metodológicos y referencias sobre un caso latinoamericano: Monterrey (1850-1910)," in *Revista Mexicana de Sociología*, 45:1 (1983), "Aduanas, poder regional y estado nacional en México a mediados del siglo XIX," en *Trienio. Illustración y Liberalismo*, 4 (1984), "División capitalista de la producción, industrias y mercado interior. Un estudio regional: Monterrey (1890-1910)," in *El siglo XIX en México. Cinco procesos regionales*, Mario Cerutti, ed. (Mexico City, 1985), "El préstamo prebancario en el noreste de México: la actividad de los grandes comerciantes de Monterrey (1855-1890)," in *Banca y poder en México (1800-1925)*, Leonor Ludlow y Carlos Marichal, eds. (Mexico City, 1985), "Producción capitalista y articulación del empresariado en Monterrey (1890-1910)," in *Grupos económicos y organizaciones empresariales en México*, Julio Labastida, ed. (Mexico City, 1986), "Militares, terratenientes y empresarios en el noreste. Los generales Trevino y Narano (1880-1910)," in *Monterrey, Nuevo León, el Noreste. Siete estudios históricos*, Mario Cerutti, ed. (Monterrey, 1987).

to the international economy and the consolidation and expansion of an internal market;

c) the beginning of a remarkable outburst of industrialization with a peculiarity not found in the other parts of Latin America during this period: large-scale production of inputs and capital goods directed towards heavy industry.

The bourgeoisie, from an industrial base which was one of the most powerful and autonomous to emerge in Latin America, had sufficient strength and stability -in social and economic terms- to face the vicissitudes unleashed by the Revolution. The industrial base of this empresarial group allowed it to maintain the conditions which would ensure its own capitalist reproduction. The recent history of this capitalist group is ample evidence of the fact that it was able to weather the revolutionary turmoil with skill and flexibility.

Before the Revolution, in the second half of the nineteenth century, the bourgeoisie passed through certain distinct phases, differentiated by its role and development. In its quest to achieve primitive accumulation, for example, between 1850 and approximately 1890, it utilized those means which were permitted by a socioeconomic structure still defined in regional terms, but which was moving toward national unification. The early phase of these forty years represented a propitious moment to carry out the reorganization required by the recent border modification in northeastern Mexico. A key figure in this readjustment was Santiago Vidaurri, governor of Nuevo León between 1855 and 1864 (he was governor of Coahuila as well, which he annexed in 1856).

## NATIONAL CRISIS, REGIONAL POWER AND CAPITAL ACCUMULATION

During the Vidaurri period the society which would form the nucleus of the national state was undergoing a crisis. In the aftermath of the military disaster following the war against the United States, the proclamation of the *Plan de Ayutla* (to which Vidaurri adhered in mid-1855) intensified civil strife. This profound crisis, characterized principally by the struggle between conservatives and liberals, was heightened by the continuing threat of further North American interventions. And from the moment that European troops disembarked on Mexican soil, it became a decisive turning point in the shaping of an independent national state.

In the far North, Santiago Vidaurri took over the government in the name of liberalism after having rebelled against president Antonio López de Santa Ana in May 1855. Two months later he extended his domain to Coahuila, which was to be integrated into one state -formally- in February 1856. His pretensions to annex Tamaulipas as well, towards the east, were checked by local leaders, linked, occasionally, to leaders of the centre of the country. But the repercussions were important for this coastal state, whose harbours on the Gulf of Mexico gave it special significance. So it can be affirmed that Vidaurri, despite ups and downs, implemented a visible regional political hegemony in the northeast between 1855 and 1864. On the one hand this hegemony was favourable to the liberal cause as a whole; on the other, it was directed at strengthening a power-group with regional dimensions which refused to submit to the liberal national governments trying to consolidate themselves in Central Mexico.

How were the businessmen who established themselves in Monterrey able to operate in such chaotic state of affairs? Under these circumstances, what permitted them, whether they were Mexican or foreign, to rapidly multiply their fortunes? With little effort the answer can be found in the archives of Monterrey. The prosperity of this group had two basic sources: commerce and speculation with the material needs of the regional political and military administration. It is clear from the outset, that, until the decade of the 1890s, commerce and management of cash money were two permanent elements among the activities of this incipient bourgeoisie.

*Border Custom Houses, Tariffs, Military Needs*

It is impossible to talk about an effective national market during this period. The most profitable sector of the mercantile trade tied Monterrey and its surrounding area much more firmly to the world market than to other regions of Mexico. Gradually, Monterrey became the commercial centre not only of Nuevo León but of the entire northeast. And this was made possible by its proximity to the border of the United States and to the growth of the harbours of Matamoros and Tampico. But it was also made possible by the policies of Santiago Vidaurri, who, as head of a large military force in constant need of considerable resources to wage war against the conservative enemy, to protect the border against constant threats from Texas, or to repel the attacks of semi-nomadic indians who frequently besieged the surrounding area of Monterrey, quickly demonstrated that regional power could assume control over means and instruments which belonged usually to the domain of the central government. Under these circumstances, the central government could not make its presence felt, was hostile, or, if it was liberal, was unable to exercise its prerogatives.

An example of this is the establishment of new custom-houses on the Rio Bravo, and the management of their resources: what later became known as the *Vidaurri-tariff*. This emerged as a result of a combination of regional and national precedents; modifications that in the course of events were incited by the governor and other local leaders and suggested by leading northeastern merchants. When the tariff was operating most effectively, around 1857, it permitted the introduction of goods with much lower charges than those determined by general prescription, enacted by liberal president Ignacio Comonfort in January 1856. According to references of the time, confirmed by our calculations, the *Vidaurri-tariff* represented a discount of about 60 percent in relation to the federal tariff. The *Vidaurri-tariff* was applied at all border points dominated by the governor of Nuevo León and, after he had extended his power to Tamaulipas, he put it into effect in the ports of Tampico and, above all, Matamoros.

Furthermore, Vidaurri established Monterrey as the administrative centre of these custom houses and the funds they provided. Declaring illegal those shipments which had not been taxed in Monterrey, he could appropriate the taxes imposed on the trade and export of silver and gold. As compensation, to those engaged in commerce -and especially to export trade- he offered protection against the danger of marauding indians, the menace of bandit groups, the threat of opposing armies and the fiscal greed of the government of central Mexico.

From the perspective of a strong regional power, the policy of both the governor and military leaders was coherent. The supervision of the custom houses, Vidaurri's tariff policy, and the control of something as strategic as the currency utilized in the international markets, provided him not only with needed funds but also with a mutually-advantageous relationship with important merchants, particularly those established in Monterrey. Upon these foundations, Vidaurri equipped his armies and strengthened his political base assuring him a significant role in the national liberal movement.

*Commerce and Loans*

In exchange for the advantage of the tariffs granted by the administration of Nuevo León, resources were obtained to meet the permanent deficits caused by warfare. Until the *Vidaurri-tariff* was systematized (in 1855 and 1856), ammunition supplies were obtained during the most pressing times by means of special contracts: the governor would concede drastic and unregulated discounts on import duties to certain merchants, as a way of compensating for the introduction of armaments. A second mechanism, which would slowly replace the former, was to apply for cash credits and loans to cover war expenditures. In this case the devolution was effected through certified papers which, when presented afterwards at the custom houses of the Rio Bravo, permitted massive imports within the scope of the ever more liberal *Vidaurri-tariff*.

The governor and commander of Nuevo Léon not only had to resort frequently to merchants of the area, he also had to acknowledge their contributions with another form of compensation: the high bonus (a kind of high short-term interest rates, because of the high risk involved in the operation) added on by the intermediaries, thus transformed into the inevitable financiers of regional power. Although Vidaurri supposed that these bonuses would not be higher than 11 percent of the money provided, at times of high tension they came to 50 percent. In this context, conditioned by necessities of warfare, the merchants of Monterrey and their agents at the border knew how to capitalize on this opportunity with the skill and rationality characteristic of men with a bourgeois mentality, whose principal aim was the continued expansion of their capital. The benefit to them was obvious. They were rewarded for their loans receiving merchandise with duties so low that it allowed them to extend their markets to various northern states and the interior.

At this point we can trace the formation of a regional sphere in which the specific interests of the members of this incipient bourgeois group would intertwine. Beyond Nuevo León, Tamaulipas and Coahuila, this sphere would include Durango, Zacatecas, Chihuahua and, to a lesser degree, San Luis Potosí. The most important merchants of Monterrey, like Patricio Milmo, Valentín Rivero, Gregorio Zambrano, Mariano Hernández, Brach y Shonfeld, became to compete the businessmen of central Mexico. In the extended market, rooted in the unique application of regional power and the strategic location acquired from the adjustment of the northern border, the merchants would also regulate the flow of goods produced in the region (for example, *piloncillo* -a sugar product). But the primary means of accumulation derived from the trade in articles introduced from England, France and the United States. The management of capital, speculation with governmental needs and the movement of goods combined to form a single action when the buyer was the regional political and military authority. The trade with articles of war, carried out during a critical period for Mexican society and national government, contributed to the formation of great fortunes.

The readjustment brought on by the modification of the border also provided the opportunity for the Monterrey merchants to take advantage of the American Civil War (1861-1865) which produced a dramatic increase in mercantile trade and stimulated rural production in northeastern Mexico. The trade in cotton was the key to this commerce. But added to it was the exchange of arms as well as the sale of mules, horses, flour and hides, which were consumed in great quantities by the Confederates, with whom Vidaurri always maintained excellent relations.

*Vidaurrismo* was in its heyday at the beginning of the sixties. Vidaurri's regional arrangements anticipated in a way the system Porfirio Díaz created later on a national scale. And the governor, together with allied and befriended merchants, knew how to take advantage of the conjuncture. Evaristo Madero (grandfather of the revolutionary chief) and Patricio Milmo, Vidaurri's son-in-law, were among the main beneficiaries. Thirty years later, both would participate actively in setting the industrialization of Monterrey into motion. It should be said that the War of Separation simultaneously yielded the experience of the contacts with Texas, a state that in fact formed part of the *regional territory* that surrounded the embryonic *regiomontana* bourgeoisie. Its significance for the primary accumulation of capital in Monterrey is a topic worthy of detailed investigation.

## AFTER THE FRENCH

A second phase of the period prior to 1890 begins in the 1870s, when the problems and structural changes caused by the Reform began to be resolved. Possibilities arose for the continuation of the expansion of capital and the concentration of wealth. Its mode of operations also changed although the general conditions were not yet suitable for the transfer of that capital to modern production on a large scale, as would occur in the 1890s. Although commerce continued to be the economic base of this bourgeoisie, two other related activities stand out during this time: the appropriation of large tracts of lands and growing financial enterprises, which usually went hand in hand with commercial ventures.

In the 1870s and 1880s an important number of wealthy families became owners of land in Coahuila, Tamaulipas and Durango as well as in Nuevo León. The vast appropriation of rural land passed three stages:

- it required the expulsion or extermination of the seminomadic indians who, if they survived at all, were pushed increasingly to the west;
- it was bolstered by the policies and possibilities emanating from the Reform which included the expropriation of large landowners who had supported Maximilian's Empire;
- it was completed by the operations of the *compañías deslindadoras* which, by the 1880s, included the participation of some of the future industrialists.

For example, Patricio Milmo created a veritable empire along the northeastern border. His cattle *haciendas* in Coahuila were already prosperous by the 1890s when they multiplied in value, due to the coal found in their subsoil. This was sold to the railroads and smelting plants. Evaristo Madero, the Hernández family and the Zambranos followed a similar path. Madero already owned land by the end of the fifties, when he lived in the neighbourhood of Piedras Negras. He went on extending his holdings uninterruptedly.

There was an interesting involvement in the rich Laguna lands. As in other fields, the Madero family were pioneers in this respect. Already in 1868 -when the Madero and Company firm still functioned in Monterrey- Evaristo and his associate Lorenzo González Trevino, signed a *contrato de habilitación* with the blanket factory "La Estrella," in Parras. Later they took charge of the factory and bought the *haciendas* "El Rosario" and "San Lorenzo" in the same locality. After the Maderos others came: González Trevino (associated with the Zambranos in commerce and linked through marriage with the majority of the relevant Monterrey families around 1890), the Zambranos and the Hernández family. From 1886, the latter owned the *hacienda* Santa Teresa in San Pedro de las Colonias: with more than 100,000 hectares, their investment in the state around 1896 reached 400.000 *pesos*.

The appropriation of land was also an upward step taken by individuals of different descent, of non-bourgeois origins, but who finally had the possibility of associating themselves with the nascent entrepreneurial class through joint stock companies. A telling case was that of General Gerónimo Trevino. Together with his wartime comrade Francisco Naranjo, Trevino went through the struggles of the Reform, fought against the French, contributed decisively to the expulsion of the Comanches and Apaches during the seventies, assumed the governorship of Nuevo León on various occasions, joined the rebellions that brought Porfirio Díaz to power and ended up as minister of War and the Navy of president Manuel González (1880-1884). It was at this moment -when Trevino enjoyed the highest level of political and military prestige- when he led a *compañía deslindadora* that enabled him to appropriate enormous estates in Coahuila. His *hacienda* La Babia was the main example, but his interests -which simultaneously extended to banks, industries and mining- involved vast areas in the desert, formerly roamed by semi-nomadic groups.

After engaging in the acquisition of large landholdings, the bourgeoisie was no longer interested in the regional sphere for strictly commercial reasons (as in the Vidaurri era). Its activities, which began to differentiate it as a separate social class, were no longer absorbed exclusively by trade which created limited ties to far-off regions: now it was also concerned with the ownership of property and, inevitably, with production. Therefore, its expectations extended beyond issues such as import duties, the *alcabalas* and taxes on the circulation of currency. The members of the bourgeoisie were now also preoccupied with such matters as the purchase and scale of land, property rights in rural areas, the juridical order which would govern the relations of production, the functioning and profitability of the *compañías deslindadoras*, the support and advancement of mining (owing to the mineral wealth located in the appropriated lands), and the potential industrialization of agricultural goods, livestock or subsoil products (as would occur at the end of the 1880s in the Laguna zone where the factory of *La Esperanza* was established for the production of soap and oil, derived from the cotton seed). And the new ties would allow them to operate in a space not bound by geographic limits.

The widening of the material base of the *regiomontana* bourgeoisie accentuated the reshaping of a regional outlook quite distinct from that of the Vidaurri era. The conditions required to establish an investment climate and an extended capitalist production based in Monterrey, which would become principal features of the 1890-1910 period, began to emerge. Within this developing bourgeois group there also arose a long-range vision which would facilitate its acceptance of the national project implemented by the Porfirio Díaz regime: the Mexican national state would cease to be afflicted by movements for regional autonomy -at least in this part of the country- like those which marked the Vidaurri era.

The financial operations of this group between 1870 and 1890 went hand in hand with commerce, so various Monterrey merchant establishments performed functions ordinarily supplied by a modern and diversified banking system. No longer dependent solely on governmental needs (although maintaining ties to this source of accumulation), the Monterrey commercial barons often provided capital to lesser merchants, operated within the urban sphere, and, above all, they financed the agricultural sector. Toward the end of the 1860s, for example, we begin to see a growing connection with the *Laguna* agricultural zone, where cotton and, to a lesser extent, wheat were produced. The businessmen not only purchased the cotton fibre: they also provided commodities and financial backing to these producers. The transformations taking place in the *Laguna* zone, particularly those pertaining to the subdivision and commercialization of the soil and the irrigation projects, required financial support that, at that time, could only be provided by the big merchants.

The archival documents that I have analyzed bear witness to the impact that Monterrey capital had on the surge of production. Contracts, located in notarial records, refer to these credits granted to agricultural producers in cash or goods as *préstamos refaccionarios* or *habilitaciones*. The following represent some of the main characteristics of these contracts:

1) The *habilitaciones* or *refacciones* involved the use of cash or goods or both (which was most often the case). The commercial houses granted their *refacciones* gradually as they were required by the agricultural producers. The requirements of these producers became more critical during the harvest or, since most of them were renters, when the rent was due.
2) The repayment of the loans was assured by the cotton crop which served as collateral. When the amount of the loan was considerable or when greater guarantees were required, the collateral could take the form of future harvests or other crops like wheat, corn or beans.
3) Moreover, the producer would accept that mortgages be placed on his various holdings, such as land, if he was a landowner; or on other property

or instruments of production in order of importance (machines, animals, implements); or, if these were insufficient, on urban property or other assets.

4) On some occasions, the lender would pay for the cotton in advance. He would pay it in installments in keeping with the needs of the agricultural producer.

5) When the amount of the loan was increased, either because the producer could not pay or when he sought to augment his production (which was frequently the case), the lenders made sure they increased the guarantee on their loan. In these instances, apart from accepting the crop as collateral and mortgaging the borrower's holdings, they would designate an administrator who would be charged with ensuring the correct application of the loan on the cotton crop. These were stern provisions and failure to meet them led to a cancellation of the loan.

6) Although part of the crop could be sold independently by the producers, in fact what often occurred was that the lender became a monopolist middleman. He would assure himself of acquiring a product in great demand at prices usually below the market value. The lender (or lenders, since on occasion these were joint ventures) became, in this way, the only channel for the producer to get his goods to market. Added to this was the stipulation of certain clauses which required the borrower, during the period of the agreement, to purchase merchandise only from the lender. In this way, the circle of relations was closed.

The unification of the national market after the completion of the railroads (with two important junctions in the northeast: in Torreón, the centre of the Laguna district, and in Monterrey) accentuated the cultivation of cotton allowing the zone to produce around 75 percent of the national cotton fibre by the 1890s. Perhaps for this reason the loans granted by the merchants never ceased. The growing investment needs of the producers of the Laguna could not be met solely by the nascent banking system created toward the end of the century. As stated earlier, the most important Monterrey merchants also participated in the acquisition of property in the zone. In some instances the land was earmarked for production, or else rented or sold.

In sum, it still was a turbulent period. But it was during these trying times (which lasted till the mid 1880s) that enormous fortunes began to be made. Starting in 1890 this situation would change: for the first time the accumulation process would be centered on capitalist production. Industry and mining would form the nucleus of this new process.

## THE BRIDGE BETWEEN TWO CENTURIES

Between 1890 and 1910 the course of events in Monterrey resembled those of a few other Latin American cities, though at times one gets the impression that this was a very significant case. The economic opportunities produced at the end of the nineteenth century, motivated by diverse factors, were seized upon with great skill by the former merchants/lenders/landowners, now joined by new entrepreneurs who merged with the old group. An initial element in this progression was the possibility that arose in 1890 to establish a link with another sector of the international market: the northeast of the United States. This connection was to be substantially different from previous commercial ties and would become a key factor in the kind of industrialization which occurred in the city.

The demand for industrial metals in the northeast of the United States, added to the American import restrictions on ore, provided the opportunity to establish smelting plants in northern Mexico. The most important smelters were located in Monterrey. The opportunity to satisfy this market was facilitated by the policies of the State government led by general Bernardo Reyes, who adopted laws declaring manufacturing investment as having a *utilidad pública* and offering generous tax exemptions to investors. In the same decade of the 1890s the railroad connected Monterrey to the United States by way of various borders points, and brought it unexpectedly nearer to a prosperous area extending from Texas to New York, New England and the cities around the Great Lakes. At the same time, the railways placed Monterrey in the centre of a vast mining area (composed of Zacatecas, Durango, Chihuahua and Coahuila as well as Nuevo León). Hundreds of mines were activated to produce minerals for the smelting plants, placing Nuevo León at the head of the metal-producing states in the country. This became a principal source of industrial wealth at the turn of the century.

But it was not only due to this international market that the Monterrey bourgeoisie was impelled to channel a large part of its fortunes toward capitalist production in mining and industry. A growing internal market had by now developed, at least between certain regions, and was spurred on by these same railroads, by the abolition of internal tariff barriers, the order which now prevailed along the trade routes, the elimination of danger posed by indian and bandit marauders and by the surge in production experienced by various regions. New demands were created by this capitalist development as well as an expansion of the internal market. Some of these demands, primarily in products of mass consumption, and for which there was no competition from foreign producers, could be satisfied by the light industry rapidly gaining a foothold in Monterrey. Another area of consumption, one of enormous importance, would originate within this same productive process involving the goods that these capitalists purchased from one another. So, what began as a process linked to North American capitalist production, now also involved an extension of the Mexican market. It was this continually expanding national market which inspired the Monterrey bourgeoisie (and its foreign backers) to undertake the most ambitious project of that time: the *Compañía Fundidora de Fierro y Acero de Monterrey*, which required an investment of 5,000,000,000 dollars and promoted an iron and steel industry that would anticipate other Latin American cities by several decades.

The socio-economic panorama of Monterrey at the beginning of the twentieth century can be summed up by the following points:

- The city was converted into the geographical axis of the productive capacity of Nuevo León. Industry had largely displaced the agricultural sector from the vanguard position it had occupied approximately up to 1885: in 1908 the value of its output was almost ten times higher than that of agriculture (41,429,116 *pesos* against 4,339,024).
- The factories and workshops of the city of Monterrey formed the principal foundation of the industrial production of Monterrey. Of the almost 40 million *pesos* which the state registered in 1906, 36 million were generated in the capital.
- At the same time, heavy metallurgy constituted within this sector the fundamental element. Of the previously mentioned 36 million (in 1906) more than 25 million were produced by two large steel mills. If we add what, already during these years, was being produced by the *Compañía Fundidora de Fierro y Acero* (iron metallurgy), the importance of these plants in the manufacturing context of the city becomes even clearer.
- The importance of Monterrey went beyond the Northeast. Statistics for the beginning of the century show that Nuevo León was one of the states with the highest industrial values in the country: it reached 13.9 percent of the total

while the Federal District and the State of Mexico accounted for 11.7 and 11.2 percent respectively; Veracruz produced 10.6 percent and Puebla 7.7.

- Similarly, Monterrey was the major metallurgic centre of the nation. According to the *Cuadro Sinóptico y Estadístico de la República Mexicana*, published in 1901, the exploitation of steel mills in the years 1897, 1898 and 1899 showed an amount of 216,007,952 *pesos*. Of this, Nuevo León accounted for 50,847,178 *pesos*, which represents 23.5 percent. Sonora, in second place, accounted for less than 20 million *pesos*.
- The development of capitalism in Monterrey and its area of influence, and the process of industrialization, changed the human panorama of the capital of Nuevo León. Between 1883 and 1910 its population increased by 112 percent, and with about 90,000 inhabitants it made up 24.3 percent of the state population just before the fall of Díaz.
- At the time of the Revolution, it was the fourth city in the country and occupied the same rank with respect to the annual population growth rate (3.7) in cities with more than 25,000 inhabitants during the 1895-1910 period.
- The demographic growth of Monterrey was not exclusively based on natural expansion. Migration from neighbouring and nearby states was highly significant. The majority of the arrivals came from San Luis Potosí, Coahuila, Durango, Tamaulipas, Zacatecas, Guanajuato and Aguascalientes. In 1900, 33 percent of the inhabitants of the city came from other states.

Those who had featured in primary accumulation during previous decades had modified their way of operating. Playing the role of a modernizing core within the framework of a class that was shaped by the development of capitalism itself, they decisively channeled their resources to productive sectors. There can be no doubt that this displacement was within the reach of these men. Patricio Milmo, Valentín Rivero, José Calderón, the Zambranos, Evaristo Madero and his sons, the Hernández family, etc. were the owners of fortunes which were sufficient to allow them to enter profitable activities.

But the enormous amount of investment required, not only by the more sophisticated part of industry, but also by mining, transportation and the foundation of banking facilities, obliged them to become associated. The process involved men and families with concrete histories. Immigrants from long ago, in certain cases: Patricio Milmo, of Irish origin, or Valentín Rivero, a Spaniard, found themselves in this situation. In other cases, heads of a family group and their descendants were natives: Evaristo Madero and the Zambranos were among them. However for the majority, if not all, of the family groups that have been researched, the basis of their capital had been the fruits of economic activities developed in the northeast of the country. These clusters of capital, in terms of their history, can be considered as regional. That twofold opportunity -international trade possibilities and a growing internal market- definitively transformed this bourgeoisie into large-scale producers obliging it to modernize its means of production while assuming the social relations that this entailed.

The Porfirian order effectively facilitated this process by providing the framework which stimulated the shift toward capitalist production. The joint stock company, which during this period acquired legal status, contributed to the concentration of Monterrey's existing capital in association with revenues from other Mexican and foreign sources, particularly the United States. The magnitude of the investments in industry and mining required it. These joint undertakings could be clearly seen in the creation of the banks (The Nuevo León Bank in 1892; The Mercantile Bank in 1899) in which local capital was predominant. The financial system was also being modernized and the branch banks would cover part of the regional sphere that I have referred to and would reinforce the conversion of the Monterrey bourgeoisie into a hegemonic group in a broad geographic area.

But it was the big steels mills -a fusion of manufacturing industry and mining- which epitomised both the investments and the process taking place in Monterrey. The importance of these enterprises in the economic growth of the city and in the development of capitalism in the regional space that surrounded it, must be emphasized: they required the most advanced technology, they produced for external (lead, particularly) and internal (the *Fundación de Fierro y Acero*) markets, they stimulated mining production not only in the north but also in other parts of the country, they required improvements in the regional transport-systems and large injections of labour, they accelerated the exploitation of coal and they supplied many medium and small scale industries. Moreover, this heavy industry singled out Monterrey within the context of Latin America at the beginning of the century. Together with other plants of somewhat lesser importance (production of glass and cement, and machinery on a limited scale), they characterized the bourgeoisie that took shape during this cycle of modernization.

From a historical as well as structural perspective, between 1890 and 1910 Monterrey and its bourgeoisie experienced the fusion of two levels of capitalist production: one which was common in the industrializing nations; the second, the product of Mexican economic and social development. This resulted in the overlapping of an international market with an extended regional market coupled with the increasing circulation of all types of goods. It also gave rise to the harmonious association of local and foreign capital, the establishment of manufacturing plants with modern technology in a country still unable to generate its own, and the utilization of a labour force in which a German or North American specialist might intermingle with workers recently arrived from San Luis Potosí or Aguascalientes. It is in this context that a solid bourgeois group, one of the most dynamic among the Mexican pre-revolutionary bourgeoisie, was consolidated in Monterrey. Its composition as a modernizing sector of this class was fashioned by the premises inherent in the *Porfiriato*. The rules of the game established by the Díaz regime -and which were profitably advantageous in a given international context- were not only accepted by that group of families, but contributed to the rise of the modern corporate sector of Monterrey.

From the moment of its conversion to a production-oriented bourgeoisie -that is, as a cohesive group of social agents identified by their position with respect to the management, ownership and advantageous use of capitalist production- this entrepreneurial class tended to diversify its investments and utilize the association and centralization of capital as a way to expand with minimum risks. It became necessary on occasion to unite with foreign capital and acquire foreign machinery and technology for the needs posed by mineral and manufacturing production. This was also clearly stimulated by the Porfirian system, which facilitated these mechanisms. The Monterrey capitalists learned that the benefits accruing from modernization were compatible with a harmonious relationship with capital and economic interests of other countries. In any case, one thing is clear: linkage with capital from other regions or from other countries does not imply that the Monterrey bourgeoisie lost control over that process responsible for its prosperity. And this became another important historical experience: the capacity to unite on approximately even terms with capital from other areas.

## REVOLUTION AND CARDENISMO

Joined by ties to the world market, a beneficiary of a growing internal market, recognized at the turn of the century for its influence in the northeastern border region, an enthusiastic contributor of the relative modernization sanctioned in Mexico by the Porfirian system and satisfied with the existing social and political order, it is not surprising that this regionally-based bourgeoisie embraced without major reservations the national state that Díaz succeeded in unifying. There was no reason in 1900 to promote alternative projects or autonomous schemes like those, for example, put forth by the Catalán bourgeoisie based in Barcelona. Perhaps this explains in part the future disagreement with another national project, which originated in the Mexican Revolution and seemingly reached its maximum expression during the Cárdenas period.

Recent studies indicate that the Monterrey entrepreneurial group managed to preserve a great deal of autonomy relative to the growing power of the revolutionary government. There was a dispute centered basically on two points:[2]

a) the preservation or suppression of concessions and privileges obtained during the *Porfiriato* which had been instrumental in the growth of manufacturing industry (especially the limited taxes paid by the Nuevo León businessmen and which were required in increased quantities to satisfy the needs of the revolutionary government);

b) the relations that this group had with a working class which could no longer be deprived of its rights and negotiating capacity, and which had been totally isolated in the context of the oligarchic control of the social relations imposed by Porfirio Díaz.

The Revolution obliged the Monterrey businessmen to undertake an enormous effort of adaptation which they were able to do because the state after 1910 was not interested in attacking all owners of property but particularly those owners whose land was brought under the plough or located in regions of intense social conflicts. The frictions that the bourgeoisie experienced with the political power of the post-revolutionary government, did not lead them to question the incorporation into the nation state which had been consolidated during the *Porfiriato*. Their response, in any case, consisted of working to extend their influence at the national level. And they would accomplish this by taking advantage of the definitive articulation and expansion of the internal market -brought about in the 1930s- and by promoting organizations representative of the Mexican entrepreneurial class.

Developments during the 1920s and 1930s were sufficiently vigorous to convert the Monterrey bourgeoisie into one of the principal opposition groups during the second great period of the Revolution: the Cárdenas years. On more than one occasion the businessmen of Monterrey headed the opposition to social reforms advocated by Lázaro Cárdenas while benefiting from the economic policies promoted by his government to convert Mexico into an industrial nation. The culmination of this dissension occurred in 1936 involving a conflict produced in *Vidriera de Monterrey*. Cárdenas was compelled to travel to the capital of Nuevo León in the midst of a convulsive climate of strikes and social antagonism and declared in a famous fourteen-point document his conception of what the *new* relations should be between the employers, other classes (especially the working class) and the state. In harsh terms, the president stated that: *"the government is interested not in debilitating the industry of the nation but in increasing it ..."* (point 8); *"the employers who are tired of the social struggle can deliver their companies to the workers or to the government"* (point 14). I have referred to this conflict -sparked by the demand of the *Vidriera* workers that they be allowed to form a union independent of employer control -because it posits in a concise manner one of the basic disagreements with Cárdenas: his advocacy of social reforms emanating from the revolutionary movement of 1910 and which could no longer be put off.

Nevertheless, these disagreements did not impede the Monterrey-based bourgeoisie from becoming one of the principal beneficiaries of the implementation of new economic development policies. The conspicuous growth in manufacturing in the city beginning in 1940 verifies this assertion. With the *cardenista* social policies at a low ebb and

2. For this point see Oscar Flores Torres, "De la edad del acero a los tiempos revolucionarios. Dos empresas industriales regiomontanas (1909-1923)," en *Monterrey, Nuevo León, el Noreste.*

social conflict redirected along more tolerable and manageable lines, the entrepreneurial group, which sprang from the *Porfiriato* -and now joined by new groups born of the same Revolution- would, with singular skill, take advantage of the economic policies put into effect beginning in the 1930s.

## REGIONAL RESEARCH AND METHODOLOGY

The rise, growth and articulation of this bourgeoisie can be seen clearly through a regional study. Before acquiring national influence (in diverse forms), this entrepreneurial class operated effectively in that regional sphere to which we referred earlier. This is surprising, when we observe the conditions which prevailed in Mexico during the sixty years prior to the Revolution -and indeed until 1930- and if we also consider that all bourgeois groups arise and expand in accordance with the markets to which they gain access.

For the merchants who prospered in Monterrey in the times of the revision of the border, there was no lack of regional market opportunities: first in terms of consumption, in which this group acted as intermediaries, then of land, to which they gained ownership, of credit, in their role as moneylenders, of mass consumption -in a later period- to which they acquired access as producers on a large scale channeling investments toward capitalist production, and of a labour force, as opportunities arose for a market of potential workers in mining and manufacturing. Without overlooking the fact that these developments were conditioned in large measure by relations established with the world market, the obvious conclusion is that this bourgeoisie followed the same path which led Mexico to the definitive formation of the national state. This process, moreover, was commonplace in other Latin American and European countries during the nineteenth century: in all of these cases it is intertwined with the consolidation of capitalism, notwithstanding that capitalism emerged to produce raw materials or manufactured goods.

This set of socioeconomic and political modifications -with their fits and starts, their inequalities and imbalances- was sustained by regionally-based movements. Thus in observing what transpired in given regions we are witnessing processes which are structurally significant in explaining reality. And because we should recognize their importance in structural terms, I insist on the methodological value of the regional perspective for the study of the period in question. The reason is simple: the method should effectively respond to the complex reality that it attempts to deal with and explain. A considerable share of the research currently underway in Mexico -and becoming more prevalent in countries like Argentina and Colombia, added to the significant work carried out in Spain during the last fifteen years- bears witness to the growing acceptance of the value and usefulness of this perspective. Another issue is whether this approach -valid for the nineteenth century- would provide similar results for more recent periods in Latin America. Finally, I would add the suggestion that interaction with European nineteenth-century specialists be intensified, that contacts be broadened and the flow of information increased.

CHAPTER FIVE

# *Montaña* and *Llanura* in the Politics of Central Mexico: The Case of Puebla, 1820-1920

GUY P. C. THOMSON*

## INTRODUCTION

Party political nomenclature in nineteenth-century Latin America was generally drawn from differences of ideology rather than geography. In this respect, the two rival regional party groupings which emerged in the state of Puebla after the European intervention command attention for being based upon topographical differences. Rivalry -often violent- between the *Montaña* and the *Llanura* lasted from 1867 until the mid 1880s. This is the only example, to my knowledge, of nineteenth-century Mexican political parties receiving a non-personalist or non-ideological labels. The *Montaña* was organised by a group of liberal military leaders from the mountainous north of the state who rose to prominence during the two decades between the American War and the expulsion of the Austrians. The *Llanura*, was a more nebulous group of liberal professionals, merchant-manufacturers and landowners from the central plateau region who, backed by federal force, held power in the state between 1867 and 1876. With Díaz's accession to the presidency, *Montaña* leaders, loyal *Porfiristas* since 1862, assumed control of state politics until the two party groupings were conciliated and incorporated into the *Pax Porfiriana* by *jalisciense* governor, Rosendo Márquez, during the late 1880s.[1]

These two regional party groupings present an attractive paradigm for analysing not only provincial politics over a critical period of transition from the *ancien regime* to the liberal state but also for examining the divergent social, economic and cultural contexts which nurtured these parties. *Montaña/Llanura* rivalry in mid-nineteenth-century Puebla also has a wider resonance when one thinks of the protracted conflict between the landed interests of central Jalisco and the peasant forces of Manuel Lozada in the *Sierra de Alica*, the challenges similar landed groups in the central areas of Querétaro, Mexico, Hidalgo and San Luis Potosí faced from rebellions in their mountain districts, the rivalry between central Oaxaca and the *Sierra de Juárez*, and between highland and lowland Guerrero and Chiapas.[2] In this chapter I shall explore the

* *Historian, Department of History, University of Warwick, Coventry, CV4 7AL United Kingdom.*

1. The politics of mid to late nineteenth-century Puebla are tackled in some depth by Laurens B. Perry, *Juárez and Díaz. Machine Politics in Mexico* (DeKalb, 1978); and Daniel Cosio Villegas, *Historia Moderna de México a República Restaurada, Vida Política*, and, *El Porfiriato. Vida Política Interior, Primera y Segunda Partes* (Mexico City, 1969-1970).

2. **General:** Leticia Reina, *Las rebeliones campesinas en México (1819-1906)* (Mexico, 1980); John Tutino, *From Insurrection to Revolution. Social Bases of Agrarian Violence, 1750-1940* (Princeton, 1986). **Jalisco and Nayarit:** Mario Alfonso Aldana Rendón, *La rebelión agraria de Manuel Lozada, 1873* (Mexico City, 1983); Jean Meyer, *Esperando a Lozada* (Zamora, 1984);

origins of the disequilibrium between the central plateau of Puebla and the *Sierra* Norte from late eighteenth century, the experience of the two regions during the Reform Wars and the European Intervention with the emergence, in the *Sierra*, of a particular kind of liberalism, the power struggle between the two parties between 1867 and 1884, the conciliation of regional rivalries under Porfirio Díaz, concluding with a glance at the recrudescence of regional rivalries during the Revolution.

## THE EMERGENCE OF THE NORTH IN PUEBLA POLITICS AND SOCIETY BEFORE THE REVOLUTION OF AYUTLA

For most of the colonial period, European settlement in the Puebla region concentrated in the central plateau region. The northern *Sierra* and the rolling tropical lowlands stretching to the Gulf of Mexico and the southern *Sierras* reaching to the Pacific proved unattractive to European settlers. They were deterred by their lack of easily exploitable precious metals or other cash commodities as by their remoteness and inaccessibility. Only the bureaucratic and economic ties established at first by the religious orders, and later renewed by the secular Church and the colonial state, brought these immense regions into the tenuous orbit of the colonial order. Thus, even by the mid eighteenth century, the province of Puebla remained little more than a geographical expression, with the non-Indian population concentrated almost exclusively in the provincial capital and cereal growing districts of the central valleys. Given the enormous productive capacity of these valleys, which even today yield grain surpluses exported to neighbouring states, it might have been expected that this pattern would have endured. However, a prolonged economic crisis, which gripped the province's central zone with growing intensity from the late seventeenth century, substantially modified the settlement pattern established during Puebla's Golden Age (taken, rather arbitrarily, as falling between 1532, the year of Puebla's foundation, and 1632, the year intercolonial trade, upon which much of the wealth of the province had been based, was abolished).[3] The repercussions of this crisis laid the basis for later rivalry between the *Sierra* and the plateau.

---

Jaime Olveda, *Gordiano Guzmán. Un cacique del siglo XIX* (Mexico City, 1980). **Querétaro:** Marie-France Houdart-Morizot, "Du bon usage des movements indiens: rebelles et rebellions de la Sierra Gorda, Mexique (1847-1849)," in *Cahiers des Ameriques Latines*, 23 (1981), 47-100. **San Luis Potosí:** Donald F. Stevens, "Agrarian Policy and Instability in Porfirian Mexico," in *The Americas*, 39:2 (1982), 153-166; Romana Falcón, *Revolución y caciquismo. San Luis Potosí, 1910-1938* (Mexico City, 1984). **Oaxaca:** Rosendo Pérez García, *La Sierra Juárez* (2 vols., Mexico City, 1956); Ismael Brachetti and Abraham Muñoz, *Tres intentos pro-soberania del estado de Oaxaca, 1857, 1871 and 1915* (Oaxaca, 1980); Paul Garner, "Autoritarismo revolucionario en el México provincial: el Carrancismo y el gobierno preconstitucional en Oaxaca, 1915-1920," in *Historia Mexicana* (hereafter *HMex*), 34:2 (1984), 238-299; Ronald Waterbury, "Non-revolutionary Peasants: Oaxaca Compared to Morelos in the Mexican Revolution," in *Comparative Studies in Society and History*, 17:4 (1975), 410-442. **Guerrero:** Ian Jacobs, *Ranchero Revolt. The Mexican Revolution in Guerrero* (Austin, 1982); Jaime Salazar Adame, "Movimientos populares durante el Porfiriato en el estado de Guerrero, (1885-1891)," in *Porfirio Díaz frente al descontento popular regional (1891-1893)*, Friedrich Katz and Jane Dale Lloyd, eds. (Mexico City, 1986). **Chiapas:** Jan Rus, "Whose Caste War? Indians, Ladinos, and the 'Caste War' of 1869," in *Spaniards and Indians in Southeastern Mesoamerica. Essays on the History of Ethnic Relations*, Murdo J. MacLeod and Robert Wasserstrom, eds. (Lincoln, 1983); Alicia Hernández Chávez, "La defensa de los finqueros en Chiapas, 1914-1920," in *HMex*, 28 (1979), 335-369.

3. All colonial data of Puebla in: G. P. C. Thomson, *Industry and Society in a Mexican City: Puebla de los Angeles, 1700-1850* (Syracuse, NY, forthcoming).

The development of commercial cereal production in the diocese of Michoacán during the seventeenth century, and in the Audiencia of New Galicia during the eighteenth, confined the market for Puebla's principal staple, wheat flour, to the limited bread consuming population of the south-east and the irregular and volatile needs of Spanish settlements and garrisons in the Caribbean. Depressed domestic and fitful overseas demand caused Puebla and Tlaxcala's estate agriculture to veer between stagnation and crisis during much of the eighteenth and nineteenth centuries. Only with the construction of the Puebla-Mexico City railway in 1869, bringing the reopening of the market of *tierra adentro* from which Puebla farmers had long been excluded by excessive transport costs, combined with the rapid growth of Mexico's urban population, did the market improve for Puebla's estate produced cereals. Agricultural depression was compounded by stagnant or declining demand for Puebla's traditional industrial staples -woollen cloth, hats, pottery, glass, soap, metal work and leather goods- in the face of competition from Peninsular imports as from other regions of production within New Spain. The only bright spot in Puebla's otherwise depressed eighteenth century was the cotton textile industry which, as a subsistence, merchant-dominated 'proto-industry', developed as much as symptom of the crisis as solution to it.[4]

The social consequences of the economic crisis afflicting the centre were the following. The demographic preponderance of the centre-west of the province (including Puebla, Cholula, and Huejotzingo) was reversed with its share of the population declining from 60 per cent in 1743 to 30 per cent in 1793. The principal cause of demographic wastage was emigration, both to the *barrio de los poblanos* in Mexico City as to the northern districts of the province (including Zacatlán, Huauchinango and San Juan de los Llanos) whose overall share of population increased from 18 per cent in 1681 to 32 per cent in 1824, with a marked increase in the non-Indian population, comprising 10 percent of the North's overall population in 1681, increasing to 20 per cent in 1793. This pattern of internal migration, characterised by whites and mestizos settling, over the eighteenth century, as farmers and artisans, in the hitherto neglected *Sierras* of central and southern Mexico, has only recently begun to be studied.[5]

Another consequence of the stagnation of Puebla's agricultural sector, and in part a result of this demographic trend, was a critical labour shortage, as Indian cultivators concentrated upon community agriculture as a steadier and more reliable source of subsistence than work on estates. Indian population recovery made this concentration upon community needs doubly necessary. The system of widespread rental of *hacienda* land to tenants, a possible solution to the labour shortage opted for elsewhere in Mexico, appears not to have developed in the Puebla region. This was for these reasons. First, Indian communities either possessed adequate land, precluding the need for rental of estate plots. Or, they sort to reclaim *hacienda* land, for which their villages possessed title deed, from the weakened estate sector. Hamnett shows this strategy to have sometimes met with success. A third explanation is that market conditions were too depressed and unstable, and cash too scarce (remember Puebla was not a mining region and local commerce frequently suffered from an acute shortage of circulating medium), to support a viable small-farming rental sector of the kind that Brading and Miller have found in the silver rich Bajío. Puebla's estate owners had therefore to concentrate upon demesne production, rather than rent, as their principal source of income. And for this they required a flexible seasonal labour supply, particularly during brief wartime booms when Caribbean demand for flour and wheat prices would

4. Thomson, *Industry and Society*, and, "The Cotton Textile Industry in Puebla During the Eighteenth and Early Nineteenth Centuries," in *The Economies of Mexico and Peru During the Late Colonial Period, 1760-1810*, Nils Jacobsen and Hans-Jürgen Puhle, eds. (Berlin, 1986), 169-202.

5. Thomson, *Industry and Society*. Frans J. Schryer, "From Rancheros to Pequeños Propietarios: Agriculture, Class Structure and Politics in the Sierra de Jacala, Mexico," in *Boletín de Estudios Latinoamericanos y del Caribe*, 34 (1983), 45.

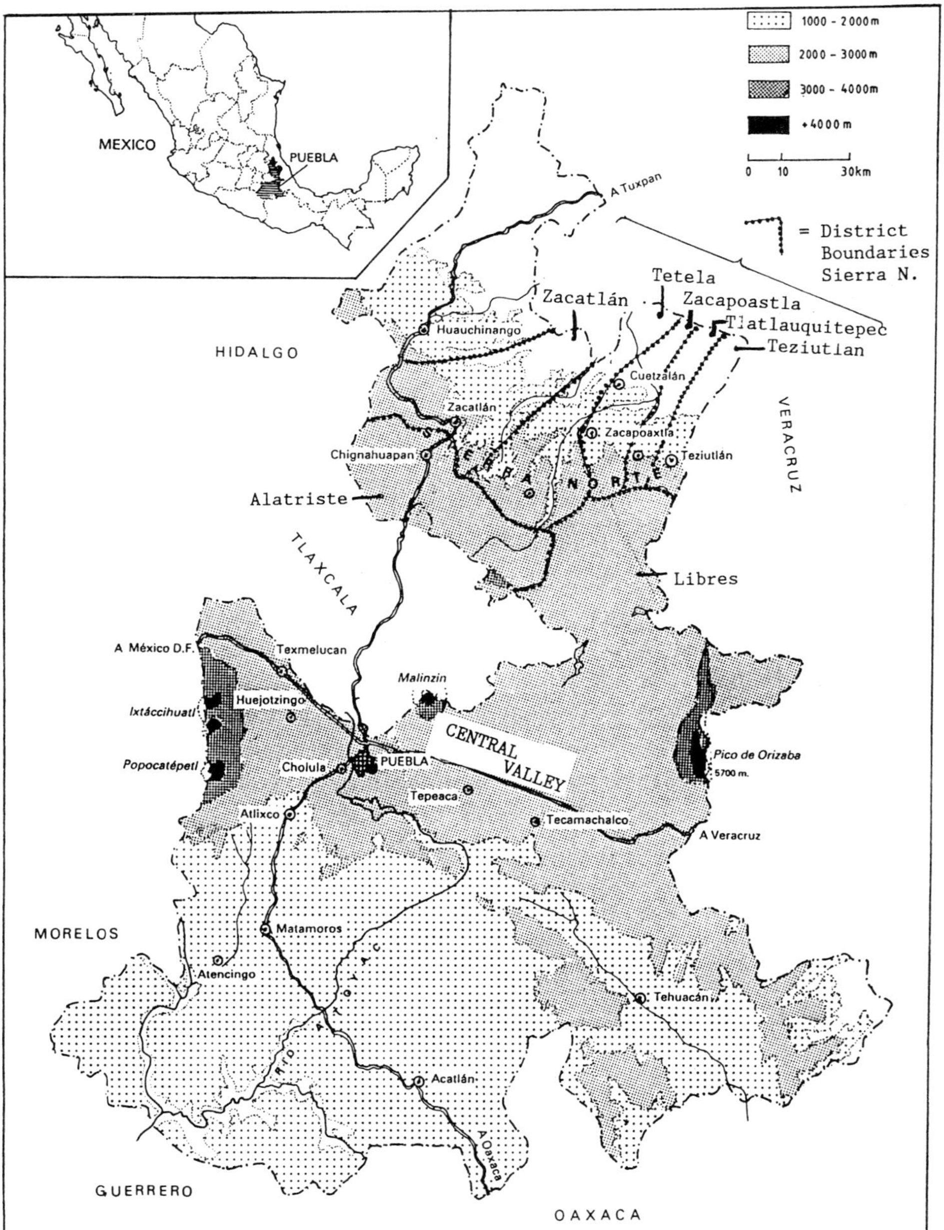


Design : Paul Wartena

suddenly increase. Scarcity of field labour became the great bain of Puebla's cereal agriculture. Landowners attempted to counter labour scarcity by coercion, often of a brutal and quite illegal kind. The *hacienda* jail -the *tlapixquera*- became a much hated feature of Puebla rural life, serving as a focus for Insurgent activity after 1810. Brian Hamnett has recently shown how Indians resisted coercion and bad treatment through the courts, often receiving judicial resolution, albeit much delayed, in their favour.[6]

For the purpose of the argument of this chapter, three important observations can be made about the social consequences of Puebla's eighteenth-century depression. The first is that no settled intermediate class of white and mestizo tenant farmers or *rancheros* emerged on the tableland of Puebla and Tlaxcala over the eighteenth century. Rather, whites and mestizos either migrated to the *Sierra* or the interior of New Spain, chiefly Mexico City, or remained bottled up in the villages, towns or provincial capital, engaged in proto-industrial activity, chiefly textiles, or, in commerce and transport. The second observation is that the relations between the Indian village population and the estate owning class, particularly in the cereal zones, were tense and mutually hostile. The third is that the economic position of the owners of cereal estates was at best precarious, and at times quite untenable, Puebla's landowners becoming a byeword for bankruptcy by the end of the eighteenth century.[7] Thus, the Puebla estate owning class, although much larger than its *oaxaqueño* counterpart, resembled it in its failure to establish a dominant relationship over Indian village agriculture of the kind Eric Van Young has observed for the Guadalajara region over the eighteenth century.[8] The post Independence political implications of these three factors -the absence of a significant intermediate class of *rancheros* and tenants, the unstable and mutually hostile relations between estate owners and Indian villagers and the fragile economic basis of the estate owning class- will shortly be appraised.

The picture for the northern *Sierra* on the eve of Independence was altogether different. No longer an inaccessible and unattractive Indian pale but a zone of immigration for Spaniards, mestizos and, indeed, Indians, expelled from the tableland by economic depression and harsh labour conditions. Censuses reveal an impressive increase in the number of *ranchos*, cattle *estancias* and small sugar mills (*trapiches*) between 1791 and 1804. Tithe records confirm a marked expansion of the non-Indian rural economy in the *Sierra* over the second half of the eighteenth century. This was the period during which the commodities which would become the North's staples -sugar loaf (*piloncillo*), aguardiente, coffee and vanilla- were pioneered in response to rising sub-tropical and tropical commodity prices, contrasting with the stagnant price level for temperate cereals on the plateau through to the 1850s. During the wars of Independence, the *Sierra* region further benefited from the breakdown of long distance interregional trade, particularly from the collapse of the cattle trade from the northern provinces which stimulated cattle raising in the gulf lowlands, closer the urban meat-consuming markets of Central Mexico. Dealing in contraband imports also became a

---

6. Puebla's deputy to the Cortes reported in 1814 that *"Se ha visto ahora que al entrar los Insurgentes al saqueo de una finca, lo primero que han hecho has sido variar las Tlapixqueras, romper los libros de gobierno e inbuir a los Indios en ideas lisongeras,"* quote from *Colección de documentos para la historia de la guerra de Independencia de México, 1808-1821* Juan E. Hernández y Davalos, ed. (Mexico City, 1877-1882), vol. V, 552. Günther Vollmer, "La évolución cuantitativa de la población indígena en la región de Puebla (1570-1810)," in *HMex*, 23 (1973), 43-51. Brian Hamnett, *Roots of Insurgency. Mexican Regions, 1750-1824* (Cambridge, 1986), 85-86 and 89-90. David A. Brading, *Haciendas and Ranchos in the Mexican Bajío* (Cambridge, 1978), 61-114; Simon Miller, "The Mexican Hacienda between the Insurgency and the Revolution: Maize Production and Commercial Triumph on the *Temporal*," in *Journal of Latin American Studies* (hereafter *JLAS*), 16 (1984), 309-336.

7. Thomson, *Industry and Society*.

8. William Taylor, *Landlord and Peasant in Colonial Oaxaca* (Stanford, 1972); and Eric Van Young, *Hacienda and Market in Eighteenth-Century Mexico. The Rural Economy of Guadalajara, 1675-1820* (Berkeley, 1981).

lucrative activity among the *Sierra*'s merchants as the wars disrupted the colonial trading system and as the smaller Gulf ports -Tuxpan, Tampico, etc.- increased their share of overseas trade.[9]

The relative vigour of the economy of the *Sierra* and the *tierra caliente* and the first signs of the emergence of a very distinct socio-political personality from that of the plateau can be observed in the important part played by the *Sierra* in the insurgency. Particularly prominent was the Osorno clan of Zacatlán who mobilised mestizo tenant farmers and Indian villagers in one of the most sustained popular movements of the wars of Independence. This movement had a very similar social basis and political character to the Márquez-Galindo rebellion in the same region, examined later in the chapter. The resilience of Guadalupe Victoria's insurgent fiefdom in Papantla, which contributed importantly to the success of the Army of Three Guarantees in 1821, was also made possible by the bouyancy of the lowland cattle and vanilla economy and by the support of *rancheros* and merchants. The first governor of the independent state of Puebla, Carlos García Arriaga, was a liberal militia officer and merchant from Cuetzalán, the *Sierra* town which would become the centre of the coffee zone later in the century. At this point, however, *Sierra* interests were still in no position to project themselves as a leading political force in the province, in spite of the North escaping the economic and political disruption afflicting the central plateau region during the wars of Independence. Nor, for a decade following Independence, were the merchants, manufacturers and landowners of the centre able to effectively regroup and propose a solution to the economic crisis facing the plateau region.[10]

After a short-lived bubble of prosperity accompanying the Napoleonic wars, the central plateau tumbled, after 1810, into a social crisis of unprecedented proportions, lasting until well into the 1830s. The demographic wastage of the state capital and centre west accelerated, with a mass migration of artisans to Mexico City or their recruitement into the army. The secular problems facing estate agriculture and manufacturing were aggravated by the loss of the Caribbean market for flour and increased competition from imported manufactures. By the early 1830s, Puebla's population had fallen to half of the level at which it had stood at the turn of the century. The city had become the epicentre of the struggles between Conservatives and Liberals. The cotton textile industry was all but extinguished and the estate agriculture lay abandoned.[11]

The intensity of the crisis provoked a vigorous response from what remained of Puebla's political leadership after the collapse of the colonial state and the flight of Spanish merchants who had dominated Puebla politics before Independence. Perched on the edge of an abyss of seemingly irredemiable economic decline and social crisis, economic interests began, in the mid-1830s, to regroup and reassert themselves, with the help of centrally imposed protectionist policies, secured in large part by Puebla's powerful lobby in the capital and considerable influence upon General Santa Anna. Elite and middle-ranking families with widespread interests spanning the Church, whole sale trade, flour milling and cereal agriculture, the manufacturing industry, the provincial militia and the national army formed the core of a provincial political leadership whose influence was perhaps unmatched by any other Mexican regional group through until the Revolution of Ayutla. They comprised a pragmatic political caste whose principal objective was to ensure the recovery of the economy of the provincial capital and the plateau region through a combination of tariff protection, a positive attitude towards Church wealth and a flexible and circumspect attitude towards the political and ideo-

9. Thomson, *Industry and Society*; Aristides Medina Rubio, *La iglesia y la producción agrícola en Puebla, 1540-1795* (Mexico City, 1983), 158-170.

10. Hamnett, *Roots of Insurgency*, 139-142. Jorge Flores, *La revolución de Olarte en Papantla (1836-1838)* (Mexico City, 1838), 8-11, 51-58.

11. Thomson, *Industry and Society*.

logical conflicts between federalism and centralism and liberalism and conservatism.[12] The bourgeoisie of the plateau met with some success in securing the reconstruction of the economy of the state capital but this was insufficient to provide a basis for any sustained growth of the provincial economy as a whole. The fragmentation of the national market, recurrent civil war and backward communications ensured that the rural economy of the plateau remained depressed, while imposing an early limit upon the modernisation and expansion of the textile industry.

How did the north of the state fare over the three decades following Independence? In spite of the steady growth of its population, its continuing attraction of immigrants from the centre, as from Europe, and the continued expansion of the northern economy, there was widespread opposition in the north to protectionist policies designed principally to benefit industrial and landowning interests in the provincial capital and the plateau. *Sierra* producers sought freer and easier access to the overseas market for tropical commodities and consumers preferred cheaper contraband imported goods to expensive highland manufactures. Policies from the centre, favouring the continued clerical administration of Indian districts, direct taxes on sugar and alcohol production, a prohibition on tobacco production and the maintenance of a centrally administered head tax, antagonised the growing non-Indian (as well as the Indian) population of the *Sierra.* In particular non-Indians sought greater participation in local and district government and a reduction in the over-bearing influence of the clergy. A broad spectrum of grievances, among both the non-Indian and Indian population, was behind the rebellion occurring in Papantla between 1836-1838, led by Mariano Olarte, whose father had fought with the Osorno clan. Olarte received support from throughout the *Sierra.*[13]

While northern interests disputed the protectionist and centralising policies of the centre, which offered them so little, the southern districts along the Pacific coast became more closely integrated with the manufacturing economy of the centre as raw cotton producers. Political centralisation and expropriation of village lands for cotton production, coupled with frequent disruption to cotton production caused by legal and illegal raw cotton imports, provoked a rash of rebellions, met by harsh military repression, during the 1840s.[14] Thus, narrow protectionist policies, political centralisation and military repression provoked general antagonism in the north and the south of the state towards the centre and a broad sympathy for the Ayutla rebellion led by the old insurgent leader from the Costa Chica of Guerrero, Juan Alvarez, in 1854.

## THE *MONTAÑA* AND THE *LLANURA* DURING THE *LIBERAL-PATRIOTIC* REVOLUTION, 1854-1867

The Revolution of Ayutla precipitated a process of realignment in provincial politics with the central plateau losing its historic, albeit often tenuous, political ascendancy

12. Guy P. C. Thomson, "Protectionism and Industrialisation in Mexico, 1821-1854," in *Latin America: Economic Imperialism and the State*, Christopher Abel and Colin Lewis, eds. (London, 1985), 125-146; Carmen Aguirre y Alberto Carabarin, "Propietarios de la industria textíl de Puebla en el siglo XIX: Dionisio José Velasco y Pedro de Zuñiga," in *Puebla en el siglo XIX*, edited by the Centro de Investigaciones Históricas y Sociales, Universidad Autónoma de Puebla (Puebla, 1983), 177-224; and, for the influence of the Haro y Tamariz, a family of Puebla industrialists, upon Santa Anna, see Jan Bazant, *Antonio Haro y Tamariz y sus aventuras políticas, 1811-1869* (Mexico City, 1985), 24-74.

13. Flores, *Revolución de Olarte*, 11-13, 58-68.

14. Ana María Dolores Jaramillo, *Insurrecciones rurales en el estado de Puebla, 1868-1870* (Puebla, 1985), 5-6; Reina, *Rebeliones campesinas*, 117-120, 245-246; and Hamnett, *Roots of Insurgency*, 211-213.

and the north of the state gaining increasing political weight. At first, however, the renewal of the armed struggle between Liberals and Conservatives obeyed no clear geographical logic with both Liberals and Conservatives seeking and finding support within the *Sierra*, the plateau region and in the south of the state. The Liberals found support among the merchant group in the city of Puebla, the young educated professional groups throughout the state and lower level military officers, particularly the commanders of units of the National Guard formed to combat the North Americans in 1847. The Conservatives drew upon the clergy, the old army (rather than the recently established National Guard), merchant-industrialists and large landowners.

The intensification of the struggle between Liberals and Conservatives brought a radicalisation of the Liberal's Reform programme which shattered the pragmatic consensus which had existed in the central region of Puebla since the 1830s. The attack upon Church wealth, the erosion of protectionism and the reassertion of economic liberalism, and the state of Puebla becoming the central theatre of the civil war, posed unprecedented threats to the landowning and industrial interests of the centre. Underlying the centre's loss of political control of the state was the continued weakness of the economy of the plateau and the political ineffectiveness of the landed, mercantile and industrial elite in a period of sustained civil war broadening, after 1862, into international conflict. Between 1854 and the end of the Three Years War, party affiliations both became more ideologically polarised as well as spatially extended as conflicts spread over state, and eventually, with the European intervention, over national boundaries. Politics also deepened as both Conservatives and Liberals, for reasons of military necessity, sought to draw upon hitherto untapped popular political reserves. This extension of hitherto largely intra-elite squabbles into deeper social conflicts contributed importantly to the political differentiation between the north and centre over the late 1850s and 1860s. The rise of the north in Puebla's politics has therefore three principal explanations: an economic, a political, and a social explanation.

First: economics. Economic instability on the plateau became more critical after 1857 as a result of the disruption caused by the nationalisation of Church wealth, the intensification of military conflicts, and the delay these caused to the introduction of transport improvements. In contrast, the economy of the *Sierra* continued to develop with the development of mining and the expansion of cattle and coffee production. Not too much, however, should be made of these regional economic disparities since the northern extractive economy was still in its infancy while the engine of the provincial economy, however rickety, still remained on the plateau region. The point to make is that Reform legislation and military conflict undermined the cohesion which had characterised the central region's social elite over the 1830s and 1840s, destroying its ability to act as a class. In contrast, *Sierra* interests drew strength from liberal reforms while warfare proved less damaging to *Sierra* interests, many, indeed profiting from supplying armies. Indeed liberal legislation, combined with loosening of fiscal and administrative controls traditionally exercised from the centre of the province, created a basis for the emergence of an autonomous *serrano* bourgeoisie of the kind analysed by Frans Schryer in the *Sierra de Hidalgo*.[15]

Second: politics and war. The strategic importance of the *Sierra* to the Liberals during the Three Years war and the European Intervention, and to Porfirio Díaz during the *República Restaurada*, served to entrench a circle of military leaders and their followings -chiefly the locally organised units of the National Guard- whose organisation and political effectiveness were unmatched elsewhere in the state. The plateau region, apart from the misfortune of becoming the power base for the 'losing' side in these conflict

**15.** Frans J. Schryer, *The Rancheros of Pisaflores. The History of a Peasant Bourgeoisie in Twentieth-Century Mexico* (Toronto, 1980).

-first the Conservatives, then the Europeans and finally the Juarista-Lerdista civilista Liberals-, proved much less amenable to mobilisation and militarisation. Ten years of involvement first with the liberal, then with the patriotic struggle endowed the *Sierra's* military commanders and political leaders with impeccable ideological credentials which could not be ignored after the expulsion of the Austrians in 1867. Conversely, the legitimacy of the *civilista* leaders of the central plateau, tainted by collaboration with a discredited conservatism and with the European Intervention, proved impossible to establish during the *República Restaurada*. Moreover, Juárez' choice of Puebla as the first candidate in a centralisation policy involving federal intervention in the internal politics of the states, made it doubly hard for plateau leaders to establish their legitimacy, strengthening the *serranos*' claim to be the true heirs to the liberal and patriotic struggle.[16]

Third: society. The people of the *Sierra* proved more responsive to liberal reforms, more amenable to military recruitment and more manageable in party politics than the inhabitants of the plateau. This, at first sight, may seem paradoxical, since the plateau had for centuries been much more directly exposed to colonial administrative control, taxation, forced labour and military recruitement. The *Sierra*, in contrast, had only been loosely integrated within the colonial system, only recently linked to the wider national and international economy, only recently exposed to a more direct external political control, and, only since the mid eighteenth century, had the *Sierra* experienced any appreciable immigration of non-Indian colonists. Moreover, it was generally the case that the less accessible Indian districts, throughout Latin America, were more averse to liberal reforms than central and more Europeanised regions.[17]

How, then, was liberalism introduced, armies mobilised and the 'political machine' of the *Montaña* contracted, in this apparently inhospitable terrain? And why were the leaders from plateau unable to match the *Sierra* leaders in harnessing the population to the 'ideas of the age'? There are, it seems, three keys to understanding *Montaña* political and military effectiveness and *Llanura* weakness over this stormy passage from *Ancien Régime* to the liberal state. These are:

1) Effective leadership in a period of liberal revolution.
2) Reciprocity between leaders and their following.
3) A unifying myth associated with the *Sierra* region.

### *Effective leadership*

The nineteenth century leaders which every *poblano* can name are Juan Nepomuceno Méndez, Juan Crisóstomo Bonilla and Juan Francisco Lucas, *'Los Tres Juanes de la Sierra.'* They are chiefly remembered for their heroic participation in the victory against the French Army on the heights of Loreto and Guadalupe above Puebla on the 5th of May 1862 and their prolonged resistance to the invader from their *Sierra* stronghold until the eventual defeat of the Austrian army in 1867.[18] They serve as an important antidote to a belief, widely held elsewhere in Mexico, that Puebla was (and is) a conservative, clerical stronghold where leaders more often were to be found collaborating with, than resisting, foreigners. *'Los Tres Juanes'* were representative of a

16. Cosio Villegas, *HMM República Restaurada, Vida política*, 168-174; Perry, *Juárez and Díaz*, 75-88.

17. For the hostile reaction among Indians to liberal reforms in Guatemala, see R. L. Woodward, "Central America from Independence to c. 1870," in *The Cambridge History of Latin America* (hereafter *CHLA*), Leslie Bethell, ed. (Cambridge, 1985), III, 484-490; in Mexico, see Charles Hale, *Mexican Liberalism in the Age of Mora* (New Haven, 1968), 215-247; and in Bolivia, see Heraclio Bonilla, "Peru and Bolivia from Independence to the War of the Pacific," in *CHLA*, III, 572-576.

18. Jesús Ferrer Gamboa, *Los Tres Juanes de la Sierra de Puebla* (Mexico City, 1967).

broader caste of liberal *Sierra* leaders who emerged as commanders in the National Guard as early as the American War, serving during the Three Years War and the European Intervention, attaining after 1867 state and federal deputyships, *jefaturas políticas* and state governorships. They formed the core of the *Montaña* party in state politics.

What did this conspicuously successful group of leaders have in common? Most *Sierra* leaders were from modest backgrounds, mostly descended from white and mestizo colonists who had settled as farmers, petty merchants and artisans on the southern edge of the *Sierra* in the later eighteenth century. These families faced, in the five districts which make up the southern *Sierra* -Teziutlán, Tlatlauqui, Zacapoastla, Tetela and Zacatlán- a narrow elite composed a handful of families in each district, descended from earlier Spanish settlers, who had occupied the small amount of land suitable for *haciendas* and *ranchos*. This elite, in hand with the Church, occupied the few available administrative posts and enjoyed privileged access to the labour services (*tópiles*) of the Indian population, whose religious festivals and confraternities they patronised. The enthusiasm of non-elite white and mestizo *serranos* for the establishment of the liberal state on the local level can in part be explained by the challenge liberalism posed to the dominance of these elite families, to the clergy and the monopoly access enjoyed by both groups to the Indian population. The separation of Church and state, the establishment of secular education, the formation of the National Guard, the abolition of compulsory labour services, the sale of municipal and Church property, the establishment of a local bureaucracy, all promised a range of opportunities which proved particularly attractive to this class of white and mestizo settlers facing social ostracism and cultural isolation.[19]

Liberalism thus created a political space, particularly in its military guise in the National Guard, for the demographically aggressive yet hitherto culturally and politically marginal non-Indian population of the *Sierra*. Since the bulk of land in the *Sierra* belonged to Indians, the avenues of career mobility offered by the liberal state were doubly attractive. This, I feel, explains the enthusiasm for liberalism in certain districts such as Zacatlán, Huauchinango and Tetela and the energy with which liberal leaders established *Juntas Patrióticas*, as guardians of the ceremonies of the liberal-patriotic state, *Cuerpos Filarmónicos*, to ensure that the clergy no longer enjoyed a monopoly of music and ritual, and, schools, to ensure a liberal-patriotic version of past, present and future. Liberal leaders formed masonic lodges which served almost as 'Committees of Public Safety', necessary guarantees of the liberal-patriotic state against clerical and conservative reaction. And in districts such as Zacapoastla, where the Catholic Church continued to work hand in glove with conservative families, Methodist congregrations were formed to ensure to complete break with the old order.[20]

Liberalism was not embraced with the same single minded purpose among corresponding social groups in the central plateau, nor could it meet with the same success. I can only surmise the reasons for this. As I have already suggested, the combined dominance of the *hacienda* and the Indian community left less space for the accommodation of intermediate social groups, which traditionally had chosen migration as a solution to limited local opportunities. Migration fragmented the social constituency which might have embraced liberalism in the rural areas of the plateau. Those on the *Llanura* seeking a 'liberal political sociability' tended, therefore, to concentrate in the state or federal capitals, or, to gravitate to liberal districts in the *Sierra*. The latter course was followed by Alberto de Santa Fe, later renowned for his attempt to organise

19. I have made a preliminary analysis of the social bases of *Sierra* liberal leadership in G. P. C. Thomson, "Mobilización conservadora, insurrección liberal y rebeliones indígenas, 1854-76," in *America Latina dallo stato coloniale allo stato nazione*, Antonio Annino et.al, eds. (Torino, 1987), 592-614.

20. Jean-Pierre Bastian, *Protestantismo y sociedad en México* (Mexico City, 1983), 87.

a socialist uprising on the Puebla plateau. He was born in Puebla in 1840 but chose to live in Tetela for much of the 1860s and 1870s, where he served as *Jefe Político* for a short time before the Revolution of Tuxtepec.[21] In the state capital, liberalism faced the barriers of the continued corporate importance of the Church, a largely unreformed institutional heritage accumulated since early colonial times and the continued existence of conservative social elite, struggling over this period to maintain its dominance. In contrast, liberal leaders in the *Sierra* confronted a much more fragile 'old order' and could design their version of liberalism on a clean slate.

The effectiveness of *Sierra* leadership was further strengthened by use made of kinship ties. The families descended from immigrants from the plateau, tended to compensate for their cultural marginality by demographic aggressiveness. Not only do we find in the principal areas of white and mestizo settlement on the temperate southern margins of the *Sierra*, a dense concentration of families of common descent, but these families sent off advance guards from their 'home bases' into the *tierra caliente* to develop sugar, coffee and aguardiente production. This combination of concentration and dispersal of kinship ties was of great strategic value to *Sierra* leaders in their military control and, later, civil administration of districts. This was the patrimonial side to *Sierra* liberal leadership which eventually gave it such a bad name.[22] On the plateau, the entrenched pattern of out-migration and mobility among intermediate groups, from whom liberal leadership was recruited, would have tended to reduce the potential use of kinship ties in war and politics.

### *Reciprocity*

The liberal state required a liberal citizenry. The *Sierra*, with its majority Totonac and Nahuatl speaking Indian population, would seem, at first, to have offered little potential in this area. And yet, *Sierra* liberal National Guard commanders were much more successful than their *Llanura* counterparts in forming Indian fighting units, which remained in military formation over prolonged periods, and in receiving material support from Indian communities in the provisioning of military campaigns. *Montaña* success in this area has sometimes been put down to the way liberal leaders harnessed the Indian warrior traditions of an area which had never successfully been vanquished by the Spaniards. The kind of warfare favoured by the largely Indian National Guard units organised by Juan Francisco Lucas, characterised by great mobility punctuated by short skirmishes, in which the machete and the pike were favoured over the rifle and the sword, would seem to give some credence to this idea.[23] However, if one examines the way recruitment and the provisioning of armies were managed by the *Sierra's* liberal leaders and how, over the same period, liberal reforms were introduced in such a way as to create minimum disruption to Indian communities, it becomes easier to understand why most Indians at least did not oppose liberalism, even if they showed little interest in becoming full citizens of the liberal state.

It is not possible to give more than the briefest explanation of this crucial factor in the *Montaña's* political success. The first point to make is that the non-Indian economy of the *Sierra* accommodated itself to, rather attempted to supplant the Indian economy. Non-Indian pressure upon Indian land existed on the northern and southern margins of the *Sierra*, from the cattle breeders of the tropical lowlands and the mestizo peasant farmers of temperate fruit and cereals in the hills and narrow valleys just below the

21. *Archivo Municipal de Tetela de Ocampo*, legs. 1876-1877; Reina, *Rebeliones campesinas*, 255-268; and, Gastón García Cantú, *El socialismo en México, Siglo XIX* (Mexico City, 1969), 220-234.
22. Thomson, "Mobilización conservadora."
23. For a brief biography of Juan Francisco Lucas, see: David LaFrance and G. P. C. Thomson, "Juan Francisco Lucas, Patriarch of the Sierra Norte de Puebla," in *The Human Tradition in Latin America. The Twentieth Century*, William H. Beezley and Judith Ewell, eds. (Wilmington, 1987).

*altiplano.* In the extensive mountainous region in between, although non-Indians had begun to pioneer small coffee plantations, their demand for land was limited to a series of small pastures needed for grazing and corralling cattle brought up from the lowlands, and to sites for small sugar mills and aguardiente factories. Non-Indian settlers would, undoubtedly, have liked more land, judging from the prolific filing of denunciations of common land following the enactment in 1868 of the 1856 law instructing common and communal lands to be subdivided among individual owners. However, a protracted Indian rebellion in the Xochitlan/Cuetzalán area between 1868 and 1871, with overtones of a 'Caste War', appears to have deterred non-Indians from making any substantial encroachments upon Indian lands. In fact, Indians came out of this stormy periods with most of their village land intact, now held individually rather than corporatively. So when coffee production took off in the *Sierra* towards the end of the century, the crop was grown on Indian lands with non-Indians largely confined to the more profitable processing and marketing.[24]

So, nothing corresponding to the gulf existing on the plateau between the *hacienda* and the Indian village existed in the *Sierra.* Economic relations between Indians and non-Indians in the *Sierra* were characterised by much more regular, if sometimes unequal, commercial exchange rather than the intensive seasonal labour demand, generally involving an element of coercion, which was the basis of economic relations between estate owners and Indians on the plateau. A stronger basis of economic reciprocity therefore existed in the *Sierra* than on the plateau. This eased the task of military and civil administration.

The commercial and administrative ties which formed the basis of relations between non-Indians and Indians in the *Sierra*, served also to sustain a network of *compadrazgo*, linking Indians reciprocally with non-Indians over wide areas. While *compadrazgo* undoubtedly existed upon *haciendas* and within villages on the plateau, it is doubtful that it played any significant role in defining and stabilising the relationship between Indian villagers and the landowning class. A landowner's principal concern was the maintenance of horizontal ties with other landowning families, merchants, the Church and the state, with vertical ties extending no further than his small resident labour force but not with quarrelsome and ill-disciplined villagers. And since only a very small proportion of the plateau's population resided on *haciendas*, this limited the range and depth of direct reciprocal ties between the elite landowning families, their estate managers and overseers on the one hand, and the mass of the rural labouring populations on the other. Thus *Sierra* leaders were likely to be tied much more closely and reciprocally to the people they sought to influence, organise, arm, tax, etc., than their counterparts on the plateau.[25]

*Sierra* liberal leaders not only ensured that liberal land legislation did not lead to Indian land despoliation, but attempted to accommodate the military organisation of the *Sierra* to Indian sensibilities. In 1857-1858, forced military recruitment, and unpopular liberal legislation, such as the liquidation of the capital funds of the religious confraternities, under an insensitive liberal state governor from the plateau, Miguel Cástulo

24. For twentieth-century political and economic developments in the coffee region, see: Luisa Paré, "Caciquismo y estructura de poder en la Sierra Norte de Puebla," in *Caciquismo y poder político en el México rural*, R. Bartra et.al. (Mexicc City, 1982), 31-61, and, "Inter-Ethnic and Class Relations (Sierra Norte Region, State of Puebla)," in *Race and Class in Post-Colonial Society*, UNESCO, ed. (Paris, 1977), 377-420.

25. According Tannenbaum, only 20 percent of the rural population of Puebla resided on *haciendas* in 1910, see: Frank Tannenbaum, *Peace by Revolution. Mexico after 1910* (New York, 1968), 192-194. Ties of *compadrazgo* between liberal military leaders and Indian village authorities can be observed in correspondence during military campaign. *Lucas Papers, Familias Manzano y Ayala* (Puebla), and *Archivo Municipal de Tetela de Ocampo* (hereafter *AMTO*), legs. 1868-1872, containing material for the *Sierra* rebellion of 1868-1870 and the revolt of La Noria in 1871-1872.

Alatriste, had threatened to propel many of the *Sierra's* Indian communities into the conservative camp. As a result, *Sierra* liberal leaders were later much more cautious. They weaned the Indian population into the liberal camp by abolishing ecclesiastical fees, tithes, *alcabalas* and *igualas* (sales taxes) replacing them with two taxes, one for funding secular education and the other for funding the National Guard. The Guard was recruited voluntarily, with peace loving Totonac Indians exempted from service. National guardsmen were exempted from all taxes. This proved a powerful inducement to Indian communities along the southern flank of the *Sierra*, who, because of land shortage, had been obliged, for generations, to work on *haciendas* for the cash needed for payment of taxes and the purchase of maize. Apart from freeing the Indian from taxation, service in the Guard could bring greater rewards. There is some evidence that guardsmen received preference or used their influence in gaining individual title to communal land, and, in the district of Zacapoastla, guardsmen serving the successful Indian leader, General Juan Francisco Lucas, received an entire *hacienda* which was subdivided among them according to rank. The undoubted popularity of the National Guard among certain groups of *Sierra* Indians is attested by the resistance put up to its partial demobilisation and incorporation within the national army during the 1880s.[26]

The National Guard was the keystone of the *Montaña's* political control of the *Sierra* and was used routinely at election time to deter opposition throughout the 1860s and 1870s. The failure of *Llanura* leaders to establish a military formation of corresponding effectiveness goes a long way to explaining the ability of the *Montaña* to retain the political initiative over the period between the Revolutions of Ayutla and Tuxtepec. For the landowners of the *Llanura*, military service, forced or voluntary, threatened to distract their resident labour forces while the chaos of civil war threatened to disrupt already tense relations between *haciendas* and neighbouring villages. The National Guard was also viewed with distrust by *Llanura* leaders, since it threatened to embody and give voice to social forces which were best left undisturbed. Indeed, for much of this period, '*peones de fincas rústicas, acortizados, casilleros y calpaneros*' in *hacienda* districts were exempt from the state of Puebla's National Guard law, as a result of pressure from landowners. For the landowning class, the ideal military formation was the mounted Flying Squad, the 'contra-guerrilla,' recruited *ad hoc* from among the resident work forces of an *hacienda* zone, of the kind organised by General Cuellar of San Martín Texmelucan and General Antonio Rodríguez Bocardo of Cuyoaco (San Juan de los Llanos) during the 1860s and 1870s. The very idea of the National Guard, of a permanently organised, liberal patriotic 'people at arms,' was anathema to most *Llanura* leaders.[27]

---

26. For fears of a Caste War resulting from liberal reforms, see correspondence between Rafael Avila, *Jefe Político* of Teziutlán, and Miguel Cástulo Alatriste, March 1860, in *Archivo de la Defensa Nacional*, Cancelados, caja 67/111/2/442, fs. 15-19. For Totonacs and military service, see *AMTO*, caja 9, exp. 4: Tiburcio Reyes, Tuzamapa, to *Jefe Político*, March 10, 1866. Lafrance and Thomson, "Juan Francisco Lucas."

27. For a denunciation of Manuel Márquez Galindo's use of the National Guard to secure the election in Zacatlán in favour of General Juan N. Méndez in 1880, see: *Periódico Oficial* 11:51 (1880), 3. For the pressure from landowners, see *AMTO* leg. 41bis, 1871, Corresp. de varias autoridades, L. Flores, sec. de Hacienda, Gob. Est. de Puebla, to *Jefe Político*, Tetela de Ocampo. For General Cuellar's role in containing the *Sierra* rebellion of 1868-1870, see: Huerta, *Insurrecciones rurales*, 72-73. For General Rodríguez Bocardo, *hacendado* from Cuyoaco and commander of a formidable cavalry battalion, see Miguel Márquez Galindo, *La gran década nacional, o relación histórica de la Guerra de Reforma, intervención extranjera y gobierno de Archiduque Maximiliano, 1857-67* (Mexico City, 1906); and, Antonio Carrión, *Historia de la ciudad de Puebla de los Angeles* (Puebla, 1897; repr. Puebla, 1970), II, 497-553.

*Unifying Myth*

Some sense of the self confidence of *Sierra* leadership will have already emerged. Contemporary literature often portrayed the people of the *Sierra* as an egalitarian, united, harmonious, liberal and patriotic community, accounting for their effectiveness against the foreign invaders and for their political ascendancy over the class divided society of the *Llanura*. While clearly this view is nonsense if taken to describe the entire society of the *Sierra Norte*, it nevertheless approximates the kind of social and ideological climate which developed within the areas of white and mestizo settlement of the southern *Sierra*, as a result the successful accommodation of liberal reforms and the prominent participation of these areas in the patriotic struggle against the Europeans. It is not unusual to find in contemporary documentation this period referred to as 'the Revolution.' It is not difficult to imagine how this sense of a sharp break with the past arose.[28]

The overbearing position of the Church had been successfully challenged. The dominance of traditional elite families in most *Sierra* districts had been shattered. Many ordinary men, including mestizos and Indians, had achieved positions of influence. But, above all, an area of 'political sociability', to use François Fûret's term, had been created, a cultural breathing space for the hitherto marginal descendants of the settlers who had moved into the region in the eighteenth century. Liberal leaders of the *Sierra* held the confident conviction that they had participated in great national events and contributed to the success of the liberal revolution and the recovery of national sovereignty. Accordingly, we find *serranos* writing the first histories of the state. On the plateau, no such sense of a heroic break with the past existed, merely one of disquiet and uncertainty as the central region remained locked in economic recession and faced, after the expulsion of the Austrians, mounting social and political unrest, converting Puebla into one of the most repressive regimes of the *República Restaurada*. Idealistic *poblano* Liberals, such as Alberto de Santa Fe, travelled to the *Sierra*, ambitious ones went to the Federal District.[29]

## THE ECLIPSE OF THE *MONTAÑA* IN STATE POLITICS AND THE RECOVERY OF THE *LLANURA*

Between 1867 and the late 1880s the *Montaña* and *Llanura* labels approximated two broad and fluid party groupings representing liberals in the north and the centre of the state. From the 1850s there had been a shift, not so much in the balance of power in the province, but in the geographical source of political initiative. But the *Montaña* and *Llanura* division reflected, above all, the distinct nature of liberalism in the two areas.

28. For a good example of *Sierra* 'boosting', see the 1874 report of French geologist F. Estragnat, "La Sierra del Estado de Puebla," in *El Minero Mexicano*, II, 429. Two events are referred to by contemporaries as *revolutions*: the period of the radical liberal governor Cástulo Alatriste, who introduced a programme of liberal reforms in the *Sierra* between 1857 and 1858, with dramatic consequences, and the 'revolución regeneradora' of Tuxtepec in 1876.

29. Two histories written by the National Guard commanders Colonel Lauro Luna (from Tetela de Ocampo) and General José María Maldonado (from Tecamachalco, but c. in c. of patriotic resistance in the *Sierra* in 1863-65) have yet to be published, for extracts see Ramón Sánchez Flores, *Zacapoastla. Relación histórica* (Puebla, 1984), 139-219. The best known liberal patriotic history of the Reform/Intervention Period is by Márquez Galindo, *Gran década*, from the leading liberal clan of Zacatlán, published in 1906. For the *Llanura*, see Perry, *Juárez and Díaz*, 161. Puebla, under the *Llanura* governorship of Ignacio Romero Vargas (1868-1876), was described in the newspaper *Siglo XIX* as *'el supulchro de los vivos.'* For a defence of Romero Vargas's governorship, see *Periódico Oficial* 7:53 (1876).

In the north, liberals had emerged as the dominant force as a consequence of successful armed struggle, military leaders proceeding to refashion the government of their districts to the model of the liberal state. In 1867, they expected to assume immediate control of the state government as a recognition of the unchallenged control they exercised over their districts and as a reward for their services to the patriotic struggle. In the centre, *Llanura* liberals took power in 1867, not because they possessed a popular base of support or patriotic credentials, but because of the vacuum left by the defeat of the region's conservatives. They were aided in this by the decision of Benito Juárez to support a group of *civilista* liberals, rather than military men, as the favoured party of government.

Puebla's *jarista-lerdista* state governor over the *República Restaurada* was a talented and autocratic small town lawyer from Acatzingo: Ignacio Romero Vargas. He was obliged to work with conservative landowners and industrialists in order to govern. For much of this decade, Romero Vargas' effective political control extended no further than the central valleys of the state. Liberal military leaders from the north and south mounted prolonged rebellions, requiring federal intervention to prevent the *Llanura* from being toppled. As a result of federal intervention on the *Llanura*'s behalf, the displaced *Montaña* party became a natural ally for Porfirio Díaz' broader political ambitions. Thus *Montaña* leaders and National Guard units featured prominently in the *porfirista* revolts of La Noria and Tuxtepec. These external political influences, resulting from an appreciation by Juárez, Lerdo and Díaz of Puebla's critical strategic location, attenuated regional ideological rivalries between the north and centre which, if left to themselves, would probably have reached a much earlier resolution.

By the time *Montaña* leaders finally took up the reins of state government in 1876, the economic and political equilibrium was already shifting markedly back to the central plateau. The opening of the Puebla-Mexico City railway in 1869 and the completion of the Mexico-Veracruz line in 1873 had begun to exercise a dramatic effect upon Puebla's long depressed cereal agriculture as a national market became accessible. The few studies so far to have emerged of Puebla's *haciendas* over the forty years before the Revolution of 1910 are providing a picture of the reemergence of estate agriculture as the leading sector of Puebla's economy, a position it had not enjoyed since the seventeenth century. The textile industry also arose from its lethargy with a growth spurt in the 1870s and again in the 1890s. Many old elite families recouped their fortunes. But more significant was the emergence of a group of immigrant families, chiefly Spanish and French, but also a few North American, German and British, who succeeded in establishing veritable family empires on the basis of a judicious combinations of cereal agriculture, flour milling, sugar growing and refining and textiles.[30]

This was not a political caste: the *Porfiriato* was not a period of 'politics'. The political direction of the state of Puebla, after the eclipse in 1884 of the last *Montaña* governor, General Juan N. Méndez, was in fact taken out the hands of *poblanos*. Rosendo Márquez, governor between 1884 and 1892, was a *porfirista* general from

30. Roberto Vélez Pliego, "Rentabilidad y productividad en una hacienda mexicana: Hacienda y Molino de Santa Cruz," in *Puebla en el siglo XIX*, CIHS, ICUAP, ed. (Puebla, 1983), 289-313; Antonio Serafín Sodi, *'Tu ya no sopla.' Monografías de San Martín Texmelucan y hacienda de San Antonio Chautla* (Puebla, 1978), containing useful material on the highly productive *haciendas* of the Gillow family; *The Rosalie Evans Letters*, Daisy Caden Pettus, ed. (Indianapolis, 1926), for the *hacienda* of San Pedro Coxtocan, Huejotzingo, acquired and restored by the retired banker, Harry Evans, in 1904, becoming the 'show place of the Puebla Valley' by 1910; Hans Günther Mertens, *Atlixco y las haciendas durante el Porfiriato* (Puebla, 1988), the estate of Emilio Maurer; Jesús Ricardo Rendón Garcini, "Dos haciendas pulqueras en Tlaxcala" (Tesis de maestría en historia, Universidad Iberoamericana, Mexico City, 1986); and Margarita Menegus Bornemann and Juan Felipe Leal, "Las haciendas de Mazaquiahuac y el Rosario en los albores de la revolución agraria, 1910-1914," in *HMex*, 31 (1984), 233-277. Leticia Gamboa Ojeda, *Los empresarios de ayer. El grupo dominante en la indústria textíl de Puebla, 1906-1929* (Puebla, 1985).

Jalisco, who had begun his career modestly as a textile worker in Tepic. He understood the subtleties of Puebla's regional conflicts and worked effectively to conciliate them. In the *Sierra Norte*, Márquez won the support of the *cacique-maximo*, General Juan Francisco Lucas, since the 1860s the political lynchpin of the *Montaña* party as a consequence of the respect and obedience, he commanded among the Indian population. On the central plateau, Márquez was first to appreciate the political importance of factory workers, a resource hitherto neglected by *Llanura* leaders.[31] In 1892, as a result of pressure from Puebla City commercial and industrial interests, who complained of high taxation, Díaz eased Márquez out and replaced him with far more ruthless and less politically astute, General Mucío Martínez, a soldier from Nueva León. Martínez had made his name in the brutal pacification of the rebellious and bandit prone districts southern of Puebla. With a 'contra-guerilla' in the governorship between 1892 until Díaz removed him in 1910, Puebla's liberals, whether *Montaña* or *Llanura* were obliged to lie low.[32]

How can we account for the eclipse of the *Montaña* in state politics? The first reason is that the 'developmentalist' dreams of *Sierra* leaders did not reach fruition. In spite of projects for linking the *Sierra* by modern communications with the central plateau and the Gulf coast, the area did not share in the benefits of the Centre's transport revolution, Tezuitlán only receiving a railway connection in 1902, and Chignahuapan in 1908. The other district capitals (Zacatlán, Tetela, Tlatlauqui, Zacapoastla, Huauchinango) were accessible only by mule tracks until well into this century.[33] As a result, the development of the *Sierra's* commercial tropical agriculture, particularly coffee, lagged far behind that of more accessible regions such as Coatepec (Veracruz), or regions where land was more abundant, such as Soconusco (Chiapas). Had the *Montaña* retained control of state politics beyond 1884, then investment might have been directed at overcoming these obstacles. Instead, the central plateau appears to have received the lion's share of investment, with the *Sierra*, apart from the coffee district of Cuetzalán, the copper town of Teziutlán and the hydro-electric plant at Necaxa, near Huauchinango, sharing little in Porfirian economic modernisation. In a sense, the *Montaña* fell victim to its political success. Its influence in the *Sierra* was based upon maintaining a balance between the ambitions of the non-Indian population for a greater stake in economy and politics and the Indian population which favoured as little change in the status quo as possible. Beneath the veneer of the liberal administration of *Sierra* districts was a historic compromise by which the Indian monopoly of land would not be significantly modified. This imposed a slow pace upon the commercial development of the *Sierra*, confining non-Indians to commerce, fruit and small scale coffee farming, cattle fattening and *aguardiente* production. These were activities which, although sufficient to guarantee the continuing control of the *Sierra* by '*gente de razón*,' hardly provided a spring board for competing with the impressive enterprises being established on the *altiplano*. Thus, from the mid-1880s, the *Sierra* liberal *caciques* turned inward, guarding their own patches and eschewing any wider political ambitions.

---

31. Cosio Villegas, *HMM El Porfiriato. Vida Política interior*, Ia parte, 626, IIa parte, 96-99, and 447-449. *Manzano-Ayala Family Papers*, Puebla: Correspondence between Juan Francisco Lucas and Rosendo Márquez, 1884-1892.

32. Cosio Villegas, *HMM El Porfiriato. Vida Política interior*, IIa parte, 447-449. For Mucío Martínez' pacification of the bandit-prone southern districts of the state, see *Archivo de Porfirio Díaz*, Universidad Iberoamericana, Mexico City, L12 C25, 012212. For a succinct analysis of the Mucío Martínez regime, see: Roberto Parra Gómez, *Puebla en cifras* (Mexico City, 1944), 41-42.

33. Enrique Juan Palacios, *Puebla. Su territorio y sus habitantes* (Mexico City, 1917), I, 240-247.

## THE REVOLUTION AND THE POLITICAL REEMERGENCE OF THE *SIERRA*

Over the first decade of the twentieth century, while the *Sierra* slumbered in a complacent *caciquismo*, with few signs still remaining of the energetic liberalism which it had fostered during the Reform, the *Llanura* for the first time witnessed the emergence of a popular liberal movement which played a large part in the overthrow of Porfirio Díaz in 1911. The recovery of estate based cereal agriculture, and the reassertion of the *hacienda* had renewed the ancient tensions between the *hacienda* and the village over labour control and land-use. The harsh policing of the countryside by the *Guardias Rurales*, the practice of the courts of sending prisoners beyond the region to work off their sentences, the systematic violation of village autonomy, the revived influence and wealth of the Church, the repression of the industrial labour force, all pointed to how little the liberal reform of the mid-nineteenth century had served to establish a 'new circuit of political sociability' in the plateau region within which grievances could be voiced and different social sectors represented.[34]

Prosperity disguised the fragility of the political system of the *Llanura*. Leading manufacturing and landowning families, many of them first generation immigrants and largely ignorant of the province's people and history, with a few exceptions, kept an aristocratic distance from politics, which they expected to be managed by Próspero Cahuantzi and Mucío Martínez, the long-serving and repressive governors of Tlaxcala and Puebla.[35] The elite's political vision and involvement went no further than coordinating labour policies and representing their particular economic interests. They were ill-equipped for confronting the political crisis which broke in 1910. Such was not the case with the mass of Puebla's urban and rural population. The work of Rodney Anderson, Raymond Buve, Jean-Pierre Bastian, David LaFrance and others is revealing how the Revolution gave voice to a popular political culture, which, like the 'agro-industrial' elite, recognised no boundary between city and countryside. To judge from its energy and articulateness, this 'revolutionary liberalism' had been brewing long before it flowed forth into militant agrarian and labour movements during the Revolution.[36]

---

34. David G. LaFrance, "Madero, Serdán, y los albores del movimiento revolucionario en Puebla," in *HMex*, 29 (1980), 472-512. François Fûret uses the term 'new circuit of political sociability' to highlight the differences between the *ancien régime* and an emerging liberal and revolutionary political order in France. He contrasts the 'old circuit of political sociability,' arranged concentrically and hierarchically around the monarch, with the 'new circuit,' composed of masonic lodges, philosophical societies, etc., its lines of communication with the traditional circuit broken. The point that can be made is that in the *Sierra* region during the 1850s and 1860s the 'new circuit' was permitted fuller expression and the 'old circuit' more convincingly broken than was the case on the plateau, where conservatives recouped their fortunes after the European intervention. Liberalism was therefore still at a conspiratorial, 'pre-revolutionary' phase on the central plateau at the turn of the twentieth century, when the 'liberal-patriotism' of the *Sierra* had already become complacently middle-aged. See, François Fûret, *Interpreting the French Revolution* (Cambridge, 1981), 36-40.

35. Reina, *Empresarios de ayer*, 192-195.

36. Rodney Anderson, *Outcasts in Their Own Land: Mexican Industrial Workers, 1906-1911* (DeKalb, 1976); Raymond Buve, "Peasant Movements, Caudillos, and Land Reform during the Revolution (1910-1917) in Tlaxcala," in *Boletín de Estudios Latinoamericanos y del Caribe*, 18 (1975), 112-152, "'Neither Carranza nor Zapata!': the Rise and Fall of a Peasant Movement that Tried to Challenge Both, Tlaxcala, 1910-19," in *Riot, Rebellion, and Revolution. Rural Social Conflict in Mexico*, Friedrich Katz, ed. (Princeton, 1989), 338-375; Jean-Pierre Bastian, "Metodismo y clase obrera en el Porfiriato," in *HMex*, 33 (1983), 39-71, and "Metodismo y rebelión política en Tlaxcala" (Paper given at *I Simposio Internacional de Investigaciones Socio-Históricas sobre Tlaxcala*, 1985); David LaFrance, "Labour and the Mexican Revolution: President Francisco I. Madero and the Puebla Textile Workers," in *Boletín de Estudios Latinoamericanos y del Caribe*, 34 (1983), 59-74, "Germany, Revolutionary Nationalism, and the Downfall of President Francisco I. Madero: The Covadonga Killings," in *Mexican Studies/Estudios Mexica-*

Francisco Madero, like Benito Juárez, put his faith in educated, *civilista* lawyers from the state capital, three of whom occupied the governorship in succession until Madero's assassination ushered a military governorship under the Huertista General Joaquin Maas. Madero, like Juárez, considered the control of the state of Puebla as a crucial first move in the securing of his regime and in the imposition of his moderate, *civilista* and constitutional brand of liberalism. Madero's nominees in Puebla faced the same problem which had dogged Juárez's appointees, Rafael García and Romero Vargas, during the *República Restaurada*. They were unable to control the process of political fragmentation and radicalisation beyond the state capital. The difference in 1911-1912 was that the emergence of autonomous, agrarian movements was occurring *within* the central region rather than in the remote north. Particularly active was the west-centre, focussing on the old agrarian trouble spot of San Martín Texmelucan and south-western Tlaxcala. Under these circumstances, the relatively orderly *Sierra Norte* offered attractions to state governors attempting to reestablish order in the state and searching for allies beyond the unstable central region. Thus the *Montaña* reemerged in state politics, just as it had originally appeared in 1855, as means of breaking the political deadlock on the plateau.[37]

The intensification of the military struggle after 1914 caused a further reappraisal of the strategic importance of the *Sierra* as of its potential as a source of military recruits. The Mucío Martínez regime had been able count on what remained of the *Sierra* forces controlled by General Juan Francisco Lucas, as a kind of 'palace guard', obviating the need for local recruitement. All of his successors attempted to establish contact with Lucas, known as the Patriarch of the *Sierra*, and understood to possess keys to its cornucopia of men and supplies. They faced, however, competition from other bidders. As a result, by 1915, the *Sierra Norte de Puebla*, like the *Sierra de Juárez* in Oaxaca, had become divided into two extensive *cacicazgos*. The west was controlled by the Márquez-Galindo brothers, an old liberal family of *rancheros* and muleteers from Ototlan, who organised an agrarian movement in the *hacienda* district around Chignahuapan, while also counting on the support the land-holding Indian population of Zacatlán and Huauchinango. In 1915 the Márquez brothers joined the Conventionalists, establishing close links with the *zapatista* leader in Tlaxcala, Domingo Arenas. The centre and east of the *Sierra* remained the territory of the now octogenarian veteran of every liberal campaign since Alvarez' Revolution of Ayutla in 1854: General Juan Francisco Lucas. Lucas, after giving much consideration to overtures from every party, joined the Constitutionalists on the agreement (which Carranza kept too) that Lucas' soldiers in the *Brigada Serrana* would not be called upon to serve beyond their own territory.[38]

The Márquez-Galindo and Lucas spheres of influence in fact replicated a division which had existed since the mid nineteenth century between the Márquez-Galindo clan of Zacatlán and the Méndez fiefdom in Tetela. The successive defeats of the conventionalist forces elsewhere in the republic left the Márquez brothers increasingly exposed and isolated in the face of the consolidation of *carrancismo* in the centre of the state.

---

*nos*, 2:2 (1986), 59-81, and "A People Betrayed: Francisco I. Madero and the Mexican Revolution in Puebla" (Ph.D. diss., Indiana University, Bloomington, 1984).

37. David LaFrance, "Puebla: Breakdown of the Old Order," in *Other Mexicos: Essays on Regional Mexican History, 1876-1911*, Thomas Benjamin and William McNellie, eds. (Albuquerque, 1984), 77-106. *Rosalie Evans Letters*, 3. Facundo Arias González, "Historia de las relaciones del movimiento obrero con el campesino. El caso de la CROM y la Confederación Social Campesina 'Domingo Arenas': 1920-1929" (Paper given at *I Simposio Internacional de Investigaciones Socio-Históricas sobre Tlaxcala*, 1985); Buve, "Peasant Movements," and, "'Neither Carranza nor Zapata!'."

38. LaFrance, "Puebla: Breakdown," 81. Waterbury, "Non-Revolutionary Peasants," 434-435. LaFrance and Thomson, "Juan Francisco Lucas," passim, and Ramón Kuri Camacho, *Micro historia de Chignahuapan* (Chignahuapan, 1986), II, 76.

Their survival as an autonomous force until 1917 probably owed much to Carranza's confidence in Lucas' overall influence in the *Sierra*, to Lucas' respect for traditional spheres of influence, as to his insistence upon *Sierra* autonomy. The death of Lucas in February 1917 removed these restraints and signalled the end of the autonomous Márquez-Galindo fiefdom.

Before his death, Lucas had made the fateful appointment of Gabriel Barrios as his successor in command of the *Brigada Serrana*. Barrios was an Indian from Cuacuilo, an outlying Indian barrio belonging to the Márquez stronghold of Ototlan. After Lucas' death, Barrios relentlessly consolidated his military control throughout the entire *Sierra*. On the 12th of August 1917, the four remaining Márquez brothers, who had laid down their arms once it had become clear that *villismo* in Central Mexico was a spent force, were assassinated by a group of *cuacuileños* under Barrios' orders. This was followed by a purge of the Márquez' relatives and friends who had fought with them since 1914.[39] The purge of an entire *cacique* clan and its principal fighters, an act of unprecedented violence and thoroughness, was the beginning of a different kind a *caciquismo* in the *Sierra* which would play a vital role in Puebla politics through until the 1940s. The *caciquismo* which had arisen under the veneer of patriotic-liberalism during the second half of the nineteenth century was based chiefly upon the desire of leading liberal families to maintain their autonomy from outside interference and to guarantee a stable relationship with the Indian population. The kind of *caciquismo* which became synonymous with Gabriel Barrios' hold over the *Sierra* had much more to do with the attempt by external political forces to use the disposable political and economic resources of the *Sierra* to further their ambitions beyond the *Sierra*. Thus, during the Revolution, and throughout the 1920s and 1930s, the *Sierra* regained the importance it had in the mid nineteenth century, as a springboard for new political initiatives and as a simpler area to control than the complex and conflict-ridden communities of the plateau. Today, the *Sierra* continues to offer a potential anchor for the politics of the state, explaining the careful attention the PRI pays to bringing *Sierra caciquismo* 'up-to-date'. But it is still an area which offers prospects for the realization of alternative political visions, both on the left as on the right.[40]

## CONCLUSION

Alan Knight distinguishes between two principal kinds of popular movement occurring during the Revolution: the agrarian and the *serrano*.[41] The division between the *Llanura* and the *Montaña* during the *Reforma* and its aftermath is helpful in explaining the background to the agrarian and *serrano* movements which controlled so much of the state of Puebla during the revolutionary period. I have attempted in this essay to show how quite different societies and political cultures emerged in the plateau and the *Sierra* regions over the late eighteenth and nineteenth centuries. In spite of its portentous agricultural resources and industrial specialisation, for much of this period the

39. Kuri Camacho, *Micro historia*, II, 85-87.
40. For post-revolutionary *Sierra caciquismo*, see Paré, "Caciquismo y estructura de poder"; and for the *Sierra* as a spring board for the Avila Camacho dynasty, see Jesús Márquez, "Los origines del avilacamachismo. Una arqueología de fuerzas en la constitución de un poder regional: el estado de Puebla, 1929-1941" (Tesis de licenciatura, Universidad Autónoma de Puebla, 1983); and the essay of Wil Pansters in this volume. Recently the PAN has won municipal elections in Teziutlán and Zacatlán. On the revolutionary left, a movement called 'Antorcha Campesina', based in Huitzilan (ex-district of Tetela), has attracted much attention and considerable support.
41. Alan Knight, "Peasant and Caudillo in Revolutionary Mexico, 1910-17," in *Caudillo and Peasant in the Mexican Revolution*, D. A. Brading, ed. (Cambridge, 1980), 17-58.

economy of the central plateau was stagnant or in crisis. Only in two periods, during the protectionist interlude of the 1830s and 1840s and the period of growth from the 1870s to 1910, did the plateau region receive effective political leadership, mostly from professional military men from beyond the state. For much of the rest of the time, during the wars of Independence, the Reform wars, the European Intervention, the *República Restaurada*, and for much of the Revolution, the authority of the centre collapsed and the focus of political initiative shifted northwards.

The political weakness of the centre has complex structural explanations which this chapter has only hinted at: the decline of the Church as a force of cohesion, the problem of the *hacienda* as a source of irreconciliable discord between the landowning class and the village, the unstable and changing composition of the urban working class, the political disinterest and cosmopolitan detachment of the immigrant entrepreneurs who were attracted to the central valley in periods of economic recovery, the frequent federal interventions, the result of Puebla's strategic importance. Mid nineteenth century liberalism found little space for accommodating itself within this highly stratified and divided social context. Indeed anti-reelectionism and revolutionary agrarianism represented the plateau's first modern popular movements, attracting a wide spectrum of support from among social sectors who had gained nothing and remained unrepresented during the liberal *Reforma*.

In contrast, the *Sierra* underwent, during the mid nineteenth century, the liberal-patriotic revolution which passed the plateau by. The 'new circuit of political sociability', enjoyed by *Sierra* leaders, was constructed over a period of armed conflict, giving the region's liberalism a marshal character. This was highlighted during the Revolution by the *serrano* movements headed by the Márquez brothers and Juan Francisco Lucas whose autonomous brigades, recruited from the same barrios that had mustered units of the National Guard in 1857, 1862-1867, 1872 and 1876, claimed to be defending the liberal freedoms and autonomy gained during the nineteenth century. Effective leadership and the organised and stable relationship between this leadership and the mass of non-Indian and Indian society made the *Sierra* particularly attractive to outside forces lacking or facing much more uncertain power bases elsewhere.

Thus, from this examination of the political history of Puebla over some hundred years, it is clear that the *Sierra* served as an important political resource over periods when economic and political crisis afflicted the centre of the province. For almost forty years during the mid nineteenth century, *Sierra* leaders succeeded not only in controlling their own districts but projecting themselves beyond their region. During and since the Revolution, *Sierra* leadership has been defensive but no less important in providing the political means for moderating the conflicts of the central plateau.

Region, State and Capitalism
CEDLA, Amsterdam, 1989



CHAPTER SIX

# Constitutionalist Reconstruction in Oaxaca, 1915-1920

PAUL GARNER*

## INTRODUCTION

This chapter deals with the period 1915-1920 which has received far less attention than the period 1911-1915, largely on the assumption that after the military victories of Constitutionalism in 1915 there followed an inexorable process of political and economic reconstruction which was completed by 1920. The evidence from Oaxaca seems to prove otherwise. There are four principal sections:

1. A brief summary of the impact of regionalism on revolutionary historiography, and of the participation of Oaxaca in the Revolution.
2. The political and military context of the occupation of the state in June 1915.
3. The ideology of Constitutionalism.
4. The practice of Constitutionalism, and the corresponding gulf between ideology and practice.

In the areas of labour, anticlerical, educational and agrarian reform, Constitutionalist practice in Oaxaca broadly conformed to the general preoccupations of Constitutionalism on a national level, although the impact of such policies obviously dependent on local conditions. However in the areas of political representation and economic recovery, Oaxaca's experience appears to be different from that of other states or regions. In short, I shall argue that the process of reconstruction in Oaxaca before 1920 had been a failure, due to:

- i The limitations of effective political jurisdiction.
- ii The authoritarian and arbitrary implementation of *carrancista* policy by the military authorities.
- iii The lack of resources available to the authorities (especially after 1917).
- iv The strength of internal resistance, manifest (although not exclusively) in the Oaxaca Sovereignty Movement (1915-1920).

## OAXACA AND THE REVOLUTION

Those with only the briefest of confrontations with the historiography of the Mexican Revolution cannot have failed to notice the predominance of regional history and the corresponding revisionism. As one of the guilty parties, I must obviously concur with

* *Historian, University of Wales, School of European Languages, University College of Swansea, Singleton Park, Swansea SA2 8PP, Wales, United Kingdom.*

the view that only with a clear appreciation of the internal dynamism of regions and sub-regions can we begin to recreate a convincing analysis of the true significance of the conflict.[1] Despite this trend we still continue to be generally ignorant of the details of regional conflict. As Simon Miller commented in 1985, *"one of the areas most urgently in need of detailed attention is the period of the Revolution itself... not so much in terms of what the Revolution signified, but rather in terms of what actually occurred on a routine basis during the turbulent decade."*[2]

Although it appears by no means certain that anything happened on a 'routine basis' during the revolutionary decade, the point is clear: it is only a brave and confident historian who would attempt a definitive synthesis, as Alan Knight's extensive and anti-revisionist study has attempted.[3] This is specially true, given the fact that any synthesis or national history of the period is bound to be contentious, given the lack of consensus in the historiography. Despite these caveats, it is nonetheless both appropriate and necessary to draw some conclusions from recent regional investigations in order to provide the context for the participation of Oaxaca in the Revolution. Regional studies from Chihuahua to Chiapas have shown that those groups throughout the republic which rose up in arms to overthrow the dictatorship of Porfirio Díaz in 1910-1911 did so for very different reasons, and in very different environments: dispossessed *campesinos* in Morelos, dissident *hacendados* in Coahuila, and upwardly-mobile *rancheros* in Guerrero. Collectively therefore, regional perspectives have demonstrated that the genesis and expression of revolution were neither universal, nor homogeneous, but rather a reflection of the disparity in regional development throughout Mexico during the nineteenth century, and particularly during the *Porfiriato* (1876-1911).[4]

The case of Oaxaca vividly highlights that disparity. It is evident, for example, that the limited evolution of systems of land tenure and modes of agricultural production in Oaxaca prior to the Revolution meant that the agrarian conflicts between *hacienda* and *pueblo* in nearby Morelos were largely, if not entirely absent. Although agrarian tensions existed throughout the state -mostly between rival *pueblos* over atavistic territorial disputes- these were insufficient to generate, and indeed incapable of generating, a sustained agrarian movement. Similarly, because of the limited degree of industrialisation and commercial exploitation of agriculture within the state, and the erratic revival of mining during the period, the *Porfiriato* in Oaxaca had not witnessed the growth of a coherent opposition groups within the small urban or rural middle-class which sought access to the political power denied by the Porfirian regime, as has been suggested as an essential factor in revolutionary mobilisation in Sonora.[5] As elsewhere in Mexico, and throughout the continent, there had been substantial growth in the export sector but its impact within the state had been diverse. The areas of most substantial transformation were those on the geographical fringes of the state, e.g. the North-East on the border with Veracruz, the Pacific Coast, and the Isthmus of Tehuantepec. It was in these regions that the response to the Madero Revolution of 1910 was most vociferous.

1. Barry Carr, "Recent Regional Studies of the Mexican Revolution," in *Latin American Research Review* (hereafter *LARR*), 15:1 (1980), 3-14; for a characteristically provocative review of recent historiography, see Alan Knight, "The Mexican Revolution: Bourgeois? Nationalist? Or just a "Great Rebellion"?," in *Bulletin of Latin American Research* (hereafter *BLAR*), 4:2 (1985), 1-37.

2. Simon Miller, "Revisionism in Recent Mexican Historiography," in *BLAR*, 4:1 (1985), 77-88.

3. Alan Knight, *The Mexican Revolution* (2 vols., Cambridge, 1986).

4. For a thorough analysis of the breadth, scope and influence of regional historiography in Mexico, see the chapter by Thomas Benjamin, "Provinces of the Revolution: Provincial, Regional, and Local History in Revolutionary Historiography," in *Mexican Revolutions: Essays on Regional Mexican History, 1911-29*, Thomas Benjamin and Mark Wasserman, eds. (Albuquerque, forthcoming).

5. Hector Aguilar Camin, *La frontera nomada: Sonora y la revolución mexicana* (Mexico City, 1977).

In other areas of the state, Porfirian development appears to have had only marginal impact, but the picture is still by no means clear.[6]

Superficially at least, Oaxaca appears to have been a provincial sanctuary of the *pax porfiriana*, although we shall not know this for certain until we have in our hands the micro-history of the Porfiriato in Oaxaca. In the state capital, a small provincial oligarchy had been the promoters and the beneficiaries of the limited expansion of the local economy during the last decades of the nineteenth century, and their interests were fully represented through the political elite which dominated the state legislature in 1910. The degree of identification of the provincial elite, and indeed from all levels of Oaxacan-society -*campesinos*, artisans, merchants, clerics, miners, and professionals-, with the regime, and the degree of personal loyalty to Díaz, is confirmed by the president's private correspondence.[7] The use of *Oaxaqueños* at all levels of the Porfirian bureaucracy throughout the republic was notorious. Of the 277 federal deputies in the National Congress in 1886, for example, no fewer than 62 were from Oaxaca. Although the precise nature of the relationship between regional and national elites in the *Porfiriato* awaits further investigation, it is possible to suggest that this intimate relationship helped to prevent any major or coherent political challenge to the Díaz regime emerging from the dictator's native state. As Francisco Madero discovered for himself when he visited Oaxaca in 1909, despite a nucleus of political opponents organised in a loose coalition under the banner of the *Asociación Juárez* since 1901, Oaxaca was hardly seething with vocal opposition to the violent overthrow of the national regime. Internal opposition certainly existed, but was, however, directed almost exclusively against the state governor, Emilio Pimentel, rather than against the regime.[8]

Because of the limited degree of formal or Constitutional opposition to the Díaz regime within Oaxaca, it seems that a useful approach to the participation of Oaxaca in the Revolution is to see local political developments as a response to the catalyst of national political crisis. The framework for an understanding of the political conflicts of the period is provided by the Oaxaca Sovereignty Movement, which provided a focus for a broad spectrum of political and popular opposition to process of political centralisation pursued by the Constitutionalists: both for those in Oaxaca who were anti-*carrancista* because they were reactionaries, and for those whose adhesion to the Revolution was based regional/local and anti-centralist affiliations, a broad category which includes *villistas* and *zapatistas* and a kaleidoscope of localised rebellions.

---

6. See F. Chassen, "Oaxaca: del Porfiriato a la revolución, 1902-11" (Ph. D. diss., Universidad Nacional Autónoma de México, 1986), which provides important evidence of levels of investment, and rises in mining and agricultural production during the last decade of the *Porfiriato*, and provides new evidence of political opposition groups in Oaxaca. Nevertheless, the precise correlation between modernization, tradition and revolutionary participation in Oaxaca has yet to be established. For recent discussions of the Madero Revolution in Oaxaca, see Paul Garner, *La Revolución en la provincia: Soberanía estatal y caudillismo en las montañas de Oaxaca (1910-20)* (Mexico City, 1988); Hector Martínez Medina, "Genesis y desarrollo del maderismo en Oaxaca, 1908-12," in *La revolución en Oaxaca, 1900-30*, Raul Martínez Vázquez, ed. (Oaxaca, 1985); F. José Ruiz Cervantes, *La revolución en Oaxaca: el movimiento de la soberanía (1915-20)* (Mexico City, 1986). F. Alfonso Ramírez, *Historia de la revolución mexicana en Oaxaca* (Mexico City, 1970).

7. *Colección Porfirio Díaz*, Universidad Iberoamericana (hereafter *CPD* legajo, document number). See for example, *CPD* 36, 1195.

8. *"El General Díaz habia diseminado a los oaxaqueños como gobernadores de Estado, o Jueces de Distrito, o Jefes de Hacienda, o Secretarios Generales de Gobierno . . . para que fuesen para el, lo que los jesuitas para el Papa, encargados de sostener la fe en el heroe de la paz,"* Francisco Bulnes, *El verdadero Díaz y la revolución* (Mexico City, 1920), 181, quoted in Chassen, "Oaxaca". Expressions of political opposition could assume some rather confused forms, and often clearly misunderstood the political realignments and conflicts which were taking place outside the confines of Oaxaca. Thus in April 1911 a collective tirade from irate *Oaxaqueños* against the state governor finished with the following exhortation: *"¡Viva Oaxaca! ¡Viva Madero! ¡Viva Porfirio Díaz! ¡No-Reelección!,"* *CPD* 36, 5828.

## POLITICAL AND MILITARY CONTEXT

The Declaration of Sovereignty in June 1915 was not simply a conservative reaction to the threat of radicalism or revolution, but also the manifestation and culmination in Oaxaca of a political process initiated throughout Mexico by the overthrow of the Díaz regime in 1911 -the emasculation of central political authority which stimulated the forces of regional and provincial autonomy. Carranza's campaign during 1914 and 1915 to reestablish and recentralise military and political control thus was bound to clash with such centrifugal tendencies. With specific regard to the south-east, *carrancista* military and political strategy after the fall of Huerta was clear: the establishment of a strong physical presence, particularly in the strategically important Isthmus of Tehuantepec, from which to create a political base in the form of administrations loyal to the ideology of Constitutionalism, and most importantly, loyal to the personal authority of Carranza himself. Young *norteño* revolutionaries who had risen through the ranks of the Constitutionalist army were dispatched to Yucatán, Tabasco, Chiapas, Campeche and Quintana Roo to supervise the implementation of pro-Constitutionalist state governments.[9]

These incursions did not however achieve the desired results: instead they provoked prolonged and even intense resistance throughout the region. Already before 1915, therefore, *carrancista* strategy had been challenged. The Declaration of Sovereignty in Oaxaca, precipitated by the blatant violation of the territorial sovereignty of the state by Constitutionalist troops in Pochutla in May 1915, not only continued the trend, but constituted the most serious challenge yet mounted in the region. Ronald Waterbury has claimed that *"since Oaxaca posed no serious military threat Carranza permitted it to enjoy its sovereignty a few months while he busied himself with Villa and Zapata."*[10] In fact the day after state sovereignty was declared the June 4, 1915, Jesús Augustín Castro, who had been appointed *Comandante Militar* and pre-Constitutional governor of Chiapas in September 1914, was ordered to march on Oaxaca and establish military headquarters in the Isthmus of Tehuantepec. In August 1915, Agustín Castro was appointed *Comandante Militar* and pre-Constitutional governor of Oaxaca. By March 1916 a successful military campaign against the State Defense Forces had forced the sovereign state government to evacuate the state capital and retreat to their respective centres of power -Tlaxiaco in the *Sierra Mixteca* and Ixtlán in the *Sierra Juárez*, a geographical division which reflected a political schism within the Movement.[11]

Despite the early occupation of Oaxaca City, the areas of *carrancista* control and effective jurisdiction were considerably restricted throughout the period of pre-Constitutional government between 1915 and 1920. The areas outside the central valleys, the Isthmus of Tehuantepec, and the northern part of the *Sierra Mixteca* remained firmly outside the political control of the military authorities in 1920. This can be illustrated by the establishment of only 146 municipal based *Juntas Calificadoras del Catastro* -a register of the size and value of all property for tax purposes- i.e. in less than one third of the total of 463 municipalities in Oaxaca by 1920.[12] Contemporary accounts

---

9. Alicia Hernández Chávez, "La defensa de los finqueros en Chiapas, 1914-20," in *Historia Mexicana* (hereafter *HMex*), 24:3 (1979), 335-369; Gilbert Joseph, *Revolution from Without: Yucatán, Mexico and the United States, 1880-1924* (Cambridge, 1982).

10. Ronald Waterbury, "Non-Revolutionary Peasants: Oaxaca Compared to Morelos in the Mexican Revolution," in *Comparative Studies in Society and History*, 17:4 (1975), 410-442.

11. Details of the military conflict can be found in Garner, *Revolución en la provincia*, Chapter VII.

12. *Periodico Oficial del Gobierno Pre-Constitucional de Oaxaca* (hereafter *PO*, Volume, date), Vols. I-II Salina Cruz 1915-16, Vols. II-VII Oaxaca 1916-20.

from Oaxaca testify as to the weakness of *carrancismo* in the state after five years of Constitutionalist occupation: local historian José Tamayo wrote that in 1920 Oaxaca *"politica- y militarmente estaba por completo fraccionado."*[13] The British consul reported in late 1919 that the only reason the rebel *serrano* forces had not occupied the city of Oaxaca was because they were anxious not to prejudice the outcome of the peace negotiations with the local supporters of the national military defection led by Alvaro Obregón under the banner of the *Plan of Agua Prieta.*[14]

## THE IDEOLOGY AND PRACTICE OF CONSTITUTIONALISM

*Carrancista* ideology has proved difficult to define. Douglas Richmond has interpreted *carrancismo* as authoritarian, populist, and above all nationalist, based upon a floating urban coalition of lower-middle and working classes. However, he admits that Carranza was *"not a popular leader in the classic sense -that is, one directly from and controlled by the masses,"* which begs an obvious question as to the basis of his political support.[15] Much of the confusion over the ideology of *carrancismo* stems from its eclectic nature, it was *"un conjunto de acciones," "an infrastructure created in response to rapid politicisation," "an accretion of many acts and pragmatic decisions,"* and even as *"a mongrel ideology whelped in the heat of revolutionary conflict."* It has been argued that the key to the success of Constitutionalism was not ideological innovation, but rather an appropriate synthesis of nationalist ideology and action which was able to provide both a short-term solution to the civil war, and a long-term political solution to the reconstruction of the state.[16] It was, in other words, very much a case of *realpolitik.*

Hector Aguilar Camín has provided further insight into the nature of Constitutionalism, rooting the radical policies of the Sonora dynasty of Obregón, Calles and De La Huerta, firmly in the social and economic development of Sonora during the late *Porfiriato,* and particularly in the practical experience and exercise of political power during the civil wars of the revolutionary period. Political circumstances in Sonora after 1911 had fostered experiments in state management of both agricultural and industrial production, highlighting the need for modern commercial exploitation of land, in the absence of pressure for the re-distribution of land (seen so graphically in the case of Morelos), and the cooperation and control of organised labour.[17] This interpretation once again emphasises the essential pragmatism and flexibility of Constitutionalism rather than its adherence to rigid ideological positions. Armed with this *norteño* experience of eclectic radicalism, Jesús Agustín Castro, a former tram worker from Durango arrived with the Constitutionalist Division 21 to establish pre-Constitutional government in Oaxaca in Salina Cruz in August 1915. The establishment of pro-*carrancista* administrations in the provinces of the South East followed a standard pattern, and the

13. Jorge J. Tamayo, *Oaxaca en el Siglo XX* (Mexico City, 1956); for contemporary and eye-witness accounts, see Isaac Ibarra, *Memorias* (Mexico City, 1975); Leovigildo Vázquez Cruz, *La soberanía de Oaxaca en la revolución* (Mexico City, 1959); Saul, *Mi madre y yo. Sucesos históricos de la Mixteca* (Mexico City, 1972); O. Jimenez, "Mi actuación revolucionaria en la Sierra de Juárez de 1910-1920" (Unpublished Manuscript).

14. *Great Britain Foreign Office* (hereafter *FO*), Consular Reports 204:532, file 8 'Oaxaca 1919'.

15. Douglas W. Richmond, *Venustiano Carranza's Nationalist Struggle, 1893-1920* (Lincoln, 1983).

16. Luis González, "Los revolucionados," in *Nexos*, 104 (Mexico City, 1986); Richmond, *Venustiano Carranza's Nationalist Struggle*; Charles Cumberland, *The Mexican Revolution. The Constitutional Years* (Austin, 1972); Knight, *Mexican Revolution*, II.

17. Hector Aguilar Camin, "The Relevant Tradition: Sonoran Leaders in the Revolution," in *Caudillo and Peasant in the Mexican Revolution*, David Brading, ed. (Cambridge, 1980), 99-124.

strategy pursued in Oaxaca followed directly from the precedent set in Chiapas. The demobilisation of federal or rebel troops was followed by the assumption of control over the executive, legislative and judicial functions in the hands of the *Comandante Militar*: this was followed by the replacement of local officials with those who had proved their affinity with Constitutionalism: the establishment of the principle of government by decree in order to facilitate the publication of a series of labour, educational, fiscal, and agrarian reforms. Simultaneously, all acts of the 'rebel' authorities were decreed to be null and void.

The *Manifiesto al Pueblo Oaxaqueño* of September 1915 was typical of the revolutionary rhetoric and obvious commitment of Agustín Castro to the hybrid goals of Constitutionalism. He declared that the supreme purpose of the 'revolutionary phalanx' (of which he was a proud member) was to provide *"the greatest good for the greatest number: the improvement of the people and the well being of society in general."*[18] There was, however, an element of almost quixotic fantasy in the initial dictates of the new administration, which consisted of a small staff of nine young Constitutionalists dispatched from Mexico City, whose area of jurisdiction was restricted to the political districts of Tuxtepec (on the border with Veracruz) and those of Juchitan and Tehuantepec (on the Isthmus). The size and scope of pre-Constitutional administration increased in proportion to the extent of military success, but the degree of hostility and lack of cooperation from the local populace experienced by the military authorities remained constant. Castro's successor as *Comandante Militar*, Juan Jiménez Méndez, complained to Carranza about the campaign of obstruction carried out by *"the landowning bourgeoisie who represented the most powerful social group within the State"*. He also complained of the response of all levels of *oaxaqueño* society to Constitutionalist presence, which he characterised in terms of *"an insolent disdain."*[19]

The task facing the pre-Constitutionalist governors of Oaxaca was certainly a daunting one. Apart from the antipathy demonstrated at all levels of provincial society to their very presence within the state, and the concomitant difficulties in establishing effective political authority, the depression of the local economy in this period and the general scarcity of resources militated against even minimal implementation of the Constitutionalist programme of social and economic regeneration. Ineffective attempts in 1916 and 1917 to convince the local population of the multiple benefits of health, education and social progress fell on deaf ears, not least because they were presented through the barrel of a rifle -there can be no doubt that the basis of Constitutionalist power in Oaxaca was authoritarian military rule. Nonetheless, in suggesting that Constitutionalist practice in Oaxaca was more rapacious than radical, it would be wrong to overestimate the strength and efficiency of *carrancista* forces -known locally, but certainly not affectionately as *con-sus-unas-listas*. Repeated requests were made to Carranza for arms, supplies and reinforcements reiterating the message that a concerted military effort would crush the rebels and secure victory for the Revolution: more often than not, these requests also fell on deaf ears. As a consequence local Constitutionalist morale was low, discipline difficult to enforce, and desertions frequent, particularly after 1918. In other words Constitutionalist authorities in Oaxaca certainly did not constitute a powerful military machine. There is an obvious paradox here: Constitutionalism *a la oaxaqueño* was authoritarian in structure but impotent in practice.[20]

It is hardly surprising in these circumstances that a broad gulf developed between the ideology and practice of Constitutionalism in Oaxaca. During the course of pre-Constitutional government that gulf did not narrow but widened. The intensity of provincial

18. *PO*, I, 16-09-1915, "Manifiesto al pueblo oaxaqueño".

19. *Archivo Histórico de la Defensa Nacional* (hereafter *AHDN*), Jimenez Méndez to Carranza 17-04-1918, leg. 213, fs. 42-48.

20. Martial law was declared in the state capital in August 1916, see *PO*, III, 5. *AHDN* 213: fs. 31-34, 35-36, 42-48.

resistance and the limited resources at their disposal combined to impede progress along what Castro had initially envisaged as *"the honourable and difficult path of reconstruction."* The espousal of radical reform by local Constitutionalist authorities was soon superceeded by familiar practices of graft and venality which have been described elsewhere as a form of *"predatory militarism."* There were plenty of examples from Oaxaca of graft, malfeasance, and profiteering.[21] By 1920 the idealism and political radicalism of individual commanders stationed in Oaxaca appears to have all but disappeared. As elsewhere in the republic, enthusiastic *jefes militares* in 1916 had independently implemented both the spirit if not always the letter of revolutionary justice -the establishment of schools, the closure of churches, and the distribution of land. After 1917, however, no more revolutionary proclamations were issued by the military authorities. Persuasion and exhortation was replaced by coercion, spontaneous radicalism by bureaucracy, and idealism by frustration and cynicism. By 1920 the military authorities in Oaxaca were in disarray, and the depleted garrisons of Constitutionalist troops (Tlaxiaco, Teotitlan, Tlacolula, Ejutla, Etla) were proving unable to stem the resurgence of armed resistance from the heterogeneous collection of rebel groups throughout the state.

The obvious conclusion is that Constitutionalism in Oaxaca had been an unmitigated failure. Whilst the *Manifiesto al Pueblo Oaxaqueño* had promised sweeping social, political and administrative reform, and had compared the arrival of Constitutionalism in Oaxaca to the dawning of a new day, it was abundantly clear that profound radical change had not occurred. But was Constitutionalist practice in Oaxaca substantially different from elsewhere in the Republic? The evidence from the *Periódico Oficial* certainly appears to confirm the impression of *carrancismo* as pragmatic and adaptable. The dictates and decrees from Mexico City were dutifully reproduced in Oaxaca -although often with delays of up to 18 months- in all the areas which have been identified (*pace* Cumberland) with Constitutionalist concern -labour, agrarian, anti-clerical, educational, fiscal and political reform. However implementation was necessarily determined by prevailing local conditions. A brief examination of each of the areas of Constitutionalist policy illustrates the particular difficulties which confronted the military authorities in Oaxaca.

## CONSTITUTIONALIST POLICY

### *Labour Reform*

In the case of labour reform, the attitude of the military authorities reflected the ambivalent treatment of organised labour by the Constitutionalist leadership on a national level. Labour organisations were established in Salina Cruz in 1915 (the *Casa del Obrero Mundial*), and 1916 (the *Federación de Sindicatos Obreros*), but, leaving aside national political considerations, the cooptation of organised labour was hardly a pressing concern in Oaxaca, given the limited pace of industrialisation and urban growth during the nineteenth century, and the consequent absence of a militant and organised proletariat.[22] The only group of workers who received any tangible benefit

21. Edwin Lieuwen, *Mexican Militarism. The Political Rise and Fall of the Revolutionary Army, 1910-1940* (Albuquerque, 1968), 39. For further details, see Paul Garner, "Autoritarismo revolucionario en el México provincial: el carrancismo y el gobierno preconstitucional en Oaxaca, 1915-1920," in *HMex*, 34:2 (1984/134), 238-299.

22. Chassen, "Oaxaca," *op.cit.*, outlines the activities of Catholic Workers' Circles, organised by Archbishop Gillow, which reputedly had a registered membership of 2,000 in 1907.

from pre-Constitutional administration were state employees, who were granted salary increases (100 percent in March 1916), and most importantly, exemption from the enforced acceptance of increasingly worthless Constitutionalist bonds and paper bills, during what was unquestionably a period of chronic monetary instability and rampant inflation.

### *Anti-Clericalism*

The revival of anti-clericalism as an important plank in the Constitutionalist political platform has been widely recognised. The fact that Oaxaca was widely noted for its adherence to Catholicism seemed to auger bitter clashes between the military authorities and the faithful of Oaxaca. But although the spirit of anti-clericalism was transmitted by Constitutionalist representatives within the state, the nature and intensity of its implementation was less severe than might have been expected, and depended ultimately on the disposition of the military commanders in control. Once again, however, local conditions were the determining factor. It is evident that, the social, political, and above all economic power of the Church of Oaxaca had been undermined by the sale of Church property and the successful implementation of the Reform legislation between 1856-1876. However, the extent to which the spiritual and administrative regeneration which occurred in certain areas during the *Porfiriato* (especially in Jalisco and Michoacán) had restored the influence and authority of the Church in Oaxaca is uncertain. The energy, activity, and influence of Archbishop Gillow in local and national affairs, clearly demonstrated in his correspondence with the President, warrants a more detailed investigation and analysis.[23]

### *Education*

Jesús Agustín Castro was certainly unequivocal when he described education as the *"cornerstone of the building which represents the definitive triumph of the Mexican Revolution."* But despite the initial flurry of demagogic enthusiasm, the military authorities could not claim to have been successful in *"spreading educational and moral enlightenment to the Oaxacan people."* At the end of 1915 the pre-Constitutional government had announced the establishment of 73 primary schools (*rudimentarias*) in the Isthmus region -but no other such announcements were made before 1920.[24] Once again, the lack of political authority and jurisdiction was largely responsible for the failure of educational reform, although there were also financial constraints. Pre-Constitutional administration was increasingly hampered by a lack of revenue which could finance an expansion of the social and welfare programmes, including education. The ambitious and unrealistic expenditure budget from 1916 was drastically reduced in 1917 from four million *pesos* to one and a quarter million, and the proportion to be spent on education reduced from one half to one-sixth. As elsewhere in Mexico, state administrations were authorised to levy local taxes which were intended to cover local administrative costs. The basis of the local levy in Oaxaca was established in December 1916, but state taxes were however never able to sustain and support the expenditure of the military authorities. In March 1917 governor Jiménez Méndez requested a monthly loan of 30,000 *pesos* from central government to cover administrative costs.[25] Although documentary evidence of the actual, rather than the proposed, expenditure of

23. Charles Berry, *The Reform in Oaxaca, 1856-1876* (Lincoln, 1981). For details of Gillow's career, see Manuel Esparza, *Gillow durante el porfiriato y la revolución, 1887-1922* (Oaxaca, 1985). A report sent to the British Legislation in 1920 described the relationship between the Church and the military authorities in Oaxaca as *"cordial . . . all of the 22 churches in Oaxaca* (city) *are used for services,"* in *FO*, 204, 547.

24. *Manifiesto al pueblo oaxaqueño.*

25. *AHDN*, 212, f. 64-5, 16-04-1917.

pre-Constitutional administration has not yet come to light, a comparison of proposed budget expenditure indicates that both financial capacity and political will had declined substantially by 1920.

### *Agrarian Reform*

One of the largest reductions in the Constitutionalist budget was in *Fomento* (Development), which amongst other things was responsible for agrarian reform through the agency of the *Comisión Local Agraria* established in November 1916. This reduction perhaps was symptomatic of the general lack of commitment by the Constitutionalist authorities nationally to the principle of agrarian reform. There can be little doubt that, despite the revolutionary zeal of individual *carrancistas*, the incorporation of *agrarismo* into Constitutionalist ideology was a direct response to the popular *agrarista* pressure from Carranza's political opponents, and in particular from *zapatismo*. In Oaxaca, the fact that agrarian reform had not been a prominent issue in most of the local insurrections that had flared up during the *maderista* phase of the Revolution (in 1911) was reflected by the limited number of petitions submitted. Between 1917 and 1920 the Commission received a total of only 40 formal petitions, only 9 of which had resulted in land grants by 1920. It is interesting to note the approximately 3/4 of these petitions came from *pueblos* concentrated in the central valleys. This is partly explained by the limitation of the jurisdiction of the Constitutionalist authorities, and partly by the nature of land tenure in the area in the latter half of the nineteenth century.[26]

Despite the apparent increase in the number of *haciendas* in the central valleys (from 60 in 1857 to 88 in 1913), Cassidy's research has indicated that poor transportation, the slow growth of the city of Oaxaca, and the general absence of market opportunities induced low levels of prices, profitability, and land speculation. In these circumstances it was far more common for *hacendados* to dispose of their property through inheritance or sale, or to distribute it to sharecroppers or tenants rather than to encroach upon the *ejidos* and *fundos legales* of the *pueblos*.[27] Although this suggests a lack of conflict between *hacienda* y *pueblo* in the central valleys, such conflict does not appear to have been entirely absent, since a small number of *pueblos* did respond to the opportunity provided by the Constitutionalist agrarian legislation to redress their grievances with neighbouring estates, grievances which in many cases appeared to predate the *Reforma*. Twenty-eight of the petitions requested *restitución* (return of land) rather than *dotación* (grant), nineteen of which were rejected because the *despojo* (seizure) had taken place before 1856. Nevertheless, this is hardly evidence of profound agrarian unrest.

Whilst Constitutionalist policy in these four areas (agrarian reform, education, labour and anti-clericalism) appear to reflect contemporary preoccupations throughout the republic there are two areas, where the character and impact of Constitutionalist policy in Oaxaca appears to challenge previous assumptions. The first concerns political representation and the second concerns the depression, rather than the regeneration of the local economy.

### *Political Representation*

The military authorities in Oaxaca were both unwilling and unable to allow free or representative elections either at municipal, state, or national level during the period. Despite the declared Constitutionalist commitment to the *municipio libre* as the basis of local government, no state or federal elections took place, and the state legislature re-

26. *PO*, VII, 5, 21-01-1920.
27. T. Cassidy, "Hacienda and Pueblo in Nineteenth-Century Oaxaca" (Ph. D. diss., University of Cambridge, 1981).

mained closed until 1920. But the clearest example of this lack of representation was the election of delegates to the constituent convention in Querétaro in November 1916. These elections have been called *"some of the fairest elections ever held in Mexico."*[28] This was certainly not the case in Oaxaca where the elections were characterised by a combination of carpetbagging, administrative incompetence and outright electoral fraud.

In Oaxaca the elections were set for the 22nd October, and copies of the decree were sent to the *presidentes municipales* of the *cabeceras* of the electoral districts under Constitutionalist control -and it was openly admitted that ten of the 25 political districts were beyond Constitutionalist control. In only six of the remaining fifteen districts did the elections take place on the specified date. Even here there were alarming regularities -the elections were held in Tlacolula on 22nd October, but votes were not counted until 26th November, owing to the 'disappearance' of the *presidente municipal-* and this was four days after the delegate had taken his seat at the Convention. As a result, Oaxaca was represented by only nine delegates at Querétaro: even then, only two of the delegates participated actively in the debates, and neither of these were from Oaxaca -the journalist Luis Espinosa, from Chiapas, and General Salvador González Torres (from Michoacán) who acted as second vice-president of the Convention.[29]

### *The Local Economy*

With regard to the local economy, the evidence from Oaxaca challenges the assertion that the Carranza regime *"resurrected a shattered economy."* This view contrasts sharply with an eye-witness report from Oaxaca in September 1919 declared that *"the state . . . is in a very bad condition. The cattle have been destroyed, hardly any decent houses are to be seen except those stolen by the carrancistas, crops have been ruined, farmhouses burnt down, and mines closed . . . if order were restored now, it would take many years before anything approaching former prosperity could be reached."* The stark conclusion was that the local economy was *"hopelessly ruined."*[30] The establishment of pre-Constitutionalist government in Oaxaca coincided with serious famines in 1915 and 1916 - which were also related to the most intense period of military activity within the state. Memoirs and contemporary accounts tell a similar story in which the consequences of armed conflict were aggravated by drought, by epidemics of typhoid and small-pox, poor harvests and by the refusal of local traders to accept Constitutionalist paper currency. Although shortages persisted, the famines of the early years were not repeated. There is good reason to suppose that the general economic depression which characterised the Constitutionalist years restored a degree of economic self-sufficiency in the various geo-political regions within the state, especially in those areas which had begun to be transformed by the extension of commercial agriculture and mining during the 1890s.

It is also possible to speculate that the period 1915 to 1920 was another phase in the pattern of cyclical depression of the local economy during the nineteenth century. This hypothesis is supported by evidence from the *Sierra Juárez* and the *Sierra Mixteca*, particularly in regard to self-sufficiency in agricultural production. The military authorities assumed that the rebel state defense forces would be starved out when they took to their respective hills in 1916, but their assumptions proved to be mistaken. The sporadic nature of the conflict meant that the rank and file of the *serrano* militias re-

28. E. V. Niemeyer, *Revolution at Querétaro: The Mexican Constitutional Convention of 1916-1917* (Austin, 1978), 36.

29. This information comes from a *legajo* marked "Congreso 1916" in the *Archivo General del Estado de Oaxaca*.

30. Richmond, *Venustiano Carranza's Nationalist Struggle*; and, *FO*, 204, 532 'Oaxaca 1919'.

turned to their villages when not on 'active' service. When local production fell short of requirements, other locally-produced commodities, in particular ore and livestock, could be exchanged for necessary supplies and equipment. Throughout the state, but particularly in the *sierras* peasant producers demonstrated their resistance to civil disturbances between 1915 and 1920 in the same way they had responded to the endemic problems of the nineteenth century, and returned to a subsistence and barter economy. This inevitably meant that the specialist crops geared to the export market which had been introduced into certain regions during the *Porfiriato* would suffer the consequences. This has been clearly demonstrated by the introduction of coffee into the local economy of the *Sierra Juárez*, where production was severely disrupted by the upheaval of the revolutionary years. Evidence from outside the *sierra* on the coffee plantations of Cuicatlán, Tuxtepec and Teotitlán suggests that commercial exploitation on a larger scale also suffered. In 1917 alone, 8 plantations, 3 *terrenos* and 1 *finca* were intervened by the military authorities in Cuicatlán alone for failure to pay property taxes.[31]

Economic depression also had a detrimental effect on more traditional industries within the state. The mining industry in Oaxaca had been particularly subject to the cyclical depressions of the local economy during the nineteenth century, but during the first decade of the twentieth mining had proved to be the principal beneficiary of the Porfirian boom. In 1898 a total of 313 mining properties were registered in Oaxaca, but by 1909 the figure had risen to 1989. However, during the revolutionary decade; as a result of a combination of fiscal and legislative assaults from the Constitutionalist administration, and physical attacks on the isolated and unprotected mining camps from rebel bands, the number of registered mining properties had fallen to 1501 by the end of 1922; although it must be remembered that those figures represent only those mining properties upon which taxes had been paid, and therefore do not reflect levels of production for which there is as yet, no evidence. The overall depression of the mining industry in Oaxaca in this period, which contrasts with national pattern of recovery by 1920, is perhaps best indicated by the closure of the largest mine in operation in Oaxaca, the *Compañía Minera de Natividad* of Ixtlán in the *Sierra Juárez* in 1921.[32]

Economic development in general was given little stimulus by the military authorities in Oaxaca. Agustín Castro certainly recognised the abundant and under-exploited mineral and agricultural resources of the state, and in February 1916 he called upon all *"honourable capitalists"* to invest in industrial and commercial enterprises in Oaxaca. Despite these rhetorical flourishes Castro's invitation was never supported by legislative incentives or initiatives. Apart from the harsh economic realities of the period, Carranza's determination to establish central control over the exploitation of the nation's resources emasculated any role the state administration might have played in promoting regional industries. A decree of August 1916 prohibited state governments from issuing laws concerning the regulation of commerce, mining, banking, public lands, *ejidos*, labour or the exploitation of subsoil deposits. A further drain on local resources was the progressive rise in the proportion of state taxes which went directly to central government, from 25 percent in 1915 to 60 percent in 1918: an early example of the process by which individual states would become economically tied to the purse strings of central government in the post-revolutionary era.[33]

---

31. For a discussion of the agrarian economy of Oaxaca in the nineteenth century, see Cassidy, "Hacienda and Pueblo." C. Young, "The Social Setting of Migration. Factors Affecting Migration from a Sierra Zapotec Village in Oaxaca, Mexico" (Ph. D. diss., University of London, 1975). *Periódico oficial del gobierno provisional del estado libre y soberano de Oaxaca*, I (1920), No. 4.

32. *Mexican Year Book* (London, 1910), 598. *Informe del gobernador Manuel García Vigil a la XXVIII legislatura del estado libre y soberano de Oaxaca* (Oaxaca, 1921).

33. "Importantes declaraciones acerca de la verdadera misión del capital," in *PO*, II, 8, 24-02-1916. *PO*, III, 3, 5-10-1916.

## CONCLUSIONS

In the absence of precise details and statistics regarding the levels of production and actual revenue and expenditure of the pre-Constitutionalist administration, final conclusions must remain tentative. Armed conflict, epidemics, famine, and migration had undoubtedly taken their toll on the population (a rough estimate is a net demographic loss of some 60,000 from a population in 1910 of one million). It is difficult to quantify the extent to which the productive base of the state had been destroyed by 1920, although it appears that the damage was extensive. The evidence certainly indicates that the *"great work of reconstruction"* envisaged for Oaxaca by José Agustín Castro in 1915 was still a distant dream in 1920. Nevertheless the initial ideological commitment of individual military commanders and bureaucrats in Oaxaca to the hybrid social and economic programme of Constitutionalism cannot be questioned. But the populist rhetoric of 1915 and 1916 slowly but perceptibly transformed into a grim authoritarianism once the scale of the task and the scale of internal resistance were recognised. The exercise of authority within the state was severely restricted, on the one hand by strict limitations on resources available to the military authorities, and on the other by the opposition of all levels of provincial *oaxaqueño* society.

Although I have barely touched upon the extent of internal resistance, it is clear that Constitutionalism by 1920 had yet to convert, undermine or replace the forces at the root of provincial opposition: firstly, the authority of the *caudillos* from the *Sierra Juárez*, or, secondly, the balance of federal-state relations throughout the nineteenth century.[34] In fact, Constitutionalist practice had, if anything, strengthened provincial resolve. The final victory of Constitutionalism would not therefore come until subsequent decades when the slow and painful process of economic and political centralisation would finally bring Oaxaca to heel. Constitutionalist government in Oaxaca between 1915 and 1920 had certainly initiated the process, however unsuccessfully and haphazardly, but it was very far from complete in 1920.

34. These themes are discussed in Paul Garner, "Federalism and *Caudillismo* in the Mexican Revolution: The Genesis of the Oaxaca Sovereignty Movement (1915-20)," in *Journal of Latin American Studies*, 17 (1985), 111-133.

CHAPTER SEVEN

# Military *Caciques* in Magnificence and Decline: San Luis Potosí in the Mexican Revolution

ROMANA FALCON*

## DAWN OF THE REVOLUTION

San Luis Potosí is a dry and mountainous state in the central north of Mexico. More than ninety percent of the land is unworkable and supports a typically semi-desert vegetation. However, its southeastern region, the Huasteca, offers a striking contrast with its high rate of humidity and an exuberant flora and fauna which link it geographically and socio-economically more with the Huastecas of the adjoining states -Tamaulipas, Veracruz, Hidalgo- than with the Potosí highlands. This fundamental geographical distinction is the basis of a clear differentiation between the two regions, as well as to a certain rivalry between the political and social movements of the highlands and those of the Huasteca.[1] The most obvious demonstration of this separatism was the -unsuccessful- attempt by residents from the Huasteca of San Luis Potosí, Veracruz, Hidalgo and Tamaulipas to create the state of Huasteco. It was the richness of its subsoil which attracted the first European settlers to San Luis in the sixteenth century, when rich silver veins were discovered. This led to the emergence of those districts which were to become famous for their brilliance: El Catorce, San Pedro, Matehuala, Cedral, Vanegas and Guadalcazar. In the period of the rebellion of 1810 a long wave of economic depression and political instability set in which persisted right up to the end of the nineteenth century, during the long dictatorship of Porfirio Díaz. Quite similar to, for example, Nuevo León, the economy of San Luis Potosí owed its dynamism to a large extent to foreign capital. With the coming of the railways began the economic and political integration of the various regions of the state, as well as that of the state with the rest of the country and with the United States. Mines, foundries, breweries, tobacco, wool and cotton textiles flourished.

However, San Luis never lost its predominantly rural character. In 1910, on the eve of the Mexican Revolution, 80 percent of the 627,000 inhabitants of the state lived in the countryside. Like their counterparts in the rest of the country, the rural districts were dominated by extreme poverty and a high concentration of property; most of the rural families had no land, while the *hacienda* owners, i.e. those with holdings of more than 1,000 hectares, constituted barely 0.01 percent of the total. The landowners formed an aristocracy with immense power. San Luis was ruled by a small clique of families that were linked by economic, political and marriage ties. Prominent members of

* *Historian, Centro de Estudios Históricos, El Colegio de México, Camino al Ajusco 20, CP 01000 México DF.* *I would like to thank CEDLA for funding this translation by Peter Mason.*

1. The situation described here is not much different from the one described by Thomson in his essay in this volume.

this small circle were the Porfirian governors: the Díez Gutiérrez brothers, who were in control of the state for more than twenty years (1876-1898); Blas Escontría, and José Espinosa y Cuevas, who was put down by the Revolution and was owner of La Angostura, the largest *hacienda* in San Luis, covering more than 80,000 hectares.[2] The political life of San Luis Potosí was clearly determined by the interests of the large landowners, both because they held the most important positions and because, besides the formal appointments, there were personal connections between the authorities and the *hacienda* owners, thanks to which the latter exercised a decisive political influence.[3]

There can be no doubt that the large *haciendas* formed the economic, political and social axis of the San Luis Potosí countryside. Even when more than 80 percent of the rural population of the state -twice the national average- was living on these properties, generalisations on their living conditions should be made with caution, for the treatment received by the peasants was by no means uniform: it varied from region to region, from holding to holding. Besides, the complex economic organisation which was characteristic of most of the *haciendas* led to a diversified system of social stratification. The workers on the land did not take this situation lying down. Various rebellions broke out in the course of the *Porfiriato.* These uprisings were concentrated in the Huasteca and in the *Valle del Maíz* which is adjacent to the northern border of *La Huasteca.* These were areas with a high proportion of natives who, unlike the majority of the inhabitants of San Luis, retained the language, customs, a large part of their social organisation and even the power structure which they had inherited from the colonial period. These *pueblos de indios* were used to an ancient organisation as an agrarian community. They were accustomed to defend their lands against the ravages of the Spanish and *mestizos* over the centuries.

It was about the time that Díaz took power and the railways began to link the capital city with Tampico that the almost total isolation in which the small *pueblos de indios* of San Luis Potosí found themselves was suddenly broken. Tamazunchale, which became the main centre of agrarian agitation in the Huasteca, had not even had passable roads before the introduction of the railways. People simply travelled on foot or by horse through tracks in the dense vegetation. The Indians formed three-quarters of the population. They saw themselves as a separate republic and retained a strong sense of cultural identity through their language, clothes and customs. Their authorities were independent of the formal political structure of the country: they elected a native "governor" themselves, who settled local disputes in line with ancestral traditions without regard to the national or state laws. Towards the second half of the nineteenth century agrarian protest in the southeast of San Luis Potosí and the neighbouring states took a violent turn. In 1849 a rebellion broke out in the Huasteca that was known as 'the first communist experiment in the country,' and seven years later, a number of Indians from the Huasteca rose up to demand *"death to private property."* On 5 July 1879 more than four hundred Indians armed with rifles occupied the main square of Tamazunchale to the accompaniment of dancing and the pealing of bells. This action inaugurated the longest and bloodiest agrarian conflict of the period. Government forces were only able to put it down after various military campaigns and the

2. Moisés González Navarro, *Estadísticas sociales del porfiriato*, (Mexico City, 1956), 41, 217; George McBride, *Los sistemas de propiedad rural en México*, (Mexico City, 1951), 26-56; Eyler Simpson, *El ejido, única salida para México*, (Mexico City, 19xx), Tables 2, 11, 13, 15; Romana Falcón, *Revolución y caciquismo. San Luis Potosí 1910-1938*, (Mexico City, 1984), 24-25.

3. See in particular the case of Paulo Verastegui, owner of the San Diego de Rio Verde *hacienda*, and his informal influence on state affairs; Marijosé Amerlinck, "From Hacienda to Ejido. The San Diego de Rio Verde Case," (Ph. D. diss., State University of New York at Stony Brook, 1980), 129, 192; Primo Feliciano Velázquez, *Historia de San Luis Potosí, IV: De como vino la revolución*, (Mexico City, 1946), 194ff.; *El Contemporáneo*, 14/8/1907.

devastation of some Indian settlements. And in 1882 the *Valle del Maíz* became the new centre of peasant conflict.[4]

Nevertheless, the spread of discontent was not confined to the lowest strata of society during the *Porfiriato*, nor were agrarian conflicts its only source. The permanence in power of *caciques* and officials meant that political control and a considerable part of the region's wealth remained in the hands of the few. Wheeling and dealing in political life, accompanied by the frequent outrages committed by the authorities, *caciques* and public figures in the villages, were met with hatred throughout the state. The geographical peculiarities of the southeastern zone led to an especially virulent spate of *caciquismo*. A tiny power group not only monopolised deputations, leading political positions, municipal offices and electoral councils, but also held political and economic sway over these isolated regions, often by illegal means, without necessarily having to hold public office.

Besides the *caciques*, the political leaders also created considerable resentment and friction through the wide-reaching and despotic power that they enjoyed in the various parties into which San Luis Potosí was divided. These were the key figures who served to connect the small villages and regions with the state authorities and the national centre. The political leaders were direct agents of the executive authority, and their appointment depended formally on the governor, who was empowered to 'suspend or dismiss them at his pleasure'. However, the centralising influence of the president was also sizeable, which meant that the executive bodies of San Luis Potosí consulted regularly with Díaz on the choice of candidates for various functions and on the most serious problems with which these officials would be faced. Within the party that remained in his charge it was the administrative bodies which presided, which formed the 'official channels' among the authorities, and which were responsible for military recruitment and the maintenance of peace, having all the armed forces of the party at their disposal for that purpose. In short, the political leader was a fundamental figure on whom the level of integration and centralisation of the political structure depended.[5]

## THE FALL OF THE OLD ORDER AND THE DISPERSION OF POWER (1910-1925)

One of the most significant and immediate consequences of the movement that was begun in 1910 was the unleashing of numerous centrifugal policies. When Díaz left the country in May 1911, the central figure who, through the lack of genuine institutions, had given unity and coherence to all political actors and procedures for decades disappeared. The decline of the old order and the weakness of the new authorities provoked a sudden large-scale upsurge of autonomy in the various regions of the country and in its most isolated villages. In San Luis Potosí, the Revolution meant that the whole

4. Falcón, *Revolución y caciquismo*, 36-37; Rafael Montejano y Aguiñaja, *El Valle del Maíz*, (San Luis Potosí, 1967), 49, 53, 59, 63, 73, 86, 268-278; Donald Stevens, "Agrarian Policy and Instability in Porfirian Mexico," in *The Americas*, 39:2 (1982), 153-166; Leticia Reyna, *Las rebeliones campesinas en México, 1819-1906* (Mexico City, 1980), 284ff; Enríque Márquez, "La casa de los Señores Santos. Un cacicazgo en la Huasteca potosina, 1876-1910" (Tesis de maestría, El Colegio de México, 1979), 19-30, 41ff, 49-53, appendix I; *El Estandarte*, 3/8/1906, 2/9/1906, 10/9/1907; *Public Record Office* (*PRO*), F0204, V3331, N15, Wilson, Consul in Tampico to Consul General, 24/7/1906.

5. *Ley orgánica reglamentaria de la sección IX del título 2 de la Constitución del Estado sobre jefes políticos* (San Luis Potosí, 1902); Daniel Cosío Villegas, *El porfiriato. La vida política interior, Historia Moderna de México*, (Mexico City, 1972), II, 95; *PRO* F0203, V172; Wilson to Consul General, 24/7/1906; Montejano, *Valle del Maíz*, 341-342; Joaquín Meade, *Historia de Valles. Monografía de la Huasteca potosina*, (San Luis Potosí, 1970), 129ff.

power structure became centred on local conflicts for more than a decennium. This newly won independence was manifested politically in various ways. From the start, two currents were present. One of these gave expression to genuinely popular demands, while the other, which was of a more political nature, was to a large extent responsible for the intensification of *cacicazgo* that San Luis went through in these years.

Right from the start of the Revolution there were villages which demanded the restitution of the lands bequeathed to them by their ancestors. This demand raised profound questions for the whole social order. Their rebellion was concentrated in a few places in the state: basically in Villa de Reyes and in settlements in the Huasteca, like Huichamón and San Miguelíto.[6] But not all the peasants of San LuisPotosí were engaged in the struggle for land. It is important to note that a fair number of villages did not even make strictly agrarian demands at all. This phenomenon is largely due to the fact that there was a relative scarcity of long-established agrarian communities, whose identity and economic viability were essentially definable in terms of land, in a considerable part of the highland area of San Luis Potosí.

The *hacienda* was the undisputed focus of the countryside in San Luis Potosí, and the *haciendas* had frequently been able to extend without arousing excessive opposition from the local inhabitants. This factor, and the obvious paternalism which was a characteristic of many *hacienda* owners, were the two principal reasons which explain why many of the workers on the *haciendas* failed to include agrarian reform among their demands. What they did ask for, in a variety of accents, were improvements of a different kind: higher wages, reduced working hours and better rates for their products.[7] In fact, the most persistent and spontaneous action on the part of the people of San Luis Potosí to dismember the Díaz government had a basically political character, a struggle for local freedom, to 'settle accounts' with the authorities and *caciques*, especially those who had made themselves notorious by their abuses and their long periods in office.

In order to understand this relative lack of a struggle for land, and the character of the various local movements which furnished the contours of the Revolution in San Luis Potosí, we should go beyond the traditional interpretation of the Mexican Revolution, with its heavy explanatory emphasis on popular action, especially on the part of the peasants. It is necessary to introduce nuances if we are to avoid both the danger of neglecting certain specific features of the participation of the workers and -more important- that of obscuring the actions of other forces which were as decisive, or more so, in determining the form and content of political life in San Luis after 1910. Among these forces we should consider the well-off sectors, especially the middle sectors, i.e. the various beneficiaries of the *Porfiriato.*

Part of the *crème de la crème* of San Luis Potosí displayed an ambivalent attitude towards the Díaz regime. While the majority of the elite did not actively oppose the *Porfiriato* and viewed any possible fundamental social change with horror, a number of the powerful supported a moderate renewal of the political personnel as well as certain reforms which endowed their interests with a greater degree of security and perspectives. This accounts for the support which some of the most notable residents of San Luis Potosí accorded to Francisco I. Madero. At all events, this young *hacienda* owner from the neighbouring state of Coahuila, an anti-Porfirian candidate for the presidency for the *Partido Nacional Antireeleccionista* in 1910, was a member of one of the most prominent and commercially successful families in the whole of northern Mexico. Moreover, his eagerness to democratise national political life, to renew the govern-

6. *El Estandarte*, 18/8/1911, 20/8/1911, 8/10/1911, 18/12/1911, 22/12/1911, 18/1/1913, 24/1/1913, 13/2/1913; *Archivo Histórico de la Secretaría de la Defensa Nacional* (*AHDN*), e.XI/481. 5/250; ff 13, 14; *Centro de Estudios Históricos de México* (*CEHM*), f. XXI (Venustiano Carranza), caja (c) 45, legajo (leg.) 4986; Leopoldo Lárraga to Carranza, n/d.

7. Romana Falcón, "¿Los orígenes populares de la revolución del1910? El caso de San Luis Potosí," en *Historia Mexicana* (hereafter *HMex*), 27:3 (1980/114), 230ff.

ments, putting an end to the dictatorship which had been in power for more than thirty years, did not appear to pose any genuine threat to the pre-eminence of the Mexican upper classes. Rather, it seemed to offer security for the maintenance of the *status quo*.

However, the most active anti-reelection supporters in the state were members of the middle strata: Dr. Rafael Cepeda -who was to assume the governorship in the triumph of the Revolution- and the De los Santos family. The remarkable persistence and pre-eminence of this clan was the clearest proof of how the Mexican Revolution came to serve as a guarantee of the security of certain *cacicazgos*. It was as if time had stopped. In the case of the De los Santos, their capacity to retain their position, with ebbs and flows, on the crest of the political wave lasted for roughly a century and a half. It illustrates not only the enormous flexibility and capacity for adaptation of these traditional structures of power, but also the way in which they managed to keep popular demands on a secondary level.

The Los Santos were small landowners, a sector in which the so-called *Maderistas* found one of their most enthusiastic receptions and which had exercised *cacique* control over part of the Huasteca since 1829. Despite the prosperity of their estates situated in the heart of the Huasteca, there were various forces which contributed to their discomfort during the *Porfiriato*. The Los Santos were thus losing their economic primacy and their political hegemony in Tampamolón in the municipality of Tamazunchale. The clan had to contend with another local faction of *rancheros*, headed by the Martells. The point at issue was the control of the municipal government, an important function which had enabled the Los Santos to gain control of the lands of the neighbouring Indian communities and part of the municipal legal treasuries, and thus to determine the unpaid forced labour demanded of many peasants, who 'paid' their dues in this manner. Young Pedro Antonio de los Santos became one of the most important anti-reelection supporters in the state. As Gonzalo, the youngest of the family, was to put it later, his family welcomed the Revolution, not because they were dying of hunger, but in order to win back their hegemony over Tampamolón and to make good in the future the promise which the *Porfiriato* seemed to deny them. To the extent that personalities of the same type as the Los Santos put themselves forward as the principal revolutionary leaders, the movement became, to a certain degree, a simple continuation of the factional struggle which had been a feature of the small regions of San Luis Potosí during the nineteenth century.[8]

Life in San Luis Potosí acquired an intensely violent character in the Revolution, which brought a naked struggle for power into its political life in the decennium which followed the fall of the old order. In this continual conflict both political power and the military dissociated themselves from the old structures of domination and division. The intense struggle in which the nation was involved provided the political leaders in San Luis Potosí with an increasing independence *vis-à-vis* the central government, or what was left of it. This autonomy reached its peak in the years 1914 and 1915, when neither in the capital of the republic nor in many of the states was a revolutionary faction able to impose its hegemony on its rivals. A considerable part of the formal structure of government was in ruins. *De facto*, the Mexican state was no more and also in San Luis the distinction between political and military power practically disappeared, together with the theoretical distinction between the various state organs and their mutual relations. Governors and military leaders settled all kinds of questions, each in his own way: executive and judicial matters, judgements affecting life and property, military affairs, confiscation and transfer of land, appointment and functions

---

8. Márquez, "Casa de los Señores Santos," 14ff, 31ff., 53-57, 66-68; *El Estandarte*, 8/5/1911; *El Contemporáneo*, 31/5/1907; Gertrudis García, "Tetralogía potosina," in *El Legionario*, July 1910. Falcón, *Revolución y.caciquismo*, 45ff.

of the politico-administrative apparatus, and so on. Their decisions were not generally taken according to legislation. Government was spontaneous and immediate.

However, the relative independence of the events in San Luis Potosí was a corollary of the weakness of the political institutions and procedures, and the incapacity of those in power to impose their decisions, that is, to govern. This is the cause of the overwhelming lack of organisation and the power vacuum in vast regions of San Luis Potosí which managed without authorities for days, weeks or even months. In this situation, the only effective power was that of the revolutionary leaders turned regional bosses and masters. Let us take the example of *Valle del Maíz*, a region with a long-standing *agrarista* tradition and cradle of what was to become the most important military *cacique* in the Revolution in San Luis Potosí. From 1913, not only the farms in the countryside, but even the capital of the district itself were at the disposal of revolutionaries and bandits, which led to the disappearance of all public officials, from judges and prefects down to the lowest ranks of neighbourhood officialdom. By the end of the year, the rebel bands were even electing trustees and administrators for the zones under their control. Early in 1915, when no revolutionary faction in the country was able to gain the upper hand over its rivals, San Luis Potosí had to conduct its political and administrative affairs for a time without a head, since those 'in charge of' government refused to take decisions on non-military matters.[9]

The real embodiments of power were thus the military leaders who managed to control a certain region for some time. The territory of San Luis Potosí was fragmented in a mosaic of tiny military *cacicazgos* where justice was administered and decisions affecting life and property were taken. Cedillo was described during his occupation of Ciudad del Maíz as ". . . *the master of the people and leader of an Indian group which engaged in unscrupulous reprisals like the Zapatistas. The few whites of the city were shut in here, besieged and at the mercy of unofficial militia; without courts nor any guarantee of civil rights. A return to the Indian filth*".[10] The band of the Cedillo brothers did not even let *hacienda* owners out of the settlement without their express permission. José Espinosa y Cuevas, brother of the last Porfirian governor, was killed on his *hacienda* and his body exposed to his labourers. An old governor complained about how the Cedillo brothers had turned into "*bosses and masters*" of various of his estates.[11]

In the solitude and isolation of the zones under the influence of the Cedillos and their allies, the *agrarista* brothers Alberto and Francisco Carrera Torres managed to impose a social order with its own political and military norms. Largely due to the havoc caused by the 'war' in the monetary economy, it was arranged that the soldiers would continue to live from the land in their villages instead of receiving payment. On the other hand, they were given the basic necessities free of charge: shoes, hats, scarfs, blankets and calico clothing, as well as food rations and communal meals. Schools were opened and bridge construction was started. The funds for these activities, as well as for the purchase of weapons and billeting, were raised from the confiscation of *hacien-*

9. *AHDN*, e. XI/481.5/261, ff 229-230, "Acta de elección de regidores y síndicos en Ciudad el Maíz realizado por la columna al mando de los Cedillo", 17/12/1913; *PRO*, F0204, V221, 271/13, Wilson to Stronge, 29/6/1913; *Adelante*, 12/5/1913, 13/5/1913, 21/5/1913, 14/6/1913, 29/6/1913; F0371; V1673, F.6269, p30678, Wilson to Stronge, 13/6/1913. Falcón, *Revolución y.caciquismo*, 89ff.; *Archivo Juan Barragán* (*AJB*), cVI/8/ff43-48 (261), deputy of Pedro Barrenechea to Juan Barragán, 6/1/1915.

10. José Vasconcelos, *La Tormenta* (Mexico City, 1958), 282; Alberto Alcocer, *El general y profesor Alberto Carrera Torres* (San Luis Potosí, 1976), 15; *Archivo General de la Nación* (*AGN*), Fondo Gobernación, Ramo Revolución (FG-R), c6, e72, Correspondencia entre Cedillo, Galván y Aguilar, May-August 1914.

11. *AJB*, cV/21/f50-55 (132), correspondence between the deputy of Díez Gutiérrez and Juan Barragán, September 1914 to September 1915. Although the Cedillos did not allow the *hacienda* owners out of the settlement, at least a few notable ones, the Moctezuma, accepted that "... *in other respects they did not bother anyone*".

*das*, exchange, the sale of *ixtle* and livestock in neighbouring markets and even in the United States, the 'enforced loans' from the petroleum companies and the sale of 'protection' to the *haciendas*.[12]

Among the regional uprisings of a genuinely political nature which occurred during the period of armed struggle, that of Los Santos is particularly significant. Throughout the course of the Revolution, the rebellion of these *caciques* retained the traditional character that such movements had from the early the nineteenth century. Thanks to their considerable influence among the local population and to a fortune that was by no means transitory, the Indians of the Huasteca continued to form the mass of their recruits. Their revolutionary action was to a large extent the simple continuation of the factional disputes which had marked politics in the Huasteca for decennia. This interlocking of the old with the new order was particularly conspicuous during the Madero phase. Los Santos were then able to place relatives and old allies in positions as municipal presidents, as political leaders and inspectors, or simply -as an opponent alleged- as *"masters of public affairs"*. More importantly, the weakness of the authorities enabled them to ignore the decrees emanating from central government which ordered the discharge of the revolutionaries. In this way, they managed to maintain hundreds of members of the rural population under arms as the ultimate base of their growing *cacicazgo*. This independence enabled the clan to engage in armed struggle against the government of Madero. In an attempt to put an end to the effectual hegemony of Los Santos in the Huasteca, the local executive Rafael Cepeda formed an alliance with the old group of his rivals, conferring on them positions of leadership in the armed forces and in the country districts, despite the fact that these opponents of Los Santos had taken up arms in support of the Díaz regime. The Revolution thus only served to intensify this long-standing dispute among *caciques*.[13] After an unsuccessful retaliatory attempt by Samuel de los Santos to overthrow the executive by force in 1923, the youngest member of the family, Gonzalo N. de los Santos, became governor at the start of the 1940s. From then on he set up a long-lived, iron rule throughout the whole of San Luis Potosí. This dominion lasted until the 1970s.

During the period of armed conflict (1911-1920), and given the lack of laws and uniform criteria which affected the local power structure, it was natural for the governors, and at the same time for the military leaders, to exercise all kinds of functions, exceeding the prerogatives allowed them by their functions and thereby imposing a strong personal stamp on local politics. The governor Eulalio Gutiérrez, for example, who was in office from July to October 1914, gave free rein to his anticlerical ideology; he seized the possessions of the church and intervened on many of their *haciendas*; he restricted the celebration of mass; he prohibited confessions unless held in the presence of a government official to hear them; he expelled the majority of the priests and took pride in having demolished a beautiful sixteenth century temple for the purpose of *"straightening some streets"*. Even more significant was the profoundly radical mark left by Gutiérrez and the *villista* governor Emiliano Saravía on the society of San Luis Potosí. An attempt was made then to ameliorate the conditions of workers and peasants, to initiate agrarian reform, and to secure the active support of the popular

---

12. Vidal Covián Martínez, *Alberto Carrera Torres, idealista de la revolución* (Tampico, 1969), with photographs of these bridges; Velázquez, *Historia de San Luis Potosí*, 235; Alcocer, *General y profesor*, 35; *AGN*, FG-R c28, e10, letters from the Secretary of Government sent by the German consul requesting protection for the *hacienda* of Agua Buena, 7/10/1913, 13/10/1913, 25/4/1914, 30/4/1914.

13. *AJB*, cV/20ff68-111, (123.3), "Copias de telegramas relativos a Nicolas Zarzúa", November, December 1912, José Nieto, commander-in-chief in Valles, Tancanhuitz and Tamazunchale to Cepeda, 27-29/11/1912, ff 35-54(123.1), Nieto to Cepeda, 21/12/1912, ff 65-67(123.2), Cepeda to Madero, 28/12/1912; *National Archives of Washington* (*NAW*), Record Group (RG) 59, 812.00 /5575, Bonney, consul in San Luis Potosí to State Department, 18/11/1912, /5908, 14/1/1913, Bonney to State Department.

classes, in order to make them the foundations of the government.[14] The attempt was not carried through because of the short life-span and weakness of these administrations, but the precedent had been set.

One of the phenomena which most clearly shows the autonomy enjoyed by the revolutionary leaders in San Luis is the intervention in rural and urban holdings, first by the revolutionaries and later by the local governments. The high point in this factional struggle was between July 1914 and July 1915. At first the interventions had a military aim: to support the rebel parties and the war. The *Cedillistas* and *Carreristas*, for example, left *"deputies of the revolutionary services"* in the *haciendas* that they occupied who were responsible for military recruitment, for ensuring that the administrators did not carry out reprisals against their sympathisers and to appropriate part of the production and earnings. The extent and manner in which they intervened in the estates varied, but in general social and labour conditions on the *haciendas* hardly changed: the same administrators and peasants continued working and maintaining the same relations that they had in the past. There was, it is true, a fundamental difference: a large part of the profits and production were at the disposal of the revolutionaries. The changes, then, were hardly noticed, especially among the other classes. The clearest proof of the social superficiality of the majority of these 'interventions' is the fact that the workers on the *haciendas* rarely remembered them.

The governments of Gutiérrez and Saravía were an important stage in the management of the occupied estates, reinforcing the autonomy of the small regions through the municipality. Moreover, these revolutionaries legalised interventions by the revolutionary parties and gave a formal legitimacy, backed up by a constitutional government, to the changes in private property. Gutiérrez created the *Junta Calificadora de Fincas Rústicas y Urbanas*, with municipal branches, while the *villista* government passed a law in line with its decentralising stance which granted the state government control over these properties, as well as total autonomy with respect to the federal authorities in deciding on new interventions and the eventual lot of these estates. Although in practice the big landowners of San Luis Potosí tried various methods to get back their estates, in these years they had a very limited success. Some of them obtained orders to reverse the intervention from their own 'supreme leader', or from the governor, but the country was in such a disorganised state that even the decrees of its supreme authority often failed to have any effect. In January 1915, for example, after the government of San Luis Potosí had been without a head, the decree issued by Carranza himself ordering that certain *porfirista* estates be returned to him was held up. Politics thus continued to be dominated by a lack of organisation and by particular interests.[15]

Despite the fact that power changed hands at the national and local level in August 1915, the absence of a relatively centralised, consolidated and functional political system meant the persistence, although attenuated, of many of the characteristics of political life in San Luis Potosí during the phase of factional struggle. None of the ge-

14. Letter from Eulalio Gutiérrez to Carranza, September 1914, in *Documentos históricos de la revolución mexicana. Revolución y regimen constitucionalista,* Isidro Fabelo, ed. (Mexico City, 1960), 349-351; Alfonso Taracena, *La verdadera revolución mexicana*, (Mexico City, 1960), tomo relativo a 1914-1915, 60; *AGN* FG-R, c77, e8, f6, 29/10/1914, c77, e58, f12, 5/12/1914; *Periódico Oficial*, 25/1/1915, 26/2/1915; *NAW* RG59, 812.00/15374, Bonney to State Department, 25/6 /1915.

15. *AGN* FG-R, c6, e72, f72, documents on the intervention in the *hacienda* El Jabali; *PRO* F0204, V221, 271/13, "Actas levantadas por el juez auxiliar de la Hacienda La Concepción, 3, 6, 12 junio 1913," appendix to report of Wilson to Stronge, 26/6/1913; *Informe rendido por el C. Juan Barragán a la Secretaría de Hacienda y Crédito Público sobre la intervención de la propiedad raíz en el Estado de San Luis Potosí* (San Luis Potosí, 1916); Falcón, *Revolución y.caciquismo*, 94f. *AJB* cVI/8/ff 43-48 (261): deputy of Pedro Barrenechea to Barragán, 6/1/1915, cV/21/ff50-55 (132), deputy of Díez Gutiérrez to Barragán, 23/10/1914.

nerals from outside San Luis Potosí appointed as *primer jefe* by Carranza to act as governors completed a full period of service, governed with a minimum of effectivity, nor could they be controlled by the central authorities or by the legislative and judicial organs. All this meant that it was after the victory of Carranza over his old allies that a start could be made in constructing the large dykes which were to allow a return to the creation of a political system which would embrace the whole country and could tackle the complex tasks of government with a certain degree of efficiency. After the Carranza faction had become assured of its place as the triumphant faction, the *primer jefe* began to set limits to the virtually total control which local *caudillos* had acquired over armed power. In April 1915 Carranza directed the separation -though it was not always put into effect- of the duties of governor and military commander, and the dependence of the armed forces within the states on the federal army. In 1916 the large territorial divisions of the constitutionalist army were dissolved, which meant that all the generals were -formally at least- made subordinates of the minister of defence.[16]

In the political field it was also during the government of Carranza that a slow return to a constitutional state was begun. The new federal constitution emphasised the anticlerical reforms, nationalism and improvement in working conditions; it also instituted an agrarian reform to transfer the land to the villages in the form of *ejidos*, a form of landholding which was to coexist with private property. The mere existence of the 1917 constitution set limits to the extraordinarily unrestricted way in which power had been wielded up to then; it was no longer possible to continue governing simply by decree, promulgating laws which were in stark contradiction to the national system, to keep on appointing the whole personnel of government directly, nor to retain such a degree of independence at state and municipal level. A start was made in the setting up or restoration of bureaucratic machinery to organise the various duties of the state separately from one another: its judicial, legislative, agrarian, labour, economic, military and other functions. However, a long and conflict-ridden process was to be needed, requiring considerable time to mature, before this desire to organise and centralise could become embodied in actual practice. Powerful *caciques* who were still in control of parts of the country managed to find shelter in its loopholes during the 1920s and 1930s.

## THE GOLDEN AGE OF *CACICAZGO*

At the beginning of the 1930s, conditions in San Luis Potosí were on the mend. A situation bearing some resemblance to peace had been secured for the first time since 1911. Successes like this did not mean, however, that the reconstruction of a relatively stable political system was not a slow and complex process. The weakness of the central authorities and the fear of new uprisings gave pride of place to arms as the key to power and economic development. This is the reason for the rise of military-style *cacicazgos*. In fact it was these individuals who had emerged from the revolutionary estates who made it possible to give some kind of structure to national political life. They mediated between the centre and the regions, kept their territories in relative tranquillity and order, at a time when their loyalty and cooperation were in demand to help to put down the rebellions which threatened the recently won stability in these decennia. The old exchange of loyalty for independence continued.

16. *AHDN*, eXI/481.5/118, ff 39, 67; /316, f127, c129; *Periódico Oficial*, 4/11/1915; Edwin Lieuwen, *Mexican Militarism. The Political Rise and Fall of the Revolutionary Army, 1910-1940*, (Albuquerque, 1968), 34-49.

In San Luis the foundations were laid in 1920 of what was to become one of the most long-standing and disciplined *cacicazgos* of the whole Mexican Revolution: that of general Saturnino Cedillo. He retained his arms until he was won over and given revolutionary legitimacy through the Plan of Agua Prieta which led to the fall of Carranza in May 1920. It took only five years for Cedillo to obtain recognition from the central authorities for the establishment of a genuine political and military hegemony over San Luis Potosí society. This phenomenon had its roots in the early 1920s, when the successive national governments still lacked the means of bringing the country under control and lived under the threat of military rebellion, as did in fact take place in 1923, 1927 and 1929, and during the *Cristeros*-war from 1926 to 1929. This insecurity in the face of a possible rebellion led president Alvaro Obregón to try to get the generals to trade in their political independence in exchange for economic privileges and local positions of power. The effectiveness and loyalty of the *caciques* with a sizeable military force of their own, like Cedillo, were thus fundamental for the survival of the national leaders and for the integration and functioning of national political life.

From 1920, when Cedillo reached an accommodation with the government, he seized from the federal authorities what was eventually to become the key-stone of his *cacicazgo*: the agricultural-military colonies on which his armed *agraristas* lived, a body which was in practice independent of the regular army since they were responsible to Cedillo alone. The existence of this militia -whose numbers swelled to some 20,000, although few of its members were well-equipped or in possession of a horse- was in itself not a threat to the federal authorities, but still it dominated San Luis Potosí, had an influence in the neighbouring states and was a force to be reckoned with during the various crises through which the country passed in these years. The nucleus of this local force was formed by the oldest and most loyal followers of Cedillo, established in colonies and *ejidos* basically concentrated in what had been his zone of operations since 1911: *Valle del Maíz* and its environs. In 1920, this region was impoverished, isolated and almost uninhabited. The intensity of the war and its consequent economic dislocation had scored a higher death and emigration rate there than in the neighbouring regions. The former success of farming in agriculture and herds had been replaced by a virtual paralysis. Upon their return to what was left of their homes, Cedillo's supporters simply appropriated the land that had been abandoned. In the solitary expanse of the *Valle del Maíz*, the 'peasant soldiers' of Cedillo lived as if it were a deserted island with few communications with the rest of the state. Beyond the boundaries of the area it was their only contact with the world, the only guarantee they had of a minimum of security and well-being. The followers of Cedillo had to respond with loyalty, personal services and even with tribute in return for the favours received from the *cacique* and his associates. Some 'peasant soldiers' had to give between 10 and 50 percent of the harvest to Cedillo's relatives or to members of his circle of intimate acquaintances. Almost all of them had to carry out various personal services for them, such as cultivating without payment the estates of the old and intimate ally of Cedillo: Francisco Carrera Torres.[17]

The services which the *cacique* and his associates were accustomed to receive, however, were only one side of the coin, since their actions in turn were bound by traditional norms and customs which were sufficiently strong to compel them to undertake certain duties on behalf of their followers, such as humane treatment. Cedillo fulfilled these obligations zealously. It was in Palomas, the ranch where he was born and which he later made his own, where his patriarchal gifts were most in evidence. Palomas was the symbol of his traditional authority until the end of his *cacicazgo*. Like that of a

17. Victoria Lerner, "Los fundamentos socio-económicos del cacicazgo en el México postrevolucionario. El caso de Saturnino Cedillo," in *HMex*, 29:3 (1980/115), 417, 421; Carlos Martínez Assad, "Las colonias agrícola-militares. Una alternativa agrarista del pasado" (Paper presented to the World Congress of Rural Sociology, 1980), 4. Falcón, Revolución y.caciquismo, 181ff.

feudal lord, his house was always open to his friends, his retinue of clients, and politicians from every level. Food, hospitality and shelter, and even money and work where possible, were provided day and night in Palomas for those who sought them. Cedillo put his agricultural ideal into practice there in collaboration with his general staff. Whenever possible the old *guerrillero* went over the estate from the early morning to share the tasks of the day with *his* men and to supervise the corn and cotton cultivation. He laid special emphasis on modernising agriculture. Irrigation became one of his chief obsessions and he took a pride in the amount of water that he was able to divert to his ranch from the neighbouring townships. This all resulted in a large measure of respect and affection for the *cacique* in Palomas and the surrounding district. Cedillo boasted that *"no one was without his cow, his hens or his horse. Everyone has a life of enjoyment, living on the produce of his own land."* During his inspection rounds, Cedillo would stop at every step *"to ask 'how our Chon is getting on,' to see whether old Pancho had bought his hens, to give money to poor old Juana 'for her sick child' . . . 'How could I help loving them all -Cedillo used to say- since they all fought on my side: they are the orphans of old revolutionaries'."*[18] He gave everything he could to those who had taken up arms with him, and their relatives. He offered a spirited defence of his colonists against the *hacienda* owners, ranchers and holders of *ejidos* with whom they engaged in disputes over land and water. In these conflicts Cedillo always supported the interests of his own people, ignoring the verdicts of the authorities when these were contrary to his own wishes and, in the last resort, imposing his will by force.

A key year for Cedillo was 1923, since the precarious situation made him an indispensable factor for both local politicians and those in the capital of the republic. In February, governor Rafael Nieto had to call upon the support of Cedillo's *agraristas* in order to retain his own position. The assistance which these 'peasant soldiers' provided at the end of 1923 to crush the important rebellion of De la Huerta enabled Cedillo to strengthen his links with the minister of defence, general Calles, who was president from 1924 to 1928. It was during this period of government that Cedillo's relations with the capital had their hey-day. Cedillo overthrew the *agrarista* governor Aurelio Manrique with permission from the government in November 1925. This cleared the way for him to become governor in 1927 and to make use of the formal apparatus of government to complete the task of extending his power as a *cacique* throughout the length and breadth of San Luis Potosí. By comparison with other *caciques* from the 1930s and 1940s, Cedillo achieved a genuinely remarkable degree of independence. Above all, he was successful in gaining an authentic hegemony in both the political and the military spheres. He thereby destroyed what is supposed to be one of the essential attributes of a state: its control of military power. His *agraristas* formed the backbone of the state armed forces, and the minister of defence decided that it would be unwise to station federal troops in that area of operations. Cedillo appointed his old ally in the Revolution, Francisco Carrera Torres, as head of military operations in 1927, to close up any chinks in the area under his control. Carrera Torres held this post for more than a decennium, which is a clear sign of the bargaining power of Cedillo, since it was in this period that the systematic rotation of the chiefs of operations in military zones was begun as a means of preventing the formation of networks of patron-client relations under the supremacy of a *cacique*.[19]

---

18. José Pages Llergo, "Tres días en Palomas con Cedillo," in *Hoy*, 9/10/1937; *NAW* RG59-812.00 SLP/13, Shaw, consul in San Luis Potosí to State Department, 18/2/1931; Graham Greene, *The Lawless Roads*, (Harmondsworth, 1971), 55-60; Falcón, *Revolución y.caciquismo*, 182ff. A theoretical analysis of this kind of traditional arrangements can be found in Max Weber, *Economía y Sociedad. Esbozo de sociología comprensiva*, (Mexico City, 1969).

19. *NAW* RG59, 812.00SLP/13, Shaw to State Department, 18/2/1931, /14, Shaw to State Department, 28/2/1931; *Informe rendido por el C. Gobernador del Estado, general Idefonso Turrubiartes ante la XXXIV Legislatura del Estado, el día 15 de septiembre de 1935*, (San Luis Potosí,

The irregular troops in San Luis Potosí were an armed body under the command of the patron. Cedillo always dipped generously into the public treasury to maintain and modernise his militia. He bought all kinds of weapons -including planes-, constructed radio stations and made bombs. There were times when this outlay was so great that it absorbed most of the state revenues. These militia were virtually independent of the federal government and there were times when the minister of defence did not even pay their wages. This all served to compound their loyalty to the *cacique*. The militia consisted of colonists, those endowed with an *ejido*, and workers on the land who hoped to gain land and retain possession of it. The strongest enticement to ensure recruitment and loyalty on the part of the *agraristas* was agrarian reform. Right up to the end of his reign as *cacique*, and especially when he had problems with the central government, Cedillo would go through the state promising *ejidos* to those who enlisted, even in the years when the agrarian reform was officially off the agenda. Given his patriarchal responsibility, once the peacemaking campaigns were over, Cedillo made all efforts to carry out his promises and to retain the loyalty of his dependents. At the end of 1929, after the *agraristas* had made an important contribution to the quashing of the Escobar and *Cristero* rebellions, Cedillo even redistributed part of his ranch in Palomas and forced the local government to buy estates for the soldiers who had joined up on his side. The *cacique* was able to convince the majority of the rural population, i.e. the majority of the inhabitants of San Luis Potosí, of the need for his intermediary role. The *hacienda* owners needed him to protect their property; the labourers needed him for protection and the promise of land; those who were involved with the colonies and the *ejidos* needed him to obtain and maintain their land as well as for water, credit and machinery.[20]

Within San Luis, all the political mechanisms were directed by Cedillo. Central government had practically no say there. It was the *cacique* who fixed the nature and powers of state administration: military affairs, politics, judicial matters, decisions in labour, agrarian and commercial disputes. The other essential elements in this system of power, as in traditional feudal relations, were the relatives and close friends of the *cacique*, each of whom had his own circle of followers. These satellites of Cedillo, with their own networks of clients, were the actual units of political and military power, overshadowing the formal structure of the government apparatus. Cedillo not only tried to ensure that his intimate circle held the key positions in San Luis. He also got them federal positions, thereby confirming their loyalty to him at the same time as assuring himself of a presence at the national level. When Cedillo was at the head of the ministry of agriculture -for some months in 1931 and from July 1935 to August 1937- he doled out appointments in the ministry to those who had taken up arms for him. Cedillo viewed the appointments, even those of experts in agronomy, in terms of the local roots of his power, since he gave preference to "*those who have accompanied me on campaign and . . . the children of those who have fallen in the fight* [who] *are at times a better choice than the experts.*"[21]

Cedillo obviously had no difficulty in getting his associates into all the political and administrative positions in San Luis Potosí. In this way he gained control of the legal apparatus, executive power, municipal presidencies, the local branch of the dominant

1935), 2; *AGN*, Fondo Presidentes (FP), Abelardo Rodríguez (ALR), 541.3/400 Cedillo to president Rodríguez, 25/9/1934.

20. Falcón, *Revolución y.caciquismo*, 190ff. *Excelsior*, 16/9/1929; *El Universal*, 21/6/1931; *Fuentes para la historia de la revolución mexicana. I. Planes políticos y otros documentos*, Manuel González Ramírez, ed. (Mexico City, 1957), 290ff.; Marijosé Amerlinck, "La reforma agraria en la hacienda de San Diego de Río Verde," in *Después de los latifundios. La desintegración de la gran propiedad raíz en México*, Heriberto Moreno, ed. (Mexico City, 1982), 191.

21. Alfonso Taracena, *La revolución desvirtuada*, (Mexico City, 1966), tomo relativo a 1937, 198, 207, 211; Manuel Fernández Eutaquio Marrón, *Lo que no se sabe de la rebelión cedillista*, (Mexico City, 1938), 176.

party (*PNR*, the *Partido Nacional Revolucionario*), the police, etc. For roughly ten years the state was in the hands of many of those who had been unknown peasants, frequently illiterate, before the Revolution, and who had thrown themselves into the rebellion on the side of Cedillo. The rest of the country does not have many other examples of such an extraordinary rate of social mobility. Official positions changed hands within the circle of friends and relatives of the *cacique*. He appointed two of his oldest followers as governors, who had no political power of their own and owed all the power that they had to him. The first was Idefonso Turrubiartes, who had been a comrade in the campaign since 1911 and whose dependence on the *cacique* was total. Since he could neither read nor write, he had to resort to another of Cedillo's confidants for official business, who carried out the wishes of the *cacique*, dealt with the formal centres of power, took charge of requests, correspondence, decrees and even briefing the governor on the annual government report. Turrubiartes had to travel to Palomas so frequently for instructions that it was necessary to install a radio between the seat of government and Cedillo's ranch. In 1935 Turrubiartes was succeeded by another satellite of the *cacique*, lieutenant-colonel Mateo Hernández Netro, who had been head of the agricultural-military colony of El Naranjo since 1920 and who followed in his predecessor's footsteps, although to a considerably smaller degree.[22]

Despite the extremely high degree of control which he exercised, Cedillo was not able to bring all of the region of San Luis Potosí under his sway to the same extent. The zone with the highest level of economic development, the north, was the farthest removed from his personal sphere of influence and it retained a greater degree of independence. The same is true of the workers, the social sector most removed from the *caciquismo*: he was not able to incorporate them in his patron-client network as he had done with the peasants. This failure was not due to any lack of interest on the part of the general of Palomas, but to the difficulties that he encountered in adapting a traditional style of personal politics to the urban context where the workers were grouped in more solid associations. This failure was destined to become a significant weakness in Cedillo's rule. Moreover, there were regions under the traditional control of other figures who maintained an independent stance *vis-à-vis* the *cacique*. The most obvious example is that of Gonzalo N. Santos, who managed to keep some of his family's influence in the municipality of Tampamolón in the Huasteca and who was on a footing of mutual aid with Cedillo rather than one of total subordination. Santos bided his time before succeeding to Cedillo with the establishment of a new fiefdom, although the latter did not have anything even remotely resembling the same degree of autonomy.

## THE FALL OF THE *CACIQUES*

The weakness of the national political system was responsible for the fact that during the Revolution and immediately afterwards it was possible, and in fact necessary, for military *caciques* to control various regions of the country. To the extent that the state had become more centralised, stable and able to carry out its functions by the beginning of the 1930s, it drastically came to lose its dependence on the strong men of the interior. This process led to a long series of difficulties with national government which Cedillo had to face in order to maintain his power. It was an effort that was bound to fail in the long run. The year 1929 saw the end of the *Cristero*-war and the last rebellion of any importance within the federal army. In the ensuing years army morale and discipline improved notably, though they could not be called exemplary. The military intervened less in politics and the army went through a gradual process of

22. Falcón, *Revolución y caciquismo*, 194-195.

transformation from an alliance of revolutionary leaders, whose tightness varied from time to time, to a relatively unified force within the hierarchical and centralised structure that is a hallmark of the modern army. The year 1929 also witnessed the creation of what was to become the major political party: the *Partido Nacional Revolucionario* (*PNR*), which enabled the question of the presidential succession to be settled within its ranks without having to resort to violence. Although the party only really began as an alliance of hundreds of local political organisations -generally the puppet of some strong man- under the leadership of general Plutarco Elías Calles, it began a process of political institutionalisation which within a few years brought about changes in the type of personal power of the *caudillos* which had predominated up to then. Calles had just left the presidency and was now free from the shadow of general Obregón, who had been assassinated in July 1928. He invested his personal authority in the control of the party. However, the result of the institutions which were later created and the discipline generated by the *PNR* was that the presence of men like him, who continued to act outside the structures by which the Revolution was trying to become institutionalised, became superfluous. Consequently, the military-style *caciques* which were in control of certain states and regions in the country were forced to recognise the new presence in central government or to disappear.

The antagonism between the new kinds of political life and the *cacicazgo* of Cedillo reached a climax during the administration entered by Lázaro Cárdenas in 1934, thanks to the profound transformations which then took place. In June 1935 there was a confrontation between the presidential institution and the 'supreme leadership', i.e. the powerful informal influence by which general Calles had managed to create a duality of power at the highest level. In this dramatic dispute, in which a number of observers expected Cárdenas to be forced to resign, the head of the executive reaffirmed his leadership, the institutions and the presidential character of the system. Cárdenas was then able to adopt the measures necessary to ensure the loyalty of the army and to achieve an enormous concentration of power in the presidency, which in turn enabled him to impose his radical, up-to-date policies throughout the length and breadth of the country. These were: a consolidation of the organisation of workers and peasants; nationalisation of the petroleum industry; the introduction of socialist education; and -most dramatically- the transfer of land to the peasants. Cedillo sabotaged every one of these directives, which were not to his liking ideologically and which threatened his personal and local form of wielding power.

The *PNR* was transformed too; it changed from being the mere sum of local organisations to become an association which recognised the president unconditionally as its leader and which was organised in workers, peasants, popular and military divisions on a national scale. In formal terms at least, this structure meant the virtually total liquidation of the old synonymity between government and local *caciques*. Finally, it was during the Cárdenas administration that the point of culmination was reached by the process of providing an institutional answer to one of the main challenges of the Mexican Revolution: the urban and rural workers. In order to bring these popular groups within single associations linked closely to the presidency and the official party, Cárdenas created for the regime a power which had practically not been in existence before. This simultaneous diversification and concentration of his bases of support enabled him to make use of the large workers' and peasants' central union organisations to put an end to the duality of the centres of decision at the top of the political structure, i.e., to emerge victorious from his conflict with Calles, the 'supreme leader,' and -and this should probably be seen as his most important contribution to the post-revolutionary political system- enabled the state to escape from its dependence on the military-style *cacicazgos*.

These were the weapons which Cárdenas wielded to undermine the internal bases of the *caciquil* structures. Cedillo's fiefdom was crushed in a pincer movement between the powerful claws of two instruments of centralisation: the popular organisations and the party. From 1933 on, the *agrarista* wing of the ruling party in the Mexican countryside had stimulated the organisation of the peasants in the states and the reactivation of the agrarian reform. With the triumph of Cárdenas, the *agraristas* continued to gain influence, and it was at this point that parts of Mexico experienced one of its most profound transformations: the destruction of the large-scale *haciendas*. Despite Cedillo's lack of enthusiasm for the *ejido*, which formed the heart of Cárdenas' agrarian reform, the *ejido* programme was started in San Luis in 1933. Many villages, supported by *cardenista* leaders linked to the *Confederación Campesina Mexicana* (*CCM*), began to raise demands for *ejidos* in the face of tenacious opposition by the *cacique*. At the same time, individuals called 'federal employees' went from village to village organising land petitions, and even calling for the dismissal of local authorities who were obviously part of the Cedillo network. From 1934, a number of rural communities who felt that the time had come to rid themselves of the *caciques* and their authorities registered complaints with president Abelardo Rodríguez, and later with Lázaro Cárdenas, against the *cacicazgo* of Cedillo. In this way, the *cardenista* leaders came to deprive the patronage system of a sizeable part of its rural base. To the extent that basic resources like land, water and credit were now the responsibility of the national government, many peasants of San Luis Potosí came to respect the authority which emanated from the capital of the republic and loosened their ties with the structure created by the general of Palomas. This was the most effective of all the actions that were undertaken to break the system of *cacicazgo* in San Luis Potosí.[23]

Political centralisation proceeded at the same pace. It was precisely in San Luis that one of the first conventions was held in October 1935 at which the *CCM* and the official party -the *PNR*- started the process of forming the single central peasants' union which Cárdenas had called for in the middle of the year. A year later the president decided that the time had come to neutralise the most compact and loyal kernel of the *Cedillistas*: the agricultural-military colonies. The offensive was justified with the argument that they had been created without complying with *"the legal formalities and by-laws,"* occupying land which did not belong to them, leading to disputes and confrontations which must now stop. Although the colonies continued to exist, open war was declared between colonists and *ejido*-holders, since the intensification of Cárdenas' agrarian reform had multiplied boundary disputes and arguments about the use of water and land. These disputes were almost always settled by the federal authorities against the colonies. On the other hand, since the urban workers had not been properly integrated in the *cacicazgo*, the policies of Cárdenas and the growing national workers' movement met with rapid support and a clearly anti-Cedillo stance on the part of the workers in San Luis Potosí. The assault began in earnest in October 1933, when the workers organisations led by Lombardo Toledano started to gain influence among workers throughout the country. This group was one of the main allies of the president during the crisis of June 1935, when it was able to bring about a remarkable unification of workers in support of the state and a gigantic mobilisation of workers which culminated in February 1936 with the creation of the *Confederación de Trabajadores de México* (*CTM*). Cárdenas' power was unequalled by that of any other president in the Revolution. Some of Cedillo's associates urged him to abandon his post as head of the ministry of agriculture and to return to San Luis to defend his position, which was crumbling away rapidly under the assault of the proponents of agrarian reform, of the organised workers' movement, of the *PNR* and of the Communist Party, i.e. the 'left wing' of the governing group. A local branch of the *CTM* was soon set up: the *Federación de Trabajadores del Estado de San Luis Potosí* (*FTESLP*), which was to occupy a decisive role in the struggle against Cedillo. Between 1935 and 1937 seventy-

23. Falcón, *Revolución y caciquismo*, 240ff.

two new unions were established in the state, the majority of which were affiliated to this federation, which had seven thousand members.[24]

The offensive which began against Cedillo in 1937 had as its primary objective the separation of the political and formal administrative apparatus from the structure of *cacicazgo*. The workers' organisations and the official party were the instruments of this presidential policy to deprive Cedillo of his control over positions which were held as a result of popular elections. The *CTM* and the *PNR* then broke the hegemony which the *cacicazgo* had held over legislative power and the municipal presidencies for more than a decennium. This coincided, moreover, with Cedillo's departure from the cabinet, that is, with his definitive break with Cárdenas. Even more important was the success of the federal government in 1937 in undermining the personal links between Cedillo and various peasant nuclei in a way which had been tried before: control over the land. Finally, Cárdenas' finishing touch was the destruction of the *cacicazgo's* military hegemony. A vigorous anti-Cedillo election campaign was begun in San Luis in March of that year orchestrated by an alliance of the *PNR*, the *Confederación Campesina Mexicana*, the Communist Party and the *CTM*. The offensive could count on the support of the ministry of government, the ministry of defence and, in the last instance, the president himself, who allowed the attack to go ahead with his blessing. The elections for deputies and members of the municipal governments, which were particularly spirited in the north, the zone that was the most distant from Cedillo's personal sphere of influence, were violent and involved some loss of lives.[25] The circle around the *cacique* closed and in May 1937 hundreds of strikers supported by the *CTM* began a *"caravan of hunger"* from the capital of San Luis to the Mexican capital, to dramatise the *"chaotic," "repressive"* and *"antipopular"* situation that the state was in.

Cedillo's opponents were able to make skillful use of the arbitrary acts perpetrated by the associates of the *cacique*, whom he was either unwilling or unable to control. On June 20th, some of Cedillo's gunmen attacked the offices of the main candidate, Aurelio Manrique, the very same enthusiastic radical governor whom Cedillo had violently deposed in 1925. Soon afterwards, well-known supporters of Cedillo, including the head of the local *PNR*, physically assaulted Manrique while he was delivering a passionate speech denouncing Carrera and Cedillo. At the sound of the gunshots the crowd broke up and Manrique remained alone on the deserted square. There he was insulted, spat upon, beaten up and finally his hair, beard, eye-brows and eye-lashes were shaved. The whole country hummed with the protests which broke out. The federal government was not slow in replying. Cárdenas himself ordered an immediate investigation and Manrique returned to San Luis under the protection of federal troops and almost a hundred bodyguards. While the workers of San Luis Potosí were closing their ranks within the *CTM*, the state *PNR*, which was still firmly in the hands of the *cacique*, launched the counterattack with a gigantic assembly at which of thousands of peasants armed with knives, rifles, and revolvers swore their allegiance to Cedillo and his local project. Besides the settlers on the colonies, groups of professional gunmen also formed a conspicuous part of the procession. The latter were retainers of some local strong man, and formed a belt loyal to Cedillo around the state capital and *Valle*

24. Martínez Assad, "Colonias agrícola-militares," 15ff; Arturo Amguiano, *El estado y la política obrera del cardenismo*, (Mexico City, 1975); *Anuario Estadística de los Estados Unidos Mexicanos, 1939*, DGE, ed. (Mexico City, 1941), 274; *Manifiesto*, Comité Prodefensa Obrera, ed. (San Luis Potosí, 1935).

25. On the eve of the elections, the minister of defence warned Cedillo that it was not permissible for him to use his *agraristas* for political ends; *AGN*, FP, Lázaro Cárdenas del Rio (LCR), 544.4-23 "Asesinatos en las elecciones locales", June 1937; *PRO*, F0371, V20639, A2928/973/26, Gallop to Foreign Office, 5/4/1937; *NAW* RG59, 812.00/SLP/97, Montgomery, consul in San Luis Potosí to State Department, 3/6/1937.

*del Maíz*. This was their only occupation, as very few of them still worked the land.[26] The fight against the *cacicazgo* reached one of its peaks on 15th August 1937. The School of Agriculture, of which Cedillo was the head, had been hit by a student strike since July, and the strike committee had already held discussions with Cárdenas. On the 15th, Cedillo sent a deputy to discuss the problem with the president in a personal and, presumably, less drastic way. At the same time, however, Cedillo hoped to force Cárdenas to give him his public support by warning him:[27]

> *"I am prepared to use my authority as minister of agriculture, for which I hope to enjoy your support, since otherwise your lack of confidence in me would irrevocably oblige me to offer my resignation."*

The *cacique* was mistaken in his expectations. A total breach occurred when the president accepted his resignation.

At this stage, the only support on which Cedillo could still rely was his personal influence among his closest associates. Victimised by the national press and isolated by the political elite, he fell back on the ultimate legitimation provided by his traditional responsibility towards 'his' men, the human and emotional touch behind his power. He told Cárdenas about his concern for those who remained in the ministry after his resignation *"because I feel a moral obligation towards my fellow comrades under arms who have accompanied me in the struggle..."*. In reply to the repeated accusations of extravagance and corruption in the running of his ministry, and of the creation of fictitious jobs for his allies, Cedillo replied:[28]

> *"I was not minister of those who only have obligations towards their chauffeur. My long history of struggle bound me by obligations which I hold sacred. I have behind me an army of widows and orphans of those who fell in the struggle, and I feel bound to help them by an obligation that cannot be shaken off."*

But the decisive blow had been struck and Cedillo returned to San Luis to witness how the federal government settled accounts with the remnants of his old dominion. Cárdenas ordered the dissolution of his armed power after having received reports that Cedillo was planning a rebellion in September 1937. On September 8th Cedillo's twelve planes, pilots and all, were transferred to Mexico City. Immediately afterwards, the federal military apparatus came into action, forming a cordon around San Luis Potosí and thereby catching the *agraristas* of San Luis Potosí in a stranglehold and depriving them of their strength. At the same time, the *cacique* was ordered to report in person to the minister of defence.[29]

The fact that Cedillo lost his military hegemony in San Luis weakened his position considerably, but it also served to drive him on even more towards rebellion. He could not just stand by and watch the end of his reign without doing anything. With sixty

---

26. *NAW* RG59, 812.00 SLP/98, 21/6/1937, /99, 26/6/1937, /100, 29/6/1937, /103, 8/7/1937 (all reports from Montgomery to State Department); *PRO* F0371, V20539, A49796/527/26, Gallop to Foreign Office, 22/6/1937; Taracena, *Revolución*, tomo relativo a 1937, 145ff.

27. *AGN*, FP, LCR, 702.12/122, Cedillo to Cárdenas, 19/8/1937; Cárdenas to Cedillo, 16/8/1937; Avila Camacho to Cárdenas, 15/8/1937, 16/8/1937; Lázaro Cárdenas, *Obras, I. Apuntes 1913-1940*, (Mexico City, 1972), 374.

28. Taracena, *Revolución*, tomo relativo a 1937, 211; *Todo*, 26/8/1937; *Documentos de Félix Bañuelos* (DFB), "Memorandum de conversación entre Gildardo Magaña, Félix Bañuelos y Saturnino Cedillo, 7 octubre de 1937". Cárdenas had sent Magaña and Bañuelos to negotiate with Cedillo, but it was in vain since, as Cedillo himself indignantly told them, *"Cárdenas accepted my resignation which was not intended as such but was an attempt to get him to support me... Although he had it in his power to give me an honourable discharge, he preferred to let me go without honour"*.

29. *NAW* RG59, 812.00/30500, Daniels to State Department, 13/9/1937, 812.00 SLP/108, Montgomery to State Department, 1/10/1037, RG165, 2657-G-732/65, Marshburn to War Department, 14/9/1937; Cárdenas, *Obras*, I, 312, 374; *The New York Times*, 12/9/1937; *Excelsior*, 21/9/1937.

years behind him, sick and almost powerless, he regarded it as a question of honour. It was more emotionally than actually necessary to *"do something"* against Cárdenas and not to let them get away with *"making a fool"* of him. This idea, which came to take on fantastic qualities, led him to overestimate the loyalty and importance of his closest followers, from the national right -a mass of small groups like the *Confederación de la Clase Media* and the fascist *Gold Shirts* who lacked a true leader to bring them together- and even from some foreign interests, especially the American and English petroleum companies who regarded the thriving radicalism and nationalism as a threat. Cedillo saw himself as the indispensable head of this heterogeneous right wing opposition and kept up his preparations for rebellion in the face of his obvious weakness. Once again he miscalculated: instead of serving as his trump card in negotiation if all else failed, and thus as his means of protection, it was these preparations which precipitated the government reaction.

The general of Palomas was constantly losing ground. For many settlements in San Luis, especially those which were the furthest from his patronage network, the new presence of the federal government opened up interesting political and economic perspectives. *Ejido* applications multiplied: from November 1937 until June 1938, more than seventy agrarian communities demanded land. The rural districts of San Luis Potosí passed through rapid and profound changes which would confirm their loyalty to Cárdenas: the *ejido* programme was the order of the day, and there were also attempts to give the agricultural-military colonists permanent property rights. It was hoped that this would put an end to the disputes between *ejido*-holders and colonists, and, above all, deprive the colonists of the necessity of protection by Cedillo. The logic was clear: the more the colonies came to rely on the support of the federal leaders and officials, the looser their ties would become with the *cacique* and the most loyal of his followers.[30]

The government and the Mexican left wing have created a black legend on the revolt Cedillo finally launched in 1938, insisting on its intimate relation with the petrol concerns that were nationalised by Cárdenas on March 18th 1938. There is no doubt that the general of San Luis Potosí represented the most extreme internal opposition to the petroleum expropriation, and although these accusations were to a large extent just exaggerations or wishful thinking on the part of the regime's opponents, they were not entirely without substance. The American and English companies in this line -basically the Huasteca Petroleum Company and El Aguila respectively- were delighted to see that there were was opposition, who wanted the fall of Cárdenas. Cedillo and the petroleum companies established certain links and fabricated illusions, even before the expropriation. Nevertheless, the fact that Washington did not regard the overthrow of the regime as the best way of resolving its differences with Mexico put a definite limit to the chances of success of those, like Cedillo, whose ambitions were to oppose Cárdenas' reforms by force. The real obstacles which prevented the companies from doing more than providing mere circumstantial support were the lack of support from the North American government and the military ineffectiveness of Saturnino Cedillo.[31]

In May 1938, once Cárdenas considered that he was master of the enormous domestic and international crisis created by the expropriation of the petroleum companies two months before, and observing the moderate stance adopted by Washington -which was the practical obstacle to the success of the rebellion- the president decided to put an end to the military influence which the general of Palomas still held. He installed a pro-Cárdenas loyalist as Head of Military Operations in San Luis, thereby eliminating

30. *NAW*, RG165, 2655-G-217/65, Freehoff to State Department, 30/11/1937, RG59, 812.000 SLP/134, Montgomery to State Department, 8/1/1938; *The New York Times*, 28/10/1937, 10/11/1937; on the military colonies see Martínez Assad, "Colonias agrícola-militares," 12, 13, 20.
31. Lorenzo Meyer, *México y los Estados Unidos en el conflicto petrolero (1917-1942)*, (Mexico City, 1972), 362ff.; Falcón, *Revolución y caciquismo*, 259ff.

the last support of *cedillismo* in this state *cacicazgo*. In fact, the links that had enabled Cedillo to control the workers and, what was of fundamental importance, the rural districts, had already been cut earlier. By May 1938, all that was left of Cedillo's domain were appearances and pretensions: it was a part of the political and administrative apparatus of the state, but no longer had the means to exercise any substantive governmental activity. If Cedillo still retained some prestige as a political symbol, this was due to the loyalty of some peasants -mainly those of his colonies- who were concentrated around the small territory from which he had been operating since 1912. All that stood in the way were thus his traditional control of a small zone of the state, and the personal ambitions of a man who refused to recognise that he was no longer the big *cacique* of San Luis Potosí that he had once been. He decided to fight to the end for the life style which he and his followers had built up in the *Valle del Maíz* and environs. Further, he refused to renounce the state power which he considered that he deservedly enjoyed and to accommodate himself to the demands of national government. His eagerness to preserve his honour and his local project, provoked by the decided attacks to which he was subjected by the Cárdenas government, drove him to lead a suicidal rebellion in May 1938. In a poor state of health, with only a handful of followers, Cedillo was killed by federal troops on January 11th 1939 after refusing various offers of amnesty made by Cárdenas. It seems that the soldiers found him thanks to his betrayal by two of his associates. However, there were loyalties which continued after his death: the last rebel *Cedillista* did not lay down his arms and submit to the government until twenty-five years later.[32]

The destruction of Cedillo's power did not necessarily mean the end of all the regional *cacicazgos*. Some survived, and others even sprang up and flourished later. Upon the death of Cedillo another system of patronage was begun in San Luis Potosí under the leadership of a member of the Santos family. Still, there was at least one essential difference between these local systems of power and their predecessors: the new *caciques* were not given the slightest opportunity of calling what was considered to be the essential prerogative of the state into question: its monopoly control of the legitimate means of coercion within society. Thus the consolidation of the revolutionary state -which was brought to completion in general terms during the Cárdenas government- meant that the mediation and mechanisms of control of the military-style *caciques* had become anachronistic, superfluous and even dysfunctional political forms for the processes of centralisation and modernisation upon which Mexico had embarked. The big military *cacicazgos* of the Revolution had come to the end of the road.

32. *Excelsior*, 21/4/1938; *NAW* RG163, 2025-G-259/639 Freehoff to Department, 8/4/1938, RG59, 812.00 SLP/116, Montgomery to War Department, 18/4/1938. After Cedillo had been turned out of Agriculture, he had informed the president that *"if the commander of the zone is changed... I will not feel secure and will thus be obliged to go to the hills," DFB* "Memorandum de conversación entre Gildardo Magaña, Felix Bañuelos y Saturnino Cedillo, 7 Octubre 1937." It was then clear that, with the removal of Carrera Torres from the military leadership, Cárdenas was putting Cedillo in a cleft stick. Carlos Martínez Assad, "La rebelión cedillista o el ocaso del poder tradicional," in *Revista Mexicana de Sociología*, (1979), 723-725. Some months later, his traitor was hanged on the spot where Cedillo had died, Montejano, *Valle del Maíz*, 369ff.

## CHAPTER EIGHT

# Tlaxcala and San Luis Potosí under the *Sonorenses* (1920-1934): Regional Revolutionary Power Groups and the National State

RAYMOND BUVE
AND
ROMANA FALCON*

## INTRODUCTION

In this chapter we intend to compare the revolutionary processes in two Mexican states under the political era of the *Sonorenses* (1920-1935):[1] the large and distant

* *Historians. Raymond Buve: Vakgroep Talen en Culturen van Latijns-Amerika (TCLA), Van Wijkplaats 3, P.O. Box 9515, 2300 RA Leiden, The Netherlands; Romana Falcón: Centro de Estudios Históricos, El Colegio de México, Camino Al Ajusco 20, CP 01000 México DF.*
*We want to express our gratitude to Guy Thomson for the careful linguistic assistance.*

1. Analysis of the case of Tlaxcala is based on Raymond Buve, "Peasants, Caudillos and Land Reform during the Revolution in Tlaxcala, Mexico (1910-1917)," *Boletín de Estudios Latinoamericanos y del Caribe*, 18 (1975), 112-152, "State Governors and Peasant Mobilization in Tlaxcala" in *Caudillo and Peasant in the Mexican Revolution*, D. A. Brading, ed (Cambridge, 1980), 222-244, "Peasant Mobilization and Reform Intermediaries during the Nineteen Thirties: The Development of a Peasant Clientele Around the Issues of Land and Water in a Central Mexican Highland Municipio: Huamantla, Tlaxcala," *Jahrbuch für Geschichte von Staat, Wirtschaft und Gesellschaft Lateinamerikas* (hereafter *JbLA*), 17 (1980), 355-394, "Movilización campesina y reforma agraria en los Valles de Nativitas, Tlaxcala (1917-1923)," in *El trabajo y los trabajadores en la historia de México*, Elsa Cecilia Frost et al., eds. (Mexico City, 1979), 533-564, "'Neither Carranza nor Zapata!' The Rise and Fall of a Peasant Movement which Tried to Challenge Both: Tlaxcala 1910-1919," *Riot, Rebellion and Revolt: Rural Social Conflict in Mexico*, Friedrich Katz, ed. (Princeton, 1989), 341-373, "Consolidating a *Cacicazgo*: The Tlaxcala Revolutionary Ruling Group and the Issue of Peasant Mobilization under the *Sonorenses* (1920-1929)," in *Mexican Revolutions: Essays on Regional Mexican History, 1911-1929*, Thomas Benjamin and Mark Wasserman, eds. (Albuquerque, 1990). Analysis of the case San Luis Potosí is mainly based on the following publications: Romana Falcón, *Revolución y caciquismo. San Luis Potosí, 1910-38* (Mexico City, 1984), "Charisma, Tradition and Caciquismo. Revolution in San Luis Potosí", *Riot, Rebellion and Revolt*, 417-447, "Las fincas intervenidas ¿Conquista revolucionaria o botín?" in *Mexican Revolutions*, "Esplendor y ocaso de los cacicazgos militares. El caso de San Luis Potosí (1910-1938)" Spanish original of chapter in this volume, "Saturnino Cedillo, el último gran cacique militar," in *Estadistas, caciques y caudillos*, forthcoming, Carlos Martínez Assad, ed. (Mexico City, 1988); Dudley Ankerson, *Agrarian Warlord. Saturnino Cedillo and the Mexican Revolution in San Luis Potosí*, (DeKalb, 1984); Victoria Lerner, "Los fundamentos socioeconómicos del cacicazgo en el México postrevolucionario: El caso de Saturnino Cedillo," *Historia Mexicana* (hereafter *HMex*), 29:3 (1980/115), 375-446.

northern state of San Luis Potosí and the tiny central Mexican state of Tlaxcala, barely one hundred kilometers from Mexico City. Both states were profoundly affected by the Revolution. Between 1910 and 1920 there was a high degree of violence in the struggle between revolutionary forces and their enemies. It resulted in considerable costs to the local economy and society.[2] The outcome of the revolutionary process was by 1920, however, quite different in both states. In Tlaxcala, a fierce revolutionary and mainly peasant-based movement had finally been able to oust local elites in 1914. Outside *carrancista* forces had great difficulty in subduing it and by 1920 a weak *carrancista* government was barely able to impose a limited degree of control. In San Luis Potosí, after the fall of the *porfirista* régime and in the absence of a dominant local revolutionary movement, power had dissipated among locally operating revolutionary factions in loose and shifting alliances with the contending parties at the national level: *villistas*, *convencionistas* and *carrancistas*. With *carrancista* victory in 1917, a landowner governor, member of the prominent *porfirista* establishment, was able to reduce the various popular rebel movements to small-scale *guerrillas* without solid territorial control. Except for the south east of the state, the position of landowners remained largely unaffected or had even been restored.

In Tlaxcala the fall of Carranza in 1920 permitted an emerging urban based revolutionary group to push aside a governor of peasant-worker origin. Without troops of their own, and despite a rather weak popular basis, especially in the rural areas, Ignacio Mendoza and his *camarillas* faced the problem of control over a still strongly mobilized peasantry, one of the few genuine *agrarista* movements outside Morelos. Through careful manipulation of the state bureaucracy interwoven with their government party, they extended their control to the grass-roots level. With firm and continuous support from the federal government, Mendoza and his men succeeded in defusing peasant mobilization and established a statewide *cacicazgo* in 1925. In San Luis Potosí, the victory of the *Sonorenses* toppled the *carrancista* régime and in the prolonged competition for local power, urban based revolutionaries, largely of a radical signature, but with a weak popular basis in the rural areas, lost out against a traditional rural revolutionary chief, Saturnino Cedillo. As is shown in the previous chapter, he had been able to capitalize on his continuous military services to the *Sonorenses* and extend his original power domain based on strong individual relationships between a *cacique* and his peasant followers into a state-wide *cacicazgo*. In 1927 the Cedillo *cacicazgo* finally usurped the formal power structures and bureaucracy of San Luis Potosí.[3]

By 1932, both Cedillo and Mendoza had become a nuisance to *'Jefe Máximo,'* Plutarco Elías Calles, the former president (1924-1928) who continued to dominate Mexican politics as *Jefe Máximo* behind the presidency until 1935. The downfall of Mendoza was brought about in a few months but Cedillo's position, both in national politics and in local power, made a quick elimination unlikely for several years to come. Comparison of these two *cacicazgos* is of considerable value for understanding the relations between regional power groups and the national presidents, referred to as *Sonorenses*, for two principal reasons. First, the emergence of these regional power groups resulted in completely different types of relationship with the *Sonorenses*. In the case of Tlaxcala, it resulted in a stable but dependent relationship which left the regional power group few autonomous political resources. In the case of San Luis Potosí, however, the group under Ce-

2. John Womack, "La economía de México durante la revolución Mexicana: Historiografía y análisis," in *Perspectivas Marxistas,* (1978), 83-84.

3. Besides works cited from Buve and Falcón, Ankerson and Lerner, see Mario Ramírez Rancaño, "El socialismo en Tlaxcala 1926-1933," in *Secuencia. Revista americana de ciencias sociales*, 5 (1986), 62-80; Diana Juanicó, "Partidos, facciones políticas y elecciones: Tlaxcala en 1924" (Paper, 1987).

dillo succeeded in strengthening its grasp on local political resources and reached its zenith towards the end of the reign of the *Sonorenses*. Especially in Calles' eyes, the case of Tlaxcala must have been a showcase of his centralization policies based on bureaucratic control, the enforcement of a monopoly on military power and state derived sources for patronage and mobilization. The *cacicazgo* of Cedillo, on the other hand, must have been at the opposite extreme: an undesirable example of regional autonomous control over political resources and a quasi-private peasant army, one, however, that had to be tolerated for the time being. Second, the emergence and development of the regional power groups in Tlaxcala and San Luis Potosí reflects to a large degree two basic patterns for the attainment and maintenance of regional power during the *sonorenses* period. In the traditional revolutionary chieftaincy, born out of the warfare (1910-1917) and often based on nineteenth-century *caudillo* traditions, the *jefe* was the *locus* of power, although he might delegate it to loyal members of his extended family, friends and clients. His authority and legitimacy were based on personal liens of mutual, be it asymmetrical, obligations between chief, clients and followers. Distribution of wealth and favours took place on a particularistic basis and had, for that matter, preference over existing laws and bureaucratic procedures. In essence, such a chieftaincy was independent of and antithetical to bureaucratic structures such as a municipality or a state.[4]

Next to these revolutionary chieftaincies, however, new forms were emerging. It is now generally accepted that Mexican history between Juárez and Cárdenas, in terms of political modernization and centralization, can be more usefully understood as a continuum rather than a sequence of distinct periods separated by watersheds. Along this meandering line of development, the Revolution broke out and gave rise to the emergence of many different revolutionary factions and groups. When *porfirista* elites lost their grip on the national and local levels, not only the opportunities for mobility increased, but also the room for local experiments in the development of new ways for acquiring and maintaining power. With the deliberate use of the state bureaucracy, their potential for popular mobilization and their control of resources, the *Sonorenses* applied these new ways in their rebellion against Huerta (1913-1914). Their success, and the success of revolutionary movements based on gaining the loyalties of peasants in exchange for land, security and autonomy, highlighted the potential of the masses as a political resource. When the *Sonorenses* came to power, they knew this; but so did others. By 1920 civilians and military men, peasant-based chieftains and urban politicians recognized the importance of expanding their bases of power by the inclusion of masses. The way they achieved this, however, showed variety, reflecting the increasing blend of older and more recent patterns in the attainment and maintenance of power at the local level. Peasant-based revolutionary chieftaincies -like Arenas and Cedillo- continued to exist, while civilians like Emilio Portes Gil in Tamaulipas and generals like Adalberto Tejeda in Veracruz combined traditional and highly personal political authority with an increasing emphasis on creating the bureaucratic institutions which could organize the masses state-wide and implement the reforms they needed to mobilize and control them. State and mass organization were often interlocked. In some places, recruit-

4. On basic characteristics see S. N. Eisenstadt and L. Roniger, *Patrons, Clients and Friends* (Cambridge, 1984), 99-102 and 114-117; Heather Fowler Salamini, "Revolutionary Caudillos in the 1920's: Francisco Múgica and Adalberto Tejeda," in *Caudillo and Peasant*, 169-192; Raymond Buve, "Jefes Menores de la revolución mexicana, y los primeros avances en la consolidación del estado nacional: El caso de Tlaxcala (1910-1920)," in *América Latina del estado colonial al estado nación, 1750-1940*, Antonio Annino, et.al., ed (Milan, 1987), 646-677; Alan Knight, "Peasant and Caudillo in Revolutionary Mexico, 1910-1917," in *Caudillo and Peasant*, 17-58, esp. 56-58.

ment of lieutenants and officials took place on the basis of state-based rather than chief-based patronage. Moreover, the social bases of these power groups were not exclusively rural, but often included labour and urban middleclass support.[5]

Under the *Sonorenses*, however, regional power groups and their opponents faced the slow, tortuous but undeniable ascendancy of the national state in the transition from military to civilian power and from regional autonomy to increasing dependency on central bureaucracies and nation-wide mass organizations. Within this framework, the revolutionary chieftaincy, mostly based on military and peasant loyalties, faced between 1920 and 1934 a continued erosion of its power basis, particularly at the hands of Plutarco Elías Calles' military and bureaucratic reforms and most important, as a consequence of the creation of a dominant party which embraced all local revolutionaries and which provided an arena for resolving tensions and conflicts. These reforms reflected the slow consolidation of a new type of political leadership, both at the national and lower levels, its ascendancy based on the use of the state and its potential for bureaucratic organization and control.[6] Before going into the details of a comparative analysis of Tlaxcala and San Luis Potosí, it is necessary to explain the considerable room for manoeuver which the *Sonorenses* conceded to the regional power groups between 1920 and 1934, obliging the central government to postpone its objective of centralising power. The *Sonorenses* faced a crucial problem: how to consolidate their power by restoring political stability and developing a strong national state, while lacking reliable coercive instruments, a dependable popular basis or orderly institutionalized forms of succession in power.

By 1920 the revolutionary army was still a loose alliance of warlords with often strong regional roots and a degree of local autonomy which surpassed by far the confines of regular military authority. Moreover, the régime was seriously debilitated, if not threatened, by recurrent clashes between presidential hopefuls, the continuous struggle for influence and power between the major *caudillos* Calles and Obregón, and finally, the dual power structure which resulted from Calles' success in maintaining his grip on the presidency between 1928 and 1934. During the 1920s, the *Sonorenses* faced a series of military and popular revolts, and a number of radical, peasant and labour movements. These partly originated as a consequence of their own policies to strengthen the national state and impose their objectives (a monopoly on the access to the coercive instruments -army, police, *militias*- a monopoly on state patronage -better labour conditions, access to land and education- and control on the political mobilization of the masses). To realize these objectives under conditions of deficient national structure of

---

5. Romana Falcón, "Las regiones en la revolución. Un itinerario historiográfico," in *Balance y perpectivas de los estudios regionales en México*, Pablo González Casanova and Carlos Martínez Assad, eds. (Mexico City, forthcoming); Barry Carr, "Recent Regional Studies of the Mexican Revolution," *Latin American Research Review* (hereafter *LARR*), 15:1 (1980), 3-14; Thomas Benjamin and Marcial Ocasio Meléndez, "Organizing the Memory of Modern Mexico: Porfirian Historiography in Perspective 1880s-1980s," in *Hispanic American Historical Review* (hereafter *HAHR*), 64:2 (1984) 323-364; Héctor Aguilar Camín, "Constantes históricos del estado mexicano," in *Historias*, 3 (1983), 39-52, "The Relevant Tradition: Sonoran Leaders in the Revolution," in *Caudillo and Peasant*, 92-124; Hans Werner Tobler, "La burguesía revolucionaria en México: Su origen y su papel, 1915-1935," in *HMex*, 34:2 (1984/134), 213-237. For a discussion of the different kinds of authority and legitimacy embedded in the peasant organization of Veracruz see, Romana Falcón, *La semilla en el surco. Adalberto Tejeda y el radicalismo en Veracruz 1880-1960* (Mexico City, 1986); Heather Fowler Salamini, *Agrarian Radicalism in Veracruz, 1920-1938* (Lincoln, 1978).

6. Ankerson, *Agrarian Warlord*, 95; Lorenzo Meyer, "Los inicios de la institucionalización. La política del Maximato," in *Historia de la revolución mexicana* (Mexico City, 1978), XII.

power, the *Sonorenses*' only viable alternative, for the time being, was the creation of loose, often *ad hoc*, coalitions with warlords, chieftaincies and other regional power groups. These clientelistic and informal pacts were different in terms of their internal power structures, patterns of mobilization and control of political resources. Some warlords had to be bribed into loyalty. Peasant-based chieftains obtained land in exchange for military services and loyalty. Civilian politicians were able to rise in the hierarchy, gain local power and profit from the revolutionary spoils system (as long as they proved able to help with the repression of military and popular rebellions, as well as to mobilize human and material resources for the often hard-pressed national government).[7]

Under Calles' hegemony (1924-1934) the policies that enabled the régime more effectively to control the regular army, the local *militias*, and the regional *caciques*, began to bear fruit. Military zone commanders, with strong local roots, who managed to survive became an exception as local power groups were, one after another, stripped of their bargaining power. The year 1929 saw the last of the major military revolts. Calles took advantage of the political crisis provoked by the sudden death of president-elect Obregón (1928), to create a National Revolutionary Party (*PNR*) as the obligatory forum for the solution of conflict within the revolutionary family. First of all, the political machines of local bosses and governors had to join the *PNR*. Later, the control over the state level *PNR* machines was gradually wrestled from local control. The party's structure was changed. On the rise were state-wide organizations of peasants, industrial workers, and a 'popular' front which integrated women, students and so forth, into national organizations, which, in a short span of time, broke the local machines controlled by *caciques* and *caudillos*. By 1934 regional power groups had become much more dependent of the federal government than they were a decade earlier. Most of them had been disarmed and their autonomous control of regional political resources was seriously threatened. "*Cedillos*" had become an anachronism, "*Mendozas*" were the rule.

To conclude, the *Sonorenses* had to resort to pragmatic equilibrium policies of an often contradictory and *ad hoc* nature. These policies often fostered local autonomy, although the long-term end was to curb it; for the time being they kept a number of chieftaincies afoot, but they also fostered the emergence of party and bureaucracy based regional power groups, all the more attractive since they lacked access to force. For years to come, the *Sonorenses* fostered their continuous coexistence and, thereby fostered a whole gamut of interrelationships between regional fiefdoms of different composition and nature. The late 1920s and the early 1930s, however, witnessed the progressive national control over irregular armed forces and the strengthening of central bureaucratic control. This reduced the room for manoeuver of regional *caciques* and forced them to adapt to the 'new rules of the game'. The *sonorense* period is clearly one of transition in terms of patterns of mobilization and control of resources. The traditional chieftaincy (San Luis Potosí) and the civilian regional power groups (Tlaxcala) existed side by side and the ascendancy of the national state and modern patterns is undeniable. Still, it is Cedillo who stays in power while Mendoza loses.

7. Romana Falcón, "El surgimiento del agrarismo cardenista: Una revisión de las tésis populistas," *HMex*, 27:3 (1978/107), 333-386; David C. Bailey, "Mexico's Accommodating President," in *Essays on the Mexican Revolution*, George F. Wolfskill and Douglas W. Richmond, eds. (Austin, 1979), 82-99; Lorenzo Meyer, "La revolución mexicana y sus elecciones presidenciales: una interpretación (1911-1940)," in *HMex*, 32:2 (1982/126), 143-197; Linda B. Hall, "Alvaro Obregón and the Politics of Mexican Land Reform," in *HAHR*, 60 (1980), 213-238; Alicia Hernández Chávez, "Militares y negocios en la revolución mexicana," in *HMex*, 34:2 (1984/134), 181-212.

# TWO DIFFERENT REGIONAL REVOLUTIONARY PROCESSES: TLAXCALA AND SAN LUIS POTOSI 1910-1920

## *Tlaxcala*

By 1920 Ignacio Mendoza and Rafael Apango, both of urban lower class origin, controlled the regional revolutionary power group in the state of Tlaxcala. Both were civilians with experience in party and bureaucracy. Their roles in the years of warfare had been minor and they had never been in combat. Yet in 1920 they were able to pass over the revolutionary chieftains of a decidedly popular movement which had shown radical labour and agrarian objectives since 1910. Societal conditions around 1910 promoted radicalism, political conditions between 1910 and 1914 resulted in experiences varying from state power to total repression. From this emerged a radicalized movement out for revenge against the elites, but its opportunities as a small-scale movement to implement its goals were more and more restricted as wider regional and national movements reduced its room for manoeuver and autonomy. Why was the Tlaxcala Revolutionary Movement (hereafter *TRM*) originally so radical and how was it possible later to curb it? How could civilian urban leadership come to power in an originally far more radical revolutionary movement with strong popular, especially rural bases? How did the chieftain lose out to the civilian politician?

To answer these questions we must trace the local revolutionary process: Tlaxcala suffered important changes during the *Porfiriato*. Railroads integrated its elites and masses into a wider central Mexican market, which included the country's major cities. The *hacienda* dominating Northern Tlaxcala produced *pulque*, cereals, cattle, timber and charcoal, mainly on the basis of strictly controlled *hacienda* labour. The village-based peasants of the densely populated South were, however, far more affected by the joint arrival of railroads, industry and large-scale commercial agriculture. They were able to combine an increasing integration into an urban labour market with home manufacturing and subsistence agriculture. Exposed to the often quite similar conditions on *haciendas* as in workshops, and facing intervention in their village affairs (over land and autonomy), strong peasant tradition of protest fused with the emerging labour movement and found in 1910 its revolutionary leadership in the radical regional *maderista* movement led by Aquiles Serdan. Based in Puebla City, it had succeeded in creating a strong regional network of popular based clubs in dozens of Tlaxcalan villages. When Díaz resigned in May 1911, the Tlaxcalan *maderistas* succeeded in extending this network into a strong grass-roots party organization which controlled the majority of the peasantry. In the 1911 election for governor, the elites remained divided. *Maderista* victory gave a peasant worker and lower middle class leadership legal access to the state bureaucracy, attracted sympathizing -as Cockroft has put it- 'low status intellectuals' from elsewhere and created, under worker-governor Antonio Hidalgo, the conditions for political mobilization on the labour and agrarian issues against the Tlaxcalan elites. A power struggle ensued in which *maderistas* and elites were forced to mobilize resources *ad extremis*. When the elites won a temporary victory in 1913, followed by all out repression, the *maderistas* took to arms. With constitutionalist victory in mid-1914, this militarily weak, but politically strong, movement was out for revenge on the elites and hoped to regain power.[8]

The *TRM* was never able to attain a long-term autonomy comparable to the Zapata movement. The accessibility of the tiny state of Tlaxcala, and its strategic location on the Veracruz-Mexico City axis, combined with the 'economies of scale' in warfare, made complete control by local chieftains (as in Morelos), difficult to achieve in 1910-1911 and again in 1913-1914. Under constitutionalist domination, autonomy became a crucial issue and provoked generalized resentment among Tlaxcalan chieftains, whose autonomous acts of revenge against local elites and personal ambitions for local leadership clashed with constitutionalist interests. In November 1914, the major chieftains of the movement split. Domingo Arenas and the majority of the movement joined Zapata, ordered land distribution while setting fire to factories and warehouses. The governor appointed by Carranza, Máximo Rojas, stayed with the Supreme Chief, supported by most of his government, the bureaucracy and the civilian party leadership. Carranza's winning troops soon reduced Arenas' military power to a *guerrilla* level and by late 1916 Arenas rejoined Carranza in exchange for a regional constitutionalist command. This gave him, like other warlords, virtual autonomous power locally and the opportunity for wholesale occupation of *haciendas*. Arenas' commanders not only realized large-scale land distribution to villagers and *hacienda* workers - far beyond the limited *carrancista* land reform decree of 1915- but also used *hacienda* products for the provision of their local troops and for personal profit, or that of their local clienteles. This gave them solid peasant support in a situation of autonomy of the kind never enjoyed before.

Rojas' position was precisely the opposite. Distrusted by Carranza, he was kept in complete dependence. With only a small military force of his own and with even less political autonomy, he had few opportunities to create large popular support under an increasingly anti-labour and anti-*agrarista* Carranza. Rojas, his small military staff and his civilian trustees from government and party, Apango and Mendoza among them, could never regain control of the state without federal support. After Arenas had been assassinated in August 1917, Carranza transferred all local troops to other states and entrusted to a non-Tlaxcalan general the normalization of *arenista* territory and the election of a dependable constitutionalist governor and legislature. In his pacification policies Luis M. Hernández anticipated the later strategies of the *Sonorenses* by requiring the peasants' loyalty and obedience to constitutionalist agrarian laws in exchange for a quick legalization of their claims on occupied *hacienda* lands. It could have resulted in solid peasant support for a constitutionalist state government if Carranza had heeded Hernández' policies. But he refused to do so. As a result, the *arenista* villagers and *hacienda* workers clinged to their former chieftains and *agrarista* leaders. Collectively threatened in their immediate interests, they constituted a strongly mobilized popular basis for an *arenista* party which decided to oppose the official constitutionalist candidate. Under these circumstances Hernández had no option but to impose Rojas. Throughout his government, Rojas was unable to gain popular support in the *arenista* districts. Since Carranza refused to heed his pleas for land distribution, Rojas had to impose his will by bribery, selective clientelism and violence.

It is quite clear, that from 1914 onwards, *carrancista* impact on the small scale *TRM* has been decisive. It was for a large part responsible for the 1914 split; it supported the weak and dependent Rojas faction, controlled it and, finally im-

8. Raymond Buve, "El movimiento revolucionario de Tlaxcala (1910-1914). Sus origenes y desarrollo antes de la gran crisis del año 1914 (La rebelión arenista)," in *Anuario de Humanidades*, 7 (1981-1983), 141-182, esp. 172-177.

posed it as state government. By doing so Carranza enabled the small Rojas faction to monopolize power at the state level. Carranza's insistence on legal-bureaucratic procedures and his success in reducing, if not eliminating the military basis of the Rojas and the *arenista* faction, forced the chieftains to look for support of civilians with bureaucratic and party experience from the *maderista* period. They were there and ready to take over. Mendoza and Apango had acquired expertise as party leaders, bureaucrats and municipal presidents of important industrial towns. When he directed Rojas' difficult electoral campaign of 1917, Mendoza came forward as a capable political manager, captured a state deputyship, promoted his friends in the state bureaucracy and rose to be governor Rojas' substitute, whenever the governor left the state. In doing so he cleverly outwitted his rivals in the government party *PLCT* who competed with him in trying to influence Rojas, especially former governor Hidalgo and general Macario M. Hernández, an important constitutionalist general of Tlaxcalan origin and friend of Rojas. It was, however, the national crisis over presidential succession in 1920, which gave Mendoza and his clique the opportunity to gain power. Both, *rojistas* and *arenistas* had ample reasons to desert Carranza, but when Rojas decided to join Obregón in his revolt in April 1920, a large part of the *arenista* leadership did the opposite. Torn between their agrarian convictions and personal ambition they gambled on Carranza's victory and lost. Mendoza now saw his chance. The municipal and state bureaucracy were relieved of *arenista 'traidores de la patria'* and the bewildered villagers, were forced into loyalty to Obregón. While Rojas remained on military campaign outside Tlaxcala, Mendoza persuaded the party to have Apango elected as governor instead of one of his rivals.[9]

## *San Luis Potosí*

From its *maderista* origins, the Revolution in San Luis Potosí was characterised by the participation of many different social groups, who quarrelled among themselves because of different views of the Revolution and its objectives. By 1914, intra-revolutionary conflict and the collapse of the old régime had resulted in "*un mosaico de cacicazgos militares donde se impartía justicia, se ordenaba sobre vidas y bienes, y, en ocasiones, se trataba de ir creando las bases de una nueva sociedad.*" By 1918, however, most of these chiefs had been subdued, eliminated or struggled for survival on their home patches; the Cedillo's represented the latter category. Meanwhile, Juan Barragán, an important *carrancista* general from a *potosino* landowning family, had been able to gain the governorship and restore *hacendado* control in most of the state. In terms of economic destruction and loss of human life, the Revolution probably affected San Luis Potosí more than Tlaxcala. Yet, by 1920, the outcome of the regional revolutionary process was quite different. In Tlaxcala, local elites and outside forces had to work very hard to control a relatively well organized popular movement which had transformed the local *maderista* Revolution into a major rupture with the past and the constitutionalist Revolution into a radical peasant worker movement. In San Luis Potosí there was a much continuity with the past. By 1920, in essence, the *status quo* in San Luis Potosí had not been altered (with the exception of parts of the South East of the state). How can these differences be explained?

One explanation is that conditions in San Luis Potosí, although regionally varied, were in general not conducive to popular mobilization. In the arid North and Centre of San Luis Potosí, mining was important, but miners were only a tiny minority in an area of low population density. The vast majority of *potosinos*

9. Apart from Buve's work cited in note 1 above, see also Andrés Angulo, *Carta abierta a los presuntos diputados del Colegio Electoral del Congreso de la Unión*, Aug. 26, 1920.

worked on *haciendas* as *peones*, cowboys, collectors of hard fibres (*ixtleros*) and share-croppers. The treatment of these labourers varied from zone to zone, and indeed from estate to estate. Moreover, the complex economic organization of the *hacienda* resulted in a highly diversified stratification within the work force of each estate. Here lies part of the explanation of the different reactions that the *potosino* peasants' had towards the revolution.[10]

To understand the peculiarities of the peasant rural response to the Revolution, it is also vital to understand that centuries-old village-based communities -comparable to those prevailing in central Mexico- were largely absent. As is said in the previous chapter, the exception was the South-East of San Luis Potosí, basically the *Huasteca* and to a lesser extent *Valle del Maíz*, which was a rich and fertile zone suited to agriculture, cattle-raising and wood exploitation. Here, during the nineteenth century, invading entrepreneurs had competed with local *rancheros* and rural communities for resources. This provoked serious social tensions, continuous litigation for the recovery of their lands held since the early colonial period, as well as serious and violent peasant rebellions from the middle of the nineteenth century, and throughout the *Porfiriato*. But, at the same time, in this isolated area, local landowning families had been able to absorb peasant protest by establishing strong networks of vertical relations with small-holders and villagers. In exchange for access to land and security, peasants would serve as *hacienda* workers and help to defend the autonomy of their local bosses.

The Revolution in San Luis Potosí, therefore, was not characterized by a large-scale party-based popular movement, but by, first of all, separate local movements, controlled by *"beneficiarios del antiguo régimen": hacendados*, *rancheros* or other local entrepreneurs who had always disliked government intervention with their property and autonomy, had suffered from the agricultural crisis and recent droughts (1906-1908), and were now able to mobilize 'their' peasants for their own, essentially non-peasant interests. In the *maderista* movement of 1910, they joined hands with urban elite and middle-class dissenters out for moderate political reforms. A second type of movements was marked by popular protest against labour conditions in mines, industry and on *haciendas*. But except for parts of the South-East, the village-based *agrarista*-type of protest was largely absent. The popular movements were, like some of the *ranchero* movements, patria *chica*-oriented and acted in direct reaction to concrete local grievances and in response to local opportunities. Cedillo's *rancheros* band started in this way, early in 1911. Motivated by quarrels with local *hacendados* over borderlines, rights of way, rent and share-cropping contracts, it started originally on a family-and-friends basis with the support of local peasants also motivated by personal grievances against local landlords. Small scale and dispersed, they played only a minor role in the *maderista* Revolution of 1910. The *maderista* government that came to power in San Luis Potosí after the fall of Díaz, involved no rupture with the past, as was the case in Tlaxcala. On the contrary, we see it as *"una mera renovación de la misma élite"* in tacit agreement with the *hacendados*. While in Tlaxcala, municipal power and part of the bureaucracy fell in the hands of radical leadership, giving it the opportunity to use its potential for purposes of large-scale political mobilization, in the case of San Luis Potosí, the popular movements were virtually excluded. The failure of the conservative *maderista* government to improve rural conditions alienated popular and *ranchero* support and provoked rebellions.[11]

---

10. Apart from the works of Falcón mentioned in note 1 above, see Ankerson, *Agrarian Warlord*, 13-15.

11. For a discussion of the different types of reactions of the peasantry in San Luis Potosí towards the revolution see Falcón, "Charisma, Tradition and Caciquismo," and, *Revolu-*

When Huerta came into power, as in Tlaxcala, the Porfirian elites of San Luis Potosí intended to return to the *status quo* and consolidate it. The big *hacendados* and their clients held key positions in the state government and many lukewarm *maderista* leaders were jailed or killed. The severe neo-*porfirista* reaction provoked widespread resistance and deprived the government of potential support and legitimacy. The Barragán and other *hacendado* families, *Huasteca caciques*, and their Indian troops joined Carranza, finally followed by the Cedillo and Carrera bands. By late 1913 landlords lost control to *guerrilla* bands who remained in power in their small, local fiefdoms for two years. After Huerta's fall in July 1914, the "War of the Winners" resulted in short-lived constitutionalist, *villista* and conventionist governments, which only achieved limited control over the countryside and left the regional chieftains largely untouched. With Carranza's victory, constitutionalist troops pacified the North of San Luis Potosí, but the Cedillo and Carrera bands managed, with ups and downs, to resist all pacification campaigns in the South-East until the fall of Carranza and his governor Barragán.[12] This long period of a power vacuum at state level enabled chieftains, who at first had survived by robbery and assault, gradually to control their areas of influence and to organize the exploitation of local resources. The *Carreras* and *Cedillos* occupied dozens of *haciendas*, kept production going by imposing a system of military share-cropping, and bartered agricultural products for rifles and ammunition.

This was not unlike what Arenas did in Tlaxcala between 1914 and 1917. But Arenas did more. A short comparison between Cedillo and Arenas may help to highlight a crucial difference between the two movements. Cedillo did not change the unit or the organization of the agricultural production: instead of for the *hacendado*, the *hacienda* workers or share-croppers now worked for the chieftain. Cedillo showed interest in land distribution and, with Carrera Torres, promulgated a radical land reform decree, but it was never implemented on any scale. On some occasions their forces occupied abandoned *haciendas* and *ranchos*, but for the time being this was done on a temporary basis, and without a legal status. Arenas, however, did make a systematic effort to combine the take-over of *haciendas* with land distribution. He distributed land to villagers and founded colonies of *hacienda* workers on the estates, while the beneficiaries had to give part of their production to the chieftains. By doing so he fundamentally altered the unit and organization of the production. The major reason of why this did not happen in a significant way in San Luis Potosí will, most likely, have to be found in the absence of a strong village-based *agrarista* tradition among most of the *potosino* peasants. However, also the ideology and views of the chieftain may be relevant in explaining the differences. Cedillo could have taken the initiative in founding agricultural colonies for *hacienda* workers, the way Arenas did in Tlaxcala, largely independent of military service to the chief. Cedillo was sympathetic to land reform, and this was one reason why he defected Carranza in 1914. On the other hand, he did not seem to be representative of a strong peasant movement from below, nor did he have clear and major social objectives beyond the maintenance of his *militia* and the redress of local grievances. In the case of San Luis Potosí, the military colonies, and the land distribution which took place under the long-lived Cedillo's *cacicazgo* (1920-1938) were strictly linked to the rendering of military service to him and his major chieftains.[13]

---

*ción y caciquismo*, 62, 58-70, 88, 273; Ankerson, *Agrarian Warlord*, 53-58; Lerner, "Fundamentos socioeconómicos del cacicazgo," 397-398.

12. Falcón, *Revolución y caciquismo*, 70-127; Ankerson, *Agrarian Warlords*, Ch. 3.

13. Falcón, *Revolución y caciquismo*, 273; Ankerson, *Agrarian Warlords*, 73, 100, 139.

When Barragán came to power (like Rojas in Tlaxcala *"con la presión del ejercito"*), his régime (1917-1920) soon developed into what we now consider a fine example of a constitutionalist military fiefdom. After the collapse of the old régime, followed by a protracted war *"de todos contra todos,"* forced loans, deliveries to chieftains and occupation of their estates, wealthy *potosinos* welcomed the return of their bourgeois governor. But, they had to pay for his support. The Barragán clique accumulated wealth by negotiating the return of occupied *haciendas* and exploiting them through local clients. Control over the railways was a resource for favouritism and for profit in mining and commerce. Thus, by 1920, most *haciendas* had been returned to their previous owners and in large parts of San Luis Potosí the *status quo* had been restored to a much higher degree than in the southwestern half of Tlaxcala. At that time, Barragán was a strong *carrancista* governor and an intimate of the president. His local social policies were in line with Carranza's conservative views. In essence, the traditional elites were included in his power groups. Barragán gave only lukewarm support to labour and did virtually nothing with respect to land reform. In part, this was due to his inability to control the *agrarista* zones in the South-East and to the legal exclusion of *hacienda* workers from Carranza's land reform legislation. But even where Barragán could have promoted land distribution he often refused to do so out of fear for disrupting food production as well as his, and his own friends' estate interests. Rojas, on the other hand, distrusted by Carranza, disliked by the local elites, and with scant military support, badly needed land distribution and improved labour conditions to reinforce his popular basis. Carranza prevented this, thereby leaving the dependent Rojas in a position of essential weakness. Since he could not show his peasants and workers real results, he was unable to reinforce his popular base. Yet, at the same time, as a peasant-worker chieftain, he did not want to restore *hacendado* control. The *Sonorenses* offered Rojas an attractive way out; Barragán on the other hand could only lose.[14]

These crucial differences in their position and views determined not only the decisions Rojas and Barragán took in 1920, but also the options of their local opponents in their attempts to come to power. In Tlaxcala, Rojas joined Obregón and, in doing so, induced a large part of the *arenistas* to stay with Carranza. The victory of the *Sonorenses* wiped out the *carrancista* state government in San Luis Potosí. As in the case of Puebla, this left the state in the hands of regional *caciques*, revolutionary radicals and bosses, who had joined the *Sonorenses* and now vied for power, looking for external support. Cedillo was one of them. In the case of Tlaxcala, a timely switch to Obregón saved the state government and gave the revolutionary power groups opportunities for reinforcing its position.

## THE EMERGENCE OF REGIONAL POWER GROUPS IN TLAXCALA AND SAN LUIS POTOSI: DIFFERENT PATTERNS AND RELATIONS WITH THE *SONORENSES* (1920-1929)

### *Tlaxcala*

Once in power, the Mendoza group faced serious problems in maintaining and consolidating their position. Apango and Mendoza did have popular support in their own industrial municipalities, but many of Rojas' peasants, bound to their

14. Falcón, *Revolución y caciquismo*, 78-86, 125-127, 143; Ankerson, *Agrarian Warlords*, 82-87.

chieftain, distrusted them. The *arenista* villagers in the South had every reason for dislike and their leaders, thrown out of their jobs by Mendoza, joined hands with disappointed Rojas' clients and looked for support in Puebla and Mexico. The elites, however much horrified by the popular background of the emerging power group, did have some reason for cooperation and support. In the South and West of Tlaxcala many landowners had lost their estates and their authority under Arenas. Carranza had ordered the return of the *haciendas* to the owners, but had apparently been unable to force governor Rojas to support the landowners in their struggle to regain control. It would, for sure, have spoilt whatever popular support Rojas still had. Under Obregón, with *agrarismo* on the rise and land distribution stepped up, an obliging military commander or governor seemed to be the only hope for these *hacendados*. The northern landowners were better off. Carranza's land reform decree excluded their *hacienda* workers, many *haciendas* had not been abandoned and their administrators had learned to negotiate with revolutionary chieftains. Moreover, with southern *haciendas* partly abandoned or in peasants' hands, the state government needed the production of the northern ones for tax income and food. Gradually a system of clientelism developed between *hacendados* and the emerging revolutionary power group. Landowners received support and protection in exchange for regular gifts, contracts, participation in profits and tax payments in advance. In local industry we can also observe a dependent position which became a starting point for state clientelism. By 1917, entrepreneurs were back in production but were still beset by reconstruction problems and scarcities (transport, raw materials). Labour relations remained an especially delicate point because Rojas' clients, of peasant worker origin, controlled labour organizations and municipal power. Research is still incomplete but there are indications that under Apango and Mendoza, entrepreneurs tried to join hands with the state government. Up to a certain extent, control over the labour movement was in the interest of both. Mendoza's challenge was how to defuse a high level of radical peasant and worker organization in a period (the Obregón years) when this phenomenon was on the rise at the national level and in neighbouring Puebla.[15]

The *Partido Nacional Agrarista* (*PNA*) and a radical *Comisión Nacional Agraria*, the national committee in charge of land distribution procedures, became the rallying point for a fierce landreform movement, while the *Confederación Regional Obrera Mexicana* (*CROM*) tried to organize labour as a support to Obregón and Calles. Because of their services to the *Sonorenses*, a radical labour leader, José Maria Sánchez became governor of Puebla (1921-1922), and the *agrarista* leader Manuel P. Montes succeeded in virtually dominating the Atoyac valley on the Tlaxcala border (1923-1927). Both leaders clashed with the, in their eyes, 'reactionary' government of Tlaxcala and offered the Tlaxcala opposition protection

15. *Archivo Histórico Tlaxcala, Universidad Iberoamericana* (hereafter *AHT-UIA*), 1.1.9.36, 1.1.9.37 and 1.1.10.38 correspondence management *haciendas* Mazaquiahuac and El Rosario, Tlaxco, with state government Tlaxcala. Rojas and Apango's top official Octavio Hidalgo received regular payments and gifts; Apango fostered cordial relations, see also Buve, "Peasant Mobilization," 367-368; Ricardo Rendón Garcini, "Tenencia de la tierra y organización agraria de dos centros de producción agrícola en el Estado de Tlaxcala: Mazaquiahuac y El Rosario (1876-1941)" (Ms. Mexico City, 1983), Ch. 5.5 y 5.6; Juanicó, "Partidos," 12. Workers' support for Rojas seems to have been weak, see Buve, "Jefes menores de la revolución mexicana," 669-670. On the tense relations between the local *CROM* federation and the state governments headed by Apango y Mendoza, see *Lucha Social, Organo del partido Laborista de Tlaxcala*, 1a época, tomo 1o, núm. 1-7 abril-junio 1924, 2a época, tomo 2o, núm 1-5 oct-nov 1924; *Archivo General de la Nación, Ramo Presidentes, Fondo Obregón* (hereafter *AGN-RPOC*), 408-T-33 file on the electoral struggle in Tlaxcala: Tel. Part. Lab. Tlax. to Pres. Calles, Jan. 12, 1925; Interview with Amado C. Morales, former local *CROM* official, Nov. 1967.

and a basis for action. On the other hand, we may assume that the fate of Puebla's entrepreneurs (invasions of lands and plants, endless strikes and exceedingly high taxes) induced the local Tlaxcalan elites to support Apango and Mendoza more than ever. It is doubtful, however, if this support, in the absence of solid popular or military support, could have saved the Mendoza group. Two factors seem to be of considerable importance for the explanation of Mendoza's success. The first was the absence of a prestigious chieftain. This was largely due to the pacification policies of Carranza mentioned earlier, the execution of *arenista* rebels and Rojas' early death in combat (1923). The second factor was federal support for a dozen years (1920-1932).[16]

Why did Apango and Mendoza obtain this federal support? First of all, from a *sonorense* point of view, they did not have to worry about Tlaxcala in a decade when the existence of autonomous local control over military resources was still their major concern. Mendoza had no access to the military or peasant based *militias*, counting only upon a tiny state *gendarmerie*. Secondly, in terms of their local policies, Apango and Mendoza anticipated later *callista* policies. That is, they foresaw development along capitalist lines and sought no *"grand restructuring of society."* This resulted in a rather uneasy relationship during Obregón's Presidency, but governor Mendoza (1925-1929) and his hand-picked successor Adrian Vásquez (1929-1932) fitted nicely into Calles' views on law, order and development. Obregón's insistence on creating peasant loyalty by land distribution in the *arenista* districts of Tlaxcala clashed seriously with governor Apango. The latter saw it, not without justification, as an attempt by his local *agrarista* opposition to gain clients and prestige among 'his' peasantry with the support of Mexico and Puebla radical *agrarista* leaders. In 1923 these leaders would join hands with others to dislodge Apango and his government party. Apango, however, survived because he seems to have served Obregón's and Calles' national and regional interests in several ways.

The delicate political situation in Puebla may have been a major reason. This represented a regional incarnation of the worst fears of the *Sonorenses* in terms of political polarization, instability and loss of control. In 1920, the state government of Puebla stayed with Carranza and in 1923 it joined De la Huerta. In both cases labour and agrarian bosses enlarged their military power and autonomy when fighting for Obregón. Power dissipated among local *caciques* and bosses, polarization fanned conflict between *hacendados* and radical armed *agraristas*, industrial conflict deepened, while labour and agrarian bosses clashed over their spheres of influence. This all became entangled with the recurrent issue of presidential succession in 1923 and 1927. For years the *Sonorenses* were unable to control politics in Puebla -the state had 20 governors in 10 years- but they succeeded in eliminating acute threats and keeping it in quarantine. By doing so they served the interests of Apango and Mendoza. Radical governor Sánchez was toppled in the midst of his all-out war against the Puebla elites in 1922. Montes and his *agrarista* army were finally dislodged by Calles' minister of labour, Luis N. Morones, and the *CROM* in 1927, much to the relief of Mendoza. In 1923, the National Cooperatist Party had successfully, and with Obregón's consent, dislodged the Liberal Constitutionalist Party from its dominant position in the Federal Congress and in the states. Puebla governor Froylan N. Manjárrez, an important national *cooperatista* leader, joined hands with the Tlaxcalan opposition in 1923 to dislodge Apango's Liberal Constitutionalist Party. The case dragged on for months until Obregón finally joined Calles in his support for Apango, most

16. Juanicó, "Partidos," 23-25; Buve, "Consolidating," 30-32.

probably because of Manjárrez and his party's support for De la Huerta as candidate for the presidency against Obregón's wishes.[17]

Finally, we have to mention the coincidence of the terms of government in the state of Tlaxcala and the national presidency. This meant an inevitable conflict between emerging rivals in the second half of a term in office, and the equally strong efforts of the new incumbent to impose his authority, coincided at the state and federal level. The Calles-De la Huerta conflict may have saved Apango in 1923, Calles' firm intention to impose his authority brought Mendoza to power in 1925. With the open support of the ex-*zapatista* chieftain Genovevo de la O, the military commander of Tlaxcala, all the oppositional groups in Tlaxcala and their *agrarista* and labourite partisans in Puebla tried in 1924 to prevent Mendoza from being elected as Apango's successor. When Apango and his *PLCT* rigged the elections, civil disobedience, attempts at rebellion and mass protest flared up. Calles, after only one month in office, ordered his new minister of labour, Morones, to reimpose order, insisting upon the disarmament of the state forces and of all Tlaxcalan volunteers and activists of the *PLCT* and the opposition.[18] From then on, Calles' firm support gave Mendoza, stripped of every access to armed force, his chance to consolidate his power into a civilian party-based but dependent *cacicazgo*, in several respects a prelude to the *PNR*.

Internal consolidation of the Tlaxcala regional power group was a process which took at least five years, because the system of mobilization and control of resources still had to be created. The first stage was the creation of a party and bureaucracy based system of mobilization and control, or, as the opposition formulated it, *"el gobierno local convertido en partido político."* From 1920 onwards, Mendoza succeeded in establishing his control over the government party *PLCT*. His rivals, one after another, joined the opposition or left Tlaxcala. The leadership of the Tlaxcala labour and *agrarista* parties consisted largely of disappointed *pelecistas*. For that same reason the Tlaxcala *agrarista* party never gained a firm foothold among the peasants in *arenista* districts. They tended to stay with the discredited *arenista* party. Some joined Montes' radical peasant organization *"Domingo Arenas"* in Puebla. Strict control of the government bureaucracy was another point. Apango and Mendoza forged a political machine of *caciques* who controlled the state's fifteen districts and the corresponding municipalities. With Apango, control was sometimes deficient and, in those cases, elections were annulled and loyal 'provisional' councils installed. In the South-West this was the rule and in the 1924 elections governor Apango had to use massive imprisonment, force and fraud in the face of fierce opposition in *agrarista* and labour districts. After Mendoza's imposition, and with Calles' firm support, electoral victories could be ensured more easily. In the northern *hacienda* districts, Mendoza ensured electoral control by making it clear to administrators that only his party was to be voted for. Dependence on government favours and the *hacendados*'

17. *AGN-RPOC*, 408-T-33: Gob. Mendoza to Pres. Calles, Jan. 16, 1925; Alan Knight, *The Mexican Revolution* (Cambridge, 1986), II, 518; *Excelsior*, Jan. 14, 1922; *La Vida Nueva*. núm. 322 3a época, tomo VII, Aug. 1923 dedicated in its Tlaxcala number an article to Apango's prudent agrarian policies, not inciting the peasants, etc.; Interviews Ez. M. Gracia, deputy under Apango, Nov. 1967; Apango had serious conflicts with the *CNA* and its delegate in Tlaxcala under the radical S. G. Miguel Mendoza López S.; see *TB/MWO* Dec. 20, 1922 in Summerlin, Mexico to SoSW (*NAW-DF* 812.00: 26161) and *El Látigo*, semanario político de combate, México núm. 2, Feb. 11, 1923 on anti-agrarian policies of the state Government; *El Demócrata*, Nov. 8, 1922, *Excelsior*, Nov. 24, 1922, *El Pueblo*, semanario del Partido Reinvindicador Tlaxcalteca, núm. 2, Nov. 1, 1930; For an eulogy on governor Vásquez' work, see *El Noticiero*, periódico de información, Tlaxcala, núm. 280, Feb. 13, 1932. This *gobernista* paper did not even mention agrarian reform among the governor's merits. Buve, "Consolidating," 15-20.

18. Buve, "Consolidating," 19-20; Juanicó, "Partidos," 17-21; *AGN-RPOC* 408-T-33.

fear for Puebla-like conditions if the opposition should win, did the rest. Mendoza remodeled the *PLCT* on Garrido Canabal's Socialist Party in Tabasco. In 1927, the government party, renamed *Partido Socialista* (*PST*), had about 300 local clubs or *uniones de resistencia* and it claimed 20,000 affiliated peasants. Those who refused to comply faced strong-arm methods, the remainder was generally disorganized or passive.[19]

Although Obregón and especially Calles succeeded in enforcing a stronger federal grip on land distribution, Apango and Mendoza were able to use it as a major political instrument in enforcing loyalty. Land distribution, the corresponding bureaucratic interventions and procedures, and the obligations imposed by law, made the peasants more dependent than ever before. The first half of the procedure took place at the local level and was controlled by the state government and its *Comisión Local Agraria.* Since the *CLA* had to prepare the state governor's decision on petitions for land -to be confirmed or rejected by the *CNA* and the president -it became a key instrument for clientelist politics. The same can be said of the implementation of presidential decisions on land grants, since the state government was, in practice, quite often capable of delaying the transfer of these lands as *ejidos* to the peasants or have them distributed among peasant clients. No wonder many *agrarista* committees of *arenista* origin complained that they were *"victimas de nuestro gobierno y de las oficinas agrarias del Estado."*[20]

The administration of *ejidos*, however, provided the most adequate instrument of control. Scarcity of land for a dense peasant population, limited water supplies, arrears in payment of taxes and conflicts over the election of *ejido* officials, all promoted the emergence of competing interest groups based on family, *barrio* and friends, looking for mediation and support. Whatever the interests of the *PNA* and the federal agrarian bureaucracy, Mendoza's regional power group controlled the local agrarian bureaucracy. Land distribution diminished during the late 1920s, president Ortiz Rubio announcing the end of the reforms in 1930. Those who held plots and power within the existing *ejidos* tended now to safeguard their interests by an alignment with the ruling group. Moreover, their enemies had been stripped of opportunities for mediation since strong exclusive local control by the Mendoza group went together with federal anti-*agrarista* policies. As far as labour was concerned, research is still fragmentary. It seems, however, that the pragmatic Mendoza, in the face of the all powerful *CROM*, consented in leaving the local *CROM* federation in exclusive control over labour in exchange for loyalty. The local *CROM* saw to loyal voting patterns and controlled many *ejidos* in peasant-worker villages.[21]

---

19. Observation made by the opposition party *Partido Laborista de Tlaxcala*, Dec. 1924 cited by Juanicó, "Partidos," 15, 19-20; Buve, "Consolidating," 12-20, based a.o. upon *El Disco Rojo* (1920) y *El Gladiator, órgano del PLC de Tlaxcala* (1921-1925), and based o.a. upon *AGN-RPOC* 408-T-19 and 33, 428-T-46 and FGdO cajas 92 y 93; *Lucha Social, órgano del Partido Laborista de Tlaxcala* (1924-1925) y *El Combate, órgano del Partido Nacional agrarista, México*; interviews with Amado C. Morales, local *CROM* official 1920s, Nov. 1967 and Candelario Reyes, Agrarian official and delegate 1918-1921, Nov. 1967 and Nov. 1979. Ramírez Rancaño, "Socialismo en Tlaxcala," 69.

20. *ASRA* DT 213 Pdt. Agr. Comm. Atoyatenco, Tlax. to Pres. Obregón, Nov. 1, 1922; Buve, "Consolidating," 22-28 and based on archival research in the *ASRA*, Mexico and in Tlaxcala, and interviews 1967-1968 in the municipalities of Nativitas and Calpulalpam, Tlaxcala.

21. In Nativitas alone five clear cases of *ejido*-elites can be found, mostly linked to the government party; *Excelsior*, July 7 and Oct. 3, 1921 and Feb. 1, 1922 give fine examples of *ejido*-elites; *El Gladiator*, the government party paper confirms the trend to join the government party. The Liga archive of the *Confederación Nacional Campesina* and the archive of the local Federation of the *Confederación de Trabajadores de México* in Tlaxcala have a number of documents about their struggle to wrest control over *ejidos*

As far as the elites were concerned, Mendoza and Vásquez clearly tried to find a balance between the minimal functional needs for maintaining civilian control over popular forces and a support generating relationship with the local elites. On the one hand, Apango, Mendoza and Vásquez repeatedly expressed their dislike of *"agraristas furibundos,"* maintained cordial, friendly and profitable relations with a number of *hacendados* and, the three of them, became owners of *haciendas*. On the other hand, actual land distribution never stopped. Between 1920 and 1925 about 22,000 peasants received lands in 98 *ejidos*. It may sometimes have hurt their relations to landowners, but the three governors did not hesitate to reap the political reward from the annual transfer of roughly 5000 hectares, ordered by presidential decree, to the peasants. What is more, on the northern *haciendas*, the socialist government party under Mendoza and Vásquez promoted the unionization of *hacienda* workers. Together with radical Marxist phraseology in the government party paper *El Socialista* and a peasant congress authorized by Mendoza in the *hacienda*-surrounded town of Huamantla (1927), unionization provoked resentment among landowners. In reality, however, changes were minor for the time being: northern *haciendas* were still exempt from land reform by 1930, and even by 1935, only five percent of the 2900 *hacienda* workers had been unionized. Nevertheless, some groups of *hacienda* workers had profited from government party mediation in obtaining better wages, schools and other social improvements. These gains were, of course, widely mentioned in government propaganda.[22]

In Tlaxcala, during the early 1920s, the regional power group needed a few years to consolidate. In the absence of strong popular support or access to force, the Mendoza group carefully avoided confrontation with the local elites and became especially dependent on federal support. During these crucial years, it was not so much unequivocal support from president Obregón, as the partially accidental coincidence of national and regional level interests of Obregón and Calles with those of the Tlaxcala power group, which saved governor Apango. Between Calles and Mendoza a firm axis of complementary interests and support developed. This gradually robbed the local opposition of its external political bases and gave Mendoza the opportunity for creating a state-wide *cacicazgo*. Internal consolidation and the resulting *cacicazgo* reflect the pragmatic policies and the bureaucracy and party based model which Calles envisaged with the *PNR*. The Mendoza group inherited a party with considerable experience in organization and policy. They acquired control over the state bureaucracy and extended the party like *"un auténtico pulpo"* down to the grass-roots.[23] This bureaucratic-party machine enabled them to achieve a high level of clientelistic control because it provided the opportunity to monopolize mediation and access to resources. By 1930 it was clear that *ejidatarios* and industrial labourers had been included in Mendoza's system. Those who did not have land remained disorganized and discouraged. Landowners and industrialists had been induced to give limited conces-

from the local *CROM* federation in 1936-1940. Even in 1937 the local *CROM* was still very powerful and the *CTM* did never succeed to replace it in important sectors as textiles; see Raymond Buve, *Boeren-mobilisatie en landhervorming tijdens en na de Mexicaanse revolutie: de Vallei van Nativitas, Tlaxcala, tussen 1910-1940* (Leiden, 1977), 154; Buve, "State Governors," 233-234.

22. Apango's secretary of government Florencio Zainos y Lumbreras cited in *Excelsior* Jan. 14, 1922. Buve, "Peasant Mobilization," 365-368 on the *hacienda* district of Huamantla; Ramírez Rancaño, "Socialismo en Tlaxcala," 73-78 on land reform and syndication; landlords reaction, see *AHT-UIA* 1.1.19.45; propaganda, see *El Campesino, órgano de la D. G. de Educación en el Edo. de Tlaxcala*, 1a época, núm. 2, Feb. 28, 1929 and *El Noticiero* various numbers between 1927 and 1932.

23. Ramírez Rancaño, "Socialismo en Tlaxcala," 69.

sions and lend political loyalty in exchange for a workable relationship with the state government.

*San Luis Potosí*

When the *carrancista* state government under Barragán fell from power, Cedillo's position remained what it had been throughout the Revolution: that of a locally rooted rural chieftain in the South-East of San Luis Potosí. His power and authority was based on a strong personal *compromiso* with his peasant soldiers, now on the winning side. His experience in politics did not go beyond his *ranchero* 'action kindreds' and their peasant clients in an isolated back-yard of the state. Yet, under Obregón, Cedillo was able to enlarge this rural chieftaincy against the rising tide of *agrarista* and labour mobilization inspired often by radical urban leaders. In only five years, he succeeded in consolidating his power domain into a state-wide *cacicazgo*, which endured throughout the transition from military to civilian power and from regional autonomy to dependency on a centralizing bureaucracy. How did he manage to do this?

The national government still lacked the means for controlling the country either politically or military, and lived under the constant threat -and reality- of armed rebellions. This fundamental insecurity led the presidents to pursue a policy of encouraging revolutionary generals to exchange their political independence at the national level for a guarantee of economic privilege and political autonomy in their home states. Under these conditions, military power continued to serve as the basic vehicle for political and social mobility. The efficiency and the loyalty of local *caciques* such as Cedillo, who had substantial military backing of their own, was indispensable to the very survival of the national leadership, as well as, paradoxically, to the restoration of an orderly political process in the country.

Cedillo proved to be particularly astute in this bargaining process. By joining the winning side in 1920 he obtained payments for his troops, confirmation of his military rank as a general, the military command of his natural zone of operations, land for settlement of his peasant soldiers in military colonies, and most important of all, permission to maintain, a small but private armed *militia* which was independent of the regular army and responded only to his call. While he consolidated his strong grasp over the *Valle de Maiz*, he cemented his clientelist relationship with the *Sonorenses* by military services in the repression of revolts. Cedillo's role on the side of the government in the De la Huerta revolt (1923) was crucial, his force doubling in size. As a reward Cedillo obtained the state level *Jefatura de Operaciones Militares*. This provided him with all the available military means in San Luis Potosí, permitting him to impose his will outside his *patria chica*. Serving the *Sonorenses*, his troops kept alive their considerable *guerrilla* experience, an asset which became most important in Cedillo's contribution to the military containment of the *Cristero*-revolt, as well as the Serrano and Escobar revolts between 1926 and 1929. This dependence of the federal government on the *potosino 'agraristas'*, enabled Cedillo to rise to a position of military prominence while most of the *militia* based chieftains, Montes in Puebla, for instance, were subdued, stripped of their command and troops, or eliminated.[24] The *potosino* warlord was able to bargain increasing services for more local control and finally extend his power over all San Luis Potosí. By 1929 Cedillo had over 6000 *militia* men who were rewarded by president Portes Gil with 100,000 hec-

24. On Montes see Facundo Arías González, "Historia de las relaciones del movimiento obrero con el campesino: El caso de la CROM y de la Confederación Social Campesina Domingo Arenas," (Paper Tlaxcala, Oct. 1985); *El Universal*, Apr. 21, 1926 and *Excelsior*, Jun. 30, 1927.

tares of land. Meanwhile, in 1925, with Calles' permission, Cedillo was able to depose governor Aurelio Manrique (1923-1925), install a client governor and have himself elected as governor in 1927. In the following years, in order to preserve Cedillo's loyalty and military backing, presidents Calles and Portes Gil helped to maintain the legitimacy of his *cacicazgo* by permitting him to reap the fruits of autonomy and patronage of which others were increasingly deprived.

The second explanation of strength of Cedillo's fiefdom was that his civilian, urban-based competitors were not able to create sufficiently independent power bases. In the countryside, they were up against a still strong *hacendado* clan and an even stronger array of local *caciques*. This was due to the joint effects of isolation, regionalization and depression. Agriculture in much of San Luis Potosí remained stagnant, often reduced to subsistence or characterized by regional markets, insecurity and lack of investments. This itself was a consequence of the radical program of a clientelist based land distribution. Bad harvests and the economic crisis of the 1930s completed the sombre spectre. Moreover, regional *caciques*, often the earlier *hacendado* and *ranchero* chieftains like the Santos clique in the *Huasteca*, were virtually autonomous. They had their own *militias*, imposed municipal authorities and had 'their' deputies elected for the State Congress.

Rafael Nieto, a Calles protegé who became governor in 1920, reflected Calles' views on economic reconstruction and moderate reforms. He issued legislation to promote the development of an independent rural middle class of farmers, but proved unable to enforce his views on a *cacique* ridden State Congress and countryside. His successor Aurelio Manrique (1923-1925), helped to power by Cedillo's peasant *militias* (his famous '*agraristas*') and by Obregón, intended to promote labour and peasant organization and implement radical reforms as Tejeda had done in Veracruz. He was successful in land reform (12,000 *ejidatarios* obtained together about 300,000 hectares), but this was due more to Cedillo's support than to his own organizational talents. In Tlaxcala, as we have demonstrated, the situation was quite different. Due to the size of this state, its location near large urban centres and a dense network of communications, isolation and regionalization were less of a problem. Moreover, with a considerable percentage of the peasant population village-based and with experience in local politics and defence of their resources since long before the *maderista* Revolution, Apango and Mendoza faced a different problem. They did not have to create a rural power base. They had to conquer one which enjoyed a considerable degree of autonomy.

A third point which helps to explain Cedillo's rise to power on the state level were the hostile relations between his opponents and Obregón and Calles. In the 1923 electoral contest for governor, the powerful Santos family from the *Huasteca* competed with the radical *agrarista* party leader, Manrique, who had Cedillo's support in return for promises of more land reform. When the *Santistas*, believing they had Obregón's support, staged a pre-emptive coup, Obregón supported Cedillo and the *Santistas* had to withdraw. They henceforth gave their support to a friend of De la Huerta, the *cooperatista* party leader, Jorge Prieto Laurens, who had the support of the traditional elites and other Cedillo enemies. Prieto Laurens claimed to have won the elections, but since he did not want to fight De la Huerta, by late 1923 Obregón cautiously supported Cedillo in his attempt to remove him. The De la Huerta rebellion was a victory for Cedillo, who was then able to install a governor dependent on his military backing: Manrique.[25]

Cedillo and Manrique soon quarrelled. This was not so much over land distribution, which was indeed promoted in a radical fashion, but over Manrique's insistence on civilian state government authority in Cedillo's domain and over the governor's intentions to organize peasants into a mass association, a *liga*, which

25. Ankerson, *Agrarian Warlord*, 104-108, 114-117.

threatened to undercut Cedillo's monopoly on using the peasantry as a political resource. What was perhaps more important, Manrique irritated Obregón, and certainly Calles, because of his ideological and political extremism, which he also tried to export to neighbouring states. Once in power, Calles decided to curb Manrique and permitted Cedillo to depose him, thereby leaving Cedillo the road to state power. Manrique and Mendoza were both civilians who could not stay in power without firm federal support. One faced a strong peasant chieftain, the other confrontated joint peasant and labour mobilization. Within Calles' pragmatic policies to *"remove whoever was less valuable to the central government,"* the weak dissident, Manrique, lost and the weak but more conformist Mendoza stayed in power.[26]

What was the basis of Cedillo's power as it grew to span the state level? How were resources mobilized and controlled? His original local nucleus of soldiers-*colonos* gradually extended. But it did so, without significantly changing the original principle of particularistic distribution of favours in exchange for loyalty and services. This was possible because the pragmatic *Sonorenses* permitted him (and the idealist Manrique helped him) to satisfy the distributive demands which had increased because of the enlargement of his forces. Once in state power, the large majority of the rural population was completely dependent on Cedillo for solving their problems or conflicts. A quarter of the rural *potosinos* were *colonos* or *ejidatarios*. For them, tenure of plots, posts in the *ejido* administration or *militias ejidales*, seeds, a school, electricity, money, a job, a personal favour all depended on Cedillo and his hierarchy of local *caciques ejidales*. Landless *hacienda* workers and share-croppers constituted about three quarters of the rural population. For the most part, still excluded from land distribution, they were even more at the mercy of Cedillo who might give them land when he needed more soldiers. It is quite possible, that peasants, weary of warfare, did not want to pay this price. The *hacienda* élite by now had learned to reckon with Cedillo. In 1923 they had supported his enemies and paid for it (as victims of Manrique's reforms, supported by the *agraristas* of *Valle del Maíz*). As Cedillo became military more powerful and politically more influential, the *hacendados* grew to esteem his enlarged capacity for mediation. It became clear to them that Cedillo could, up to a degree, ignore presidential policies and laws. To avoid the threat of land distribution, embargos for fiscal reasons and extortions, they tried to obtain guarantees in exchange for gifts, profitable contracts and political support. Until the end of the *sonorense* period the large *potosina hacienda* remained basically unaffected. This was due to the legal limitations regarding *hacienda* workers, but also to the limitations of clientelist *cedillista* land reform which focused on 'his' south-eastern peasants. The *hacienda* workers of the *altiplano* remained largely outside the *cedillista* clientelist system, but were often controlled by clients of Cedillo who sometimes showed a much more pronounced *"enrichissez vous"* attitude in deals with local entrepreneurs.

Even business interests in mining and industry began to look to Cedillo's mediation, especially after two years of harassment by *manriquista* labour unions. After the fall of Manrique, Cedillo and the *CROM* vied for control over labour, but, as in Tlaxcala, Calles seems to have preferred 'his' governor over the *CROM*. The state level federation of the *CROM* was dismantled by Cedillo when Morones lost his power in 1928 and labour became gradually neutralized under the joint impact of the economic crisis and complete dependence on Cedillo mediation. Unlike Tlaxcala, the local *CROM* was never integrated as an instrument in the state *cacique* system. In the long run, this failure to integrate industrial workers

26. Ankerson, *Agrarian Warlord*, 116.

into the power structure proved to be one of Cedillo's weakest points, labour providing the platform from which his network would, eventually, be destroyed.

In terms of their control over the various social classes and groups, the *cacicazgos* of Cedillo and Mendoza looked quite similar. In the face of the increasing power of the regional strongmen and peasant and urban organizations, and the prospects of the possibility of worse experiences under somebody else, like Manrique or Montes, the elites of rural and industrial entrepreneurs preferred *Real Politik* and sought mediation with the *caciques*. The peasants who had received lands as *colonos* or *ejidatarios* were now bound to the *caciques* through a hierarchy of local clients. The landless remained largely outside the system, unorganized and, sometimes, discouraged. For those who did not conform to the rules there were the *fuerzas rurales* or professional gunmen.[27] Both *caciques* also had their weak points in terms of control. The *ranchero* Cedillo was popular with the majority of the peasants, even those who had not yet received land, because he had the aura of an *agrarista* chieftain. Mendoza was disliked by most of the peasants, even those who had received land, because he was generally perceived as anti-*agrarista* by *arenistas* and *rojistas* alike. Mendoza, of urban origin and with experience in party and bureaucracy, knew how to handle industrial workers and officials. He forged a clientelist élite of bureaucrats, party activists and union leaders who henceforth served as an instrument of control. Cedillo, however, never succeeded in creating a real party. With state power he inherited a bureaucracy, but never integrated industrial labour and bureaucrats as crucial instruments in his system. It was on these weak points mentioned above, that the enemies of Mendoza and Cedillo, particularly the stronger federal government, would begin their attacks on these *cacicazgos* in the 1930s.

## THE *CACIQUES* AND THE *PNR*: OBEDIENCE OR ELIMINATION?

By the beginning of the 1930s, when the post-revolutionary state had grown more highly centralized, and more capable than a decade before, of exercising its functions, the government became correspondingly less dependent on the support of local strongmen. By 1932, both Mendoza in Tlaxcala and .Cedillo in San Luis Potosí had become a nuisance to Calles. How then, was the *potosino cacique* able to keep his grasp for six more years, while the *tlaxcalteco* fell swiftly from grace? After Obregón's assassination in July 1928, Calles was skillful enough to take advantage of the resulting crisis for the creation of a political instrument to discipline the revolutionary family. Within a few months most revolutionary parties and groups joined the *PNR* and had to accept the centralizing authority that emanated from it. In Tlaxcala, the government party *PST* adhered to the local *PNR* and Ignacio Mendoza became local *PNR* president. It was the struggle for power between the partisans of president Ortiz Rubio, aided by the powerful defence minister Joaquín Amaro, and the ambitious Portes Gil, with the *Jefe Máximo* as the decisive mediator, which provided the Tlaxcala opposition between 1930 and 1932 with new opportunities. Calles used Portes Gil to prevent Ortiz Rubio and Amaro from becoming too independent. He imposed him as president of the *PNR* in 1930 and permitted him to oust the *'blancos' Ortizrubistas* by his

27. On the basis of the national newspapers and the local political leaflets and reviews the same can be said about Apango's and Mendoza's image, see Buve, "Consolidating."

more radical '*rojos*'. It resulted in fierce struggle and mobilization in all Mexico, especially in Tlaxcala.[28]

Dissatisfied *socialistas*, old *maderistas* and *agraristas*, attracted by the banner of the '*rojos*', founded in October 1930 the *Partido Reinvindicador Tlaxcalteca* (*PRT*) to compete with the ruling group, which had, at least in part, strong *ortiz-rubista* sympathies. At least a hundred representatives, especially from southern villages, incensed by governor Vásquez' anti-*agrarista* attitudes, joined the convention of the *PRT*. When Portes Gil grew too independent, Calles replaced him as president of the *PNR* with the more neutral General Lázaro Cárdenas. At the end of 1931, Calles imposed his own reliable instrument, General Manuel Pérez Treviño, who was no friend of president Ortiz Rubio. The Tlaxcalan *PRT*, with an eye on the 1932 elections for governor and state deputies, sought adherence to the *PNR* and local recognition. Local *PNR* president Mendoza could not ignore this and tried to impose on the *PRT* total obedience to his socialist leadership and program within the local *PNR*. At first, *PRT* leadership was inclined to accept this. But some of the leaders revolted and headed for an open confrontation with the socialists. The *PRT* then launched the former *arenista*, General Adolfo Bonilla, a Pérez Treviño protégé, as their candidate for governor. The socialists launched Moises Huerta, a federal *ortizrubista* congressman and put behind their campaign the party and state bureaucracy, the local *CROM*, the *ejido* committees and the *uniones de resistencia*. With strong federal *PNR* support and military vigilance on election day, Bonilla won. The *socialistas* staged a coup to prevent Bonilla from reaching power but federal intervention installed a provisional governor who purged the local *PNR* and the bureaucracy and Bonilla became governor in 1933. Meanwhile, the opposition press highlighted the "*enrichissez vous*" mentality of the socialists mentioning, above all, the many rural estates of the now deposed ruling group.[29]

Why did the socialists lose? Mendoza did something which, by 1932, was already considered as particularly dangerous. This was ". . . *desobedecer las directivas del CEN del PNR, cuando éstas contaban con el apoyo del general Calles*" While Calles might have hesitated in the case of a *militia*-based chieftain or general, in this case a rebellion was quite unlikely and Calles used Pérez Treviño to apply the modern techniques of extending central control by mobilizing popular forces under *PNR* protection against the local *cacique*. Moreover, Calles and the *PNR*, the latter with an emerging more populist left-wing, did not have to look for local support. Governor Vásquez and his socialists certainly had merits because of their encouragement of education in the countryside, but Vásquez, in his anti-agrarian attitude, was even "*plus royalist que le roi*" (Calles), and known for his anti-*ejido* declarations and his strong compliance with Ortiz Rubio's policy to end land distribution. The opposition party, with support from the federal *PNR* was able to mobilize many peasants, even though they were threatened by socialist *ejido* committees, union leaders or "*gobiernista*" officials.[30]

How did Cedillo manage to maintain his fiefdom over San Luis Potosí? In the early 1930s, the power of Cedillo reached its zenith. It rested on a strong *cacicazgo*, with a private army, and, on a state-wide system of loyalties, mechan-

28. Meyer, "Revolución mexicana," 132-136; Ankerson, *Agrarian Warlord*, 141-142.

29. *El Noticiero* cit. 252 Jun. 27, 1931, 280 Feb. 13, 1932; *El Pueblo* cit. núm. 2 Nov. 1, 1930, núm. 8 Apr. 30, 1932; *El Socialista, órgano del Partido Socialista de Tlaxcala*, 67 Nov. 12, 1932. Meyer, "Revolución mexicana," 141-144; *El Pueblo* and *El Socialista* cit.; Ramírez Rancaño, "Socialismo en Tlaxcala," 78-80; Buve, "State Governors," 233-234.

30. Meyer, "Inicios de la institucionalización," 144; Buve, "Peasant Mobilization," 367-373; interviews with Ruben Carrizosa, Feb. and Mar. 1968. Carrizosa was a partisan of Bonilla. In 1930 governor Vásquez issued a strongly worded anti-*ejido* decree which was discussed by the opposition in the press: *La Prensa* and *El Universal*.

isms and checks, which in essence, operated outside the state, agrarian and *PNR* bureaucracies. Furthermore, Cedillo had become a pillar of the national régime playing an important role in Calles' policy of checks and balances to maintain his control over the presidency of the republic between 1928 and 1934. Cedillo's military autonomy, his independence of central bureaucracy and his often divergent local policies went against Calles' policy of bureaucratic centralization and control. However, Calles' attempts to retain power over his presidential successors made him vulnerable to the *"chantaje de los poderes locales"* as long as his *PNR* did not yet control local politics and popular mobilization at the grass-roots level. Moreover, the independence of Cedillo's *cacicazgo* probably would have left the federal government no option but military force. This could still provoke turmoil or even prompt other rebellions. During the *Maximato*, Cedillo's autonomy in crucial issues was impressive. He enlarged his *militias* to abôut 15,000 men and had complete control over the federal military in San Luis Potosí through his trusted friend and state military commander Alberto Carrera Torres. Cedillo was able to impose an illiterate *ranchero* as governor against the will of president Ortiz Rubio. He simply refused to antagonize the Church and private education by implementing the anti-clerical policies of the federal government. And he upheld the prestigious military status of his *agraristas*, while virtually all the others were eliminated by the federal government.

All this autonomy, of course, annoyed *Jefe Máximo* Calles and 'his' presidents, but for reason of *Real Politik*, the parties who vied for power over the *PNR* and the presidency often hesitated to touch a real or potential ally of importance. Cedillo, therefore, remained loyal, first to president Portes Gil, with whom he shared the idea that it would be advisable for the time being to stay with Calles. Cedillo served Portes Gil militarily against the *Cristeros* and the Escobar revolt (1929), supported Calles in his successful attempt to have Ortiz Rubio elected president (1930) and sided with Calles in his struggle to retain control over him. When Calles removed Ortiz Rubio in 1932, Cedillo loyally supported the new president Abelardo Rodríguez. Along with Portes Gil, he advocated the nomination of general Lázaro Cárdenas as the official candidate for the 1934-1940 presidential term. In doing so, the rural chieftain Cedillo aligned himself with an emerging group of '*agrarista*' radicals within the *PNR* who wanted to mobilize the masses and consolidate this power-base with important reforms in the fields of land, labour, religion and education. Quite a number of these radicals were civilian politicians with views and ways of organizing power-bases which were in opposition to Cedillo's interests.[31]

As is shown in the previous chapter, Cedillo lost the struggle with Cárdenas in 1938. Why then, did Cedillo opt for Cárdenas and these radicals? First of all, Cedillo wanted to safeguard his *cacicazgo*. In this he was no different from other *caciques* like Mendoza. Cedillo only had to read the newspapers or hear the Mexico City political gossip, to know that, whatever his own privileged position, the *callista* policy of bureaucratic centralization was encroaching upon him. By 1933 many of his fellow *caciques* had fallen. Himself an *agrarista*, be it of a conservative clientelist type, he found allies among the radicals who saw in the fall of the *agrarista* governor, Tejeda of Veracruz (1932) and the disarmament of his *militias*, another *callista* assault on reforms and local control over popular mobilization. On the other hand, personal motives may also have been involved. It is doubtful if Cedillo ever harboured real presidential ambitions, but he was certainly aspiring to a cabinet post or some national level position of corresponding

31. Falcón, *Revolución y caciquismo*, 223-230; Ankerson, *Agrarian Warlord*, 134-144, 149, 152-153.

political influence. But he did not use his position to seek a federal level power-base, but more to reinforce his local patronage: jobs and favours for 'his' men.

Calles and 'his' presidents only once invited Cedillo to a cabinet, and only for a short time. Cárdenas might reward him better and did so in 1935. Once in office, Cárdenas restored power to the presidency by removing Calles from his informal but spectacular influence in Mexican politics (1935). He reorganized the *PNR* into a strong presidential tool for popular mobilization and his reforms gave peasants, industrial workers, soldiers and government employees reasons for loyalty. By 1938, Cedillo had no other options but to follow the strategy of his local *potosino* competitor Gonzalo N. Santos. This *Huasteca cacique* recognized early that the only way to ensure his permanence in local power, and a future fiefdom over his home state, was to respect and use the new political rules: disavowal of independent armed force, the agreement to control and mobilize peasants and workers only through the official party' channels, and recognition of the central government's supremacy. Given the bases of the *cedillista cacicazgo*, its clientelistic network, and its traditional political culture, it would have been impossible to adapt the *potosino* fiefdom to this modernizing impulse. The era of independent, military-based revolutionary *caciques* had come to an end.[32]

## CONCLUSION

When taking the presidency from Carranza, the *Sonorenses* faced a whole gamut of different power situations at state level. It took about twenty years to forge and coordinate the many different regional political and military situations into standardized bureaucratic dependence on the central government. The *Sonorenses*, therefore, hesitated to intervene directly at the state level, since it might stir local *caciques* to revolt or create regional alliances against the central government. If possible, Obregón and Calles tried to remove enemies or less valuable contenders by careful manipulation of competing interests at the state level. Long-term objectives of transition from military to civilian power and from regional autonomy to dependence on a centralizing bureaucracy could only be realized by pragmatic policies. In each state level case, these policies had to take into account the real or potential power-bases of local contenders and the possible entanglements of local level interests with those emanating from the presidential palace.

In these respects, the cases of Tlaxcala and San Luis Potosí were strikingly different. To begin with, Carranza had already achieved by 1918 in Tlaxcala what Cárdenas only achieved between 1936 and 1938 in San Luis Potosí: the elimination of autonomous local power-bases. Apango and Mendoza, like Rojas before them, could only reach power by accepting full dependence on the central government, a situation not yet common in the Mexico of 1920. Since they had no military autonomous base, no peasant *militias* or significant popular bases of their own, they lacked the resources which Cedillo in San Luis Potosí could generate and exchange for almost complete autonomy and increasing national prominence. As a consequence, Calles could fully apply his policies in Tlaxcala, but he was forced to accept an independent development in San Luis Potosí. Whatever nuisance the *potosino cacicazgo* provoked to Calles, by 1934 Cedillo's power-base still had pre-1920 dimensions in terms of local control over armed forces, a pervasive revolutionary militarism in social and economic matters, and independence from

32. On Santos, see Meyer, "Revolución mexicana," Ch. II, 85-189; also Carlos Loret de Mola, *Los caciques* (Mexico City, 1979), Ch. 1.

federal bureaucracy and party organizations. Mendoza's power was internally based on control and extension of a government and party bureaucracy which used all instruments of state-derived patronage available through his connections with the federal government. When Calles decided to dislodge the Tlaxcala socialists he only had to wrest the state and party bureaucracy from their grasp. In sharp contrast, Cedillo proved able to construct and maintain his clientelistic network largely independent of the federal army and bureaucracy, as well as of the national and centralizing peasant and workers' organizations. Unlike Mendoza, he was basically autonomous of the mechanisms by which the *Sonorenses* concentrated power. As long as he managed to keep control over his political and military bases in San Luis Potosí, and to offer valuable services to the central authorities, it proved impossible to destroy his powerful *cacicazgo*. This was a task which awaited Cárdenas.

Whatever the difference between Tlaxcala and San Luis Potosí in terms of their relations to the *Sonorenses* and their internal patterns of reaching and maintaining power, it seems important to stress that both cases represent contrasting but characteristic forms of Mexican post-revolutionary *caciquismo*. To that extent they provide models of analysis that may shed light upon other regional power-bases of this era. Mendoza and Cedillo sought strong local and exclusive domains. They sought a monopoly of access to local political resources and to relations with the federal government. Cedillo managed, for the time being, to impose his own terms. This permitted him to remain distant from an emerging political culture quite alien to his ways. The result was a chieftaincy, turned into a state-wide *cacicazgo*, based on quite identical principles. Mendoza, on the other hand, had to accept the *Sonorenses* terms. The fact that his own political culture and that of his *camarilla* were much more in line with that of Calles, always more of an administrator than a general, may certainly have facilitated the development of a dependent civilian bureaucracy-based fiefdom. The latter political development anticipated a new form of *cacicazgo*: a weaker, less dependent, non-militaristic structure integrated in the national state, and subservient to its interests, but still able to use its dependent power for its local interests. To conclude, both in terms of their internal patterns and of their relations to the federal authorities, the cases of Tlaxcala and San Luis Potosí reflect the transitional character of the *sonorense* period: while Tlaxcala was much of a *novum* in 1920, San Luis Potosí was an anachronism when Cárdenas took office. In few years his once mighty fiefdom was wiped out.

Region, State and Capitalism
CEDLA, Amsterdam, 1989

CHAPTER NINE

# Paradoxes of Regional Power in Post-Revolutionary Mexico: The Rise of *Avilacamachismo* in Puebla, 1935-1940

WIL PANSTERS*

*"However, the predominance of central power is not synonymous with the absence of regional power."*

*Irma T. Corrales*[1]

## INTRODUCTION

In the conclusion of his study on the *cacicazgo* of Saturnino Cedillo in San Luis Potosí, Dudley Ankerson stated that at crucial moments Cedillo's military force contributed to the forging of a strong central state which, in turn, was able to oust him from his regional fiefdom.[2] As can be deduced from studies on regional *caciques* and movements led by men like Tomas Garrido in Tabasco, Saturnino Osornio in Querétaro and Adalberto Tejeda in Veracruz, the paradoxical process described by Ankerson in the case of San Luis Potosi applies to other regional contexts as well.[3] These *caciques* all rose to power as a result of their relations with the dominant faction of the revolutionary forces after 1920, i.e. the Sonoran group. Once in power, they implemented specific social and political projects -mostly in the agrarian field- radicalizing elements from the Constitution of 1917, and thus created a firm social base in their regions.

During the military uprisings of 1923 and 1929, the peasants and workers led by the *caciques* supported the presidents in office at the time and constituted a

---

* *Political Scientist, Center for Caribbean and Latin American Studies, University of Utrecht, Heidelberglaan 2, P.O. Box 80.140, 3508 TC Utrecht, The Netherlands.* *This essay is a slightly revised version of a chapter of a dissertation in progress.* *I would like to thank Sheila Gogol for her linguistic assistance.*

1. Irma Teresa Corrales, "Heterogenidad del estado y conflictos regionales. Desaparición de poderes en Hidalgo," in *Revista Mexicana de Sociologia* (hereafter *RMS*), 44:1 (1982), 120.

2. Dudley Ankerson, *Agrarian Warlord. Saturnino Cedillo and the Mexican Revolution in San Luis Potosí* (De Kalb, 1984), 197.

3. Carlos Martínez Assad, *El laboratorio de la revolución. El Tabasco garridista* (Mexico-City, 1979); "Los caudillos regionales y el poder central," in *Revolucionarios fueron todos*, Carlos Martínez Assad et.al., eds. (Mexico-City, 1982), 147-233; Romana Falcón, *El agrarismo en Veracruz. La etapa radical (1928-1935)* (Mexico-City, 1977).

major force in the defeat of the rebels. But the foundation of the *Partido Nacional Revolucionario* (*PNR*) in 1929, and to an even greater extent the start of large-scale reforms in the political system and agrarian policies during the Cárdenas period, challenged the legitimacy of the *caciques* which the previous political machinery of Calles and Obregón was based upon. Since they constituted powerful agrarian and military forces that could eventually endanger the process of centralization and institutionalization, they came to be viewed as a threat to the federal state.

Thus, ever since the beginning of the Cárdenas-*sexenio*, they all clashed with the federal army, the *PNR* and, later, the machinery of the *Partido Revolucionario Mexicano* (*PRM*), with its newly founded corporate peasant and labour organizations. The *Liga de Comunidades Agrarias*, the *Confederación Campesina Mexicana* (*CCM*) and the *Confederación Nacional Campesina* (*CNC*), which were set up on the regional level, all received full support from the Cárdenas government and attracted masses of peasants, thereby depriving the *caciques* of their power base. By 1940 the leaders of the regional movements had gone into exile, or been imprisoned or killed.[4] One might get the impression that by 1940, Mexico had been liberated from regional bosses and the path had been cleared for a smoothly operating centralized state. This suggestion is, in part, related to the fact that most studies limit their historical analysis to the crucial 1920-1940 period. The defeat and disappearance of important regional political movements by the end of the period seems to justify this.

However, the defeat of these particular regional forces did *not* imply the complete disappearance of regional power structures. It only implied that the conditions under which they could develop had substantially changed. The new rules in the recently founded state and party structures allowed for the development of new regional *cacicazgos*. In fact, paradoxical processes developed, whereby regional politicians aware of the political potential of the new situation were able to assert themselves in their respective domains. In this article, I want to illustrate this process with the case of Puebla, where the foundations for a *cacicazgo* around the family Avila Camacho were laid during the 1930s, when the aforementioned regional political movements were considered a threat to the centralization and institutionalization of state power and were subsequently eliminated. During the next three decades, the *avilacamachistas* became the dominant political force in Puebla. They managed to reserve the governorship for the members of a tiny clique of politicians, established around 1940, which controlled the key positions in the institutional and social system. The case is particularly interesting because it concerns the rise of an openly conservative *cacicazgo* during the heyday of *cardenismo*.

My main object is to analyze the circumstances and mechanisms that facilitated the emergence of *avilacamachismo* as the leading political force in *poblano* politics. For that purpose, I shall examine *avilacamachista* labour politics, the composition of the regional bourgeoisie and its relations with the political elite. In the final sections, I shall focus on *avilacamachismo* as it extended its political network to several crucial institutions in civil society, and shall examine how its discourse was organized.

4. Carlos Martínez Assad, "La rebellión cedillista o el ocaso del poder tradicional," in *RMS*, 41:3 (1979), 709-728, esp. 728.

## THE FORMATION OF A POLITICAL GROUP

The *Avila-Camachos* came from Teziutlán, a town in the *Sierra Norte de Puebla*, where the family was engaged in small-scale muleteering. One of the firms they worked for was a mining company, owned by the family of Vicente Lombardo Toledano. Maximino Avila Camacho later frequently used this fact to attack the political radicalism of one of Mexico's most prominent union leaders and intellectuals. In his youth, Maximino had thus worked with his father as a muleteer, and as a cowhand on nearby *haciendas* and, by the time the Revolution started, as a salesman for a foreign company.[5] Although he took part in the Revolution, very little is known about his military career. Even one of his most faithful followers, a local journalist, was not able to produce any detailed information about him, and simply concluded that Avila Camacho was said to have always been *"present at the places of utmost danger and responsibility."*[6] However, the complete lack of references to his military achievements during the Revolution and the fact that his brother Manuel is considered a general who made his career within the military bureaucracy and party system rather than on the battle fields, point in another direction: Maximino was just another *Artemio Cruz*.[7] Except for his most docile admirers and followers, he has been described as a harsh and ruthless *caudillo militar* who did not hesitate to eradicate any opposition to his policy. As a dedicated admirer of bullfights and *charro*-costumes and a man not free of vanity, he responded to the image of the 'new self-made strongman' needed to put the political and social instability in Puebla to an end.[8] In 1931, a group of local politicians and journalists already invited him to become governor of Puebla because:[9]

> *" . . . hace algunos años, cuando algunos poblanos veíamos con profundo dolor la tragédia moral y material, en que se debatía nuestro Estado . . . nos echamos a cuestas la difícil tarea de buscar al Hombre excepcional que pudiera salvarlo. De este modo fue como . . . fuimos a peregrinacion romántica . . . a la ciudad de Aguascalientes, a ofrecer al señor general Maximino Avila Camacho que a la sazón era jefe militar de aquella entidad, su candidatura para gobernador del estado de Puebla."*

The romantic admirers had to wait another six years before their 'exceptional man' would make it to the top.

This then raises the question of the conditions that eventually led to Maximino Avila Camacho's rise to governor. This can only be answered by a brief description of the political situation in Puebla from the end of the 1920s until 1937. Unlike the neighbouring state of Veracruz, where Tejeda established solid control during the second part of the 1920s, Puebla was characterized by a high degree of political instability and factional disputes at the time. No less than nineteen governors 'ruled' this strategically important state between 1920 and 1930, some

5. Daniel Blumenkron, *Maximino Avila Camacho. El hombre, el militar, el estadista* (Puebla, 1943), 64. See also, Jorge Arrazola C., "La formación del poder político en Puebla (1934-1940)" (Unpublished thesis, Universidad Autónoma de Puebla, 1987), 16-22.

6. Blumenkron, *Maximino*, 15.

7. With respect to Manuel Avila Camacho, see Alicia Hernández Chávez, "La mecánica cardenista," en *Historia de la Revolución Mexicana*, (Mexico-City, 1979) XVI, 113.

8. These remarks have been taken from conversations with former collaborators of Maximino and witnesses. The image of the 'ruthless macho' is excellently described by Angeles Mastretta in her novel *Arráncame la vida* (Mexico-City, 1985), based on the life of Maximino's wife Margarita Richardi.

9. Blumenkron, *Maximino*, 5.

of them following a radical *agrarista* course, as was the case with Sánchez and Montes. In response to the sudden death of Obregón (1928), Calles' national policy of checking a renewed dispersion of power and a possible revival of armed factional disputes, was thus highly relevant for the state of Puebla. The notion of founding a new revolutionary party coincided with the regional elections for governor in 1929 in Puebla. Two factions, both linked to the *PNR*, vied for the official nomination: one led by *callista* politician Mijares Palencia and the other by Leonides Andrew Almazán, who was connected to Tejeda in Veracruz. Since the latter had a difficult relationship with the political centre of the country, in which *callismo* was strongly entrenched, it seemed likely that Calles would support Mijares, thereby counteracting the spread of *tejedismo* to Puebla. However, things turned out differently, probably because Calles realized that an Almazán-Tejeda alliance *outside* the *PNR*-machinery would endanger his policy of unification and institutionalization even more.[10]

As a result, Almazán was elected governor in 1929. During his term in office, Puebla was confronted with grave economic problems caused by the international depression of the 1930s. Puebla was one of the states with the highest levels of urban and rural unemployment.[11] In response to this critical situation, Almazán launched a radical land distribution programme affecting 210,000 hectares between 1929 and 1933, a dimension that was not even reached during the Cárdenas era. The policies produced sharp conflicts, not only with the more moderate leaders in Mexico City, but also with the *poblano* deputies to the federal congress, clearly identified with *callismo*. Because of this pressure, Almazán finally had to resign in January 1933.[12]

In the meantime the federal deputies from Puebla, including Gonzalo Bautista Castillo, who was to become one of the leading politicians in the years to come, had created the *Centro Encauzador de la Opinión Revolucionaria de Puebla* in order to influence the electoral process of 1932. The *Centro Encauzador* successfully supported Mijares Palencia in his second attempt to become governor against the candidate from the Almazán faction. During the regime of Mijares (1933-1937), control by the centre over *poblano* politics increased and the influence of the *PNR* was augmented. The foundation of municipal committees of the *PNR* in the state of Puebla was one of the main instruments in this strategy. During the municipal elections at the beginning of 1937, the *PNR* nominated candidates in 203 of the 215 electoral districts.[13] Parallel to the national developments, agricultural redistribution policies slowed down tremendously during the Mijares government. (Only a third of the quantity distributed by Almazán).

However, during the 1933-1937 period an important change in the relations of power occurred on the national level. The attacks by Cárdenas on the political strongholds of *callismo*, in combination with an outburst of strikes during the first half of 1935, provoked Calles' well-known intervention in June of that year, criticizing Cárdenas and the working classes for destabilizing the country's economic and political system. In response to this challenge, Cárdenas mobilized the rural and urban masses in support of his policies, replaced *callista* followers in the *PNR* and started the large-scale removal of governors strongly identified with Calles. By the end of 1935, the relations of power favoured Cárdenas and Calles left the country. During this period, Cárdenas started with the replacement of

10. Julio Glockner, "La presencia del Estado en el medio rural (Puebla, 1929-1941)," (Unpublished thesis, Universidad Autónoma de Puebla, 1982), 19-20.
11. Victor González Lara, "La desocupación en Puebla durante la depresión de los años treinta," in: *Boletín de Investigación del Movimiento Obrero* (hereafter *Boletín IMO*), 7:10 (1987), 120.
12. Hernández Chávez, "Mecánica cardenista," 86.
13. *Diario de Puebla*, 1/II/1937.

*jefes militares* in order to fortify his position in the states. As part of this reorganization, Maximino Avila Camacho was stationed as new *jefe militar* in Puebla in 1935. He thus entered state politics at a decisive moment to ensure support for Cárdenas in Puebla.

Once Maximino had become *jefe militar*, he began to organize the first (informal) layers of what was to become an enduring regional power structure. He restructured the military organization of Puebla and thus obtained control over the entire state. Before this reorganization, the *Sierra Norte de Puebla* was under the command of the Tlaxcalan military and the city of Puebla was controlled by the *Guarnición de la Plaza* directly under the command of the governor. Avila Camacho simultaneously stimulated the creation of *guardias blancas* -armed peasants and workers who supposedly were there to maintain law and order but operated in fact on behalf of local *caciques* and landowners. He furthermore restructured the *defensas sociales*, which depended directly on the army, and thereby enlarged his personal influence. Maximino was thus able to build up a rural paramilitary force that was ready to support him in subsequent years and to suppress rural dissent.[14]

It is important to note that the appointment of Avila Camacho did not trigger off a clash between *callistas* and *cardenistas* in Puebla. Although the members of the majority faction of the state congress, including Bautista Castillo, had supported Calles after his violent intervention of June 1935, they shrewdly switched their loyalties, becoming the *Bloque Cardenista*, when it became clear that Calles was fighting a losing battle. They were soon to become an essential part of Avila Camacho's group. The absence of any opposition between *cardenistas* and *callistas* in Puebla can be understood if we take into consideration the existence of a more radical *PNR* faction. This *poblano* left wing, represented in the local and federal parliament by followers of Almazán, was linked to an active labour movement.[15] So, within the political arena of Puebla around 1935 and 1936, two opposing currents existed that could not be reduced to the same ones as on the national level. There was the dominant faction that had jumped from the *callista* to the *cardenista* bandwagon and the *almazánistas*, whose main fortress was in the *Frente Regional de Obreros y Campesinos* (*FROC*).

In 1936, these two factions, one led by Maximino Avila Camacho and Gonzalo Bautista Castillo and the other by Gilberto Bosques and Leonides Andrew Almazán, competed for the nomination of a new governor and senator of the state of Puebla. Avila Camacho was supported by the local congress, the *Confederación Regional de Obreros Mexicanos* (*CROM*), several newspapers and peasant organizations, including the *Confederación Campesina Emiliano Zapata*. Bosques received the support of the *FROC*, its political arm, the *Alianza Revolucionaria de Obreros y Campesinos del Estado* (*AROCE*) and the influential regional newspaper *La Opinión*. But when the support given by the leader of the *Confederación Campesina Emiliano Zapata* to Avila Camacho was withdrawn by his constituency, the relations of power changed completely. With Bosques backed up by the most important peasants' and workers' organizations, Avila Camacho virtually stood no chance of winning the nomination. In order to reverse an imminent defeat, the *avilacamachistas* triggered off a wave of violence and intimidation against the *bosquistas*, resulting in numerous fatalities. Moreover, a day before the internal *PNR* elections, dozens of buses from Mexico City and elsewhere, carrying hundreds of *avilacamachista* 'voters,' poured into the city of Puebla, making the elections a complete sham. However, a few weeks later Portes Gil, president of the *PNR* at the time, conceded victory to Avila Camacho.

14. Arrazola, "Formación," 24-30.

15. I will elaborate upon this point in the next section.

Despite frequent denunciations and massive demonstrations, some of which were in the country's capital, Portes Gil was able to stand by his decision. And Cárdenas . . . he was said to be ill, when 30,000 members of the *FROC* marched through the streets of Mexico City. Why? Cárdenas had expressed confidence in Avila Camacho by sending him to Puebla as *jefe militar*, in return for loyalty to his faction. As long as Maximino Avila Camacho did not betray his adherence to Cárdenas, there was no reason to switch his support to another local faction. An underlying factor was also the intimate relationship between Cárdenas and Maximino's brother Manuel, who had by then become Secretary of War in the national cabinet. Viewed from the regional angle, this alliance constituted the critical leverage for Maximino in carrying out his policies. The defeat of Bosques and Almazán implied that internal partisan divisions were coming to an end, although it would be another four years before things would be completely settled.

Once in power, Maximino Avila Camacho appointed friends, relatives and fellow *teziutecos* to key positions in the state and party bureaucracy. His brother Rafael became head of the *poblano PNR* and, later, mayor of the city of Puebla. Another brother, Gabriel, was appointed chief of police. Others, like Díaz Pumarino and Fausto M. Ortega, became mayor of Teziutlán and later federal deputy, and several comrades in arms occupied important public positions. Maximino carefully prevented his collaborators from forming their own personal clientèle so that only he continued to be the central figure within the clientelistic network.[16] Using this network, he controlled departments, parliament and the main cities, i.e. the most important political institutions of the state. In the end, the result was the complete dominance of Avila Camacho's group in *poblano* politics. An example of this is the fact that in 1939, a *Pacto de Honor* was signed by the members of the state parliaments between 1937 and 1940, stating that,[17]

1. they will act and direct their followers to act in a coordinated and united manner during the coming social and political events, pertaining to the elections of 1940;
2. they will recognize Maximino Avila Camacho as the exclusive leader in political and social affairs and will respond to him with loyalty, cooperation and discipline;
3. they will do their utmost to struggle for the group as a collectivity, and be willing to sacrifice one of its members;
4. they will form a closed group and exclude people from outside the state of Puebla in its political affairs.

Concepts such as unity, discipline, loyalty and closure clearly reflected the coherence and hierarchy involved in the 'political pillar' of a regional power structure.

Exactly one year later, a group was formed that was to guide the elections process for governor, called the *Comite Directivo Electoral*. Its president was Gonzalo Bautista Castillo, who was simultaneously nominated candidate and actually became governor between 1941 and 1945. The group also consisted of Carlos I. Betancourt of the popular sector of the *PRM*, Fausto M. Ortega, parliamentary representative of the *PRM*, Antonio Nava Castillo representing the military sector of the *PRM*, Aaron Merino Fernández of the agrarian sector of the *PRM* and Gustavo Díaz Ordaz representing the labour sector of the same party. The significance of this group in terms of political dominance and stability is illustrated by the following data: the man behind the group, Maximino Avila Camacho, was governor between 1937 and 1941, Gonzalo Bautista, governor between 1941 and 1945, Carlos I. Betancourt, governor between 1945 and 1951, Fausto M. Ortega,

16. Arrazola, "Formación," 90-95.

17. *Diario de Puebla*, 3/I/1939.

governor between 1957 and 1963, Antonio Nava Castillo was governor in 1963 and 1964 and Aaron Merino Fernández was governor between 1965 and 1969. If we add to this that Maximino's younger brother Rafael governed the state between 1951 and 1957 and that another brother, Manuel, was president of Mexico between 1940 and 1946, as was Gustavo Díaz Ordaz between 1964 and 1970, it becomes clear what a powerful political group was formed in Puebla at the end of the 1930s. This can be partly explained by the links between Maximino Avila Camacho and the central state. However, the emergence of this political group as the core of a *new power structure* can only be understood if its regional articulation is fully taken into consideration. For that purpose, I shall examine *avilacamachista* labour policies, the composition of the regional bourgeoisie and its relations with the political group. In the final sections I shall focus on how the *avilacamachistas* were related to crucial institutions of civil society and their political discourse.

## URBAN AND RURAL LABOUR

Before I proceed to discuss the *avilacamachista* labour politics, I would like to briefly describe the history of *poblano* unionism during the 1920s and the first half of the 1930s in order to put the subsequent developments in their historical perspective.

During the presidency of Obregón, the increasing influence of the *CROM* was clearly evident in Puebla, where it operated under the name *Confederación Sindicalista del Estado de Puebla*. These were years of political instability, largely due to the struggles among local *caciques* linked to different factions on the national level. Governor José María Sánchez, who assumed power in 1921, had a secret mutual support agreement with the *CROM*. The activities of the *CROM* in those days mainly consisted of fighting for the recognition of unionism, especially within the important industrial region of Atlixco. When Sánchez started openly pursuing *agrarista* policies, the agreement with the *CROM* was abandoned, as the union became hostile to the *Partido Nacional Agrarista* (*PNA*) during the second half of Obregón's regime. Froylan Manjarrez, who succeeded Sánchez in 1922, also entered into an alliance with the *CROM* and supported the struggle against recalcitrant entrepreneurs unwilling to recognize the right to unionize. But when the governor claimed to be a partisan of De la Huerta during his revolt, the agreement came to an abrupt end; the *CROM*, mobilizing approximately 10,000 workers in Puebla, supported Obregón and Calles.[18]

But the *poblano agraristas*, led by Montes and Sánchez, also contributed to the defeat of De la Huerta. Nevertheless, it was the *CROM* that was able to capitalize on its decisive role in the defeat of the revolt: *CROM* militant Vicente Lombardo Toledano was governor in 1923 and 1924. In the meantime, the clashes between the *CROM* and the non-affiliated workers had reached a peak. This undoubtedly contributed to the political instability in the state during the next two years, a period in which Puebla had no fewer than six governors. In the course of 1925 the struggle against the non-affiliated workers was won by the *CROM*, which thus gained control of the textile workers. It should be noted that in 1924, Calles had assumed the presidency, a fact that enormously increased the influence of the *CROM* throughout the nation. While the *CROM* largely controlled the urban

18. Fabio Barbosa Cano, *La CROM, de Luis Morones a Antonio J. Hernández* (Puebla, 1980), 25-26.

workers, the *agraristas* still held the strongest positions in the countryside. These relations of power were to see to it that *agrarista*-leader Montes assumed power as governor in 1926. His government was characterized by polarization and the battle between the *agraristas* and the *cromistas*, especially in the countryside. It even led the *cromistas* to proclaim their own governor in 1927. In fact, it was a reflection of the conflict that took shape on the national level between Calles (supported by the *CROM*) and Obregón (supported by the *PNA*). Montes, like Tejeda, Mugica and Carillo Puerto, belonged to a clique of important *agrarista* leaders, who had become highly influential on the national level and had founded the *Liga Nacional Campesina* (*LNC*). The *CROM* opposed Montes' *ejido*-policies and accused him of cultivating communist sympathies. The *CROM* was involved in the assassination of Montes in 1927. The murder was followed by the nomination of Donato Bravo Izquierdo, of *callista* origin, as governor.[19] With the arrival of Bravo Izquierdo, the *CROM* received the full support of the regional state and started an offensive against the *agraristas* in the countryside. That is why the *CROM* in Puebla changed its name into *Confederación de Sindicatos de Obreros y Campesinos del Estado de Puebla* in 1927.

However, the tide turned in 1928 and 1929, when the *CROM* was hit by a severe political crisis caused by the murder of Obregón and Portes Gil seized power. That was when two currents within the *poblano CROM* became discernible. Their roots went back to 1925, when radical *poblano cromistas* refused to submit to the centralized and reformist line of their national leader (Morones). The first current, led by Limón, pursued a reformist line and continued to exist under the name of *Confederación de Sindicatos*; secondly, the radical and dissident faction, led by Escamilla and Coca, founded the *Confederación Sindicalista*.[20] This union entered into an alliance with governor Leonides Andrew Almazán (1929-1933).[21] The years of Almazán's rule in Puebla were not only characterized by a growing fragmentation of the labour movement as a result of the fissures within the old *CROM*, but also by a severe economic crisis. On the other hand, the fragmentation itself pressed the working class to construct a new umbrella organization.[22] From 1929 onwards, the dissident faction became dominant in the city of Puebla, and the weakened *CROM* withdrew to smaller cities such as Cholula, Atlixco and San Martín Texmelucan.

In 1934, the *Confederación Sindicalista* joined the new national *Confederación General de Obreros y Campesinos de Mexico* (*CGOCM*) founded by Lombardo Toledano. It changed its name to *Frente Regional de Obreros y Campesinos del Estado de Puebla* (*FROC*). The *FROC* exercised predominant influence on the arbitration board for capital and labour disputes, the *Junta de Conciliación y Arbitraje*, and during Mijares' term in office it played the role of the radical ideological vanguard of the working classes. The governor, unable to put an end to

19. Barbosa Cano, *La CROM*, 38-41; Clark, *La organizacion obrera en Mexico* (Mexico, 1984), 109-121; Leticia Gamboa, "La CROM en Puebla y el movimiento obrero textil en los años 20," in *Memorias del encuentro sobre historia del movimiento obrero* (Puebla, 1980) I, 53.

20. Gamboa, "La CROM en Puebla," 57.

21. There are various opinions on this problem. Cano argues that Almazán and the *CROM* were both involved in a struggle against the recently formed *PNR* and thus agreed on an alliance, whereas Gamboa (1980) puts forward that Almazán's victory implied a marginalization of the reformist *CROM*. Probably the controversy is related to the split in the *CROM* in 1929. In the light of subsequent developments, I prefer the second interpretation. See, Gamboa, "La CROM en Puebla," 33-67.

22. Teresa Bonilla, "La desorganización de los trabajadores poblanos durante la gran depresión de 1929 a 1933," in *Boletín de IMO*, 6:9 (1986) 93-103; Samuel León, "Cardenas en el poder," in *Evolución del Estado Mexicano*, Javier Garciadiego et.al (Mexico, 1986) II, 224.

the violent animosity between the *FROC* and the *CROM*, turned to Abelardo Rodríguez. However, the president refused to provide federal intervention and left the solution of the problem to the state authorities. When the *FROC* refused to accept the compromise proposed by Mijares at the beginning of 1935, it called out a general strike. It was the imminent threat of another outburst of inter-union struggle and violence, that made the *CROM* appeal for government protection. Since the *FROC* had rejected proposals for a compromise and negotiations, and had thereby gone beyond the limits of state corporatism, the army fiercely repressed the strike. Being *jefe militar*, Maximino Avila Camacho was responsible for the military action. As a consequence, his relations with the *FROC* were antagonized. At the same time friendly relations between the future governor of Puebla and the *CROM* were established.

However, the change in the relations of power on the national level that took place in the midst of 1935, favoring the *Cardenistas*, and the concomitant strengthening of the working classes, bore fruit in Puebla as well. The *FROC* was able to capitalize on the intense mobilization of the working classes and win the municipal elections for the 1936-1937 period. Despite the opposition from the regional parliament and the governor, who cut financial resources to the municipal government, a workers council ruled the city of Puebla for one year.[23]

During the first half of 1936, the *FROC* was thus confident enough to confront a possible candidacy of Maximino Avila Camacho to succeed Mijares and nominated its own man: Gilberto Bosques. Avila Camacho reacted immediately by launching severe attacks against the *FROC*. In this strategy, and in the light of the events during the general strike of 1935, the *CROM*, arch-enemy of the *FROC*, turned out to be an ideal ally for Maximino, causing a renewed explosion of inter-union conflict, mainly in the Atlixco region. The weakened position of the *CROM* made it relatively easy for Maximino to discipline and mobilize the union in his struggle against Bosques. Conversely, the alliance was welcomed by the *CROM* because it provided the opportunity to strengthen its position *vis-a-vis* the *FROC*. The essential political dilemma the *FROC* found itself in was that, as a member of the *CTM* it did not subscribe to the official -i.e. *PNR*- candidate, Maximino Avila Camacho, who could thus effectively claim political action from the centre against supposed lack of discipline, when 30,000 *froquistas* demonstrated in Mexico City against his nomination.[24] From this moment on, differences between the *FROC*-Puebla and the *CTM*-Mexico became painfully clear and future divisions were in the air.

The *poblano CROM* took advantage of this course of events. When Avila Camacho finally won the elections, the *FROC* suffered a severe blow. Cárdenas' refusal to intervene left the union virtually without powerful allies. At the same time, however, the *froquistas* Blas Chumacero and Francisco Márquez were *PNR* candidates for the local parliament. When they agreed to support the candidacy of Avila Camacho, the road for cooptation was free and the threat of divisions within the *FROC* became imminent. Once in power, Maximino not only put political and physical pressure on the *FROC*, he also made use of legal manoeuvres to favour the *CROM* and reduce *froquista* influence. In 1938, the *Junta de Conciliación*, which had been the domain of the *FROC* for many years, was restructured in a way that favoured the *CROM*. In the same year, a well-known anti-*froquista* was appointed government representative on the important board of arbitration: Gustavo Díaz Ordaz. These decisions led to a considerable increase in the amount

---

**23.** Jorge Arrazola C., "La Comuna de 1936 en Puebla: un ensayo de gestión obrera," in *Boletín IMO*, 7:10 (1987) 39-52.

**24.** Teresa Ventura Rodríguez, "La FROC en Puebla, 1942-1952," in *Memorias del encuentro sobre historia del movimiento obrero* (Puebla, 1980) II, 234.

of 'illegal' strikes.[25] Furthermore, the governor proposed to the regional parliament in 1938 that local elections in the districts where the *FROC* was strongly represented be declared null and void.

Although the *FROC* had suffered several setbacks since 1935, when it first felt the aggression of the rising *avilacamachista* group, the decisive blow did not come until 1939. In that year, Manuel Avila Camacho was nominated as presidential candidate for the *PRM*. Maximino's brother received full support from the *CTM*, led by fellow *teziuteco* Lombardo Toledano, while the *CROM* supported the opposition candidate Juan Andrew Almazán, a brother of the former governor of Puebla. In Puebla, however, the situation was just the reverse. The *FROC* (*CTM*-Puebla) was unwilling to back Avila Camacho, because it was aware of the fact that with a triumph of Manuel in Mexico City, *avilacamachismo* in Puebla would certainly continue to be in power. Thus it rebelled, and in the end, supported Almazán because of their good political relations in former years.[26] At the same time, Antonio J. Hernández, the local leader and future strongman of the *CROM*, signed a secret pact with Maximino Avila Camacho promising to stand behind his brother.[27] This situation may seem paradoxical at first, but is completely comprehensible if the histories of the relations of power on the national and regional level are taken into consideration.

The dilemma the *FROC* faced at the beginning of 1939 was whether to follow the course set out by the *CTM* and to stand behind Manuel Avila Camacho, or to maintain its independent anti-*avilacamachista* stance, which implied a rupture with the *CTM* and an affiliation with the right-wing opposition led by Almazán. Within the ranks of the *FROC*, adherents of both options were present. The majority formed the *almazánista* wing headed by Escamilla and Rivera. They refused to subscribe to the *CTM* directives with respect to the presidential elections, but in general resisted the tendency of centralized union control. The minor *avilacamachista* current, led by Coca, Chumacero and Márquez -the last two had become strongly articulated with governor Avila Camacho since they signed the significant *pacto de honor*- proclaimed obedience to the national confederation and consequently supported Manuel Avila Camacho. The inevitable result was that the majority group separated the *FROC* from the *CTM* in July 1939. The *CTM* was then forced to found a new union in Puebla that would be loyal to the central decision-makers. The *Federación de Trabajadores del Estado de Puebla* (*FTP*) was born.[28] The *FTP* received the full support of the local government, while the dissident *FROC* could only count on another wave of violence from the regional state.

One could say that, by the end of 1939, the *avilacamachistas* had managed to dramatically modify the relations between the different unions to their own advantage and to increase their influence on the labour movement. The *avilacamachistas* had had an alliance with the *CROM* since 1936. During the 1940s, the *CROM* was able to regain considerable influence in cities like Atlixco, San Martín Texmelucan and Cholula *"a la sombra del cacicazgo avilacamachista."* The revival of the *CROM* was also due to the policy of national unity put forward by the president. In fact, the *CROM* from Puebla turned into be the strongest faction within the national union and, as a consequence, Antonio J. Hernández be-

25. D. Malpica, "Las Juntas de Conciliación y Arbitraje en Puebla, 1931-1940," in *Memorias*, II, 143.

26. Jesus Márquez Carillo, "Los orígenes del avilacamachismo," (Unpublished thesis, Universidad Autónoma de Puebla, 1983), 211; Ventura, "La FROC en Puebla," 215; Malpica, "Las Juntas de Conciliación," 143.

27. Barbosa Cano, *La CROM*, 68.

28. Teresa Ventura, "La consolidación de la FTP-CTM en Puebla, 1938-1952," in *Boletin IMO*, 7:10 (1987), 54-55.

came federal deputy for the *CROM* in 1943 and actually took over the union. In contrast, from the day it was founded, the *avilacamachistas* built up a close relationship with the *FTP*. In the years to come, the *FTP* was to be a highly important ally of the regional state and a vehicle for workers' control. With it, Blas Chumacero became the most salient labour leader in Puebla since the early 1940s. Under his regime, the *FTP* was to identify itself with the interests of the 'official' party (*PRM-PRI*). Finally, the recalcitrant *FROC* was successfully weakened in a series of conflicts. After the defeat of the *almazanistas* in the elections of 1940, it received the final blow. Several leaders, including Escamilla, were killed by *avilacamachistas*. Moreover, the *FROC* was deprived of its seats in the regional congress and the *Junta de Conciliación* and its strikes were declared 'illegal'. With no organizational links to a national union, the *FROC* thus entered a period of serious decline. When it finally became part of the *Confederación Proletaria Nacional* in 1942, it was soon to lose its radicalism and start to function within the borders of official labour politics.[29]

To sum up, the fragmentation of the *poblano* labour movement, which followed the disintegration of the *CROM* in 1929, brought with it an intense and violent struggle between rivalling factions. It was during the government of Maximino Avila Camacho that a process of re-unification and 'pacification' took place by way of coopting some unions and attacking others, which in the end resulted in an increased control of the labour movement by the regional state.

Tendencies towards the encapsulation of the rural masses into the state machinery were similar to those witnessed in urban areas. During the 1920s, various peasant organizations were active in the *poblano* countryside: the *Liga de Comunidades Agrarias*, which was linked to the *Partido Comunista Mexicano* (*PCM*), the *Confederación General de Trabajo*, with anarchist tendencies, the *Partido Nacional Agrarista*, linked to Obregón and obviously the *CROM*. During the governorship of Almazán a great deal of attention was devoted to agrarian policies. After Mijares Palencia had come to power, however, things rapidly changed as the more radical organizations, especially the ones linked to the *PCM*, were harassed and repressed by the regional state. These developments were exacerbated by the grave effects of the world-wide depression on the rural economy in Puebla, causing unemployment, a fall in real wages and tense relations between the social classes.[30]

During the 1930s, the Puebla countryside was characterized by multifarious conflicts among peasants, *caciques*, *ejido* leaders and large landowners. Furthermore, there were *bandoleros* roaming rural Puebla when Maximino rose to power. In an attempt to pacify and subject trouble-ridden areas to his influence, the new governor immediately launched a military campaign against these groups. A second mechanism to diminish rural unrest was the articulation of the local *caciques* to his government, as happened for example in Zacapoaxtla. It was actually a two-sided process. In order to incorporate their constituencies into the system, regional and national power-holders articulated the existing local *cacicazgos*. Many *caciques* understood that serving as intermediaries within the new state and party structures would enable them to maintain local control. Those who were unwilling to adjust to Avila Camacho's supremacy suffered repression.[31]

---

29. Barbosa Cano, *La CROM*, 73, 83-88; Ventura, "La FROC," 236.

30. Julio Glockner, "Presencia del Estado," 1-17, 55-56; Márquez, "Orígenes del avilacamachismo," 212-219.

31. For an excellent analysis of the struggle in the context of an *ejido*, see David Ronfeldt, *Atencingo. La política de la lucha agraria en un ejido mexicano* (Mexico City, 1975). Márquez, "Origines," 152-155; Luisa Pare, "Caciquismo y estructura de poder en la Sierra

The third and most important mechanism to cope with rural conflict was the government's effort to check the wide range of rural organizations frequently operating with conflicting strategies in different regions. This effort was completely in line with *cardenista* policies to unify and bring the peasant masses under state tutelage.[32] The first step in that direction was the foundation of the *Confederación Campesina Emiliano Zapata* during the electoral campaign of Maximino Avila Camacho. Although it exhibited signs of dissidence towards Maximino at the beginning, it became the most important peasant union during the 1936-1938 period in promoting the land distribution policies. However, an organization was founded in 1938 that was to group together the whole array of small peasant unions: the *Liga de Comunidades Agrarias y Sindicatos Campesinos del Estado de Puebla* (*LCA*). This umbrella league entered into the *Confederación Nacional Campesina* and thus automatically into the federal machinery of the *PRM*. On the regional level, this organization became directly linked to the *avilacamachistas* as Sacramento Joffre, leader of the *LCA*, signed the *pacto de honor* with Maximino, which tied him to *avilacamachista* policies.

## THE BOURGEOISIE

The overlapping of the politically and economically dominant classes has been put forward as the determining feature of *avilacamachismo*. Although other domains of influence -for example in the labour movement- are equally important, the relations between the *avilacamachistas* and the regional bourgeoisie were excellent and deserve special attention. Although at the threshold of the 1930s Puebla, as the rest of the country, had a predominant agricultural economy, it was also one of Mexico's most highly developed industrial states.

Like in colonial and porfirian times, *poblano* industry mainly consisted of the production of textiles. The dominant fraction of the *poblano* bourgeoisie owned the medium and large-scale textile enterprises, approximately twenty in number.[33] The families were of Spanish origin and controlled their capital investments in a traditional 'family-centered' manner. In economic terms, the group was closed, leading to oligarchic tendencies. It implied that a small number of families -Conde y Conde, Rivero Quijano, Gavito Quijano, Gavito Méndez, Díaz Rubin, Artas Sánchez, Arce Pellon- actually dominated the *poblano* bourgeoisie at the time. These families not only constituted an economically closed entity, but also one that was socially and culturally closed. Marriage within the Spanish community was the rule, and a great deal of energy was devoted to retaining Spanish ethnicity, mainly by founding such institutions as the *Sociedad de Benificiencia Española*, the *Casino* and *Círculo Español*. Furthermore, conservative Catholicism was essential to the cultural identity of the group. These characteristics are all indicative of an inner-oriented class consciousness, in which the compartmentalization and hierarchization of society were central values. The strong involvement with the narrow *poblano* context added to this a regional characteristic.

Politically, this fraction had excellent relations with important politicians during the porfirian age, the period during which they made their fortunes. When the

---

Norte de Puebla," in *Caciquismo y poder político en el Mexico rural*, Roger Bartra et.al., eds. (Mexico City, 1985), 47; Arrazola, "Formación," 116-120.

32. Arnaldo Córdova, *La política de masas del cardenismo* (Mexico City, 1984), 116.

33. Leticia Gamboa, *Los empresarios de ayer. El grupo dominante en la industria textil de Puebla, 1906-1929* (Puebla, 1986), 51-76.

Revolution broke out, some of its members left the country, but returned after military hostilities came to an end. They soon regrouped and reorganized in order to counteract the revolutionary transformations proposed by the regime. A powerful organization that served their interests was the *Centro Industrial Mexicano Puebla*, (*CIMP*), founded in 1906. The *CIMP* survived until 1936, when the *Cámara de Industria Textil de Puebla y Tlaxcala* was founded. The attitude towards the new regime can be illustrated by the resistance against the more radical policies of the *agrarista* governments during the 1920s, whereas they welcomed *callista* Mijares Palencia in 1933. It was from this moment on that the *poblano* bourgeoisie started renewing its close links with the politically dominant group, a process that intensified during the government of Maximino Avila Camacho. It was in particular the establishment of political and social stability in the state of Puebla that earned him the confidence of the porfirian economic elites and created the basis for unproblematic capital accumulation. The suppression of violent inter-union rivalries, the elimination of rural *bandolerismo*, the disappearance of political factionalism and an accentuated anti-reformism constituted the most important elements in this respect. With Avila Camacho, the interests of the regional bourgeoisie were safe, because " . . . *desde que se inició mi gestión, la actividad de los hombres de negocios, ha sido rodeado de todas las garantías que concede la ley y ha gozado de una protección moral gubernativa, favorable a su desarrollo.*"[34]

A second group that needs to be discussed shortly, is the Lebanese one. It differed substantially from the former one in that during the 1930s, it had hardly begun to enter into productive activities. It was, in fact a fraction *in formation*. Having arrived in Mexico at the end of the nineteenth and the first decades of the twentieth century, Lebanese immigrants were engaged in the textile and clothing trade. They functioned as intermediaries between the producers, the scattered settlements throughout the state and the revolutionary troops. These commercial activities rendered them considerable profits and encouraged them to found the *Cámara de Comercio Libanés* in 1926. At the end of the 1920s, they succeeded in diversifying their economic activities to include the production of textiles, thereby using their contacts with textile producers, their knowledge of production techniques, and the economic crisis of the time that had caused financial problems for too many companies. Predominantly between 1928 and 1932, Lebanese capital penetrated the *poblano* textile industry, often by taking over companies formerly controlled by Spanish or French capital. Alonso Palacios emphasized the modernizing steps taken by the new industrial entrepreneurs, facilitating greater and cheaper production. In these years, the foundations were laid for the subsequent expansion and consolidation during the Second World War and for the displacement of the traditionally dominant capital groups in later years. The penetration and modernization brought about by the Lebanese can not be understood solely in terms of an economic conjuncture. In non-Lebanese circles in Puebla, emphasis is frequently put on their alleged ruthless entrepreneurial mentality, which contributed to an astonishing amassing of capital, mainly between 1930 and 1945.[35]

However, a more important general political factor must be mentioned. The Lebanese became part of the *poblano* bourgeoisie during the time of the consolidation and formation of a new political regime. For Lebanese capital as well as for the 'revolutionary family,' the 1920s and 1930s were the years of the start of a new societal configuration. The two groups fought for the powerful positions

---

34. *Diario de Puebla*, 1/X/1939.

35. Alonso Palacios, *Los libaneses en la industria textil* (Mexico City, 1983), 112, 144-146. My data are based on interviews with several politicians and industrial entrepreneurs in Puebla between 1985 and 1987.

within the post-revolutionary state and economy. Since the regime was not only interested in stabilizing the system politically but also in strengthening the productive apparatus, the new industrial entrepreneurs, who had not suffered from the hostilities during the Revolution, participated in the new developments without prejudice. At the moment the revolutionary elite had taken over the role formerly played by the porfirian oligarchy, the Lebanese capitalists were to assume the task of displacing, although partially, the old porfirian bourgeoisie in Puebla. The Lebanese were to become the 'revolutionary' or 'nationalist' fraction of the bourgeoisie, which made them the most loyal ally of the regime, up to the present time.[36]

Finally, I would like to draw attention to the rise of an economic empire of the North American William O. Jenkins in the small city of Atencingo in the south of Puebla. As United States consul in Puebla, he had already acquired considerable influence when he bought a sugar factory and *hacienda* in Atencingo from textile entrepreneur Díaz Rubin in 1921. This changed the political relations in the Atencingo area, an area torn apart by the continuing conflicts between *zapatista* peasants and *hacendados*. Jenkins encouraged the peasants to increase the pressure on the *hacendados*, who then returned to Jenkins for financial help or to sell their property. Within a short period of time, Jenkins was able to amass the largest agricultural property in *poblano* history, covering 123,000 hectares. He subsequently founded the *Compañía Civil e Industrial de Atencingo*, an integrated complex of sugar *haciendas* and alcohol factories. The illegal export of alcohol to the United States during Prohibition increased his fortune even more. In 1931 the enterprise owned by Jenkins was the biggest of its kind throughout Mexico.[37]

The tide turned against Jenkins with the ascent to power of Lázaro Cárdenas, which revitalized the *zapatista* movements in the Atencingo region. It created the threat of a total expropriation of his agro-industrial property. However, Jenkins arranged to bring some of the agricultural and industrial workers under his control by organizing them with the help of regional *FROC*-leader Blas Chumacero. But Jenkins' most important political resource in his struggle against expropriation was undoubtedly his strong alliance with governor Maximino Avila Camacho. With his help, and against the will of the local *zapatistas* and national labour leader Lombardo Toledano, Jenkins retained indirect but effective control of the sugar producing and processing complex. At the beginning of the 1930s, together with two young *poblanos*, Manuel Espinosa Yglesias and Gabriel Alarcón Chargoy, Jenkins started entering new branches. Together they set up a cinema enterprise. Later Jenkins went into banking, appointing Espinosa Yglesias to the board of managers of the *Banco de Comercio* and Alarcón Chargoy headed the cinema enterprise. In 1954, in an effort to evade taxes, an enormous sum of money from the various enterprises was transferred to the Mary Street Jenkins Foundation. In 1958, Espinosa Yglesias virtually took over BANCOMER and introduced a modernizing policy. With Jenkins' death in 1963, the same Espinosa Yglesias assumed the presidency of the foundation, which already administered 500,000,000 *pesos*. By way of its voluminous contributions to the municipal budget, the foundation continued to play an important political role in Puebla. In 1965, Alarcón Chargoy entered the newspaper business and founded the right-wing *Heraldo de México*.[38]

This case clearly illustrates how Maximino Avila Camacho's protection of befriended entrepreneurs gave rise to an important *poblano* capital group. In the

36. Interview with Rodolfo Budib, one of the most salient Lebanese entrepreneurs, Puebla, 3/XII/1985.
37. Ronfeldt, *Atencingo*, 19-23.
38. Ronfeldt, *Atencingo*, 28-45; Miguel Angel Granados Chapa, *La banca nuestra de cada día* (Mexico City, 1985), 73-74; Fátima Fernández Christlieb, *Los medios de comunicación masiva en Mexico* (Mexico City, 1982), 51-54, 70-73.

case of Jenkins, personal relations were decisive, whereas in the case of the Spanish and Lebanese industrial entrepreneurs, the more structural alliance was based on the creation of favourable conditions for the accumulation of capital. Maximino's intimate contacts with the captains of *poblano* industry conversely meant that, in political and economic terms, his position was fortified. He owned, or so he said, four ranches, various houses, packing and refrigerating companies and large bull and horse stables. His links with the bourgeoisie were strengthened through his daughters' marriages. One married Justo Fernández, a rich farmer from Veracruz, and another married Romulo O'Farrill Jr. from Puebla, nowadays one of the most important shareholders of TELEVISA and, since the mid-1940s, of the national newspaper NOVEDADES. His father, who was mayor of Puebla in 1925, had had business dealings in automobile retailing with Jenkins since the 1920s. The link between the political group and the bourgeoisie is also clear in the case of Gonzalo Bautista Castillo, who married a sister of Romulo O'Farrill. Finally, the integration of the political elite with members of the industrial and commercial bourgeoisie took place at the social clubs. The Lions Club of Puebla, for example, was founded in 1933. Mijares Palencia and Avila Camacho were both heavily involved in this organization, which brought together people like Jenkins, O'Farrill, Lebanese textile entrepreneur Abed and the owner of a large-scale wholesale house, Rodoreda. These clubs were the site of frequent personal meetings between political and economic leaders.[39]

## CIVIL SOCIETY

In this section, three specific institutions within civil society -the news media, the school system and the Church- will be briefly analyzed. Since they are not involved with the production and distribution of commodities (with the exception of newspapers) and not formally linked to the state apparatuses, their roles are in the field of the cultural texture of society. The analysis of how the new relations of power affect these institutions, which are primarily concerned with the production of political, cultural and symbolic discourses, can simultaneously reveal how power is exercised hegemonically.

During the 1920s and 1930s, newspapers were by far the most important means of mass communication. In the early 1930s *La Opinión*, *Diario de la Manaña*, founded in 1924, was the most important newspaper in the Puebla area. It had a localist perspective and hardly devoted any attention to international affairs. In the 1930s, it was heavily influenced by the ideas of *FROC* leader Leobardo Coca Cabrera, and consequently became linked to the *almazánista* wing of the local *PNR*. When the political struggle around the 1936 elections erupted, *La Opinión* supported the candidacy of Gilberto Bosques and attacked Maximino Avila Camacho's campaign. Understanding the importance of favourable information on his political activities, Avila Camacho started threatening the owners and editors of *La Opinión*. It was then that a former employee of the opposition newspaper, Julian Cacho, offered Avila Camacho to found a loyal newspaper to be printed on state-owned premises. Maximino agreed. The *Diario de Puebla* was born in 1935. Cacho and his staff backed Maximino and promised him absolute loyalty during his regime. It was to become the mouthpiece of the *avilacamachista* doc-

39. Some even speak of the Avila Camacho-Jenkins 'project,' which aimed at the conquest of influence on national politics. Interview with Horacio Labastida, Mexico City, 21/III/1987. For a fictionalized version of these events see Mastretta's, *Arráncame la vida.*

trine. Julian Cacho was rewarded with a political career that made him local and federal deputy and the president of the *PRI* in Puebla. The opposite happened to the owners and journalists of the *La Opinión* who, for continuing to support Bosques, were forced to leave the state of Puebla, leaving the newspaper in the hands of the workers. Another critical journalist, José Trinidad Mata, director of the weekly magazine *Avante*, was killed in 1939. Although Maximino was generally considered the brain behind the murder and was sharply criticized by the national press, his political contacts in Mexico City kept him from being prosecuted. Convinced of the successful role a local newspaper could play in constructing and cementing a power structure, Maximino repeated the same formula a few years later, but now tailored to the national level. Together with the *poblano* José García Valseca, he worked out a plan to found a chain of newspapers to prepare the political ground for Maximino's possible presidential candidacy. In the beginning, Maximino gave García Valseca financial support. Soon the newspaper expanded into different parts of the country, arriving in Puebla in May 1945 with *El Sol de Puebla*. With a pervading influence on public opinion, it was to become the most important regional newspaper. With the *Diario de Puebla* and the *Sol de Puebla* the *avilacamachistas* were thus able to exercise decisive influence on the public opinion.[40]

The importance of the printed media is even greater if we consider the fact that until 1958, there were only five local radio stations in Puebla. The first one, founded in 1939, was linked to a national chain dominated by Emilio Azcárraga, a prominent entrepreneur who was closely connected to the political regime. Likewise, the cinema industry was dominated by Jenkins and Alarcón, who controlled the large distribution networks and were intimate allies of Maximino Avila Camacho and his political group. Thus, within a period of ten years, the *avilacamachistas* managed to penetrate the crucial means of communication.[41]

One of the central political issues during the 1920s and 1930s was the dispute on the school system. At the beginning of the 1920s, José Vasconcelos initiated a plan to federalize primary schools. It was not only a clear attempt to raise the people's educational level, but also to expand the revolutionary state to the most remote areas of the country. But it would be another decade before the literacy programs were carried out with vigor, followed by the effort to control secondary schools and the introduction of socialist education. In Puebla, there were ample grounds for these policies, since almost 1200 small communities still had no educational facilities at the start of the 1930s. However, it was in these areas, specifically the *Sierra Norte de Puebla*, that the penetration of schools and teachers provoked such a violent reaction on the part of the communities themselves and the local power holders, who saw their influence threatened. Despite the fact that rural teachers were harassed, tortured and sometimes murdered, they could never rely on effective protection from the regional state. Neither Mijares Palencia nor Avila Camacho were interested in supporting radical changes in the countryside headed by the teachers, a task assigned to them in *cardenista* ideology. The project of socialist education, based on a constitutional amendment, was approved by the regional congress during the Mijares government, but never materialized in Puebla. This was due to the fact that the *avilacamachistas* had established close

40. *Diario de Puebla*, 11/I/1935, reprinted in Blumenkron, *Maximino Avila Camacho*, 23-24. Data based on an interview with the ex-director of *La Opinión*, *Diario de Mañana* and actual director of the *Opinión de Puebla*, Manuel Sánchez Ponton, Puebla, 23/III/1987. Cordero y Torres, *Historia Compendiada*, 410. Fernández Christlieb, *Medios de difusión masiva*, 32, 77.

41. Fernández Christlieb, *Medios de difusión masiva*, 190-191. Arredondo Ramírez et.al., *Comunicación social, poder y democracia en México* (Mexico City, 1986), 69-78.

relations with the conservative bourgeoisie and the Church, who strongly opposed the policy of socialist education. The acceptance in Puebla was an example of the classic colonial credo *'obedezco, pero no cumplo'*. As a result, the teachers in Puebla hardly conducted any significant anticlerical actions, nor were they effectively involved in the regional peasants' and workers' organizations, as they were in other states.[42]

Nevertheless, the important role played by the teachers in spreading new ideas and in molding the students' perception of the world made the *avilacamachistas* want to control them politically. Moreover, teachers in the city of Puebla had formed the *Sindicato de Maestros Revolucionarios del Estado de Puebla* (*SMREP*), which adhered to the *FROC*. As Maximino was engaged in a harsh struggle against the *FROC* in view of the coming elections, a *SMREP* strike was bitterly repressed in 1936. In order to isolate the small but radical teachers' union, Maximino did not recognize it officially and supported a larger and more moderate organization, part of the *Confederación de Maestros Mexicanos* (*CMM*), which was controlled by the Molina Betancourt family from Zacapoaxtla, close allies of the *avilacamachistas*. Although the family Molina Betancourt had previously been linked to the *callista* faction in Mexico, it was able to maintain its influence in Puebla after 1935. Fausto Molina Betancourt was director of federal education in the state of Puebla during the *cardenista* period. His friend Victor Sosa was director of education during the governments of Mijares Palencia and Avila Camacho. In order to diminish the *FROC* influence among the teachers, Avila Camacho worked with Molina and Sosa to bring the *poblano* teachers together in one union (*SUTEP*) in 1937, which operated under firm state tutelage. Together with the decree (1938) that made secondary schools directly dependent on the executive and thus authorized the intervention of the governor in administrative and teaching policies, the *SUTEP* became another element in the *avilacamachista* machinery.[43]

The modern university was founded when the *Colegio del Estado* was transformed into the *Universidad de Puebla* in May 1937. Maximino Avila Camacho had just assumed power and was determined to keep it under his firm control, largely because ever since the beginning of the century, university students had agitated on the side of the popular masses. He was partly able to do so because of the dependence of the *Universidad de Puebla* on regional state resources. It was perhaps for this reason that the governor felt it was justified to exert decisive influence on academic appointments. The law on the new university gave the governor the right to appoint the director and to overrule decisions made by the university council. The first director was Manuel L. Márquez, who had been a legal advisor of the extremely right-wing, anti-communist organization *Camisas Doradas*. In an attempt to regulate university and student life, Márquez did not hesitate to proclaim a series of strict rules. The students, however, resisted the measures and expressed doubts on the academic qualifications of Márquez. In direct negotiations with the governor, student leaders successfully demanded the replacement of Márquez by Alfonso Alarcón in 1938. The existence of student groups that opposed the *avilacamachistas* in their effort to seize control over the university, made them want to adopt a strategy to get hold of the students directly. Af-

---

**42**. Glockner, *Presencia del estado*, 81-82. With respect to the influence of rural teachers on local power systems see Ulrich Kohler, "Ciclos de poder en una comunidad indígena de México: política local y sus vínculos con la vida nacional," *América Indígena*, 46:3 (1986), 435-451. Mary Kay Vaughan, "Actuación política del magisterio socialista en Puebla y Sonora, 1934-1939," in *Crítica*, 32-33 (1987), 90-100.

**43**. Rafael Molina Betancourt had been a high official working directly under Secretary of Education Narciso Bassols before Cárdenas came to power, see Vaughan, "Actuación política," 99.

ter some initial problems, the regime -working through the *PRM* machinery- managed to unify the *poblano* student population in 1939. The *Confederación de Estudiantes Revolucionarios del Estado de Puebla* immediately exhibited its adherence to the regime by promoting the candidacy of Manuel Avila Camacho to the presidency. As in the case of the urban and rural workers, unification became almost synonymous to subordination to the state.[44]

The aim of the government to keep the educational institution, so important for the breeding of useful intellectuals, under tight control, became very clear in 1941 when governor Bautista Castillo backed a new university law that reduced the decision-making power of the council and the students to an even greater extent. With the motive of bureaucratic simplification, all the decision-making power was put into the hands of the director of the university, who was obviously appointed directly by the governor. Gonzalo Bautista explicitly sought to crash all the political movements at the university by issuing military-like regulations. In defense of these rules, the governor stated:[45]

> *"El sometimiento de la juventud universitaria a las normas estrictas de una disciplina severa, además de significar un mejoramiento importante de su aptitud para asimilar las ensenanzas impartidas, constituirá también una ayuda valiosa para facilitar la asimilación de los propósitos que persigue la ley del servicio militar."*

In 1942 he even went so far as to appoint military officials in the university hierarchy. The regulation allowed almost no space for university autonomy. The absence of democratic procedures provoked a student strike in 1943. The governor threatened if the protests, *"evolving from a centre of disorder,"* continued, the university would be closed by direct police intervention. In the end, the regulations were adopted, which showed that just as in the case of the labour movement, the Second World War served as an excuse to curb calls for democratization and to limit and neutralize demand-oriented movements. In spite of these disciplinary measures, the *avilacamachistas* never managed to obtain complete control over the university. In fact, it was to become the nodal point for future revolts against the *cacicazgo*.[46]

A third topic to be discussed is the relationship between the state and the Catholic Church. Throughout the *Porfiriato*, the clerical influence on Puebla's social and political life was considerable. With the advent of the revolutionary changes and the rise of anti-clerical forces between 1914 and 1935, however, it decreased substantially. Especially between 1914 and 1917, the clergy was persecuted, the Catholic university was attacked, libraries were destroyed and buildings were closed down. It is interesting to note that the Church intended to keep pace with new developments, such as tenets of socialist ideology and the liberal economic policies, manifest throughout the world and leading to growing secularization. The papal encyclical letter *Rerum Novarum* was the principle source of the reforms within the Catholic doctrine. *Poblano* archbishop Sánchez Paredes (1919-1923), confronted with the inevitable changes and with the demands of the

---

44. Based on remarks made by Maximino Avila Camacho when the foundation of the university was officially celebrated, *Diario de Puebla*, 17/IV/1937. Márquez, "Los origines," 198.

45. Vélez Pliego, "La sucesión rectoral," 53. *Diario Oficial*, 18/IV/1941, as cited in Vélez Pliego, "La sucesion rectoral," 52-58.

46. According the new law: *"Como una de las transformaciónes necesarias de la mentalidad actual, la adquisición de una disciplina severa que subordine todos los actos de la conducta pública o privada a la obtención rápida y armónica de los fines de utilidad colectiva que se adopten," Diario Oficial*, 18/IV/1941, cited in Vélez Pliego, "La sucesión rectoral," 52.

peasants and workers, emphasized the social doctrine of the Church, which proposed the improving the conditions of the working classes without abandoning the principle of private property. The reorientation put the 'social question' on the agenda of the Church authorities, who consequently produced statements on the relations between capital and labour and on the agrarian problem. According to them, capital and labour supposedly had a mutual interest in cooperating in harmony. Class struggle could only be legitimate if and when workers struggled to obtain the rights and goods that rightfully belonged to them. The formulation of the proper criteria to embody the common good was the task of the Church and the state. Around the agrarian problem, a whole body of propositions was produced, which made bishop Sánchez Paredes known as the *obispo agrarista*. When he proposed to the landowners that they cooperate in land distribution programmes, it provoked a radical denial on the part of the most reactionary elements of the rural and urban bourgeoisie.[47]

During the 1920s, the Mexican Catholic Church founded several organizations aimed at winning back territory in a societal context that was not particularly benevolent. Just as the relations between the Church and the state became increasingly tense and were eventually to lead to the *Cristero* movement in the western states of the republic, the *Liga Nacional de Libertad Religiosa* was founded in 1925. Several organizations in Puebla took part in this movement. After the agreement between Rome and the political leaders in Mexico put an end to the *Cristero* revolt in 1929, clerical leaders focussed their attention on the revitalization of lay organizations. So at the end of 1929, *Acción Católica Mexicana* was newly founded, aimed at increasing Church influence among laymen by 'preparing them politically'.[48] The same can be said of the *Caballeros de Colón*. The contact between the Church and the *avilacamachistas* took place largely by way of these lay channels. The association between Bautista O'Farrill and Díaz Ordáz and the *Caballeros de Colón* was an irrefutable example.

Although the reconciliation between the Church and the state was formally established in 1929, there were still pockets of radical anti-clericalism in the country (for example the radical policies enacted by Garrido in Tabasco). In Puebla, Mijares Palencia was the last governor to pursue an anti-clerical policy by closing down Catholic institutes and nationalizing Church property. When Maximino Avila Camacho rose to power, the relations finally normalized. During his regime, Catholics were permitted to open their schools again. Furthermore, the rapprochement between the *avilacamachistas* and the Church became manifest when Maximino and Manuel, the presidential candidate at the time, declared publicly that they were religious Catholics. A few years later, Bautista Castillo stated that religious Orders should no longer be excluded from educational activities. On a different level, the *avilacamachista* and Catholic discourses coincided on at least two crucial points: the corporativist organization of society and a deeply entrenched anti-communist attitude. In summary, at the end of the 1930s, the relationship between the Church and regional the state was redefined, and the foundations were laid for a long-term alliance. It was to clearly re-emerge during the years of Archbishop Octaviano Márquez y Toriz (from 1951 to the end of the 1970s). He revived the conservative tradition of the *poblano* clergy and initiated an intense anti-communist purge in close collaboration with the highest state officials.[49]

47. Cordero y Torres, *Historia compendiada*, II, 432-437.
48. Márquez, "Origines," 78.
49. Cordero y Torres, *Historia Compendiada*, II, 440-442. Márquez, "Origines," 188-189. Martínez Assad, *El laboratorio*, especially 15-55.

## DISCOURSE

Besides an articulated circuit of institutional power positions, *avilacamachismo* also encompassed a discourse with a set of distinctive characteristics, designed to legitimize authoritarian rule. The first element was tantamount to a clear anti-radical and anti-communist position. It emerged against the background of the experiences of the workers' council that had ruled the city of Puebla in 1935 and 1936 and the government of Almazán between 1929 and 1933. These experiences were discursively constructed as an antithesis to the *avilacamachista* project; *'Puebla libre contra el comunismo'* was a slogan used during the electoral campaign of Maximino Avila Camacho. When addressing the *Congreso de Unificación Campesina*, Avila Camacho criticized the divisions and conflicts in the rural areas, inherited from previous governments. He referred to the agrarian policies of Almazán and warned the peasants that the communist danger had not yet disappeared completely. On another occasion, he stated that his regime was unlike those of former governors in that they had lost their authority and had thus made way for left-wing currents and disorder. In 1939, Bautista Castillo produced a sharply different picture of the immediate past, stating that during the government of Almazán *"fueron sacrificados revolucionarios representativos y hombres honestos, sólo por oponerse al desbarajuste económico y a la bancarota moral que caracterizó aquel régimen."* The hidden message was just the opposite: the *avilacamachistas* were the true revolutionaries who would restore moral values to Puebla and stimulate renewed economic development.[50]

Contrary to conceptions of social division and struggle, *avilacamachista* discourse evolved around harmony, reconciliation and unity. Harmony among the workers themselves after a period of violent inter-union struggle and harmony between capital and labour were the central propositions. The aim was to deny opposing radical discourses by blurring the existence of class conflict. At a meeting of the regional Chamber of Commerce, Avila Camacho accurately expressed this idea: ". . . *la filosofía de nuestro movimiento social aconseja la colaboración de los que poseen el capital y los que ayuden a conservarlo y acrecentarlo, sobre bases de comprensión, de equidad y de justicia social.*" During the same meeting, the contrast with former governments was brought to the fore:[51] " . . . *mi gobierno, desde un principio, cambio la* ***conducta de regimenes anteriores****, procurando hacer efectivos para patrones y proprietarios las garantias constitucionales.*" This conception closely resembled the social doctrine of the Church which, based on papal encyclical letters written at the end of the nineteenth century, propagated the collaboration of mutually dependent groups.[52]

Furthermore, the discursive elements of social harmony and class reconciliation are linked to such concepts as state tutelage and corporatism. The state as the embodiment of the Revolution assumes the role of arbitrator between the conflicting classes and between the rivaling unions. The state represents the masses and Maximino represents the state in Puebla: he is thus entitled to act and judge on the people's behalf. But the criteria of judgment are linked to another important element:[53] " . . . *contarán con el respaldo de mi gobierno, todos los directores de*

50. *Diario de Puebla*, 14/III/1938; *Diario de Puebla*, 30/XI/1938; *Diario de Puebla*, 31/XII/1939.

51. *Diario de Puebla*, 1/X/1939 (my emphasis).

52. Márquez, "Origines," 6.

53. "Mensaje a los trabajadores poblanos de Maximino Avila Camacho," reprinted in Blumenkron, *Maximino Avila Camacho*, 26 (my emphasis).

*las organizaciones obreras, que ajustando sus actos a* **los dictados de la moral** *cumplan a satisfacción de sus representados con la delicada misión que les corresponde . . . ."* What was defined as morally acceptable and justifiable was determined by the 'embodiment of the masses' and the traditional 'specialists' on moral issues, i.e. Church authorities. Besides, what was morally responsible was synonymous to what was good for Mexico. And Mexico needed peace to rebuild its shattered economy rather than a class struggle that would jeopardize this enterprise.

In this respect, the necessity of order and the prevalence of the law appear as crucial elements of the *avilacamachista* discourse. Order refers to social harmony and unity, whereas struggle and conflictuality represent disorder. Thus, *conflictuality*, which implies the breaking of the rules of morality, requires the enforcement of the law by invoking disciplinary and punitive measures and regulations: *" . . . quiero advertir que a partir de este momento tomaré medidas que sancionaran enérgicamente, de acuerdo con nuestros leyes, toda vejación o vituperio que se lance contra actos del gobierno . . . "* As a leading businessman phrased it, when speaking about the days of Maximino and his attitude towards law and order: *"Era una época difícil y el era un hombre de orden, que le gustaban las cosas muy firmes. El quería que el país caminará dentro del orden y la constitución. Era alguien que no quería huelgas, ni desordenes pero si orden y trabajo."* So here the symbol of the *'mano dura,'* of a 'strong man' enters the discursive field: the man who is going to save Puebla from immoral disorder that lasted more than twenty years. This man can only successfully confront this difficult task of re-establishing harmony by ruling with an iron fist. Maximino Avila Camacho, the 'exceptional man', complied with the requirements: the *torero*, the ruthless *macho*, the purposeful general who survived the Revolution. These symbols were articulated and legitimized within a broader political discourse. In fact, all together they formed a perfect guise for authoritarian rule, which was only to be accentuated by a characteristic of closure, referring to the fact that no one from outside the state was to be tolerated within the *poblano* political group and that Maximino was to be recognized as the exclusive authority.[54]

In summarizing, I would argue that the re-establishment of law and order by the representatives of the revolutionary state in Puebla, informed by Catholic doctrines, corporativist and authoritarian ideologies, constitutes the guideline of *avilacamachista* discourse. These discursive elements were produced and disseminated throughout a wide range of institutions. So in an apologetic booklet on Maximino Avila Camacho, Julián Cacho was thanked for having made of the *Diario de Puebla " . . . una bandera esforzada y viril de la doctrina avilacamachista."*[55] A local newspaper was the principal vehicle for transmitting the dominant discourse throughout the *poblano* social fabric. Furthermore, the leading unions, strongly articulated with the Avila Camacho group, channeled their part of the general discourse to the workers and peasants, particularly in the field of capital-labour relations. The same goes for the university, the state and the party bureaucracy, which had constant access to instruments to reproduce their discourses on a variegated spectrum of topics.

54. *Diario de Puebla*, 30/XI/1938. Quotations from an interview with Rodolfo Budib, Puebla, 3/XII/1985.
55. Blumenkron, *Maximino*, 3.

## CONCLUSIONS AND COMMENTS

By the time the armed stage of the Revolution came to an end, the centralized political system of the *Porfiriato* had collapsed. Individual revolutionary leaders with their followings, dispersed over the country, formed the elementary political entities. It was during the presidencies of Obregón and Calles that the dispersed power structure started to be redefined. The foundation of the *PNR* in 1929 was a decisive step in the direction of institutionalization, although the revolutionary party consisted of multifarious local and regional political parties and military *caciques*. Yet it was an attempt to restructure the political configuration from the centre. With the arrival of Cárdenas, the process initiated during the *Maximato* acquired a new dimension with the *organized* appearance of the popular masses on the political stage and the installment of a corporativist structure in the new revolutionary party (*PRM*). Mass mobilization served Cárdenas well in his struggle against the *callista* faction and it decreased autonomy of the regional strongbosses. By 1938, the major exponents of the 1920s style of regional and local bossism had been eliminated.

However, the new political conditions, notably the rupture between Cárdenas and Calles and the corporativization of the masses, contained the seeds of similar phenomena. In fact, what had been eliminated by the end of the 1930s was the almost autonomous -politically and sometimes militarily- independent position of the regional strongbosses.[56] It was, paradoxically enough, the domination of the corporate organizations, within a regional context but according to central political guideline, that constituted the cornerstone for the rise of the 'modernized' *cacicazgos*.

In order to destroy *callista* strongholds and ensure lower-level support of his policies, Cárdenas appointed loyal followers on the regional level. As part of this reorganization, Maximino Avila Camacho became *jefe militar* in Puebla in 1935 and governor in 1937. In subsequent years, he was able to build a *cacicazgo* according to the new rules of the game. It consisted of a set of strategic interventions, which were to eventually serve as the pillars of the new regional power structure: corporatist control of the working classes, disciplinary regulations within the party structure and the school system, the amalgamation of the interests of the bourgeoisie and the political elite, the subordination of key elements of civil society and the diffusion of *avilacamachista* discourse. The key positions within this new political organization and the relations among them formed a pyramidal grid articulated by the Avila Camacho clique that included the governorship, the cabinet, departmental heads, the mayor of the city of Puebla, the president of the *PRM*, regional and federal deputies, senators, union leaders, the director of a local newspaper, the director of the local university, the church hierarchy and leading members of the bourgeoisie.

Although the formation of the *avilacamachista* machinery was opposed by a local newspaper, an active union (*FROC*), students, and a group of teachers, their resistance was never effective because the central state refused to act on their behalf. Cárdenas did not enforce his reformist project in Puebla but, on the contrary, supported the *avilacamachistas*, who founded an authoritarian and conservative rule. In other words, the relations between the regional and the central state were crucial for the development of the regional *cacicazgo*.

The factors explaining the *cardenista* policies towards Puebla are not difficult to understand. In the first place, Puebla never experienced a struggle of any importance between *callistas* and *cardenistas*. After the arrival of Maximino Avila

56. See also the essay by Falcón elsewhere in this volume.

Camacho in 1935, politicians of *callista* origins rapidly switched their loyalties, knowing that with Maximino no drastic changes were to be expected. The mobilization of the masses to oust followers of the former *Jefe Máximo* -a task the *FROC* would have fulfilled so well- thus became redundant. The specific local conditions did not leave any political leeway for militancy backed by the president. This leads to the conclusion that Cárdenas' reformist policies should be viewed as an instrument to strengthen his own position. If Cárdenas, as Vaughan stated, had followed the logic of his reforms, he would have encountered sufficient reasons to intervene in Puebla.[57] But, as we saw, he did not. Secondly, the strong personal ties between Cárdenas and the *avilacamachistas* provided the main insurance for *avilacamachista* politics in Puebla. Manuel Avila Camacho had played an important role in bringing Cárdenas to the presidency, and Maximino paid tribute to the *PNR-PRM* and backed the president despite their divergent political conceptions. In this patron-client relationship, loyalty, and support to Cárdenas on the national level was exchanged for Cárdenas' non-intervention in Maximino's regional domain.

This raises the issue of the relationship between *avilacamachismo* and *cardenismo*. Can *avilacamachismo* be viewed as a regional expression of *cardenismo*? If one takes the relationship between the state and labour as the criterion for comparison, the question can not be unequivocally answered. Seen from one perspective, *avilacamachismo* in Puebla was indeed an expression of *cardenismo*. The relationship between Cárdenas and the labour movement has been referred to as the implementation of a corporativist policy, since the working class was absorbed into the *PRM* as a separate sector. This process actually boiled down to the submission of the working class to the state. As I have tried to show, these processes can be clearly identified in the case of Puebla. Maximino Avila Camacho exploited and sometimes exacerbated the conflictual relations between the different unions in Puebla. In this way, the *avilacamachistas* managed to first achieve control over the *CROM*, then the *FTP* and finally the decimated *FROC*. From the point of view of the unions themselves, it became clear that the possibility of controling (part of) the working class was largely dependent on the nature of their relationship with the regional state. In the end, they willingly or unwillingly agreed with Avila Camacho who, on the first of May 1937, stated:[58]

> *"Por eso los revolucionarios de México hemos comprendido la necesidad de organizar el gobierno en tal manera que siempre desempeña el estado un papel tutelar para las masas."*

On the other hand, *avilacamachismo* cannot be characterized as a reflection of *cardenismo* for the simple reason that the national and regional levels had their own political logic and their own relations of power, which could easily result in different and sometimes contradictory alliances. On the national level, Cárdenas sought and promoted an alliance with demand-oriented movements within the working classes and among the peasants, partially in order to gather sufficient power to confront Calles. In Puebla, however, the working-class organization that continuously mobilized workers (*FROC*), organized strikes and the like, and which, on these grounds, could be considered an 'ideal' ally for Cárdenas, was systematically excluded from participation in this kind of alliance, mainly after the appearance of Maximino Avila Camacho in *poblano* politics in 1935. The exclusion of a union that suited *cardenista* mass politics so well could largely be explained by the fact that the *avilacamachistas*, and not the active labour leaders, had excellent relations with the political heart of the country. Moreover, the *FROC* suffered severe repression during the 1935 strike, for which Avila Cama-

57. Vaughan, "Actuación política," 92.

58. *Diario de Puebla*, 2/V/1937. Barbosa Cano, *La CROM*, 77.

cho was responsible. The *FROC* subsequently tried -almost successfully- to win the elections in 1936, leaving an unbridgeable gap between the *avilacamachistas* and the most active segment of the *poblano* working classes. These specific relations of power created the possibility for an alliance between the regional state and the *CROM*, indeed one of the most hated remnants of *callismo*!

But perhaps a more fundamental reason can explain the political exclusion of the most articulate union in Puebla during *cardenismo*. The simple change from *callista* to *cardenista* political factions in the state of Puebla made an alliance with active parts of the working class in order to break *callista* power *unnecessary*. Although the government of Maximino Avila Camacho was embedded in *cardenista* discourse, it did not actively seek support among the region's most highly mobilized sector. On the contrary, this sector was systematically opposed and repressed. This explanation sheds some light on the political priorities of Cárdenas. Essentially, he seemed to be interested in 'keeping the system together' rather than in demanding the implementation of his general political guidelines. His commitment to a strong and secure ally, like Avila Camacho, in exchange for loyalty, heavily outweighed meeting the demands of the more radical factions of the *poblano* labour movement. This then explains the absence of any effective intervention of the president in favour of the FROC, which has puzzled others in the past.[59]

This brings me to my final and more general comment. The development of 'modernized' *cacicazgos* illustrates the persistent tension between the growing centralization of state power and the existence of centrifugal forces. This is closely related to the persistence of personalist political relations that check increasing institutionalization, mobilization on the basis of programmatic interests and the professionalization of politics. The personalist relations between the *avilacamachistas* and Cárdenas excluded the reformist factions in Puebla from an alliance with the centre. They prevailed over and contradicted the programmatic logic of *cardenismo* and blocked the tendencies of institutionalization, as they made possible the birth of new regional *cacicazgos*.[60]

---

59. A similar conclusion can be drawn from Cárdenas' treatment of the Atencingo land distribution conflict, in which he finally conceded to the wishes of Maximino Avila Camacho and William Jenkins. See Ronfeldt, *Atencingo*, 28-45. Arrazola, "Formación," 84.

60. Schryer similarly noted that Cárdenas was linked through personal informal networks to the most anti-agrarian politician in the *Sierra Alta* of Hidalgo, *Rancheros of Pisaflores*, 92-95; see also his essay in this volume.

Region, State and Capitalism
CEDLA, Amsterdam, 1989

CHAPTER TEN

# A *Ranchero* Elite in the Region of Huejutla
## [THE CAREER OF GENERAL JUVENCIO NOCHEBUENA OF ATLAPEXCO]

FRANS JOZEF SCHRYER*

### INTRODUCTION

During the Mexican Revolution, a *ranchero* elite came to power or consolidated its position in many parts of rural Mexico. In this chapter, I will analyze the relationship between the Mexican state and such an elite in the district of Huejutla, a region inhabited by both Nahua Indians and Spanish-speaking *mestizos*. This region experienced a violent peasant revolt in the 1970s, culminating in the expropriation by the state, in 1981, of most privately owned land. Elsewhere I have described this revolt and analyzed its ethnic dimensions in considerable detail.[1] However, we need to examine more closely the evolution of class relations and cultural values between 1920 and 1970. This chapter will therefore trace the recent history of Huejutla, prior to the peasant uprising, to show how the economic structure and political system of a *ranchero* region changed as a result of its greater integration into the national and international market through the process of 'modernization'.

The *ranchero* economy of Huejutla underwent a qualitative change between 1930 and 1960. This transformation, whereby *mestizo rancheros*, rich Indian peasants and former *hacienda* owners became 'modern' businessmen, involved a process of increasing concentration in land ownership. At the same time the cultural system became characterized by a differentiation in life style between a new economic elite and the majority of peasants who continued to practice small-scale subsistence agriculture. Initially, the members of both ethnic groups experienced improved standards of living and opportunities for economic advancement despite the appearance of greater class differences and the corresponding system of status distinction. During this period of economic growth, landowning farmers and ranchers were able to reward their part-time labourers with access to land and short-terms loans, usually in the form of advances on wages. They also provided other forms of assistance and advice to their economic subordinates. Economic exploitation -from the viewpoint of an outside observer- was thus compati-

* *Anthropologist, College of Social Science, Department of Sociology and Anthropology, University of Guelph, Ontario N1G 2W1, Canada.* *Based on the anthropological study* ***Ethnicity and Class Conflict in Rural Mexico*** *(Princeton University Press, 1989). Research in the region of Huejutla was conducted between 1980 and 1987 and was largely financed by grants from the Social Science and Humanities Research Council of Canada.*

1. See Frans J. Schryer, "Ethnicity and Politics in Rural Mexico: Land Invasion in Huejutla," in *Mexican Studies/Estudios Mexicanos*, 3 (1987), 99-126.

ble with a set of cultural values that have been referred to as the 'moral economy'.[2] However, further economic developments along capitalist lines, especially the rapid expansion of modern cattle production (the most profitable economic activity) eventually brought about a break-down of the apparent social harmony and ecological equilibrium characteristic of the *ranchero* economy. After 1960 patron-client ties rapidly eroded, setting the stage for the development of overt class conflicts.

The three decades between 1930 and 1960, which witnessed the most rapid changes in both the economic structure and the cultural values in Huejutla, coincided with the career of general Juvencio Nochebuena. A leading *ranchero* from the small town of Atlapexco, Nochebuena became an important politician on both the national and the regional levels. Indeed, his social origins, political rise and subsequent decline (including his failure to become the governor of Hidalgo) epitomizes the changing relationship between the Mexican state and a class of *mestizo rancheros* who became modern businessmen, i.e. modern farmers, cattle ranchers and merchants.

## HISTORICAL BACKGROUND AND THE EMERGENCE OF REVOLUTIONARY STRONGBOSSES

The district of Huejutla, today comprised of nine *municipios*, is located in the larger semi-tropical region known as the Huasteca. This district, located in the northeastern corner of the state of Hidalgo, has been a single administrative unit since approximately the beginning of the nineteenth century. I found it useful to conceptually divide Huejutla into two parts: a southern zone, also slightly more mountainous, and a northern zone. During the colonial era, the southern zone consisted of what were the called *pueblos de indios*, whose inhabitants paid various forms of tribute to the Spanish crown and to Church authorities. These *pueblos de indios* administered their own communal lands. The main subsistence activities were the slash-and-burn cultivation of maize, beans and squash which are still the main staples today. Less than ten percent of the land in this southern zone was privately owned in the form of *haciendas* or *ranchos*, many of which produced *pilón* (sugar loaf). In contrast, the land tenure system in the northern part of Huejutla was quite different prior to 1800. Here all land was obtained by a handfull of Spanish families who established cattle *haciendas*. Although many were subsequently divided through sale and inheritance into smaller estates of varying sizes, by the beginning of the nineteenth century, each *hacienda* still included at least several communities of resident peons or sharecroppers.[3]

2. See Edward P. Thompson, "The Moral Economy of the English Crowd in the Eighteenth Century," in *Past and Present*, 50 (1971), 76-136; George Rudé, *Ideology and Popular Protest* (New York, 1980); James Scott, *The Moral Economy of the Peasant: Rebellion and Subsistence in South East Asia* (New Haven, 1976); Arij Ouweneel, *Onderbroken groei in Anáhuac. De ecologische achtergrond van ontwikkeling en armoede in Centraal-Mexico (1730-1810)* (Amsterdam, 1989).

3. The nine *municipios* are: San Felipe Orizatlán, Jaltocan, Tlanchinol, Huazalingo, Huejutla, Atlapexco, Huautla, Yahualica and Xochiatipan. The combined population of these *municipios* in 1980 was 191,345; see data in Secretaría de Agricultura y Recursos Hidraulicos (Comisión de Estudios del Rio Panuco, Huasteca Hidalguense), *Datos Estadísticos Generales de la Huasteca Hidalguense*, July, 1982. The figure of land tenure in the southern zone was taken from a study of the former *Alcaldía Mayor* of Yahualica, most of which corresponded to what I call the southern zone; see Ludka de Gortari, *Pueblos de indios en la jurisdicción de la alcaldía mayor de Yahualica (1650`1800)* (Mexico City, 1983), 61. The *pueblos de indios* were part of what was called the *República de Indios*, a segregated administrative unit in the Spanish system; see Ouweneel, *Onderbroken groei in Anáhuac*, 153-178. For the part of the former *Alcaldía Mayor* of Huejutla corresponding to this same predominantly communal southern zone, the only *haciendas* or *ranchos* mentioned in the *Archivo General de la Nación* are Zitlan and Vinasco. These small private

Throughout the nineteenth century, and especially after 1850, the Huasteca also became a frontier area which attracted numerous settlers from other parts of Mexico and even abroad. In Huejutla, these settlers established themselves in the southern, communal part of Huejutla where they set up small craft industries like wood-cutting, soap-making and liquor distilling). These newcomers (mainly *mestizos*) also got involved in a variety of agricultural activities and the raising of cattle which grazed freely in unfenced pastures and forests. At the same time, better-off Indian peasants started to raise livestock (especially pigs and goats) and to grow new cash crops such as coffee and sugarcane. Many Indians also became increasingly involved in petty commerce. While poor peasants continued to have access to the communal lands for swidden cultivation, both outsiders and better-off Indians established more permanent farms and ranches generally referred to as *ranchos*. Their owners, the *rancheros*, were a class of entrepreneurial farmers who employed seasonal wage labourers. The lifestyle of this class of small property owners did not differ radically from that of their economic subordinates.[4]

The same economic changes which transformed the economic structure of formerly communal Indian villages altered relations of production within the *haciendas* (mainly located in the northern zone) in less drastic ways. The *hacendados* (who lived in the town of Huejutla and maintained a distinctive, more Europeanized lifestyle) became increasingly involved in commercial agriculture (as well as cattle raising) using a combination of wage labour and non-capitalist forms of surplus-extraction such as servile labour and labour rents. However, such commercial *haciendas* only expanded into a very small section of the southern zone which had already become transformed into a *ranchero* economy.[5] While *hacienda* owners continued to dominate political life at the level of the district as a whole, *mestizo rancheros* managed to gain direct control over several new *municipios* of Huejutla (Huazalingo, Atlapexco and Xochiatipan). These *rancheros* benefited from the liberal land reform laws initially introduced by Benito Juárez. Not only did this land reform legalize the *de facto* usurpation of formerly communal lands by *mestizo rancheros* and their Indian counterparts -who ruled Indian *pueblos* -but it allowed these new landowners to purchase additional titles originally issued to poor Indian peasants. However, sections of communal land did remain intact; in some cases all or some of the new private land titles were simply kept by a single representative while in other cases, Indian villages bought already existing privately owned lands in common and then registered such land in the form of a corporate partnership. In most cases such sections of communal land represented a reserve set aside for poor peasants to practice subsistence agriculture.

Despite a change in the legal status of landholdings, the traditions and administrative boundaries of Nahuatl villages remained intact.[6] For example, the *rancheros*, who originally took possession of land inside the communal boundaries of Nahuatl villages, continued to recognize such boundaries even though most communal land legally became private property. Such village boundaries had to do with judicial authority as

---

properties also represented less than 10 percent of the land area of this sub-region. A more detailed analysis of the history of land tenure in the region of Huejutla appeared in Frans Schryer, "Peasants and the Law: a History of Land Tenure and Conflict in the Huasteca," in *Journal of Latin America Studies*, 18 (1986), 283-311.

4. The *rancheros* of Huejutla were very similar to those in the *Sierra de Jacala* region described in my book, *The Rancheros of Pisaflores. The History of a Peasant Bourgeoisie in Twentieth-Century Mexico* (Toronto, 1980).

5. The owners of already existing *haciendas*, dating back to the colonial era, appropriated formerly communal land only in the northern section of what is today the *municipio* of Jaltocan.

6. For a more detailed description of the culture and the social organization of these Nahuatl *pueblos*, see Frans Schryer, "Class Conflict and the Closed Corporate Peasant Community: Disputes over Land in Nahuatl Villages," in *Journal of Anthropological Research*, 43:2 (1987), 99-120.

much as with rights of access to land. In fact, *mestizo* towns and villages established within the original communal boundaries of former *pueblos de indios* continued to recognize the authority of Indian representatives of Nahuatl *pueblos. Mestizo rancheros* even used to give these Indian representatives monetary contributions to defray ceremonial costs or for the upkeep of local chapels. Such authorities, who were usually rich Nahuatl-speaking peasants who also owned small *ranchos*, were in turn subject to more powerful *mestizo rancheros* who either dominated or directly ran municipal governments. Thus, the original communal boundaries of Indian villages continued to be used for administrative purposes by both Indians and *mestizos*. Everyone who lived within such village boundaries participated in the same set of rotating civil and religious posts and were responsible for performing communal labour (usually one day a week) to maintain their rights of membership in local communities. *Mestizo* authorities continued to use this institution of communal labour or the *faena*, which had originally been part of the tribute exacted by Spanish rulers, for building muletrails and the upkeep of public buildings.

Notwithstanding a great deal of political dissatisfaction, there were no peasant uprisings in Huejutla during the Mexican Revolution and the local class structure and systems of land tenure remained intact. This continuity can be explained by the existence of paternalistic patron-client bonds between the majority of landowners (including *hacienda* owners) and their economic subordinates.[7] However, the small commercial landowning farmers or *rancheros* who controlled the predominantly Indian *municipios* in the southern zone played an active part in the Mexican Revolution which started in 1910. Indeed, the strongmen who ended up ruling various parts of the Huasteca at the end of the Revolution were all *mestizo rancheros*.[8]

During the decade following the Mexican Revolution, the state of Hidalgo was controlled by Matías Rodríguez. This left-leaning, populist leader, elected governor in 1925, was a *callista*. During this period, the district of Huejutla was in turn politically controlled by a *ranchero* revolutionary, Wenceslao Martínez. Martínez, originally from Jacala, first served as military commander of Huejutla under Carranza and later became municipal president of Huejutla on four separate occasions. While he did not take advantage of his political position to amass wealth, like so many former revolutionary commanders, he also did not attempt to change the local political and economic structures inherited from the *Porfiriato*. Some peasants in the northern zone gained access to land by default since many *haciendas* were left abandoned by their owners. However, those who returned (and some wealthier *rancheros* as well) again demanded labour services from the inhabitants of both *mestizo* and Nahua villages under their direct jurisdiction. In the southern zone, Martínez also allowed local authorities to collect head taxes officially abolished by the Revolution. Like Matías Rodríguez on the state level and Plutarco Calles on the national level, Wenceslao Martínez only paid lip service to the ideal of land redistribution.[9] For example, Martínez allowed an agrarian leader

7. See Frans J. Schryer, "Peasant Quiescence in the Huasteca" (Paper presented at the 1988 Americanista Congress, Amsterdam; to be published in a book by Simon Miller and Arij Ouweneel, 1990).

8. Most of these *rancheros* are mentioned in an account of the Revolution in the Huasteca written by a local historian; see Eutiquio Mendoza, *Memorias de la revolución mexicana en las Huastecas. Gotitas de placer y chubascos de amargura* (Mexico City, 1960).

9. Matías Rodríguez was elected governor after a particularly bitter electoral dispute between his Labor and Agrarian Party of Hidalgo and the Confederate Party, representing the powerful Azuara clique, a family of *hacienda* owners who came from the Huejutla area. This factional dispute is discussed in Ernest Gruening, *Mexico and Its Heritage* (New York, 1928), 434-439. Wenceslao Martínez had been a closely of Nicolás Flores, the chief military commander and first constitutionalist governor of Hidalgo (in 1917). This governor was one of the *rancheros* from Pisaflores described in my earlier book cited above. At the end of the political rally by the agrarian leader from Veracruz, organized by Bernabe Sánchez, several peasant participants were assassinated; interview, Ancelmo Torres (a retired schoolteacher), Huejutla, June 9, 1985. Copies of

from Veracruz to organize a large political rally in the city of Huejutla for peasants from different parts of the Huasteca. That same year, the first petitions for land were also sent off to the state capital. But, as in so many other parts of Mexico, all of these petitions fell on deaf ears. Instead, during Calles' campaign against the clergy, Martínez channeled most of his revolutionary energies into the fight against an already powerless Catholic Church.

The *ranchero* strongbosses who came to power on the municipal level, especially in the southern part of Huejutla, included both *mestizos* and some Indians. Take for example the case of Gerónimo Lara, a former revolutionary and educated Indian, who took charge of the *municipio* of Yahualica in 1925. Lara, who was the son of an Indian *ranchero*, surrounded himself with an entourage of armed supporters and required the local population to supply the same type of unpaid services (carrying the mail, feeding his horses) that were exacted by his *mestizo* predecessors. Lara hand-picked all post-holders among his own relatives and supporters and did not allow any other families (*mestizo* or Indian) to participate in the running of local municipal affairs. In the *municipios* of Huazalingo, Huautla and Xochiatipan, *mestizo rancheros* set up similar *cacicazgos*. For example, in Huazalingo, a part-time schoolteacher and newcomer called Emilio Vargas ruled with an iron fist. Beginning as a municipal employee, he forged an alliance with the Gonzáles family who owned the small *hacienda* of San Pedro. Emilio Vargas then used his position as tax collector to acquire numerous properties. He also allied himself with prominent Nahuatl families who in turn dominated large Indian villages. Vargas charged duties on any produce sold in local markets and any critics or political opponents were ambushed and shot by his personal armed retainers or *pistoleros*. Such *pistoleros* were officially members of *defensas rurales* set up by the new revolutionary government to protect the local population from bandits and possible counter-revolutionaries![10]

The monopoly of power by families like the Lara, Vargas and González gave rise to a great deal of resentment. Every *municipio* had its share of discontented *rancheros*, including the relatives or friends of people who had been assassinated on the orders of local *caciques*. All of these opponents were waiting for an opportunity for revenge. Members of the same family sometimes also became internally divided, as in Xochiatipan, where the Bustos, who set up large ranches in the nineteenth century, were split into two opposing political factions in the 1920s.[11] These lingering hostilities broke out into a series of open confrontations with the translation of power from Plutarco Calles to Lázaro Cárdenas on the national level. After a period of factional in-fighting, the new powerholder and chief collaborator of Cárdenas in the region of Huejutla turned out to be Juvencio Nochebuena, previously out of favor on the local level.

all of the original petitions for land distribution and other documents relating to subsequent land grants are located in the historical archives (*archivo muerto*) of the Land Reform Office (*Reforma Agraria*, previously known as *Departamento de Reforma Agraria y Colonización*). Papers from this archive relating to the Huasteca region were housed in Mexico City in the 1970s, were then transferred to the state capital of Pachuca and in 1985 were in the process of again being transferred to Huejutla. This archive will henceforth be referred to as *AHRA* (*Archivo Histórico de la Reforma Agraria*). In 1926, the bishop of Huejutla, José Manríquez y Zarete (head of a new diocesis established only three years earlier) was arrested and marched off to Pachuca for criticizing the government; see Jean Meyer, *La Cristiada* (3 vols., Mexico City, 1973), I. Since the militant *Cristero* rebellion that developed in other parts of Mexico, never expanded into the Huasteca, Martínez concentrated on persecuting the only priest, Salvador Borja, who continued to operate in the area throughout this period.

10. Interviews with Juvencio Oaxaca, Santa Lucía (Calnali), October, 1981; Daniel Salazar, Mexico City, December 10, 1981; Bulfrano Coronel Ochoa, Tlatzonco (Huazalingo), May 31, 1985.

11. Interviews with Emigrio Vite, Huautla, May 11, 1983; Jesús Borja, Yahualica, June 6, 1985; Francisco Oviedo, Huejutla, June 9, 1985.

## THE *CACICAZGO* OF JUVENCIO NOCHEBUENA

Juvencio Nochebuena was a teenager when the Revolution broke out in 1910. He played a minor role in the subsequent period of civil war, but, after the Revolution, continued his career in the army (he reached the grade of general) and then in politics. General Nochebuena supported Alvaro Obregón in 1920 but left politics when he fell out of favor with Calles. Nochebuena then returned to the Huasteca to manage his family estate in the *municipio* of Atlapexco; a *rancho* called Teocuatitla. This *rancho*, which bordered on a smaller property owned by his farther, was later expanded into a sizable rural estate. In the early 1930s, Juvencio Nochebuena entered politics again and became a member of that faction of congress which supported the candidacy of Lázaro Cárdenas. He spent most of the rest of his life in Pachuca and Mexico City but continued to visit the Huasteca on a regular basis and to oversee the affairs of his properties in Atlapexco. The many posts he held included that of *presidente municipal* of the state capital of Pachuca (still under Cárdenas), *diputado federal* on several occasions (under Avila Camacho, Alemán and Ruíz Cortines), *diputado local* (under Alemán) and senator for Hidalgo (under Ruíz Cortines). During or between his various terms of office Nochebuena also served as general inspector of police, head of transit in the state capital (in the late 1940s), and he was a candidate for the post of general secretary of the League of Agrarian Communities and Peasant Sindicates of the state of Hidalgo. He also helped to set up an association of urban tenants in Mexico City. During his long political career, general Nochebuena was the chief patron and became the *compadre* of numerous individuals throughout the Huasteca and Sierra of Hidalgo.[12]

### *The Birth of an Agrarian Cacicazgo*

Juvencio Nochebuena started to establish his own powerbase in Huejutla just after completing his term of office as *diputado* under Cárdenas, when he returned home to take part in the political campaign for a new state governor. This campaign became an open contest for power between the politicians who had originally been allied to Matías Rodríguez and their opponents, led by Juvencio Nochebuena. Cárdenas' choice for governor of Hidalgo was a political protegee of Juvencio Nochebuena: Rojo Gómez, who had already played a major part in the redistribution of lands in the Laguna region of northern Mexico. Former Matías and Calles supporters in Huejutla wanted another candidate (Ordoñes) to become the next governor. When it became clear that Rojo Gómez would become the next state governor, Juvencio Nochebuena took the offensive by getting more directly involved in local politics. He not only hand-picked the first set of authorities for the newly created *municipio* of Atlapexco, where he owned his ranch, but ousted the Lara's from Yahualica and replaced them with one of his own relatives. He also personally led an armed attack on the newly created *municipio* of Jaltocan. Rojo Gómez' term of office as governor, beginning on April 1, 1936, ushered in two decades of strongboss rule by general Nochebuena in the district of

12. Interview, Nereo Nochebuena, Huejutla, May 21, 1981. Another reason Juvencio might have had to return to Huejutla is that he ran into trouble with the law. On October 28th, 1924 (while still a *coronel*), he was arrested for shooting a young man when the latter delivered his suit; see Theodomiro Manzano, *Anales del Estado de Hidalgo* (Pachuca, 1927), 2a parte. Most of the aspects of his political career were taken from letters, carbon copies of official documents and identification cards contained in a file of personal correspondence in the possession of one of his sons, Miguel Nochebuena, who lives in Mexico City. This file will henceforth be referred to as the *Nochebuena Papers*, hereafter: *NP*. There are also eight references (and photographs) of Juvencio Nochebuena in Gustavo Casasola's book, *Historia gráfica de la revolución mexicana* (4th. ed., Mexico City, 1967), IV, index on p. 2990.

Huejutla. After a short period of consolidation in 1937, Nochebuena managed to get his own supporters nominated for the next set of municipal elections and either evicted or gained the loyalty of all informal powerholders (including Martínez who stayed on as chief of police in Huejutla). Although Juvencio at that time served as mayor of Pachuca, his *ranchero* relatives, former revolutionary companions and hand-picked supporters carried out his orders.[13]

Together with Rojo Gómez, Juvencio Nochebuena implemented Cárdenas' policy of agrarianism in the Huasteca of Hidalgo which involved the transfer of portions of all remaining *haciendas* (mainly located in the northern part of Huejutla) to their peons and supervisor. Indeed, *ranchero* politicians (led by Nochebuena) suddenly became 'spokesmen' for the largely monolingual Indian peasant population of Huejutla and encouraged all villages of the region to submit agrarian petitions, if they had not already done so. *Mestizo rancheros* became *agraristas* because they realized that only in this manner could their political patron, Rojo Gómez, maintain his image as a socialist and a true follower of Lázaro Cárdenas. Not surprisingly, all of these petitions, as well as those that had been initiated when Wenceslao Martínez was still in power, received a favorable response from the state government within one or two years. In 1939, Rojo Gómez gave provisional titles to 31 villages for *ejidos* or *terrenos comunales* and an additional 66 communities submitted written requests to be included in Cárdenas' land reform.[14] Over half of these petitions came from villages in the southern part of the region. However, while radically changing the agrarian structure of Mexico as a whole, this land reform did not affect the political control or economic power of local *rancheros*.

Cárdenas' land reform was not implemented in the same manner in the two sub-regions of Huejutla. In the northern zone, Juvencio Nochebuena personally supervised the partition of most of the *haciendas* dating back to the pre-Revolutionary era. Although Cárdenas' land reform did meet with some opposition from local *hacendados*, the provisional transfer of land to peasant communities went fairly smoothly and more than half of the Nahua peasants in the northern zone received land in the form of *ejidos*. The *hacienda* owners were allowed to keep two hundred hectares but could no longer force their peons or tenants to work as servants or messengers. Legally, *hacienda* owners were thus transformed into *pequeños propietarios* (small owners) like their *ranchero* counterparts. Former peons of local *haciendas* still alive today, especially in villages like Chalahuiyapan and Otates (Huejutla) and Tamoyon (Huautla), consider general Juvencio Nochebuena to be 'a friend of the peasants' because of the role he played in the setting up of *ejidos* in this part ofthe district of Huejutla.[15]

13. Interviews, Ricardo Rodríguez, Yahualica, September 29, 1981; Maria Luisa Amador, Jaltocan, June 13, 1985; Luis Amador, Chiconcoac (Jaltocan, June 15, 1985. While the Nochebuena faction consolidated its position throughout most of the district of Huejutla, another family of former revolutionaries became the principal *caciques* in the neighboring district of Molango. This family consisted of the relatives of Honorato Austria from Tepehuacán de Guerrero, a *municipio* bordering on Orizatlán. For the next forty years the Austrias and the Nochebuenas were to each rule their respective areas of political influence, although they both tried to encroach on the others' territory whenever possible.

14. Rojo Gómez granted provisional titles to 44 of these 66 additional communities one year later. These figures were extracted from an inspection of all of the *expedientes* relating to the Huasteca of Hidalgo available in the *AHRA*.

15. According to a peasant from one northern village, interviewed on June 19, 1985, the *hacienda* owners had a peasant leader originally from Veracruz assassinated because of his attempts to organize agrarian peasants, Juvencio Nochebuena subsequently gave his full support (and protection) to another peasant leader, a bilingual Nahuatl peasant who acted as official legal advisor (*procudor indígena*) for the Nahuatl-speaking peasant population in the northern zone. However, some local landowners also sold sections of their estates to their estate supervisors or to wealthier peasants against government orders. Based on interviews, Nicolás Hernández (an older peasant who bought some of this land), El Zapote (Huejutla), June 2, 1985. Interview (in Nahuatl), Anto-

The same *ranchero* politicians who supervised the partition of local *haciendas*,'implemented' Cárdenas' land reform in the southern zone where most of the arable land consisted of farms and ranches privately owned by *mestizo* landowners and a minority of wealthy Nahuatl peasants. However, unlike the northern zone, land reform in most of the southern zone did not result in any real changes in the pattern of landholding. Local authorities declared practically the entire southern zone to be communal, as it had once been, and then persuaded the inhabitants of Nahuatl villages to petition for full recognition of their already existing 'communal lands' (for which they supposedly did not possess proper titles) in the form of *ejidos*. Many landowners added their names to these petitions as 'potential land recipients' with the understanding that land reform would be carried out 'only on paper' while others, who were illiterate, simply followed the orders of local *ranchero caciques*. The subsequent granting of land in this area therefore resulted in purely fictitious *ejidos*.[16]

The way that a large number of such fictitious *ejidos* were created illustrates the manner in which *ranchero* politicians manipulated the institutions of Nahua society. When several teams of surveyors arrived to measure the communal (i.e. judicial) boundaries of Nahua villages and to take censuses in the southern zone, they were accompanied by local politicians and schoolteachers (some of whom also owned *ranchos*). These 'peasant representatives', who acted as the guides and interpreters for these surveyors, convinced agrarian officials that no one in the southern zone owned any private properties (apart for a few very small *haciendas* dating back to the colonial era) and then directed representatives of Nahua *pueblos* to show such surveyors the existing administrative or judicial boundaries which no longer had anything to do with communal ownership of land. Technically, most privately owned *ranchos* were thereby incorporated into huge *ejidos*. Any local *rancheros* who raised questions about what implications this procedure might have for the farms they had bought or inherited, were told that the creation of *ejidos* would not change anything and would prevent the take-over of their land by so called outsiders.[17]

The largely fictitious *ejidos* in the formerly communal zone of Huejutla stood in stark contrast to the real *ejidos* established in the northern zone. This does not mean, however, that all peasants in the northern zone suddenly received sufficient land to satisfy all of their requirements. Some northern villages were granted all of the land to which they were entitled while other ended up having to wait many years for actual rights of possession. Moreover, even where *ejidos* were properly set up, they were subject to manipulation by politicians connected to landowning families. Moreover, not all northern *ejidos* were divided into parcels of equal size (as stipulated by law) and a number of communities were excluded from the original petitions altogether. The hopes of the inhabitants of such villages ever receiving their own land were dashed by the election of Avila Camacho in 1940 and the advent of more conservative regimes.[18]

---

nio Felipe Angeles, Tamoyon Primero (Huautla), May 17, 1983; interview (in Spanish) with the father of Bernabe Cruz, Los Otates (Huejutla), June 4, 1985.

16. For example, most of the original petitions for *ejidos* in the *municipios* of Atlapexco and Yahualica, include the phrase *"que se nos concede en dotación los terrenos que en la actualidad poseemos comunalmente."* These petitions were found in the archives of the state agrarian commission (*Archivo de la Comisión Agraria Mixta*) in Pachuca (hereafter *ACAM*). Most of the original petitions, as well as the subsequent acknowledgement of receipt of provisional land grants in Atlapexco and Yahualica were signed by Pedro Vélez or Pedro Larragoiti, local landowners who were henchmen of general Nochebuena.

17. Interview, Narciso Naranjo Bautista, a retired schoolteacher who accompanied several engineers and peasants to measure village boundaries in 1939, Huautla, May 13, 1983.

18. On the character of *Avilacamachismo*, see the essay of Wil Pansters in this volume.

### *The Conservative Reaction*

The process of land reform came to a virtual standstill in the 1940s. Few new petitions were sent to Pachuca and only nine villages received their definitive, final presidential resolutions. All of these *ejidos* were located in the *municipio* of Huautla and had belonged to three *haciendas* whose owners did not have political connections with the clique of people in power.[19] However, in the rest of Huejutla, former *hacienda* owners (now officially *pequeños propietarios*) started buying properties that still remained in private hands, including those located within the boundaries of fictitious *ejidos*. Some former *hacienda* owners bought land in the southern zone while southern *rancheros* bought sections of former *haciendas*. At this point it cannot be said that there were any real differences in class structure left between the two zones of Huejutla. For the next two decades landowners from both parts of the region, including Indian peasants with small ranchos, continued to create permanent, cultivated pastures and to introduce exotic breeds of cattle.

Despite the decline of agrarianism on the national level, Juvencio Nochebuena maintained his public image as an agrarian leader while he continued to be a friend of local *rancheros*. However, Nochebuena now started to emphasize the importance of education and the introduction of technological change in order to increase production. For example, Nochebuena used his connections in Mexico City to obtain scholarships for the graduates of rural schools, many of whom were his poorer relatives or the children of barely literate *rancheros*. Some of these students, as well as the children of Nahuatl families, were also sent off to residential schools.

In terms of economic development, general Nochebuena persuaded the federal government to ship Swiss bulls to the Huasteca, including those donated to Mexico by foreign governments, and encouraged local cattle ranchers to continue planting new forms of *zacate* and to fence in all pastures. Nochebuena also used his political influence to prevent the slaughter of cattle when the Mexican government signed an agreement with the United States to take drastic measures to stop the spread of a highly infectious cattle disease in the late 1940s. Since Huejutla was located just on the edge of the region considered to be infected, he arranged to have a quarantine line -used to prevent the spread of infection- to be placed just to the north of the region of Huejutla, so that cattle producers in the district of Huejutla would be immune to the obligatory destruction of cattle.[20]

The patronage of Juvencio Nochebuena extended to Nahua villages as well. For instance, he collected money to rebuild the village of Huazalinguillo (Huautla), destroyed by fire, helped the peasants of Tamoyon, who had already received their *ejido*, to get proper title to an additional 150 hectares of land, and settled numerous disputes related to boundaries, inheritance or personal animosities. In return, all of his supporters were expected to attend political rallies and demonstrations, especially those held for important politicians from Mexico City or Pachuca. These outsiders were inevitably impressed by the large turn-out of 'Nochebuena's Indians' and the hospitality provided at local banquets. Their impression of the Huasteca -one of colourful embroidered blouses of the Nahua women, the clean, white linnen trousers and shirts of their menfolk and the numerous garlands of flowers presented to any visiting dignitaries- belied the underlying current of conflict and repression that was still a part of everyday life in the Huasteca of Hidalgo. Indeed, some of the general's own relatives were professional thieves and cattle rustlers.[21]

---

19. These *ejidos* were Aquetzpalco, Ceresos, Chiliteco, El Aguacate, El Ixtle, La Mesa (all in 1944); Tamoyon Primero, Tamoyon Segundo (1943) and Tepeco (1947), *ACAM*, ramo ejidal.

20. Interview, Ezequil Reyes, one of the wealthiest *rancheros* from Huejutla who also owns the cinema and an apartment building in downtown Huejutla today, Huejutla, May 3, 1985.

21. When the general helped the peasants of Tamoyon to get an extension for their *ejido*, a piece of land that had been abandoned by the original owner after the Revolution, their completely

While Juvencio Nochebuena 'controlled' the Huasteca, local politicians took advantage of their connections with this influential leader for their own personal benefit. For example, local tax collectors confiscated rural properties from political opponents or poor relatives who did not have good connections with the general. Apart from continuing to work *faenas* in municipal administrative centres, poor peasants throughout the region were also expected to pay special taxes on the production of cash crops. Juvencio Nochebuena, presumably the most prominant 'agrarian' leader, even resorted to occasional forced labor in order to clear the pastures or to cut the cane of his own privately owned *rancho*. Almost all older peasants in the southern part of the district recall having participated in such *faenas* for the general. In some cases, his *pistoleros* simply arrived and distributed 'wages' in advance for work to be done in Nochebuena's ranch while at other times they ordered village authorities to bring day labourers to clear pastures or to carry wooden poles, used to construct fences, to his ranch without any financial remuneration whatsoever (apart from the customary drink of *aguardiente* around mid-day). Most older peasants interviewed in the 1980s, bitterly resented such obligatory labour, as well as the onerous duty of serving as messengers or couriers. Their views of the general contrast with those of the sons of Juvencio Nochebuena, most of whom were educated in private schools in Mexico City. These sons claim that most of the Indians liked their father so much that they used to come and 'work for him for free'![22]

The entire era of *Nochebuenismo* was characterized by factional disputes, frequent political assassinations and a high level of banditry and family feuds. This was particularly the case for the southern zone. Unlike the more Europeanized professionals and landowners whose families dominated the region prior to the Revolution, the *rancheros* of the southern zone were less refined in terms of speech and deportment. They also did not hesitate to use violence to settle personal disputes. Such disputes, ostensibly motivated by sexual jealousy or accusations of unfair business transactions, frequently

monolingual representative (*presidente del comisariado ejidal*) was flown in a small aircraft to be 'interviewed' by the then secretary of state and the state governor; he also personally delivered to both of them a large quantity of dried beef as a token of his appreciation; see data in tape recorded interview (in Nahuatl), Antonio Felipe Angeles, Tamoyon Primero, May17, 1983. This was also described during an interview with one such visitor, Maria Esther Fernández Nochebuena, a relative of the general who has lived almost her entire life in Mexico City, August 29, 1981. The mentioned relatives included several nephews who lived in Atlapexco and El Arenal (Yahualica); interview, Camilcar Martínez, also a relative of the general, At¡lapexco, September 23, 1981. The names first mentioned by this informant came up time and time again in subsequent conversations with people in this region.

22. Interviews, Pedro Palacios, Atlapexco, June 15, 1985; Pedro Ideroa, Huautla, May 14, 1985; David Arenas, Huejutla, May 6, 1985; Juvencio Oaxaca, Santa Lucia (Calnali), October 10, 1981; Herminio Sánchez, Mecatlan (Yahualica), April 8, 1982; Agustín Castillo, Huejutla, May 14, 1985. A head tax (called a *donativo*) was also still administered until the early fifties. Interviews (in Nahuatl), Teodolo Gómez, Mecatlán (Yahualica), April 16, 1982; Nicolás Ortega Limantzintla, Cuautenahuatl (Huautla), May 25, 1985; several older men (in a group interview), San Francisco (Huazalingo), June 7, 1985; Interviews (in Spanish), Camarino Ramos, Huautla, May 4, 1983; older peasant from Las Piedras, in La Coneja (Orizatlan), May 4, 1985; Timoteo Vargas, Yehuetlan (Huejutla), May 30, 1986; Jesús Borja, Yahualica, June 6, 1985; Ancelmo Torres, Huejutla, June 9, 1985. Taped interviews (in Nahuatl) with several older peasants in Cochiscoatitla (Atlapexco), April 7, 1982; oral interviews (in Nahuatl), Francisco Lara, Pepeyocatitla and José Lara, La Mesa Larga (both located in Yahualica), June 1, 1984; José Francisco Pascual Tepanijtic, Tlalchiyahualica (Yahualica), June 17, 1984; Interviews (in Spanish), Francisco Naranjo, Tecolotitla, September 1, 1981; Ancelmo Baltazar, Atlapexco, September 25, 1981; Sabino Longinos, Olma (Yahualica), September 27, 1981; Ignacio Gregorio Tolentino, Tlalchiyahualica (Yahualica), February 12, 1982; Clementis Ramírez, Pepeyocatitla (Yahualica), May 19, 1984; Ramón Jiménez Hernández, Audiencia Pública (Orizatlán), May 19, 1985; Juan Flores (from Jaltocan), Atlapexco, June 12, 1985. The 'Indians opinion' on their father was mentioned to me on several occasions by Juvencio Nochebuena's sons, most of whom were living in Atlapexco or in their family ranch (called Teocuatitla) in 1981.

erupted when the male offspring of landowners reached their twenties. At this point in their lives, young men had to negotiate marriages that would give them access to the maximum amount of privately-owned land. Many wealthy *rancheros* had more than one family through multiple marriages or various mistresses. Hence, each son might only inherit a small fraction of the family estate, or even end up as a landless cowboy or mule driver, unless he could marry the daughter of a landowner with no male heirs or disinherit his own siblings and cousins. Other men, born into prosperous families, turned to banditry or became *pistoleros* to avoid downward mobility into the ranks of the peasantry. Whenever such rebellious offspring robbed or killed members of other landowning families, their victims had to take the law into their own hands which would in turn trigger off family feuds.[23] Such disputes, all of which contained, to a greater or lesser degree, some combination of sexual jealousy, conflicts over inheritance and proving one's valour are a common theme in the popular culture of the region.

## THE DEMISE OF NOCHEBUENA AND OLD STYLE CACIQUISMO, POLITICS IN THE SIXTIES AND THE OUTBREAK OF A PEASANT REVOLT

Starting in 1945, economic expansion, together with the growth of the national bureaucracy and the educational system, made family feuds and the use of force in settling political disputes obsolete and unacceptable. Indeed, Juvencio Nochebuena, who represented the typical regional *caudillo* who came out of the Mexican Revolution, was himself transformed into a professional politician and an appendage of the stage on the national level, while maintaining his position of power in Huejutla through a combination of patronage, repression and piece-meal social reform. A new economic elite of modern cattle ranchers maintained good relations with Nochebuena and occasionally lent him money.[24] However, more businesslike and better educated *rancheros* became increasingly resentful of the general's political influence and his connections with local outlaws. Starting in 1950, with the election of Quintín Rueda Villagrán as governor of Hidalgo, Nochebuena's political power gradually started to decline.

In 1952 Juvencio Nochebuena still ran the presidential campaign for Ruíz Cortines in northern Hidalgo and invited all of his supporters to attend a huge political rally in downtown Huejutla. However, despite Nochebuena's background as a revolutionary and his close connections with Ruíz Cortines, an alliance of disgruntled local politicians and new men of wealth without connections to the old guard, soon disowned the general. These men gave their support to the new state governor, Rueda Villagrán, when this governor decided to reform the political administration of Hidalgo, put an end to lawlessness and cattle rustling in the Huasteca and counteract the political influence of general Juvencio Nochebuena. Not surprisingly, Juvencio Nochebuena and other high-ranking politicians connected to Nochebuena condemned Rueda Villagrán and tried to

23. The small police force stationed in Huejutla did not have the resources to undertake proper criminal investigations, and much less to apprehend suspects or known criminals. Even in the 1970s, a local businessman who had been seriously wounded in an ambush, could not convince the police to catch the man who had tried to kill him, unless he was willing to pay for their expenses and provide them with his own pick-up truck.

24. For example, this was the case for Ezequil Reyes, the man who became the wealthiest cattle producer and farmer of Huejutla; confirmed in an interview held with him on June 15, 1984. He also told me he rarely complained if minor *caciques* occasionally did not pay back small loans or if some of his cattle was stolen.

have him removed from office.[25] However, they were unable to stem the tide of political opposition and the subsequent disintegration of the Nochebuena cacicazgo.

The first action of Quintín Rueda Villagrán was to arrange to have a man from Atlapexco, whose father had been an opponent of Nochebuena, get elected as a member of the state legislature. Together, this *diputado* and the. governor nominated Nochebuena opponents as official candidates of the government party in most of the upcoming municipal elections or else persuaded former Nochebuena to switch sides. Nochebuena opponents also took advantage of a bitter dispute between several relatives of Juvencio Nochebuena and a newcomer called Crisantos. Crisantos, a reformed criminal (he had presumably repented after shooting a busload of passengers in the process of committing a political assassination in another part of Hidalgo) had originally been invited to settle in Atlapexco by the general.[26] The new governor and the *diputado local* tacitly supported Crisantos, who had already left Atlapexco, when Crisantos started recruiting a para-military band in order in wage war on the general. That same year, one of the main Nochebuena supporters, a *ranchero* from the *municipio* of Yahualica called Pedro Vélez, was assassinated while serving as municipal president of Huejutla.

Crisantos did not succeed in staging a successful military attack on the general's ranch in Teocuatitla, but he did set up his own sphere of influence in a remote part of the *municipio* of Yahualica. However, Crisantos also extorted the peasant population of Yahualica with the claim that he represented the government and then allied himself to one of the descendants of the small *hacienda* of Crisolco. Like many young *rancheros*, these descendants had turned to banditry and cattle rustling. We can thus see that, in stamping out the *caciquismo* of general Nochebuena, Rueda Villagran still had to rely the last of the old-fashioned *caciques* who resorted to such tactics as forced loans to recruit a private army. Like former *caciques*, Crisantos also used the money and animals he obtained through plunder or taxes to win friends among a significant portion of the peasant population and styled himself as an agrarian leader.[27] However, he lost credibility with the government and, as soon as he had served his purpose, he was hunted down as a common criminal.

While these events were taking place in the remotest part of Huejutla, the rest of the district remained relatively calm under a new set of officials directly appointed by Villagrán. For example, in Huazalingo, in 1954, no assassinations took place for the first time in their recorded history and cattle rustling was put to an end in Huautla. The governor also appointed a military commander, called Millan, as chief of police in

25. One of the arguments presented by these critics is that the governor was not a 'real Mexican' but of direct Spanish descent; interview, Daniel Salazar, Mexico City, May 31, 1985. Such accusations were also made in a series of letters found in the *Nochebuena Papers*. These papers also included reports with detailed information about which local politicians had supported Rueda Villagran and which had betrayed the general.

26. Crisantos, who had set up a liquor still and operated a store in Atlapexco, was a very distant relative of the general and his last name was also Nochebuena. The dispute in question started when one of the general's nephews, who was also a bandit, refused to pay back a loan and then insulted Crisantos and 'challenged his honor,' interviews, Nereo Nochebuena, Huejutla, May 31, 1981; Ildefonso Maya, March 6, 1982. Crisantos' life history was also reported in an official document, "Memorandum confidencial al C. presidente de la república (de J. Nochebuena)," *NP*, February 1, 1956.

27. Interviews, Ildefonso Maya, Huejutla, April 4, 1982; older peasant from Chipila, Chipila (Huautla), May 25, 1983; taped interview in Nahuatl with two elderly men, Cochiscoatitla, April, 1982. During the period when Crisantos was operating in the remote southern part of the *municipio* of Yahualica, several petitions on behalf of Nahua villages in this zone were set to Pachuca. All of these petitions, regarding a change of legal status from *ejido* back to communal land tenure, were completely ignored in the state capital and did not even get published in the official state newspaper (as required by law) until 1964! See *ACAM*, ramo comunal, exp. 5-2239 (Santa Teresa), exp. 5-2238 (Tlalchiyahualica), exp. 5-2239 (Mecatlan). See also *Periódico Official del Estado de Hidalgo*, 20, May 24 (1965).

the city of Huejutla. This military commander restored 'law and order' by flushing out a nest of gun slingers and cattle thiefs who had established themselves in the Nahua village of Santa Catarina as well as in the remote *mestizo* village of Las Piedras. Also, in 1955, municipal governments were for the first time given a small share of the revenues collected through state taxes on the sale of tobacco products. Most older informants (outside of Yahualica) recall this as the period when compulsory *faenas* were finally ended.[28]

The lowest point in Nochebuena's career came in 1957, when he failed to become the official candidate for the governorship of Hidalgo. Instead, Alfonso Corona del Rosal became governor in 1958, and Juvencia Nochebuena was given the less important post of senator. Juvencio Nochebuena died from illness (some Mexicans say from rage) that same year. His closest political friends attributed the political downfall of the general to his failure to get Rojo Gómez's approval for his nomination as governor.[29] However, by the end of the 1950s the general had already lost a great deal of political influence in a region over which he once had almost total control. The downfall of Juvencio Nochebuena can be better explained by the changing nature of the Mexican economy and its corresponding political system. With the rapid expansion of modern capitalism, the Mexican state no longer needed to rely on local *caudillos* for its survival nor was it to its advantage to have armed factional struggles impede the spread of economic development into hitherto remote regions.

Let us then have a brief look at the economic changes that took place in the same decade that witnessed the demise of general Nochebuena. Throughout the 1950s, Huejutla experienced a rapid growth in commercial agriculture as well as the further expansion of modern cattle production. The latter involved renting out scrubland and forest to peasant cultivators to create more permanent pastures. In this manner, local peasants continued to have access to land for subsistence cultivation and these same peasants also worked for wages in local farms and ranches. The prosperity associated with this short-lived boom is exemplified by the rapid growth of the city of Huejutla (which even had a small airfield). Other parts of Huejutla benefited as well and a large number of Nahuatl villages built schools and chapels and expanded their religious feasts.[30] This growing prosperity and better communication with the outside world undermined the informal power of local *caciques* who had been the basis of Nochebuena's political power. Under Quintín Rueda Villagrán and Corona del Rosal, a new generation of more educated politicians started to assume political control. Prominent cattle producers farmers merchants and schoolteachers who had not been revolutionary started to hold public office. Most of these new municipal authorities were more progressive *rancheros* who had been educated and had also lived in other parts of Mexico.

Despite continued growth and the end of the worst abuses of strongboss rule in the Huasteca, the decade of the 1950s did not bring about an improvement in everyone's way of life. This same decade was also characterized by an increase in seasonal migra-

28. Interview with government official (*recaudador de rentas*), Huazalingo, June 7, 1985; Cleto Mendoza (former *presidente municipal* of Huautla), May 19, 1985. Interviews, Ancelmo Torres, June 9, 1985; Teodoro Guillén, Chililico, June 1, 1985; Nicolás Hernández, El Zapote (Huejutla), June 2, 1985; Nereo Nochebuena, May 12, 1983.

29. Interview, Miguel Nochebuena, Mexico City, August 27, 1981. According to another son (Nereo), Juvencio initially helped Rojo Gómez get his education and introduced him to politics. Apparently, Juvencio also was the political patron of Suárez Molino (interim governor of Hidalgo in the 1970s) to whom he even lent his jacket when Suárez was married. Another son complained that these and other politicians eventually became rich and famous, whereas their father died penniless (comparatively speaking) and has also been forgotten in the annals of history.

30. This and other information about the economic history of the area is based on numerous interviews, conducted in both Nahuatl and Spanish, with mainly older informants in various localities between 1981 and 1987. These interviews, typed unto 160 5x8 index cards, are available from the author.

tory wage labour by land-poor peasants and the continuing concentration of land ownership. During the 1960s things got worse for the poor; an increasing number of day laborers found that they could no longer find anywhere to grow maize since most arable land and forest had already been converted to permanent pastures.[31] Moreover, local landowners shut down more labour-intensive enterprises, including tobacco growing and the cultivation of cane sugar to produce *pilón* because these enterprises were no longer profitable. The further expansion of cattle production, even in isolated Nahua villages, was given additional momentum with the completion of a paved highway in 1971 connecting Huejutla with the state capital and the port of Tampico, further integrating the region into the market. However, even seasonal employment in other parts of the Huasteca became harder to obtain as a result of the conversion from cotton to sorghum along the Gulf coast. Rising unemployment and increasing demographic pressures, at a time when the small reserves of arable land were shrinking even faster than before, meant that an increasing number of poor peasants were no longer able to improve their economic position through a combination of subsistence cultivation and wage labour.

At the same time, new roads facilitated visits to the region by outsiders, including officials from a government-affiliated organization called the *CAM* (*Consejo Agrario Mexicano*). *CAM* officials and members of other left-wing political organization, anxious to use peasant discontent to further their own political goals, organized peasants groups to petition for land and, in instances where these groups had strong legal claims arising out of earlier unfulfilled land reforms, actually to take possession of the land directly. Thus, during the second half of the 1970s, direct-action agrarianism spread throughout the region of Huejutla causing an explosion of violence as landowners attempted to defend their properties. The main complaint of the land-poor peasants who supported this agrarian movement was that local landowners no longer 'helped' the peasants by renting out land or providing employment.[32] Modern landowning ranchers, in turn, emphasized the increase in standards of living and the opportunities available to hard-working peasants and complained that Indian peasants were *"becoming lazy and no longer show any respect"*. Further political mobilization and land invasions resulted in overt class conflicts both within peasant communities and between poor peasants and absentee cattle ranchers. An escalation of violent confrontation, and the loss of legitimacy on the part of the ruling party, closely identified with the local landowning elite, finally forced the government to take drastic measures and to restructure both the economy and the administrative system of the region.

## CONCLUSIONS

*Ranchero caciques* like Nochebuena constituted an important base of support for the new regime that emerged under Alvaro Obregón and Plutarco Calles. The revolutionary strongbosses who consolidated their power in Huejutla in the 1920s represented a form of political control associated with a traditional *ranchero* economy where *rancheros* used

31. The overall population of the Huasteca of Hidalgo increased by 42% between 1950 and 1970. Yet, in this already densely populated region (higher than the state average), cattle production rose even higher (by 56.7%) in just one decade (between 1960 and 1970). See figures on a chart in Angel Bassols Batalla's *Las Huastecas en el desarrollo de México* (Mexico City, 1977) 192.

32. The outbreak of a violent peasant revolt in Huejutla can easily be interpreted in terms of the theoretical model proposed by John Tutino in the first chapter of his book, *From Insurrection to Revolution in Mexico. Social Bases of Agrarian Violence, 1750-1940* (Princeton, 1986). Most of the peasants in Huejutla in de 1970s were 'long secure dependents rapidly made to face insecurity', see 31, who rebelled under the right set of circumstances, as outlined by Tutino.

a combination of paternalism and authoritarian rule to reinforce their class interests. *Ranchero* powerholders also resorted to the use of arms to settle intra-elite disputes over power. *Ranchero* politicians, mainly *mestizos*, were in turn allied to better-off Indian peasants who used similar tactics to maintain their control over the Nahua communities which provided most of the local labour force. Nochebuena was the chief link between the state and this local power elite starting with the regime of Lázaro Cárdenas. However, after 1950, Nochebuena's strongboss rule and the type of people on whom he depended to maintain his local base of support were no longer required by the Mexican state. The political control exercised by old-fashioned *rancheros* and their traditional cultural values were also no longer compatible with the economic interests of a new type of more educated cattle rancher and commercial farmer, i.e. modern *rancheros*. Hence, both the paternalism and violence associated with the *cacicazgo* of Nochebuena faded away. Not only did modern businessmen and their political representatives have a different relationship with the Mexican state, but their links with the predominantly Nahuatl-speaking peasants population were also radically altered. This change, both in the structure of local class relations and in the nature of the relationship between a regional elite and the state, set the stage for the recent political turmoil in Huejutla.

The peasant uprising that broke out in the 1970s was primarily caused by the negative impact of modernization, especially the expansion of modern cattle production which created a polarization between economic classes. However, we must not ignore the corresponding changes in the system of cultural values which had hitherto legitimized the local class structure. Older, more old-fashioned bilingual *rancheros* frequently comment on the fact that a new generation of modern ranchers (and professionals who are offspring of *rancheros*) no longer understand either the language or the customs of the inhabitants of Nahuatl peasant communities.[33] This growing cultural gap added fuel to a class conflict which was conceptualized by many in terms of an opposition between *masehuali*, Nahuatl peasants, and *coyomej*, rich, Spanish-speakers.[34] We also cannot afford to ignore the influence of local folk interpretations of historical events. The fighting among rival factions in the 1930s, the political dominance of Juvencio Nochebuena and the short-lived economic boom of the 1950s were fresh in the memories of those who became involved in conflicts over land in the 1970s and 1980s. These memories, filtered through the perspective of people with very different class interests, were used to justify their respective political positions. Radical peasant leaders emphasized the exploitative nature of the *hacienda* system and the use of coercive forms of labour by municipal governments in the past. In contrast, commercial farmers and ranchers pointed out that servile labour and the most blatant abuses of the system of *caciquismo* disappeared long before the outbreak of land invasions. Ironically, prior to 1970, educated and progressive landowners severely criticized Juvencio Nochebuena for his abuses of power but, after 1980, these same landowners lamented that the former *cacique* was no longer alive to prevent peasant rebellions and political anarchy.

The expropriation of land in 1981, following a series of land invasions, does not mean that poor peasants have won their class struggle. Today, the people who were the

33. In my research, I observed that many young professionals whose *mestizo* parents were bilingual were no longer able to either speak or understand Nahuatl. In addition, the formerly almost completely monolingual day-laborers who in the past could only speak Nahuatl are today rapidly becoming bilingual as a result of their contact with the national culture both as migratory labourers and through the educational system.

34. Although conceptualized by many local people, as well as by most outsiders, in dichotomous ethnic terms, class conflicts in the 1970s and 1980s were much more complex. Poor, landless *mestizo* peasants also took part in land invasions, together with their Indian counterparts and in some cases, such poor *mestizo* peasants were even pitted against wealthy, landowning Nahuatl peasants. The use of ethnic labels and the complex relationship between class and ethnicity were examined in my article, "Class and Ethnicity".

most powerful landowning ranchers and farmers, who no longer own land in Hidalgo, have become commercial middlemen or run an expanded state bureaucracy in Huejutla. This government bureaucracy, including rural developments agencies and the local land reform office, functions to develop new forms of class control and ideological hegemony over a radicalized peasant population. Both the rebellion of local peasants and their ultimate subordination must be seen in the broader context of the relationship between a local political elite and the Mexican state. Although this state was originally created with the help of the *rancheros* (whose children faced a peasant rebellion in the 1970s), the very policies of this state brought about the changes that resulted in open class warfare between peasants and modern *rancheros*. Indeed, Juvencio Nochebuena himself helped to bring about the process of modernization that brought about both his demise and eventually, the disappearance of a class of *rancheros*.[35] However, although the Mexican state expropriated all privately-owned land in Huejutla in the 1980s, the new economic and political elite of Huejutla today is still largely composed of the offspring of *rancheros* who came to power at the end of the Mexican Revolution.

35. For example, Juvencio Nochebuena sent the original petitions to speed up the construction of the highway from Mexico to Tampico via Huejutla.

CHAPTER ELEVEN

# Urban *Hacendados*: The Industrial Bourgeoisie of Guadalajara

CARLOS ALBA VEGA
AND
DIRK KRUIJT*

## INTRODUCTION

In Latin America the regional issue has been a point of particular concern from the colonial period to the present. From the 1930s rural and commercial elites re-unified the regions as a territorial base of their economic and political power. The process of industrialization in the principal countries of Latin America -Argentina, Brazil, Columbia, Mexico and Venezuela- since the 1930s, strengthened the role of the state and gave rise to a process of political, social and economic centralization in the different capitals of the respective countries. The role of the landowning aristocracies, traditionally the nucleus of regional power, was consequently replaced by that of a national and regional industrial bourgeoisie, at times allied with, and at times opposed to the power of the state. From the beginning of the 1970s transnational capital, primarily North-American, Japanese and German entered this configuration of interests -partially parallel and partially antagonistic- between public and private capital.[1]

The present study is an illustrative case of the formation and consolidation of the industrial bourgeoisie in Mexico -that of Guadalajara, Jalisco, the second largest city and after Mexico City and Monterrey the third economic center of the republic. It is an attractive case because it gives us the opportunity to analyze in detail the transformation of a rural-commercial region into an urban-industrial one, where both formal and informal economies of considerable scale coexist and where regional, out-of-state, transnational and state capital also coexist, in heterogeneous and uneven levels of development. In contrast to the process of in-

* *Economist Carlos Alba Vega is researcher of El Colegio de Jalisco, Avenida de las Rosas 543, Col. Chapalita 54.000, Guadalajara, Jal., Mexico. Sociologist Dirk Kruijt works at the Center for Caribbean and Latin American Studies (CARLAS), University of Utrecht, Heidelberglaan 2, P.O. Box 80.140, 3508 TC Utrecht, The Netherlands.* *This chapter is based on the study* ***Los empresarios y la industria de Guadalajara*** (Guadalajara, *1988). We would like to thank Simon Miller for his linguistic assistance.*

1. See for further discussion Menno Vellinga and Dirk Kruijt, *Industrialization and Regional Development in Colombia* (Amsterdam, 1983); Peter Evans, *Dependent Development. The Alliance of Multinational, State and Local Capital in Brazil* (Princeton, 1979); René Armand Dreyfuss, *A conquista do Estado. Ecao política, poder e golpe de clase* (Petrópolis, 1983).

dustrialization in the national centers of Latin America, like Sao Paulo or Mexico City, or in the regional centers of industry like Monterrey or Medellin, the industrialization of Guadalajara and the simultaneous development of a formal and informal economy, is a more recent development and less well known.[2]

This essay is divided into separate parts: first, to locate the question in its context, we offer a brief sketch of the historical development of the region of Jalisco, the tradition of cattle-raising on the *haciendas*, the formation of a landowning-commercial oligarchy, the growth of Guadalajara as an administrative, commercial and religious center, the role of the Catholic Church, the direct relations among industries in the 1930s, the process of urbanization in Guadalajara, and finally the subordination of agriculture to urban-industrial economy. In the second part, which treats the present condition of industry, the themes are: comparison with other Mexican industrial centers like Mexico City and Monterrey, Jalisco's role in national industry, small, medium and large industry and the articulation between the formal and informal sector; and the presence of different forms of property and the relations of these forms in large industry. The third part of this chapter concentrates on the industrial bourgeoisie of Guadalajara -its economic interests, the formation of industrial groupings and conglomerates, its management organization and its ideology. The concluding part contains two comparisons:

- a comparison between the present industrial bourgeoisie and the rural-commercial oligarchy of the end of the eighteenth century;
- a comparison between the bourgeoisie of Guadalajara and Monterrey, the latter being a classical example of a regional bourgeoisie; since it has exercised almost absolute control over its own territory for almost a century.

## THE HISTORICAL LEGACY

Once the city of Guadalajara had been founded, within 50 years it transformed itself into the cultural, commercial, religious and administrative center of western Mexico. Jalisco was the cradle of Nueva Galicia, and the limits which set it off from New Spain were created as much by the power games between *conquistadores* as by the distance from the center of power in Mexico City.[3] The *Audiencia* of Nueva Galicia, conceded by the Spanish Court, had as much independence as various others elsewhere in Mexico. The dominant class, composed of merchants and *hacienda* owners and connected closely to the Church, sought the formation of an autonomous viceroyalty whose capital would be Guadalajara. They did not succeed, but by the end of the colonial period the merchants of the city profitted from the break of the old commercial monopoly on outside trade that had existed for centuries. In the nineteenth century the struggle between capital/centralism and federal/regionalism was located most fiercely in Jalisco. During the 1920s and 1930s the *Cristero*-movement -a religious civil war with regional roots- was centered in Jalisco.

2. Warren Dean, *The Industrialization of Sao Paulo, 1880-1945* (Austin, 1969); James Parsons, *La colonización antioqueña en el occidente de Colombia* (Bogotá, 1979); Mario Cerutti, *Burguesía y capitalismo en Monterrey, 1850-1910* (Monterrey, 1983).

3. Nueva Galicia comprised the current states of Jalisco, Nayarit, Aguascalientes, parts of Zacatecas, Sinaloa and Durango.

Jalisco is a region with strong traditions. It has the image of the most 'mexican' state of the country: cowboys in traditional costume, *mariachi* music, *machismo*, and the values of honor, loyalty and Christianity. Cattle breeding, by its very nature, called into existence the large *latifundia* on which the herds were able to expand extensively. For the origins of agricultural and breeding activity, we need to look not only at the requirements of the growing local population, but also at the urgent demands of other expanding regions in Mexico -particularly the mining regions. The majority of the production and marketing of meat and hides was in the hands of an oligarchy, simultaneously owners of the land and political decision makers. Cereals, especially wheat, were also controlled by this regional oligarchy. Cattle raised in western Mexico, one of the most important products to the entire viceroyalty, was shipped as far as the mining zones of the southeast, and other regions outside New Spain. This production was from its beginnings the property of the regional oligarchy, comprised of a few great families, the majority interrelated to each other in some way, who founded the cattle-breeding dynasties.[4]

According to Serrera we might classify two separate groups as belonging to this oligarchy: the first had its origins in the beginning of the colonial period and dated from the first appropriations of the land by the Spanish. They were able to preserve, over three centuries, the property of their ancestors using a variety of mechanisms to retain control of economic and political resources: intermarriage within the same group, primogeniture, disowning of poorer branches of the family, and relationships with godparents of their children. The second group was later in origin and with more diverse shades of extraction -any were European adventurers who had entered into mining or commerce. Miners and merchants like Cañedo and Vizcarra were typical of the colonial phenomenon of transferring capital accumulated from mining or business to the ownership of land. These new landowners lost no time in marrying into the old families of regional landholders and in sharing with them key positions of economic and political power.

Jalisco, a region with a cattle-raising and commercial tradition and characterized by an elite based in both economic sectors, highlighted its regional ambitions in the city of Guadalajara which had developed since the beginning of the seventeenth century as an administrative and commercial center. The most prosperous period of the colonial era was the second half of the eighteenth century. The city flourished as a cultural center for all of western Mexico and as an urban center for artisans. Its significance was also marked by the presence of educational services -principally the university- and for having constituted one of the most important religious centers of Mexico, perhaps of all Latin America. During the colonial era the regional clergy had succeeded in accumulating a treasure that contrasted starkly with the indigence of the state. This had been made possible by tithes, donations, legacies and inheritances, interest received on its own capital investments, and profit from its own agricultural and cattle enterprises. During

4. For a more detailed discussion on the mining sector of Zacatecas, see Peter Bakewell, *Minería y sociedad en México colonial. Zacatecas, 1546-1700* (Mexico City, 1976; transl. from the English, Cambridge, 1972). For greater detail on Nueva Galicia, see Richard B. Lindley, "Kinship and Credit in the Structure of Guadalajara's Oligarchy, 1800-1830" (Ph. D. diss., University of Texas, Austin, 1976); Ramón Serrera Contreras, *Guadalajara ganadera. Estudio regional novohispano, 1760-1805* (Seville, 1977); Eric Van Young, *Hacienda and Market in Eighteenth-Century Mexico. The Rural Economy of the Guadalajara Region, 1675-1820* (Berkeley, 1981). Several historical studies have emphasized the persistence of other forms of rural properties, especially the medium and small farm, see the review of Eric Van Young, "A modo de conclusión: el siglo paradójico," in *Empresarios, indios y estado. Perfil de la economía mexicana (Siglo XVIII)*, Arij Ouweneel and Cristina Torales Pacheco, eds. (Amsterdam, 1988), 206-231.

the eighteenth century the Church became the principal financing agent of the region. For example, between 1721-1790 of all the money loaned in Nueva Galicia whose origin has been recorded in the registries, the Church accounted for four-fifths, almost all of it coming from Guadalajara.[5]

It is worth pointing out that from the beginning of the colonial era economic and political power was linked closely to the Church. The large landowners concentrated their fortunes by giving the inheritance to one son only, generally the first born, *"according to the rules instituted by the founder of the estate, and approved by the King, through the Council of the Indies."*[6] One of the greatest of these sons of Nueva Galicia was José Rincon Gallardo, the owner of the impressive estate, the *Cienega de Mata*. Besides its importance to civil and military powers -Rincon was married to the daughter of a minister of the court-, the system of primogeniture was closely linked to the Church. For instance, Rincon's sister entered a contemplative order at the convent of Santa Mónica in Guadalajara. Like many of the rich merchants and miners, Rincon Gallardo tried to reconcile the state of his soul with the economic interest of his family, and so became the patron of five churches and monasteries. This example is by no means an exceptional case. During the colonial period, and through the nineteenth century, and even into our own century, the great landowning and former landowning families, merchants and industrial entrepreneurs have had relatives among the secular and regular clergy.

The most important economic, political and ideological changes in the region took place in the 1930s and 1940s of this century. Agrarian reform and the *Cristero*-movement coincided with the rapid urbanization of Jalisco and the growth of Guadalajara. The area was transformed from a rural region into an urban-industrial entity. Agrarian reform broke the power of the traditional elite, composed of landowners and merchants. The urbanization of Guadalajara accentuated the economic and political centralization of power and the industrialization of the metropolitan zone, achieved at the cost of the subordination of the region's agriculture. The *Cristero*-revolt was a popular movement, fundamentally rural, in which people of all ages and both sexes participated. This movement, for political and ideological reasons, threw *campesinos* and people of low income into opposition with those who had come out on top after the Revolution of 1910.[7] Above both these groups and exercising a clear influence, were the post-revolutionary

5. Rodney Anderson, *Guadalajara a la consumación de la independencia. Estudio de población según los padrones de 1821-1822* (Guadalajara, 1983); Carmen Castañeda, *El sistema universitario en Nueva Galicia* (Guadalajara, 1984); Linda Greenow, *Credit and Socioeconomic Change in Colonial Mexico. Loans and Mortgages in Guadalajara, 1720-1820* (Boulder, 1983).

6. Jorge Palomino y Cañedo, *La casa y mayorazgo de Cienega de Nueva Galicia* (2 vols., Mexico City, 1947), I, 96. Shortly after independence, an Englishman looking for business opportunities described Guadalajara, as a good Protestant, in this way: *"The population is religious almost to fanatical excesses. (...) If one were known to be Protestant one might be expelled as a leper, so easily do they believe it a duty to God to cleanse their land of Jews and heretics (among whom they include Protestants) (...). My companions and I are the first to live here in peace, treated with espect by the inhabitants. We owe this to our punctual attendance at Mass and observance of Holy Days, for which we earn the reputation of true Christians."* Quoted from T. Penney, "A Sketch of the Customs and Society of Mexico in a Series of Familiar Letters; and a Journal of Travels in the Interior, During the Years 1824, 1825, 1826," published in *Guadalajara a través de los tiempos. Tomo I: 1586-1867*, Juan B. Iguiñiz, ed. (Guadalajara, 1950).

7. See Jean Meyer, *La Cristiada* (3 vols., Mexico City, 1976); José Díaz and Román Rodríguez, *El movimiento cristero: siciedad y conflicto en los Altos de Jalisco* (Mexico City, 1979); Víctor Ceja Reyes, *Los Cristeros. Crónica de los que perdieron* (Mexico City, 1981).

state and the Church, both in process of redefining their positions and influence on civil society. The *Cristero*-revolt very possibly caused more social mobility han the Revolution. It had the immediate impact of an enormous migration from the countryside. For example, during the single year 1927-1928 there occurred the most significant social movement in the Jalisco countryside: 475,000 Mexicans emigrated to the United States. In addition to this, the large urban centers of Mexico received thousands of rural migrants seeking better living conditions. For the people of Jalisco Guadalajara was the principal center of attraction. During the 1920s the city grew by 25 percent, while the rest of the state grew by only 2½ percent.

The agrarian reform and distribution of land reached its most significant impact during the presidency of Lazaro Cárdenas, during the second half of the 1930s. The modernization of the national economy, supported by the state during the following years, resulted primarily in the industrialization of a few urban centers (Mexico City, Monterrey and Guadalajara) and in the improvement of the economic infrastructure (land transport, railroads and communications); the period was also marked by the beginning of gradual mechanization of agriculture. The petrol engine, recently arrived in Jalisco, showed its capacity to increase agricultural production at the same time it reduced the need for human labor. These modifications of the agrarian structure resulted in the proportionate and slow transformation of an extensive cattle raising enterprise into a more intensive one where it was necessary to raise cattle on smaller areas of land. In this sense the tractor caused part of a change in the ownership of land by the gradual substitution of the tractor for the enormous quantities of oxen and mules which had previously been necessary for cultivation. The gradual penetration of industrial capital into the rural context above all by means of new technology, and the attraction of the centers of urban expansion, occurred at the same time that the agrarian reform of the 1930s was being carried out.

The country and with it Jalisco, was growing rapidly, but this growth did not benefit equally the various zones, nor its diverse economic sectors, much less the classes and social groupings of the countryside. The double subordination -of agriculture to industry, and the countryside to the city- kept on pushing the growing population of the cooperative farming communities (*ejidos*) and villages into the industrialized centers. The rural areas -to their loss- aided the development of urban areas and industry thanks to the transfer of raw materials, foodstuffs and a large workforce to the more developed centers. In Guadalajara a few large agro-industrial enterprises were developed -for example, Atentique (paper), Nestlé (milk products), the Danesa creamery and others, most especially in the area of vegetable oil. All of these used the raw materials of agriculture, cattle raising and forestry. In the countryside, on the other hand, mechanization revolutionized the production processes. At the technological level, between 1940 and 1950, investment in farm machinery multiplied ten times. Besides, investment changed its orientation: from this period on, and in an increasing way, more was invested in modern, rather than traditional, technology.

At the beginning of the decade of the 1940s, there were 128 tractors and at its end that number had reached 760. The acquisition of tractors, trucks and pickups represented respectively 26 and 19 percent of regional, rural investment. The strategy of agrícultural modernization undertaken by Mexican governments at the beginning of the 1940s provoked unequal models of development. The best land and the best equipped proprietors received the most significant advantages of the technological process. That is, it was the most fertile, best irrigated land and those with the best communication systems that received the first tractors and other farming implements, the best seed, fertilizer and insecticides. For the great majority of small landholders, communal farmers and simple farm laborers, however, modernization meant simply an accelerated expulsion from the land and a migration towards the cities or the United States. The number of illegal immigrants apprehended or deported, for example, grew in a remarkable way: in 1940 the number had reached 8,000; in 1942 10,000; in 1944 40,000; in 1946 115,000; and in 1960 475,000. In the case of Guadalajara, which had become a center of attraction for a wide region consisting of Jalisco and neighbouring states, the population increased 60 percent during the same period, from 235,000 in 1940 to 380,000 in 1950. In the following decade, from 1950 to 1960, population growth was the most accelerated registered to date. The population of Jalisco went from 1,750,000 to 2,450,000; this growth took place primarily in the urban areas of the state and especially in the metropolitan zone of Guadalajara.· In this decade, for the first time, the urban population was greater than the rural. The proportion of the state population that was made up of the urban areas was as follows: 13 percent in 1910, 37 percent in 1920, 39 percent in 1930, 41 percent in 1940, 48 percent in 1950, 59 percent in 1960, 69 percent in 1970 and 80 percent in 1980. The metropolitan zone, composed of Guadalajara, Zapopan and Tlaquepaque, received between 1950 and 1960 one quarter of a million immigrants and went from 380,000 to 750,000 inhabitants. By 1970 it had 1,200,000 inhabitants and 15 years later had reached 3½ million.[8]

The tendency to substitute machine for manual labor had followed its course, but not without the participation of large national and international interests. It would appear that the years 1966-1970 were decisive: during these years the urban industrial productive apparatus broadened and diversified in Guadalajara. The production of traditional consumer goods like foodstuffs, beverages, footwear, textiles and clothing increased, but also some new industrial production intermediate goods and investment capital, made their appearance. This industrial growth, however, benefitted above all the urban population and the new industrial merchants, construction and banking elites, followed by a growing urban middle class. Profits from industry were not reinvested in the countryside. In spite of the fact that agricultural modernization reached certain areas and sectors of the countryside, it did not do much more than heighten unemployment and spur the flight to the cities. Increased technology also heightened the polarization between two types of agriculture: one modern, oriented towards the urban-industrial market, whose principal products were sugar cane, corn, wheat and sorghum (and more recently fruits for export), and the other -subsistence farming mostly on small private holdings or communal lands, alloted predominantly to the cultivation of corn, but unable to offer full employment to a peasant family.

The control of prices of some basic products -like corn and sugar- resulted in an additional kind of subsidy by the rural sector to the urban-industrial sector. Prices and production of goods were stimulated or depressed, always to the benefit of industry, whether by guaranteeing low-cost food consumption in the cities or by providing agro-industry with its necessary resources. The cases of milk and sorghum are most illustrative. As a consequence of agrarian reform under Lazaro Cárdenas, the traditional *latifundista* oligarchy had disappeared, or at least had lost a great part of its power. And following the structural changes in agriculture, there were corresponding changes in the use of capital in farming and livestock. Generally, large properties were broken up and had to make room for grazing land on much smaller acreage than before. Cattle raising, previously an extensive operation, became intensive dairy farming. In these transformations,

8. Jorge Martínez Saldaña, "Emigración de un pueblo mexicano a los Estados Unidos. El caso de Arandas, Jalisco" (Manuscript, Universidad de Guadalajara, 1976), 81ff.; Cynthia Hewitt de Alcántara, *La modernización de la agricultura mexicana, 1940-1970* (Mexico City, 1978), 99.

transnational corporations played a significant role, arriving in Jalisco at the time of the Second World War and placing themselves advantageously in expanding internal markets. Nestlé, for example, spurred the growth of dairy farming in the region and supported the creation of new farms and ranches, many of which were converted into exclusive providers to the company. Other transnational corporations which arrived in Jalisco, and had a profound effect on the rural context, were the feed industries; corporations like Anderson and Clayton and Purina pushed for the opening of the market for livestock feed. Together with many foreign and national industries, fodder business of all sizes appeared in the farming regions of Jalisco. Their requirements for raw materials spurred the introduction and growth of sorghum production. The cultivation of this crop, destined for industrial use, spread rapidly with great success. Again, it was local and transnational corporations like Anderson and Clayton, Purina and Northrop which determined the varieties of crop to be planted.

With the advantages to local, national and transnational industrial capital, and because of the attraction of greater profits for larger farmers, the last 20 years have seen the transfer of surplus from agricultural zones in Jalisco -surpluses which had previously been retained by the communities themselves. This has terminated a slow process of the incorporation of agriculture and the subordination of farming and cattle rasing to industry and the centers of industry. The relation between city and country in the west of Mexico has therefore been redefined.

## THE INDUSTRIAL SITUATION

To typify Jaliscan industry is not an easy matter. On the contrary, the industrial structure is heterogeneous in various ways. It is spread out in many branches and sub-branches. In some branches small businesses predominate, in others medium-sized businesses. In almost all branches, however, a few large businesses are present. They use different types of raw materials, different technology, social organization of labor and forms of management. Not only are they distinguished with respect to their size, but also with regard to the forms of property: as much in terms of the source of investment but also in terms of the presence of state or private capital. There are business groupings in the form of formal and informal holdings, which administer in a centralized manner other businesses of which they are majority stockholders. This presents, in general, a complicated interconnection between local, national and transnational interests, sometimes operating in alliance, at other times entering into conflict. They are further intertwined in a different manner with other economic sectors and with organizations and institutions of political power. They differ at times with respect to ideology and organization. But to characterize Jaliscan industry usefully, we will begin by typifying it in national terms. Then an analysis according to branch and size will follow. Subsequently, the articulation between the formal and informal sectors of the economy will be discussed, and we will present finally, in this section of the essay, the relation between different forms of property.

In Mexico, industry never achieved a great physical dispersion. Taken together, the data from the three most industrialized regions -the metropolitan areas of Mexico City, Monterrey and Guadalajara-, show that, according to all recent indicators, the physical plant, the bourgeoisie and the industrial working class have found themselves intensely concentrated, see Table 1. In these three regions is found 50 percent of the industrial establishments, 55 percent of fixed activity, and 67 percent of the gross worth of production and accumulated value. Sixty percent of industrial employment is generated in these three areas. Sixty percent of all workers and seventy percent of white collar workers have found work in these locations. Mexico City holds the first place according to all indicators, followed by Monterrey and then Guadalajara.

TABLE 1. INDICATORS OF INDUSTRIAL CONCENTRATION (1975)
(IN MILLIONS OF *PESOS*, 1975; PERCENTAGES OF TOTAL)

| | mumber of establishments | fixed gross activity | gross prod. | accumulated value | blue collar | white collar | non-sal. | total workers |
|---|---|---|---|---|---|---|---|---|
| Mexico City | 34% | 37% | 50% | 50% | 44% | 53% | 29% | 45% |
| Nuevo León | 4% | 12% | 11% | 11% | 8% | 9% | 3% | 8% |
| Jalisco | 8% | 6% | 6% | 6% | 7% | 6% | 8% | 7% |
| sub. total | 50% | 55% | 67% | 67% | 59% | 68% | 40% | 60% |
| total country | 100% | 100% | 100% | 100% | 100% | 100% | 100% | 100% |
| | 119.212 | 171.325 | 473.148 | 182.831 | 1.254.741 | 347.135 | 143.407 | 1.707.919 |

Source: *X Censo Industrial: 1976* (Mexico City, 1979), 97-172

It is interesting to compare the industries of Monterrey with those of Jalisco. The number of establishments is twice in Guadalajara what it is in Monterrey. Nevertheless, in terms of fixed activities, production and accumulated value, the relation is reversed. Thus we find the presence of an industry of much greater capital intensity in Nuevo León, and the existence of an extensive subterranean economy, an informal sector of great size, in Jalisco. Indicative of this fact is the number of workers without regular wages in Jalisco; eight percent of the national total as against three percent in Nuevo León.

Table 2 shows the industrial concentration according to type of industry in the three regions. In Mexico City there are branches which are ov.er-represented, that is with more than the average percentage concentrated in the city. Of the ten branches where we find more than fufty percent of the national total, four belong to the category of intermediate goods: textiles, paper, chemicals, oilcloth and plastics; and two belong to the category of capital goods: metallurgy, electrical products and electronics. In Monterrey, we find a similar profile.[9] There is a lower concentration in fewer branches, of which there are one of final consumption (tobacco), three of intermediate goods: oil, non-metallic minerals, and machinery; and two of capital goods; metal products, machinery and equipment. In Jalisco, by contrast, the major concentration of industry is in the more traditional branches: foodstuffs, beverages, tobacco, footwear and leather tanning, all of these being consumer goods. Four of the other over-represented branches are of the category of intermediate goods: wood, paper, oilcloth and plastics, and non-metallic minerals. Taking into consideration the internal distribution of Jaliscan industry over the twenty branches, one notes the importance of especially four: foodstuffs, beverages, footwear and chemicals. They represent sixty percent of the gross value of production and fiftyfour percent of the accumulated value of the entire state of Jalisco. The foodstuff branch is the most important with 32

9. For early characteristics of industry in the Monterrey region, see the essays of Cerutti and Vellinga in this volume. With different data and less comparative Patricia Arias, "El proceso de industrialización en Guadalajara, Jalisco, siglo XX," in *Relaciones. Estudios de Historia y Sociedad*, 3 (1980), 9-47, arrives at the same conclusions.

percent of the gross value of production and 22 percent of the accumulated value.

TABLE 2. CONCENTRATION OF INDUSTRY IN MEXICO ACCORDING TO BRANCH OF INDUSTRIAL ACTIVITY IN TERMS OF ACCUMULATED VALUE

| | national total in millions of 1975 *pesos* | percentage of total in all 3 regions: | Jalisco | Nuevo León | Mexico City |
|---|---|---|---|---|---|
| foodstuffs | 22.917 | 53 | 11 | 6 | 36 |
| beverages | 12.357 | 60 | 13 | 11 | 36 |
| tobacco | 3.966 | 84 | 11 | 62 | 11 |
| textiles | 12.098 | 61 | 5 | 3 | 53 |
| clothing | 4.627 | 18 | 4 | 6 | 8 |
| footwear | 2.644 | 69 | 28 | 7 | 34 |
| wood | 2.175 | 25 | 8 | 2 | 15 |
| furniture | 1.700 | 82 | 9 | 6 | 67 |
| paper | 5.508 | 81 | 8 | 11 | 62 |
| publishing | 4.772 | 88 | 2 | 6 | 80 |
| chemistry | 23.645 | 81 | 6 | 9 | 66 |
| oil | 1.151 | 61 | 2 | 24 | 35 |
| plastics | 6.705 | 94 | 8 | 6 | 80 |
| non-metallic minerals | 9.752 | 81 | 7 | 22 | 42 |
| basic metals | 15.371 | 56 | 2 | 23 | 31 |
| metal products | 11.363 | 85 | 4 | 13 | 68 |
| machinery | 8.871 | 59 | 5 | 12 | 42 |
| electric products | 10.588 | 82 | 3 | 9 | 70 |
| transport equipment | 13.002 | 63 | 2 | 7 | 54 |
| miscelleous | 2.333 | 99 | 12 | 4 | 83 |
| total | 182.831 | 67 | 6 | 11 | 50 |

Source: *X Censo Industrial: 1976* (Mexico City, 1979), 735-802

The industrial structure for each branch is different. In some cases a conjunction of businesses lead their sector. In the majority of cases only one or two businesses dominate the complete branch. In general, a great variety of small and medium businesses surround such leading enterprises. There are -using a slightly arbitrary criteria for minimum accumulated value of 5 million *pesos*, 1975- some three hundred significant enterprises. They represent, taken together, 85 percent of the total accumulated value of the state and of the gross value of production in Jalisco. Their introduction, accomplished largely in the last twenty years and above all during the period of 1966-1970, represents the 'modern' phase of industrialization. These are enterprises which require a high investment of capital, which apply relatively advanced technology, produce for an extra-regional market, national and in some cases international. These industries are located mostly in Guadalajara and its surroundings and can be classified under four headings, according to their form of property:

- the transnational corporations, above all of North-American ownership;
- extra-regional corporations, predominantly from Mexico City and Monterrey capital groups;
- para-state corporations whose investments exclusively or largely come from the state;
- local corporations, led by a few of the large Jaliscan industrial families.

In all these enterprises, workers receive relatively high salaries and enjoy more advantageous working conditions. Almost all of them are organised in unions, mostly through membership in the *CTM* (Confederation of Mexican Workers). They enjoy possibilities of negotiation within the entire urban-industrial sector of the region.[10]

The small and medium enterprises make up the 'traditional' industry. The majority of those were formed since the 1930s with small amounts of capital accumulated in the agricultural and commercial sectors. More than 9,000 establishments of this character were registered in the last industrial census of 1976; they represent 90 percent of the total of industrial establishments and employ one fourth of the work force officially registered. Their investment of capital is low: their activities in land, machinery and installation represent less than 10 percent of the regional total. The official figures, however, quite often underestimate the employment figures in traditional industry, above all in small enterprises. The extreme case is in clothing manufacture. According to the industrial census of 1970, that branch as such employed during that year some 3,500 people, while the population census of the same year showed some 20,000 people declaring that they worked in clothing manufacture as their principle occupation. What we have here is an industrial activity which, lacking a better term, we might call subterranean, clandestine, unregistered, illegal or informal. It would be, nonetheless, a mistake to think that we are dealing with two distinct economic circles, one formal and the other informal, which operate independently of each other. On the contrary, there are various mechanisms of articulation between both sectors. They are linked by their material supply, as well as by their merchandising activities. The businessmen of the informal sector acquire their merchandise, their commercial lines of credit, and industry from Guadalajara and Mexico City. They produce for a broad and diverse market, from popular markets, commercial shops in residential zones to national supermarket chains. Frequently they even work on final products for the formal industry. Among all industry -large, medium and small- there exists the custom of delegating that part of the work which is most costly, or involves a great deal of manual work, to registered establishments. Thus they resort to the *maquilas* (workshops, individuals or businesses who subcontract the productive finishing required). In Jalisco, in 1981, 11 percent of all registered enterprises transferred part of their semi-finished materials to other businesses or to homes of individuals for finished production. This has happened mostly in those branches of production where technological innovations have not succeeded in replacing in any extensive hand-work in the productive process -in the branches of textile, clothing, footwear, machine metals and jewelry. Between 25 and 40 percent of all enterprises in these branches use the system of piece-work.[11]

We are not speaking of a symmetrical relation between the two sectors. Small industry, whether of the formal or informal sector, is subordinated to the medium and large industries by chains of dependence. Between them we might

---

**10**. Qualification of Guadalajara industries according to 50 percent of the stocks, although generally there are investments mixed with local, national and transnational capital. The same could follow with state capital. See Carlos Alba Vega, "Jalisco: un caso de desarrollo contradictorio," in *Economía Informa*, 127 (1985), 13-24; and, Jaime Tamayo Rodríguez, *La estructura del sindicalismo en Jalisco* (Guadalajara, 1985), esp. 63ff.

**11**. For further discussion, see Cristina Padilla Dieste, *Marginados y asalariados. El trabajo domiciliar de maquila en una colonia popular* (Mexico City, 1978), and, *La industria maquilera del vestido. Una estrate en la industrialización de Jalisco* (Guadalajara, 1980); Carlos Alba Vega, "La importancia de la pequeña industria en sociedades dependenties," in *Relaciones*, 22 (1985), 85-112; *La situación industrial de Jalisco*, Gobierno del estado de Jalisco, ed. (Guadalajara, 1982), X, 1.1, 1.2, 1.3, 4, 5.1, 5.2, 5.3, 5.4, 5.5, 5.6, 5.7.

draw a variety of connections: towards urban and rural workshops, whether registered or clandestine, which in their turn establish contract or subcontract relations. At the end of the chain we find the piece workers, and they as well might lay off on others part of the work. 'Extramural' workers are generally married women who work as casual labor. They take on, in this way, part of the risk of the formal sector, especially during times of intensive work, immediately before summer and during the winter, when business has its major losses, and the lower and middle classes make their purchases. Workers are organized as a productive force, but not as a social force, there is no unionization, social security or benefits by law. Generally they are connected to subcontracted work through family, neighborhood or friendship ties. This explains in part the frequent turnover of employees in the informal sector. Workers, paid barely an acceptable minimum, change work as soon as they find a better offer. There is considerable crossover between formal and informal work, between small and medium businesses, between medium and large businesses, as well as crossover between private and state enterprises, and national or transnational enterprises of great industry.[12]

The character of small and medium industry is notable in that the larger the business, the fewer possibilities of encountering completely local ownership. During the last twenty years new establishments from outside have been founded. As may be observed in Table 3, the majority were first transnational, then extra-regional, followed by state or para-state businesses. The transnational penetration was welcomed: quite a few Jaliscan businessmen associated themselves discreetly with transnational capital, acquiring in this way access to more sophisticated technology. The penetration of out-of-state capital, from Mexico and Monterrey in general, was felt more painfully. A campaign against this apparent loss of local hegemony was launched publicly. If transnational capital had cast its spell over the Jaliscan bourgeoisie, capital from the Monterrey region and from Mexico City caused in time a noticeable disenchantment. The presence of four forms of property strengthened the heterogeneous image of large industry in Jalisco. According to the figures in Table 3, it is clear that this heterogeneity is found mostly in two branches, foodstuffs and beverages, but in all other branches it is present to some extent. It is remarkable as well, what economic weight such enterprises carry. The first ten industries generate a third of the accumulated value of industry in Jalisco. Taken together, the first fifty account for 60 percent of the accumulated value and the gross value of production in the state and employ a third of the labor force officially registered.

Analyzing each of the four forms of property, we can see the following: in the case of transnational corporations, in Mexico as in other countries of the Third World, they have arrived since the Second World War and especially during the 1960s. A potential market of 75 million people seems, in the logic of such corporations, to be abundant.[13] In contrast, in the case of Mexico -as in Argentina and Brazil- along with other Latin American countries, it is well known that they established themselves as industries of assembly and of advanced technology, and to a much lesser degree in the businesses of raw materials, such as metals and

12. *Situación industrial*, V, 9.1., 9.2, 9.3.

13. This market was actually captured. According to an article in *Expansión*, of August 15 (1984), pp. 130-150, of the 100 most important enterprises of the state, 34 are mostly foreign controlled, and 58 depend on foreign financing. Of the 500 most important, these figures are 150 and 253 respectively. It is well-known that the 150 completely transnational corporations are found in the most dynamic sector of the Mexican economy; see, Dirk Kruijt, "La industrialización, alianzas de clase e ideología populista. Los modelos de Brasil, México y Perú," in *Encuentro*, 3:10 (1986), 87-128; and for the mining sector Dirk Kruijt and Menno Vellinga, *Estado, clase obrera y empresa transnacional. El caso de la minería peruana, 1900-1980* (Mexico City, 1983).

non-metal minerals, for export. With respect to the region of Jalisco, additional advantages accrue to the foreign corporations: political stability, labor peace, a docile working class, an industrial and service infrastructure, access to an internal market and facilities for export. Some twenty businesses have established themselves here, with a certain ease, in positions of leadership in their respective branches. Above all in the branches which have regional and national importance: foodstuffs (Anderson and Clayton, Purina); beverages (Pedro Domecq); chemistry (Celanese, Celusa y Derivados); metals for machinery (Nibco and Protomes in association with local capital from Swecomex, Siemens); electronics (*IBM* and Motorola); oilcloth and plastics (Goodyear); and others (e.g. Kodak).

TABLE 3. CHARACTERISTICS OF THE 50 MOST IMPORTANT INDUSTRIES IN JALISCO, 1975

| | most important branch | second most important branch | principal form of property | secondary form of property | % accum. value in Jalisco | % tot. prod. in Jalisco |
|---|---|---|---|---|---|---|
| *businesses* | | | | | | |
| first 10 | food | beverages | T (5) | M (2) | 31 | 26 |
| first 20 | beverages | food | T (8) | M (4) | 44 | 37 |
| first 30 | food | beverages | T (12) | M (6) | 53 | 45 |
| first 40 | beverages | food | T (15) | M (12) | 58 | 51 |
| first 50 | food | beverages | T (18) | M (15) | 62 | 58 |

Legend:
T = Transnational Capital; M = Mexico City Capital.
Pre-Dominant Union: *CTM*, all businesses.
Time of establishment: 1966-1970 all.

In the case of extra-regional but Mexican corporations, they enter at times into association with transnational capital, but the general rule is that they establish new corporations and to a lesser degree buy local businesses. Examples are Guadalajara Glasswork, Polyurethanes of Mexico and various tequila producers. Also, they have established holdings in beverages, foodstuffs, cement (Tolteca Cement) and in chemicals and petro-chemicals. The large state corporations, few in number in comparison with the remaining groups, and less significant than in other states, were established in food industries (almost all sugar refineries were bought by the state), fertilizers (Guanomex/Fertimex), metallurgy (Condor), paper and cardboard (industrial complex of Atenquique), wood, textiles (Textil del Salto) and tobacco (La Tabacalera Mexicana). The larger companies of Jalisco origin and property have traditionally been active in foodstuffs (vegetable oils), beverages (tequila), footwear and tanning. In these branches Jalisco entrepreneurs made their fortunes. Until the 1960s the family enterprise predominated; however, from the arrival of large (trans) national capital onwards, they started to restructure their industries and formed company-groups with corporate and centralized administration by founding holdings. In the vegetable oil industry some industrial groups emerged with certain diversification; two entrepreneurs, Aranguren and Urrea, became linked to transnational companies in the branches of foodstuffs and metallurgy. Of the most important local companies two deserve special attention: Calzado Canadá -a footwear empire comparable to that of the Bata group- and the SIBEK group formed around an iron and steel complex. The first emerged from a family workshop and is the pride of the region; it is a classic example for all workers in the informal sector and small-scale entrepreneurs; the second, grouped around the Siderurgica Guadalajara, was the first enterprise in the region to become a limited liability company.

## THE JALISCO BOURGEOISIE

It becomes clear that when considering the industrial bourgeoisie as a social class, it is necessary not only to view it in terms of the position it holds in the social structure or more specifically in the structure of production, but equally to examine the position it holds in the cultural and political sphere. At this point we shall consider in particular the economic and financial bases of the Jalisco bourgeoisie, or better, its hegemonic formation. It seemed important to us to select of the elite that group, which openly, as well as behind the scenes, and together with the working class, was one of the most important social actors within the industrial process. Table 4 summarizes the diversification by sectors which the businessmen presently hold. From this one may infer that the small producers generally live exclusively from the income of their shops. Three fourths of them are found in this situation. Farming is the other important activity of the small businessmen. This is partly due to the fact that prior to becoming industrialized, they had been engaged in animal husbandry and farming, and also because for a few, buying a modest ranch strengthened their sense of origin. Hardly anyone sought to invest in other industrial sectors. In turn, a few of them are also found in commercial activities, but this was generally before they became involved in industry. A few found solution in the purchase of real estate or services. Greater diversification is found in the medium-sized industries. Those who were able to diversify did so in other industries or in farming. The real estate sector equally gained importance.

What truly holds a surprising and eloquent significance is the panorama of investment which has made up the stratum of large industry. It is impossible to find a single sector which has remained unaffected by the presence of the large industrial entrepreneurs. Two thirds hold diverse interests, predominantly in other industries. The second place is reserved for commerce. One-fifth of industry is associated with banking, one-fourth invest in real estate and land speculation: land, condominiums, hotels and housing. We may conclude that the ruling class did not 'put all its eggs in one basket'. Their investments are found in a wide area of activities: generally not in industrial sectors related or connected in terms of products, but in economic areas which are promising in the short range or which are secure: commerce, real estate, housing, hotel industry, or non-productive service sectors. The harmonizing of interests among the financial and industrial sector appears to be much more functional. In local terms, the position of stock holders, before the nationalization of the Mexican Bank in 1982, and the minority stock holders later, offered them great opportunities; information on the channelling of credit, new investments opportunities and, most important, access to personal credit for new projects. If one had to typify the Jaliscan bourgeoisie briefly, it would be necessary to describe them as a class with multiple interests: entrepreneurs involved in dispersed sectors much more than the leaders of industrial empires or conglomerates.

They have sought to organize themselves in different ways to defend their class interests. There exist three types of business organizations which stand out in Jalisco: ethnic organizations, the formation of industrial groups, and the association in industrial chambers or business centers. In all three cases, the Jaliscan industrial businessmen have not found a commonly accepted leadership nor a nucleus of power. Nevertheless, empirically, the three forms have been successful.

TABLE 4. DIVERSIFICATION OF ECONOMIC INTERESTS BY SIZE OF ENTERPRISE, 1981

| | family artesans | medium-sized manufacture | large industry | Jalisco industry |
|---|---|---|---|---|
| *undiversified* | 76 | 50 | 33 | 66 |
| *diversification in production/commerce sectors:* | | | | |
| agriculture | 9 | 14 | 13 | 10 |
| industry | 1 | 19 | 41 | 9 |
| commerce | 4 | 7 | 26 | 7 |
| *diversification in banking/finance* | 0 | 3 | 21 | 2 |
| *diversification in speculation and other sectors:* | | | | |
| housing | 1 | 7 | 23 | 4 |
| services | 2 | 2 | 18 | |
| other | 7 | 6 | 5 | 6 |

Source: *La situación industrial en Jalisco*, III, 8

In the nineteenth century, in particular towards the end, the German and the French arrived in Mexico.[14] Both groups integrated themselves into commerce; the former also in railway industry. The German community joined the Jalisco elite within a few decades, and since the first half of the twentieth century has disappeared as an ethnic group. The French, by far the most important community of foreigners in Jalisco since the *Porfiriato* until the 1940s, came to control the most important commercial activities and the textile industry of Guadalajara. In their factories they partially employed workers of their hometown -Barcelonette. They spoke French among themselves, they met daily in the French Club and married among themselves. In this fashion, the industrial and commercial enterprises remained for a long time in the hands of French families. The Spanish community was formed in a similar manner. They also came to be specialized in the textile and commercial branch. Later, they started to diversify. They became members and (often as father-in-laws) frequented the French and Spanish Clubs. In such a manner an informal trust among the ethnic businessmen was formed. And at a national level -they were present also in Mexico City, Puebla and Monterrey- they could agree on prices, outlay expenditures, production and markets. The French-Spanish community flourished until the Second World War, when textiles constituted a highly important industrial sector and when the national policy of import substitution still had not gained all its force. They were known and

14. For more on the French, see Hélène Rivière d'Arc, *Guadalajara y su región* (Mexico City, 1973); Jorge Durand Arp-Nissen, "En un pueblo obrero: de la privatización al corporativismo" (Tesis de maestría, El Colegio de Zamora, 1983); Luisa D. Gabayet, "Regional Development, Industry and Workforce: the Case of Guadalajara and Its Region" (Ph. D. diss., University of Durham, 1983); Patrice Gouy, *Le Barcelonette méxique* (Mexico City, 1983).

respected members of the Chamber of Commerce, and started to diversify their businesses by means of family connections. They acquired electricity enterprises, hotels, and real estate. Through their clever purchases of terrain in the time of the exploding urbanization of Guadalajara in the 1960s and 1970s, they appropriated new fortunes, this time through the sale of buildings, the breaking into lots of land holdings, and participation in speculative activities.

Other ethnic groups, like the Lebanese and the Jews, arrived later, also to stay and integrate with the Jalisco community; the latter have still conserved their identity by means of endogamous marriages. The Lebanese, in general, arrived after the Revolution and *Cristero*-uprising. Like the ethnic entrepreneurs of previous generations, they took shelter first in Mexico City and in Veracruz, the port of entry into the country. Kinship relations by means of inter-ethnic marriages strengthened the community through access to loans, information, purchases and sales. Their members specialized in a few traditional industrial sectors: clothing, garment and textiles. In a similar manner as previous generations, they learned of industry through commerce. The communities prospered up to the first decades after the Second World War. Generally, the second or third generations of French, Spanish and Lebanese are now wholly identified as Mexican nationals. As a result the ethnic organizations have dissolved themselves, in order to emphasize that they presently form part of Jalisco's bourgeoisie, having found their entrepreneurial vocation.

The most common organization, previously and presently, is the formation of family enterprises. Industrial groups, conglomerate enterprises, and corporative holdings are still few in Guadalajara. In contrast to the industrial empires which have their principal sites in Monterrey and Mexico City, the family enterprise continues to predominate. In this enterprise the power of *pater familias* is almost absolute in terms of administration, decision-making and daily management. The proprietor, founder, or inheritor of the business exercises his power until an advanced age. He is the principal stock holder and although his children or relatives may participate in decisions, it is only symbolically. No other partners intervene; in the family enterprise the leadership is indisputable from management all the way down to the minor posts occupied by family members.

Among the family groups and entrepreneurs in Jalisco, we wish to briefly present a few results on six of the most important ones in terms of capital, number of enterprises and capacity to mobilize economic, social and political resources which confer on them a certain hegemony in the regional industrial process. The entrepreneurial groups have been selected from statistical information, coming from business and government publications and above all from interviews with key informants. In choosing these business groups, we have wished to identify them by their names, but also by the role they play in the regional industrialization process. For this reason, we are interested in grouping types, profiles and tendencies of these social actors. The entrepreneurs selected are: Aranguren, owner of the *Promotora de Industria Nacional*, a holding company which groups 20 enterprises in the food and chemical industry; Martínez Guïtron, a group of five stock holding brothers of the SIDEK holding company and *Siderurgica Guadalajara*, grouping 15 industrial enterprises in the metal-mechanics sector, along with many hotel, building and housing enterprises; López, father and daughter, leaders of an enormous shoe business, *Calzado Canadá*; Urrea, owner of a holding company of the same name which administers 15 enterprises in the metal-machine industry; Garciarce, owner of various bottling franchises and distributor of potable water, exercised in the form of a local oligopoly, associated with transnational capital in a chemical industry and promotor of multiple hotel and tourist activities; and Gutierrez Nieto, oligopolic distributor of butane gas for domestic consumption and owner of 15 industrial enterprises related to gas consumption such as stove manufacturing factories, tanks, valves, stationary tanks and allied products.

In comparing these diverse Jaliscan entrepreneurial groups, one can observe a few similarities among them and features characterizing them individually. A few of the points on which they converge and diverge, the similarities and differences, are presented as follows:

a) All of the above mentioned businessmen and leaders of local groups were born in the west of Mexico with one exception (Aranguren, son of a Spaniard), all of them are sons of Mexicans. Two of them, Aranguren and Garcíarce, were born in Guadalajara, and the rest are Jaliscan by adoption. A few immigrated to Guadalajara from small cities of the neighboring states of Sinaloa and Michoacan (Urrea and Gutierrez Nieto). López originated from a small village in the south of Jalisco. With the exception of Garciarce, in the other cases the parents of the businessmen were born outside of Guadalajara and brought their children to the city to live.

b) None of the businessmen belonged in direct lineage to the more prosperous families of the region. In general terms, the creators of the original enterprises started on a small scale and from below. Most often it was by means of marriage that a variety of them legitimized their social relations with the regional dominant class. The entrepreneurial origins of their families are not very remote, since, putting aside Martínez Guïtron (a third generation businessman), all are second generation entrepreneurs and in the case of Urrea, the first. In fact, *none* of the industrial capital now in their hands existed before this century.

c) The accumulation of capital which was originally invested in industry was realized properly in commerce and in a small quantity in small industry; few of the founders of the enterprises were prior farmers. Four of the groups originated in industry at a small scale during the 1920s, a little after the Revolution. The other two arose in the 1940s. Nevertheless, independent of the date of foundation of the original enterprises, all really gained importance as industrial enterprises after the Second World War, above all in the 1950s, when conditions were more favourable: social violence in the countryside had decreased; agrarian reform had been implemented and the Pacific Railway and asphalt highways had reached Guadalajara; the urban population had reached an accelerated growth as a consequence of the strong increase in birth rates and migratory movements from the countryside.

d) The economic predominance of these businessmen is in traditional industry: production of goods for mass final consumption (foodstuffs, drinks, footwear) and a few goods of non-complex production (unsophisticated products of the metal-mechanics industry). In only one instance (that of Aranguren) does there exist production of complex and strategic goods such as sorbitol (a food additive) or enzymes. The metallurgical iron and steel of Guadalajara owned by Martínez Guïtron and López Chavez deserves special attention. With the base of this traditional industry, generally geared towards the satisfaction of basic necessities (but in the case of fizzy drinks also 'luxury' consumption), these Jalisco industrialists are displacing the orientation to accumulation. There also exists a strong tendency towards an orientation to invest in real estate, building production and the hotel industry. A factor that has strongly influenced this inclination has been the rapid urbanization of Guadalajara and the housing problem, the development of national and above all international tourism (especially in Puerto Vallarta) and governmental incentives, with few controls on speculation and ample credit for the development of the hotel industry.

e) Within the strictly industrial production, there exists the preponderance of a mother enterprise which has been the generator of various allied industries and which joins the others. In a few cases a vertical integration is produced such as in *Calzado Canadá* and the additional tanning, heel, glue, shoelace factories, etc. Nevertheless, in the cases presented, industrial proliferation appears more in the form of horizontal integration: enterprises which in some form are related to the mother enterprise but not among themselves.

f) In the cases studied the businessmen stand out not only in the regional context, but also in the national context. Their enterprises appear on the lists of the large Mexican firms and in the case of a few of them (López, Martínez Guïtron, Aranguren) they figure among the business elite of the country. In two cases, they are national leaders within their branch of the economy (López in shoewear, and Aranguren in the production of supplies for the food industry).

g) The ownership and the management of the firms is classically family-based and in the majority of cases the mother enterprise is exclusively reserved for family stock-holders, or even for the person (the father or his successor) who controls the stocks. The most professional groups in industrial management appear to be Urrea and Aranguren who are at the same time the two most important members of transnational firms. However, the tendency of the rest is also towards professionalization. Almost all of them profess that for the future there should prevail authentic anonymous societies and holding companies, in spite of the fact that currently most anonymous societies only conceal formally the existence of an exclusive family business.

h) The majority of these entrepreneurs arrived at this stage through practice. Almost all of them at one time in their careers have taken courses in business management or administration. All, without exception, grew up under a strong Catholic influence and maintain close ties with religious individuals and institutions. If with a few of them the influence of the social Catholic doctrine can be detected, in others the presence of *Opus Dei* is clear. Although some of them may identify with the political party *PAN* (*Partido Acción Nacional*, a right-wing party), they take care in not demonstrating their preferences. It serves their purposes to maintain good relations with the dominant political power, and its party, the *PRI* (*Partido Revolucionario Institucional*).

i) The diversity of the industrial sectors in which these businessmen are involved (foodstuffs, beverages, shoewear, basic metal, simple metal products) argues that each one exercises a certain leadership, but only at a particular industrial level. At the level of the general economy this leadership needs to be divided among 16 industrial sectors.

j) A large part of the success of this entrepreneurial group is derived from their wide connections with regional banks and national branches, of which they have been members on administrative councils, stock-holders or consultants. The nationalization of the banks up to now seems not to have radically changed their relations. Thanks to them the industrialists were able to reserve for them a considerable part of the credits destined for expansion or the creation of new projects. This was particularly clear in the last ten years, in which investments increased notably and diversified towards building production.

In Jalisco there is a surprisingly high number of institutions which group the entrepreneurs together. To start with, there are sixteen local industrial chambers. The existence of these is due in part to state initiative and on the other hand to the interests of the businessmen themselves. By law, since 1941, the working class as well as the business sector have a syndicate. In the republic, federations such as the *Confederación Nacional de Cámaras Industriales* (*CONCAMIN*), *Confederación Nacional de Cámaras Comerciales* (*CONCANACO*) and *Cámara Nacional de la Industria de Transformación de los Estados Unidos Mexicanos* (*CANACINTRA*) incorporate industrialists and merchants by obligation. The *Confederación de Centros Patronales* (*COPARMEX*) groups entrepreneurial and employer centers in the different states by voluntary means. In the Business Center of Jalisco businessmen feel at home. It is their association, while the chambers are creations of the state. Nevertheless, one may ask why there are so many different industrial chambers.[15] In Jalisco it appears to be difficult to arrive at any unity of planning, lines of action and collective policies to follow. There is no organizational unity, nor ideological congruity. As various businessmen express it: "*In times of peace we are individualists with each one looking out for himself, in times of war we are united.*" By this, one can explain, for example, the coexistence of two chambers: one of footwear and the other of tanning within the same industrial branch. When in 1984, the tanners asked to open the frontier in order to import cheap hides, the shoemakers asked for them to close. For them these differences and contradictions of interest are the reasons for disorganization. The lack of hegemony, leadership, the presence of various groups and large enterprises, each dominating one or two sectors is reflected in the diversity of chambers.

One may question the interests that these chambers are defending. To start with, the large businesses do not need Jalisco's chambers which only hold regional importance and which do not have sufficient capacity to negotiate at a higher level, in Mexico City. The large Jaliscan industrialists, on the other hand, are received at a personal level and have direct access to national levels of power. Moreover, what common interests do the large business groups hold with small industry in their sector? Hardly to share credits, import and export rights and licenses to produce with the handcraft producers. The large and small industrialists in Jalisco do not eat at the same table. The large businesses are registered with the chambers, generally in several; they pay their dues and attend the meetings. But they do this for the most part in order to have an audience. At times they hold presidential posts, but basically in order to strengthen their positions and increase their personal prestige in face of authorities in Mexico City. But they do not hold sufficient power to influence the other businessmen of their own circle. On the other hand, neither do the small industrialists appear to receive all the benefits which the chambers would wish to bestow on them. They do not desire regulation, nor planning, nor control by the state. All things considered, they feel that the chambers are creations from above. They do not sympathize with the obliged social security, and workers' benefits payments, etc. They prefer less state intervention, increased liberty and the possibility to survive and grow. In fact, Jaliscan chambers are creations of middle-sized businesses, the ones which benefit from the granted services of information about credit, financial discounts, legislation and regulation.

Of the multiplicity of chambers, the three that have the most power are: the chamber of commerce, of transformation, and of the metal industry. The first one is the oldest and most powerful, but it expresses the ideas of the conservative

15. The chambers related to food, oil, ham, tequilla, tanning, and jewelry are of local origin. Chambers related to construction, clothing, plastics, graphic arts and condiments are Jaliscan delegates to different national chambers.

sector of Jaliscan businessmen. Moreover, at times, it represents the views of the Catholic Church in Jalisco, which despite having a fraction of the clergy committed to social and progressive causes, is in general one of the most conservative in Mexico, if not of all Latin America. The chamber of transformation unites various industrial branches and is the local industrial chamber with the largest membership. In addition, the metal-mechanics chamber integrates various branches and serves as the most active of business organizations.[16]

With respect to the organization of companies of foreign origin, one can observe that in the 1960s and early 1970s, North-American firms such as *IBM*, Motorola, *TWR*, General Instruments, Kodak and others arrived. Apart from the fundamental reasons of their location, which are of an international order, they were attracted by local forces and were received with great enthusiasm. The Business Center (previously Employer Center) of Jalisco made studies of the local area for them which facilitated the choice of the most profitable location. It underscored the docility of the workforce, excellent relations with local management syndicates, the existence of various industrial services and assured the good treatment of North-American management teams. The export firms of North-American origin joined in the Association of Foreign Businesses, headed by Kodak. Transnational and local capital which exports to the United States is also found grouped in the American Chamber of Commerce in Guadalajara. Its promotor and manager was Adolfo Horn, former consul of the United States in the city and first director of the chamber. He received for his performance -as did the industrialists Urrea, Martínez Guïtron and Aranguren- the medal of industrial merit granted by the Council of Industrial Chambers in Jalisco.

In Guadalajara the large industrialists have never managed to formulate a clear and congruent ideology which would denote a united class. The absence of coherent and well-defined leadership also had its repercussions at an ideological level. Comments like: *"There is no conformity in criteria in Jalisco;" "We still need to mature;" "We are still empirical businessmen, we need development; we haven't studied sufficiently,"* are self-definitions voiced by the major businessmen of the region. The principal problem was summarized as follows: *"We have clashed with industry and have fallen into alliance with it."* It is as if industrialization of the region ran against their tastes and wishes. One could almost say that they have primarily been businessmen who have passed from merchants to industrialists, bankers and builders.

An ideologically aggressive posture towards the state has rarely been seen in Jalisco.[17] Jaliscan entrepreneurs do not confront the state as those of Monterrey, Sinaloa, Sonora or Chihuahua are in the habit of doing. When, towards the end of the presidencies of Echeverria and López Portillo, the Monterrey bourgeoisie tried to unite the different industrial centers in order to publicly condemn the government, they found little support in Guadalajara. Jalisco could not be counted on in a head-on attack. One may submit that the spokesmen of the chambers and the most important industrialists speak of defending free enterprise and express their anxiety about the omnipotence of the state and about metropolitan centralism, but never very loudly. The *Gaceta Mercantil* (Merchant Gazette) as well as the magazine *De Interés Público* (Public Interest) published by the chambers propose criticism, but always in rather bland, general terms, almost submissive. And of course, over the last ten years the state has been their benefactor.

16. By initiative of its director, this chamber put forward the idea of organizing the subcontracting market in the so-called *Bolsa de Subcontratración.*

17. Mario Ramírez Racaño, "Los empresarios mexicanos: las facciones dominantes," in *Revista Mexicana de Sociología*, 37 (1975-1976/24), 49-82; Carlos Ariola, *Los empresarios y el estado* (Mexico City, 1981), 63-160.

Entrepreneurial activity has flourished in Jalisco, because private and later nationalized banks generously granted credit in order to modernize industrial equipment, construct hotels and luxury apartments. With reason one can affirm -as did Derossi in his characterization of Mexican business- that the Jaliscan industrialists developed under the protection of the state.[18]

In Jalisco, a similar non-aggressive posture is assumed by the working class. Local businesses have a formidable ability to reach understandings without conflict in dealing with the two official labor unions, the *CTM* and the *CROC*. They emphasize 'business responsibility', and 'belonging to one big family', 'mutual respect', and the 'rights of both parties'. They receive support and gratitude from the labor sector. The few 'social extremists' are duly noted and blacklisted and their names are circulated among the offices of industrial relations of the Jaliscan businesses.

Jalisco's posture towards transnational and extra-regional capital has likewise been non-aggressive. Jalisco accepted the arrival of the Monterrey group and the Mexico City group with passivity, in the same way it accepted the purchase of local business and the foundation of new competitors. Transnational firms, whose presence did not benefit the local industry either by technological contributions or by sales of industrial by-products, were nevertheless received warmly.

## CONCLUDING REMARKS

Industry in Jalisco has a heterogeneous character. Two industrial fields co-exist: the large and the small. The last is composed of a large number of artisan workshops. Small industry, formal or informal, is subordinated to large industry through the system of *maquila* (sub-contracting). The large industry, in turn, produces basically final consumption goods: foodstuffs, beverages, clothing and footwear. In the last decades corporations were created for production of intermediate consumer and capital goods -the metallurgy industry, other firms of machine metal, and chemicals. The industry is organized in four forms of property. Transnational corporations predominate, followed by *maquiladores* or agro-industry. There are few state corporations: sugar engineering and a few tool and dye plants. The industrial complex of Atenquique, which processes forest products, is the most important one. It is well known also that extra-regional capital from Mexico City and Monterrey are present in Jalisco. Conglomerates located in these two cities absorb other business: industrial mostly, but also many commercial and financial enterprises. They are prominent in a few local industries of foodstuff production, footwear and chemical and machine metal production.

The modern version of industrialization in Jalisco has a recent history: there is no Jalisco businessman whose grandfather owned factories. On the contrary, his grandfather or his parents arose as industrialists only insofar as they began in commerce or agriculture. In the lists of the most important businessmen, we find many foreign names: French, Spanish, Lebanese and Jewish. It has only been since 1970 that the ethnic ties have dissolved and foreign families have been integrated into Jaliscan society. There are still few industrial groups. There is no hegemony or common leadership. Leading one or two branches of industry, almost all the large industry is concentrated in one mother enterprise -property of a single person. It has been only during the last decade that these groups have established links between themselves. But there have not yet arisen multi-indus-

18. Flavia Derossi, *The Mexican Entrepreneur* (Paris, 1970), 44.

trial consortia. Almost all the joint ventures of local industry are new corporations, peripheral and focused on the building industry: condominiums, hotels, housing. The formation of holding companies and corporative groups is from these last years; until recently they were dominated by large Jaliscan industry and modelled on family enterprises. In contrast with the industrialists of Monterrey, the banking system of Jalisco was never integrated into industry. The banks were developed commercially, not industrially, and this resisted the attempts of financial agents from Mexico City and Monterrey to shift its development in another direction. Until nationalization, the banking community was shared between groups of merchants, industrialists and construction companies.

Jaliscan industry has tried over the last few years to deny access into Jalisco to large transnational consortia and strong extra-regional groups: real estate and tourism (with its undeniable presence of extra-regional and transnational capital). When we compare the present Jalisco bourgeoisie to the regional oligarchy of the eighteenth and nineteenth centuries, we are surprised by certain similarities. Once more the large enterprises, industrial as well as agro-industrial, are managed as family businesses. The old fusion of rural and commercial capital is similar to the current integration of industrial and real estate groups. In a certain sense it could be said that the Jalisco bourgeoisie has been transformed into a *neo-latifundista* urban class. There exists a tendency in certain industries of Guadalajara to invest in security, not in dynamic opportunities for growth. They buy land and urbanize it, but they have to *"wait until the time is right."* From the beginning of the *latifundista* tradition it has been known that harvest follows ripening. Therefore, they build condominiums and hotels, and wait for the harvest of profits.

The ideology of the business community in Jalisco is characterized as Catholic: respect for the social order and existent religion, obedient, non-aggressive, following a tendency to accommodate and to share power. This explains its behaviour with the four regional sectors with which it is necessarily related: the Church, the working class, the state and extra-regional enterprises. The Church in Jalisco does not appear to have the economic power it once had, but it continues to exercise ideological power. Whoever seeks success in Guadalajara must first understand the ecclesiastical hierarchy. It is frequent, as in the eighteenth century, that a business family has relatives in the Church. With respect to the working class, the Jalisco bourgeoisie demonstrates a true virtuosity. It is less repressive than manipulative. They have understandings with the official unions, and thus have no need of company unions. Relations between worker and boss are generally paternalistic. They have good relations with the state; the last four governors (each with a six-year term) have come from the business community of Jalisco, and for more than thirty years the vice-president of Guadalajara has come from the ranks of the private sector. Taken all in all, with its ups and downs, there have been no conflicts of major proportion between business and local government. In actual fact, the high authorities have accompanied the business community in its attempts to resolve its problems with the center of power in Mexico City. With respect to the arrival of large capital in Jalisco, the businessmen of Jalisco have been coherent in their ideology: they accept without difficulty the advantages of 'free competition' and resign themselves to sharing economic power with the transnational and extra-regional enterprises.

It is worth the effort not only to compare historically the present bourgeoisie and the neo-Spanish elite which preceded it, but also to compare the regional bourgeoisie of Monterrey and that of Guadalajara. Monterrey is a city with a long tradition of industry. Industry arose at the beginning of the last quarter of the last century. During the North-American Civil War, the Monterrey region took advantage of international business dealings with the United States. The closeness of cheap energy sources and local coal aided the creation of heavy industry, intermediate and capital goods. The absence of a traditional *latifundista* stratum was also a decisive factor in the orientation towards industrialization, resulting in large industrial-banking consortia at the beginning of the 1920s. The typical organization is along anonymous society lines; holding companies have a decade long tradition in Monterrey and the four industrial groups -Alfa, Visa, Vitro and Cydsa, in order of prestige and importance, are all conglomerates integrated with corporate administration.[19]

In Guadalajara, the rural tradition predominates. Industry came late, at the beginning of the 1940s of this century. Since that decade, the *latifundias* and ranches, and in Guadalajara, commerce and administration have characterized the region. Agriculture, farming and commerce contributed to the original accumulation and Jaliscan industry has maintained close ties with the rural context. They are major producers in agro-industry and consumer goods for the inhabitants of the rural areas. Local industrial businessmen became urban landowners. Instead of forming industrial banking consortia, they transferred their investments to land, construction companies, condominiums and hotels, secure investments in a metropolitan city in a process of full expansion. The predominant industrial organization has been the family enterprise.

The differences between the Monterrey region and Jalisco has been reflected in organization and ideology. *CAINTRA*, the only chamber in Monterrey, brings together 8,000 businessmen, under the leadership of four industrial groups. What *CAINTRA* proposes as a line of action is docilely published in the local press, radio and television owned by the groups. The power of the groups over the other industries is immense -they dominate raw materials products, technology, sales and contracts- and their authority in the region is undisputed, and no opposition is tolerated. The working class is organized in company unions, controlled by the groups, and the ruling class of the Monterrey region dictates the norms of economic, political and even moral action in the city. In Guadalajara there are 16 chambers. Big businessmen have tried a variety of times to unify with others, but except in a situation of crisis, they prefer to act independently. Many efforts to unify business forces have failed: the principal industries are leaders in one or two branches while the others depend on them for technology, raw materials, sales and contracts. Leadership is therefore motivated by prestige, without any real power of dominance. There is linkage with other sectors of local power: real estate and commerce generally. With the public sector there exists a gentleman's agreement, and with the cultural sector, they have reached an understanding. Transnational capital and out-of-state capital meet little resistance in Guadalajara or are welcomed openly. In comparison to Monterrey Jaliscan regionalism is moderate and easily appeased.

19. Frédéric Mauro, "Le développement économique de Monterrey, 1890-1960," in *Caravelle*, 2 (1964), 35-133; Menno Vellinga, *Industrialización, burguesía y clase obrera en México. El caso de Monterrey* (Mexico City, 1979); Cerutti, *Burguesía y capitalismo*; Jean Revel-Mouroz, "Aspects de l'industrialisation à Medellin, Guadalajara et Monterrey," in *Travaux et mémoires de l'Institut des Hautes Etudes de l'Amériques Latines. L'espace Mèxicaine, questions d'actualité* (Paris, 1976), II, 19-31; John Walton, *Elites and Economic Development. Comparative Studies on the Political Economy of Latin American Cities* (Austin, 1977). See for the question how, in one way or another, the *latifundista* tradition has blocked industrial development: Hugo Cabieses, Dirk Kruijt, Raúl Lizárraga and Menno Vellinga, *Industrialización y desarrollo regional en el Perú* (Lima, 1980); as well as, Dirk Kruijt, Franklyn Maiguashca, and Menno Vellinga, *Industrialización y desarrollo regional en Colombia* (Bogotá, 1982).

Region, State and Capitalism
CEDLA, Amsterdam, 1989

CHAPTER TWELVE

# The *Regiomontana* Bourgeoisie and the State

MENNO VELLINGA*

## STATE AND BOURGEOISIE: SOME INTRODUCTORY REMARKS

The growing centralization of political power by the Mexican state in the course of the institutionalization of its political system in the post-revolutionary period, has repeatedly met with the powerful forces of regionalism. Regional powerblocs have a long history in Mexico which often can be traced back to colonial times. They persisted and even received a new impetus, in particular in those cases where they found a firm economic base and could draw on traditional regional identities as a source of legitimation, sometimes as part of a hegemonic project involving pluriclass participation. Here the relationship between both phenomena: -centralization and regionalism- became a dynamic and at the same time contradictory one. They tended to conflict and in doing so, reinforced one another. The Mexican Northeast is a case in point. The regionalist movement here was dominated by the *regiomontana* bourgeoisie. In this chapter I will analyze the evolution of its relationship with the state and try to unravel the complex interaction between the tendencies towards the strengthening of central state authority and the assertion of regional autonomy.

How to characterise the Mexican state and how to define its relationship to the political and other sectors of civil society, has fascinated analysts ever since the days this ideosyncratic creature came into the world. Especially its identification with the *Partido Revolucionario Instutucional* (*PRI*), the official government party which aims to integrate the populace across class lines in one organizational framework, has generated ample discussion on the relationship between corporatist tendencies and the struggle between social classes, in particular because the entrepreneurial sector has been left out of this official structure. The structure of the state has become a product of class contentions and the efforts to control them; once created, its operations and actions have exercised a determining influence on the patterns and issues of class conflict. Its political power and control potentialities, in their turn, have become an object of class contention.

Following this perspective, the question of the relative autonomy of the state with regard to civil society becomes primarily an empirical problem. The liberal view of the state as a neutral body, functioning on a political level where its policies are defined in response to the demands of competing interests groups without a link to social classes, is in Mexico, as in almost any other case, as untenable as the instrumentalist approach which views the state as a mere committee of the

* *Sociologist, Center for Caribbean and Latin American Studies (CARLAS), University of Utrecht, Heidelberglaan 2, P. O. Box 80.140, 3508 TC Utrecht, The Netherlands.*
*I want to express my gratitude to Frans Schryer for his careful linguistic assistance.*

bourgeoisie. The multidimensional view supported here -the state as a product, determinant and object of class conflict- does more justice to the complex structure of power relationships, with all its consistencies and its contradictions, which the state represents, and which together serve as, and are being used as, mechanisms of class control.

This view underlies my analysis of the relationship between the Mexican state and the regional powerbloc in the North of the Republic. Consequently, I will emphasize the process of class formation among the *regiomontana* entrepreneurs which, in my opinion, offers the key towards an understanding of this peculiar case of state-region relations.

## THE ECONOMIC BASIS FOR THE CONSOLIDATION OF THE *REGIOMONTANA* BOURGEOISIE

Monterrey occupies a special position within the context of Mexican and even Latinamerican development. It was in fact one of the first industrial cities in Latin America and one which took the traditional route -starting with 'heavy' industry and an organisation of production in big enterprises. In the course of this process of industrialisation, a class structure has emerged which constitutes the core of a rather peculiar socio-political system. Monterrey presents an early case of the formation of an industrial bourgeoisie: the transformation of a group of entrepreneurial families into a class in its own right. This early formation has probably contributed to the success with which they have managed to build a regional economic-political bastion, a position of strength from which they could negotiate with the state in policy areas pertaining to their interests. At the same time they managed to maintain a certain autonomy *vis-a-vis* foreign capital for a long period which lasted through the stage of industrial take-off untill the consolidation of import substituting industrialisation in the 1970s.

The origins of this process go back to colonial and post-colonial years. During colonial times, the region had been integrated weakly into the colonial system due to its location in a hostile area on the periphery, or because it was of little economic interest to those in the colonial center.[1] After Independence, the region at first experienced little economic and political stability. Economic activity was at low levels, with the exception of a relatively short quiet period (1855-1864), when under the regime of regional *caudillo* Vidaurri trade was stimulated. This situation gradually changed towards the 1870s. In this period the foundations were laid for a process of industrialisation, that within the context of Latin America, stands out up untill the present day. The question of why and how is a fascinating one, but will go beyond the object of my essay: a few major explanatory factors are expressed in Cerutti's chapter in this volume.[2]

Within a relatively short period industrial growth in Nuevo León took on a considerable magnitude. In 1892, the number of workers in industry was 800, it had increased to 13,172 in 1902, and four years later to 19,259. In 1906 Nuevo León generated 13.9 percent of the gross value of industrial production in the nation. The federal district (Mexico City) produced 11.7 percent, the state of

1. For an analysis of the frontier areas, see Enrique Florescano, et.al., *Tierras Nuevas. Expansión territorial y ocupación del suelo en América (Siglos XVI y XIX)* (Mexico City, 1969), 43-76. A contrasting view can be found in José Cuello, "El mito de la hacienda colonial en el norte de México," in *Empresarios, indios y estado. Perfil de la economía mexicana (Siglo XVIII)*, Arij Ouweneel and Cristina Torales Pacheco, eds. (Amsterdam, 1988), 186-205.

2. See also Andrés Montemayor, *Historia de Monterrey* (Monterrey, 1971).

Mexico 11.2 percent, Veracruz, in comparison, 10.6 percent and Puebla 7.7 percent.[3] Once the regional economic process had reached this momentum, multiplier effects began to work on the basis of already accumulated capitals, the expansion of the internal market and the presence of labour. These effects not only stimulated industry, but also had positive effects on production in the mining and agro sectors. Conflicts of interest did not occur. Since industrialists, mineowners and *hacendados* in many cases were the same persons, Nuevo León established itself as one of the leading economic regions of the country with Monterrey as hegemonic center. The accumulation, distribution and allocation of capital was dominated by a small group of entrepreneurial families, alert to exploit the resources of the region in accordance with their interests, enjoying an easy access to regional political power and possessed by a strong regional consciousness which included a very ambivalent attitude towards the federal center. As is concluded by Cerutti in his essay, the contours of a regional economic and political bastion which would be a competitor for power with the central government, already began to appear.

After 1910, the process of development was increasingly influenced by national political developments, which brought an end to the stability which in the years before had favored the transition of capital towards industry. The region became the scene of continuous struggle between rival armies in subsequent years. Roads and railroads to the city were repeatedly interrupted and food shortages arose in the city. Businesses and real estate property of those who were considered enemies of the Revolution, were set on fire. The occupying troops, also continuously exacted tributes from the local businessmen and industrialists, several of whom fled the city and went into exile in the United States of America. But when the most violent epoch of the Revolution had come to an end, the business people and industrialists came back to the city to pick up their affairs where they had left them. And once political stability finally returned to the region in the second half of the 1920s, the entrepreneurs responded as before. Capitals which had been brought to safety in foreign banks, returned. It is clear that for industrial take-off the developments in the political sphere have been decisive. Conjunctures of political stability which offered perspectives of virtually unbridled capital accumulation were responded to by the entrepreneurial families who took great effort to see to it that their interests were respected. When the industrialisation process gained momentum, the region increased its economic and 'political' weight in Mexico City. The entrepreneurs' dependence on these political factors changed to a capacity to actively influence these policies. The *Grupo Monterrey* had appeared as a power factor on the national political scene.

The first few decades of the twentieth century witnessed the beginnings of a modest process of industrialisation. In most places this concerned the establishment of enterprises which produced day-to-day consumption articles such as textiles, leatherproducts, foodstuffs, and clothing. This production responded to the demand created on the internal market as a result of rising incomes generated by a booming export sector. In addition, the demand for construction materials had increased parallel to the urbanisation process, giving rise to an industry catering to this increasing demand. The 1929 crisis changed all this. The collapse of the external sector and the growing difficulties in getting access to international credit made it difficult to maintain previous levels of imports. The Mexican economy reacted through an expansion of that part of the industrial sector which had been directed towards the internal market in order to substitute totally or partial-

3. Montemayor, *Historia de Monterrey*, 277; Mario Cerutti, "Frontera, burguesía regional y desarrollo capitalista: el caso Monterrey. Referencias sobre el período 1860-1910," in *La frontera del norte: integración y desarrollo*, Roque González, ed. (Mexico City, 1981), 224.

ly the articles which previously had been imported. The presence of an important metal and metallurgy sector contributed to the expansion and deepening of this substitution process. The exports by this sector to the United States had dropped dramatically after 1929 and the shift towards the national market had become a matter of survival.

The structure of production in many Latinamerican countries underwent drastic changes in the 1930s and 1940s. In these years, the volume of industrial production increased. The excess capacity of the existing industrial apparatus was put to use, but in addition new industries were organised. In Monterrey a great number of enterprises of all kinds and sizes were established. Their production was directed towards the regional and national market. The number of industries in Nuevo León was aleady 101 in 1900, and in 1937 it increased to 438. It further rose to 1509 in 1945. In the period 1937-1945 the totally invested capital in industry increased from 153 to 530 million *pesos*. The number of workers in industry grew from 800 in 1892 to 13,000 in 1900, to 24,000 in 1930 and to 40,000 in 1940.[4]

In the 1930s the role of the state in the economy also increased considerably in virtually all industrialising Latinamerican countries. Mexico formed no exception. In previous years various institutions, such as the *Banco Central*, the *Nacional Financiera*, the *Comisión de la Electrificación*, had been created to increase the hold of the state over the internal economic and financial affairs. The expansion of the role of the state came into conflict with the export sector, at that time largely controlled by foreign interests. These conflicts reached their highest levels during the days of the nationalisation of the oil interests by president Cárdenas in 1938. In this same period the growing influence of the state in the economy caused considerable tension with the Monterrey entrepreneurs, completely identified as they were with the ideology of a free market and free enterprise economy. These types of conflicts, were to characterise regional political developments all through the second half of the 1930s. They were a natural result of the entrepreneurs' determination to resist the growing political centralization and to maintain political control over the region in order to protect their interests tied up with the prevailing model of accumulation and distribution of capital.[5]

The expansion of the Monterrey industrial apparatus continued unabated during the Second World War. The metal and metallurgy sectors worked at top capacity, producing inputs for the American war industry. The import substituting sectors of industry grew thanks to the continued isolation from the world market. In the postwar years, the international economy gradually recuperated and the relative isolation of the Latinamerican economies from the world market came to an end. In most of these economies the import substitution process temporarily lost some strength. Mexico as a whole conformed to this trend, but Monterrey formed an exception. Between 1945 and 1950 the volume of total industrial investment quadrupled to an amount of 1.3 billion *pesos*. The number of industrial establishments rose from 1513 to 2440. The following period up untill the mid 1960s were the heydays of industrialisation in Monterrey. The process grew in breadth as well as in depth. Technologically advanced industries, notably in the chemical sector were established in the region, and the first steps were taken towards the establishment of capital goods production. Industrial investments grew nine times to a total of 11.5 billion *pesos* in the period 1950-1965.[6]

The metallurgy sector remained the most important branch of industry. In 1975 it accounted still for close to one third of total industrial investment and one fourth of the gross industrial production value. The concentration of production

4. Montemayor, *Historia de Monterrey*, 374.
5. See Nora Hamilton, *México: los límites de la autonomía del estado* (Mexico City, 1983).
6. Montemayor, *Historia de Monterrey*, 375.

in the other branches, however, was equally impressive. In 1984, 2.6 percent of the total number of industrial enterprises with an investment of over 50 million *pesos* accounted for 88.6 percent of the total invested capital. They employed 63 percent of the total industrial labour force. The leading industrial branches were all dominated by industrial giant companies. In metallurgy, 1.6 percent of the companies accounted for 90 percent of the capital and 60 percent of the employment in the branch, which indicates the capital intensive nature of these industries. But the trend towards concentration was also pronounced in the other branches. In textiles, for example, only two big companies accounted for close to 90 percent of the capital invested in this branch; they employed 60 percent of the textile workers in Monterrey. Thus, the dynamics of industrialisation in the region was centered in a limited number of very big enterprises managed by the traditional entrepreneurial families. The small companies with an investment of less than 10 million *pesos*, which numbered 93.3 percent, accounted for 5 percent of total industrial capital invested and employed 25.4 percent of the industrial labour force. These figures include hundreds of small shops, engaged in production and repair, which emerged as a result of the multipliers generated by the industrialisation process. This considerable degree of concentration and centralisation of capital was not only typical of the Monterrey industrialisation process in the 1950s and 1960s, but was a salient feature right from the beginning. In the course of the 1970s, however, the process assumed unparalleled proportions and the organisation and policies of the big concerns had to be adapted to the requirements of this accumulation. The emphasis shifted towards product differentiation and the creation of divisions, two processes which were usually initiated in combination. Consequently, conglomerates, the so-called *grupos industriales*, were formed.[7]

The process of conglomerate formation concerned in some cases an integration along vertical and horizontal lines of certain branches of economic activity. In others, however, it was often hard to discover a logic behind the integration of a variety of widely differing activities under one corporate umbrella, other than the one dictated by overall financial strategies. In previous decades, the Cuauthemoc and Fundidora companies had acquired interests in the commercial and services sectors, but the emphasis clearly remained on industrial-financial interests. In the course of the 1970s, some of the newly formed *grupos industriales* started emphasizing expansion in a wide range of other sectors next to their industrial interests. Branches like real estate, tourism, communications, transport were taken on and some assumed great importance. The emphasis on accumulation through financial strategies made the financial sector even more important. In addition, it served as an institution through which great amounts of foreign loans could be contracted which helped to finance the expansion programs of the *grupos*.

Thus, the association with the banking system again proved to be essential for the big companies in the Monterrey area. At an early stage, it already functioned as the vacuum cleaner of private savings all over Mexico and in addition served to contract foreign loans. In subsequent years, this function was institutionalized. In the period 1950-1980, the Monterrey banks were able to finance, in the form of loans and credits, 23.3 percent more than they received from within the region in the form of savings and deposits. Next to the cash flows of the companies themselves, these banking activities made the mushroomlike growth of the *grupos industriales* in the 1970s possible. Monterrey became a classic example of the integration of industrial and financial capital. And indeed, the trend towards concentration also presented itself in this financial sector. Big financial groups

7. Edgar López Garza and Jorge N. Valero Gil, *Situación actual de la industria en Nuevo León y su evolución en el tiempo* (Monterrey, 1985).

were formed, all of them in close coordination with industrial interests. The more spectacular examples are *SERFIN* and *BANPAIS*, which, in a few years, became two of the most powerful banking institutions on the national scene. Up untill the nationalisation of 1982 these gave the Monterrey based industries, notably the conglomerates of *VISA*, *VITRO* and *CYDSA*, a greater independence from the state and the banking system in the center of the country. *SERFIN* integrated *Financiera de Aceptaciones SA* and the *Banco de Londres y Mexico SA*, in addition to a number of smaller banking institutions. *BANPAIS* integrated nine institutions in banking, finance and savings, among them *Financiera del Norte SA*, *Banco de Nuevo León SA* and the *Banco del País SA*. Among the Monterrey based banking institutions, *SERFIN* and *BANPAIS* represented respectively 54 and 13 percent of combined total assets in 1978.[8]

The structure of the big *grupos industriales* in Monterrey at the beginning of the 1980s suggested a strategy at work which de-emphasized the exclusive importance of industry and which differentiated interests towards other sectors. At the same time, these interests were often situated in other regions of the country. The process of capital formation had acquired a truly national scope. This model of accumulation, distribution and allocation of capital functioned unharmed until the beginning of the 1980s and it served to build the economic-financial imperium of the Monterrey entrepreneurs. Starting in 1981, however, when the impact of the international economic crisis became felt, cracks began to appear in this structure. The nationalisation of the banking system in September 1982 gravely complicated this difficult situation. Things went so bad that at one point even the *HYLSA* steelplant, the pride of the Garza-Sada clan, was in danger of passing to the state. It appeared that important packages of its stock had already been given to the state as guarantee in state loans. In the other *grupos*, interests were being restructured, and improfitable branches were cut off, often at others' expense. In no few cases, the state had to bail them out, when company after company appeared unable to meet their financial obligations. Indeed, several *grupos* were thrown back to those activities which in earlier years had been their stable basis of operations. In the last few years of the De La Madrid *sexenio* (1982-1988) the big concerns were slowly recuperating from the blows suffered at the beginning of the 1980s. A return to previous expansion *bonanzas*, however, seemed far away.

## THE FORMATION AND CONSOLIDATION OF THE MONTERREY BOURGEOISIE

### *Origins*

Since the second half of the nineteenth century the small group of entrepreneurs in Monterrey had been in the position to accumulate great capitals through a variety of activities in commerce -legitimate and through contraband-, speculation, loan operations and investments in rural property. Only in a limited number of cases had they realised investments in the productive sector. In the period between 1890 and 1910 this situation changed, primarily as a result of changes in

8. Enrique Hernández Laos, "La desigualdad regional en México (1900-1980)," in *La desigualdad en México*, Rolando Cordera and Carlos Tello, eds. (Mexico City, 1984), 166; Juan Manuel Fragoso, Elvira Concheiro and Antonio Gutiérrez, *El poder de la gran burguesía* (Mexico City, 1979), 64.

the national and international economic and political conjuncture. Within a few years massive amounts of previously accumulated capitals were channelled towards new productive endeavors, initiating a process in the course of which a group of entrepreneurs developed into a class. Previously, capitals had remained in the hands of individual families. The transition towards industry required these capitals to be pooled. Integration on the basis of common economic interests was followed by social integration: families involved in the same enterprises sealed their cooperation through intermarriage. Thus a process of class formation was initiated which was to lead to the emergence of a genuine regional bourgeoisie.

In his chapter, a summary of booklength studies,[9] Cerutti has analysed the beginning phase of this process through a study of the activities of 10 Monterrey great-families who at the time took leading roles in the transition of capital towards industry. This group of families, which constitute the nucleus of what later would become known as the *regiomontana* bourgeoisie, contained the following names: Armendaiz, Belden, Calderón, Ferrara, Garza, Hernández-Mendirichaga, Madero, Milmo, Muguerza, Rivero, Sada Muguerza and Zambrano. Those of Calderón and Muguerza and those of Sada, Muguerza and Garza were combined as they virtually constituted one large-family. Within these families, Cerutti studied the entrepreneurial activities of 42 people, involved in a total of 272 enterprises during the period 1890-1905. The following sectors were represented: mining (170), the agro-sector (19), industry (40), finance, commerce, transport and other (43). A total number of 49 enterprises had a participation of at least three of the families mentioned; 55 percent of these enterprises were in mining, 25 percent in industry, and the rest was spread over finance, transport and other sectors. In one third of the mining enterprises, five families or more were involved at the same time. In industry this applied to 58 percent of the cases, indicating the greater need for capital and the spreading of risk. The centralisation of capital underlying these combinations of interest, was consolidated, in no few cases, by intermarriage. Virtually all families investigated by Cerutti were involved in this process, those of Calderón, Muguerza, Sada and Garza resulted totally intertwined. The entrepreneurs of foreign extraction who had settled in the region recently, like Kelly, Clausen, Bortoni married into the important *regiomontana* families.

The diversification of interests of the various families was facilitated by the early introduction of the *Sociedad Anónima* and the extensive web of interpersonal relationships among the small group of entrepreneurs which permitted the sharing of risks in an atmosphere of *confianza*. This made it possible to profit fully from the favorable internal and external economic and sociopolitical conjuncture after 1890. And indeed, with the growing investment in direct productive activities, the emphasis in accumulation shifted from commerce, investment in land, speculation, and contraband, towards one based on ownership of the means of production. The Monterrey entrepreneurs assumed complete control over these activities and the surpluses which were generated. They came to dominate the social relations of production which emerged in the process. In subsequent years, in the interaction with the state and with the other segments of *regiomontana* society -especially the workers in their own production centers- this group of entrepreneurial families was gradually transformed into a class, a genuine regional bourgeoisie, parallel to the process of class formation among the workers.

9. Mario Cerutti, *Burguesía y capitalismo en Monterrey 1850-1910* (Mexico City, 1983), and, *Producción capitalista y articulación del empresariado en Monterrey (1890-1910)* (Monterrey, 1985).

## *Class Formation*

The families mentioned above remained in control of the Monterrey economy all through the ups and downs of the second and third decade of the twentieth century. The expansion of the production apparatus in this period was based largely on the growth of existing enterprises and the organisation of companies that would produce inputs for them. An example was the *Cervecería Cuauthemoc* which organised the parallel production of malt, glass bottles, crowncork and carton boxes. It would last until the 1930s and 1940s before a whole new range of industries would be established. The organisation of the new enterprises, like in the case of the existing ones, was modelled along the lines of a family enterprise and basically it has remained so until the present day.

This phenomenon substantiates Dunn's observation that the structure of family wealth and power, as a mechanism for the maintenance of class control, is not a phenomenon identified only with the early stages of capitalist development. It has remained very much a leading characteristics of contemporary corporate capitalism. The kinship group provides the structure, secrecy and *confianza* to perpetuate power relations originating in upper class families and extending to other institutional structures. Obviously through time their mechanism of control and cohesion have taken on new organisational forms. For example large-scale productive property first took on the legal form of the corporation and, later on, that of *grupo industrial*, a holding company which subsumes a wide range of interests controlled by interrelated kin which combine their ownership interests and have a strategic representation in management of various companies. In their study of ownership and control of corporations and land in Chile, Zeitlin et.al. apply to this situation the concept of *kinecon group*: *"a complex kinship unit in which economic interest and kinship bonds are inextricable intertwined."* In this context, Dunn defines 'family control' as a situation in which members of the same kinship group own a combined total of ten percent or more of the common stock. Further, their capital investment must be coordinated and family members must be involved in the enterprise as managers or as directors. The percentage of ten may be considered a rather conservative figure as control is often secured by possession of five percent or more of the common stock, at least in the American situation.[10]

In the case of Monterrey the amount of control over common stock would be far higher. Traditionally the *Sociedad Anónima* had been organised on the basis of capital contributed by one family or a small group of families who did not transfer their property to others. The stock owned by them normally would not be traded on the stock market and in case the rates were listed, these would not reflect their real value. The family structure of the corporation and their control over banks and other financial institutions has eliminated the necessity for them to appeal to individual savers. This also explains why the amount of trade in privately owned stock on the stock exchange traditionally has been so small.

The rapid expansion of the production apparatus in Monterrey from the 1920s on, soon exceeded the possibilities of the traditional families to staff the managerial positions of newly established companies with family members. A segment of high-level managers came into being, who together with top-level technical specialists, corporate lawyers, and bankers, entered the existing network of entre-

10. Marvin Dunn, "The Family Office: Coordinating Mechanisms of the Ruling Class," in *Power Structure Research*, G. William Domhoff, ed. (London), 17-45, esp. 18 and 33; Maurice Zeitlin and Richard Ratcliff, "Research Methods for the Analysis of the Internal Structure of Dominant Classes: The Case of Landlords and Capitalists in Chile," in *Latin American Research Review*, 10:3 (1975), 5-61.

preneurial families. Often, as in the case of the Maldonado and Elizondo families, kinship ties developed with them. In addition, new families rose to entrepreneurial prominence. Names like Santos, Clariond, Lobo, Ramírez, Benavides, Llaguno, González had to be added to the list of well-known entrepreneurial families.[11]

The involvement of all these families in domestic and international business, control over financial resources, contacts with each other in business and social spheres, and participation in dealing with the state, has brought about their integration into a single class. The members of this class share control over production processes in the economy and over the labour of their workers. Their incomes -profits for the entrepreneurs, high salaries and bonuses tied to profitability of their firms for top executives- derive directly from this command position. This common position relative to subordinate groups and the interest it generates in preserving their status quo, unite them as members of a class in an objective sense, despite short term differences of interest and occasional internal confrontations. The manifestations of this class membership on the levels of organisation, ideology and in political practice, indicate that in the course of the industrialisation process in Monterrey a genuine regional bourgeoisie has emerged. This is a highly significant phenomenon, which has shaped their dealings with the state at an early stage.

In the classical discussion on processes of class formation, the elements of ideology, organisation and political action play a vital role. The subjective dimension of this process, i.e. the emergence of class consciousness, is thought to present itself here. Traditionally the analysis concerns the formation of a proletariat, and focusses on the organisation of a union movement, the emergence of a revolutionary ideology and the engagement in concrete struggle in defence of class inte-rests through bargaining or other forms of more militant collective action. The formation of a bourgeoisie -on a subjective level- presents itself in an analogous way, i.e. through organisation, the elaboration of an ideology and action in the political arena.

The first element to discuss is the entrepreneurial organisation, which has been crucial from the beginning. In 1883 a local *Cámara de Comercio* was founded, and in 1908 the Díaz-regime promulgated the *Ley de Cámaras de Comercio e Industrias* in which they officially recognized such organizations as service institutions for the whole economic sector. Following this legislation, the *Cámara Nacional de Comercio* was constituted in Monterrey in 1911 with participation of all important families. The law remained in force until 1936 when, the Cárdenas-regime elaborated a new legal framework for their role as genuine interest organisations. In addition, many entrepreneurial families had already become integrated into a network forged on the basis of kinship. Further social contact was cultivated through social activities, such as through the *Club Atlético Monterrey SA*, founded by Armendaiz, Belden and Milmo in 1895, and the *Teatro Circo de Monterrey SA* founded in 1900 by the families Calderón-Muguerza, Madero, Rivero and Zambrano.

Moreover, since the beginning of industrialisation in Monterrey, the entrepreneurs had operated close to the regional center of decisionmaking in economic and political affairs. Their relationship with the Porfirian state governor Bernardo Reyes was one of mutual support. The latter assumed the role of benefactor of the incipient industry and designed the legal-administrative framework that permitted an unhindered industrial expansion. The entrepreneurial families, on their turn, helped to support Reyes' political ambitions on the regional and national

11. Alonso Aguilar, "El proceso de accumulación de capital," in *México: riqueza y miseria*, Alonso Aguilar and Fernando Carmona (Mexico City, 1970), 67-70.

levels by fortifying the economic base for the power of his regime. Their close marriage of convenience was broken up through the removal of Reyes by Díaz in 1909. By that time his power had become a real threat to the central authorities. The interdependence of economic and political power was never again so complete as in the Reyes period. The Revolution and its aftermath changed this situation considerably. Since then, the central government has stepped in repeatedly to prevent the emergence of a competing power center in the North that would dispute the government initiative in policies affecting the industrial center.

At this point of developments, the Monterrey entrepreneurs had become preoccupied with the question of formally combining forces, also with other entrepreneurs from outside the region, when they saw the need to create a position of strength in an economic, social and political climate which they considered unstable and more and more dominated by what they saw as a trend towards socialism. Immediately after hostilities had ceased during the Revolution, in 1917 the *Confederacíon de Cámaras de Comercio* was founded (*CONCANACO*), followed one year later by the *Confederacíon de Cámaras Industriales* (*CONCAMIN*). Monterrey entrepreneurs played an important role within both institutions, as reflected in the presence of Enrique Sada Muguerza, first president of *CONCANACO* and Adolfo Prieto, first president of *CONCAMIN*, both representatives of leading *regiomontana* families. Their involvement with the combination of forces and organisation of entrepreneurial interests remained intense, all during the unstable economic and political conjuncture following the Revolution.

When the Revolution consolidated and the trend appeared towards the establishment of structures with a corporativist tinge (in which the entrepreneurial organisations would fulfil a role of 'official' mediator between their respective economic sectors and the state), the *regiomontana* entrepreneurs manifested their inconformity. The discussion around the elaboration of a new Federal Labour Code at the end of the 1920s brought this problem to a climax. The *Regiomontanos*, led by Luís G. Sada, again objected the public character of *CONCAMIN*, its growing integration in state-controlled networks and the increasing influence of 'radical socialist ideas'. They proposed a new organisation, in fact a union (*gremio*), which would organise all entrepreneurs, regardless of the sector of the economy or branch of activity they would belong to. The political motive of this initiative clearly emerges from the formal aims given by the members to this new *asociación patronal COPARMEX*:

a) -the necessity to study the relationship between capital and labour,
b) -to translate the results of such studies into recommendations for harmonisation of this relationship,
c) -to defend the interests of the members in a more narrow sense.

The emphasis in the activities in this period was on consultancy and advice in legal matters, in particular in relation to the *Ley Federal de Trabajo* which had been promulgated in 1931. The founding committee counted a strong *regiomontana* presence; next to Luís G. Sada, we find the names of prominent entrepreneurs like Eugenio Garza Sada, Virgilio Garza and Joel Rocha. In subsequent years the *Centro Patronal* on the regional level and *COPARMEX* on the national level became the most prominent institutions through which collective opinions of the Monterrey entrepreneurs were voiced and pressure was brought to bear on the government. In addition, they played an active role in the organisation of *Centros Patronales* in other parts of the republic.[12] In 1928 the *Asociación de Banqueros de Mexico* (*ABM*) had been founded as a civil organisation, independent from the government bureaucracy but in political practice serving as a consulting organism

12. *COPARMEX. Su origen y desarrollo* (Mexico City, 1979), 16, 23.

for the government in affairs related to interests of the banking sector. Monterrey entrepreneurs, again, were present.

The earlier mentioned law of 1936 on the *Cámaras de Industria y de Comercio* and their respective federation, emphasized their public function and integration with 'official' politics. The representation of industrial and commercial interests was combined through the creation of *CONCANACOMIN*, a fusion of *CONCAMIN* and *CONCANACO*. This fusion was undone in 1941. In this year industrial and commercial interests were again obliged to organise separately. Within *CONCAMIN*, interests were organised according to specific branches of industry, although the possibility existed of organisation on a sectorial basis, as in the case of *CANACINTRA* which came to group most of the medium- and small-sized national industrialists. In addition, the organisation of *Cámaras* of a purely local scope, in which all entrepreneurs involved in the manufacturing industry would participate, was authorised. The Monterrey entrepreneurs used that possibility and united forces within the region in order to organise more effectively the defence of their interests. A branch-wise organisation would have made this coordination of efforts very difficult if not impossible. Moreover, the more 'progressive' stands *CANACINTRA* was taking had generated their opposition. The result was *CAINTRA* of Nuevo León which soon appeared to be the only strong organisation on a regional basis.[13] Its status as a consultative organism of the state in affairs relating to the industrialists interests has brought through time a more moderate attitude towards 'official' politics and greater pragmatism in dealing with state proposals in matters affecting national policies on industrial development and national trade. The *Centro Patronal* as a 'union organisation' has, given its origins, been inspired by a more traditional and conservative attitude, in addition to an almost instinctive anti-unionism directed towards the official unions, the *sindicatos rojos*. The influence of the Monterrey entrepreneurs in the institutions on a national level, such as *CONCAMIN* and *COPARMEX*, has been differently structured. In both cases, they inspired their organisation and provided leadership during the beginning years. From the 1930s on, however, their main influence has been channelled through *COPARMEX*. Names of prominent Monterrey entrepreneurs or their representatives continue to appear in the presidency or among the members of the *Consejo Directivo*.

Within *CONCAMIN* interests are expressed through *CAINTRA* of Nuevo León. The presence on the level of the *Confederación* has varied in different economic and political conjunctures. In addition, the emphasis on negotiation and dialogue which has prevailed on the confederation level, to be expected of state integrated institutions, has not always concurred with the style of operations practiced by the *regiomontana* entrepreneurs. This style has been very much conditioned by a determination to assert independence *vis-a-vis* the government and to apply pressure in defence of their interests through open confrontation in defiance of government policies and occasionally through the organisation of mass rallies and demonstrations in Monterrey. The local *Centro Patronal* and *CAINTRA* provide a context for discussion about problems pertaining to the industrialists' interests on the basis of which a common stand is developed which can be communicated to the government and the public at large. As such they perform a vital function as a medium through which their interests as a class are articulated and expressed. In this process of articulation and expression, members of the great entrepreneurial families traditionally have performed a leading role.

In 1975 the leaders of the entrepreneurial organisations, with the exception of *COPARMEX*, founded the *Consejo Coordinador Empresarial* (*CCE*) in order to coordinate the defence of the interests of the various entrepreneurial sectors and

13. Flavio DeRossi, *The Mexican Entrepreneur* (Paris, 1971).

to increase the effectiveness of their lobbying and pressuring with the state, especially in matters of economic policy. In addition, they decided to give greater attention to the diffusion of their ideological principles, no doubt as a response to the official ideological offensive in the Echeverría period. Although the Monterrey entrepreneurs had a presence in the *CCE*, the emphasis in their activities remained with *COPARMEX*.

The second topic to be discussed is the entrepreneurial ideology of the Monterrey entrepreneurs, which has been fed principally from two major sources that are interrelated: the reaction against the emerge of socialist doctrines nationally and internationally and the social-christian doctrines figuring in the various papal encyclicals that have appeared since the end of the nineteenth century (*Rerum Novarum*, *Quadragesimo Anno*, *Mater et Magistra*). Core elements in their ideological discourse concern their position on the family, religion, private property, law and order, patriotism, and the role of the state.[14]

The ideas on the role of the family among the Monterrey entrepreneurs traditionally have been zealously conservative. The influence can be noted of a stern Catholicism which in particular had a grip on the first and second generation entrepreneurs. In its effects on values related to work, responsibility, austerity and the success of their enterprises through continuous reinvestment of accumulated savings, it reminds one of Max Weber's thesis on the role of the Calvinist ethic during the rise of capitalism.[15] The patriarch of the Garza Sada clan, Eugenio Garza Sada (who died in 1973 at the hands of urban *guerrillas*) has long been the personification of this ethic. It had its strongest expression among this clan and those families related to it. Another segment of the bourgeoisie, grouped around the *Fundidora* interests, initially supported more liberal ideas. The emphasis on the family as the cornerstone of society was projected on to the structure of the company and the socioeconomic context in which it functions. The company is viewed as one big family, one organic unit functioning on the basis of a harmony of purpose existing between the parts; a perspective which does not allow conflicts of interest. This image is carefully cultivated by the big companies in the Monterrey area. The members of the family are portrayed by company magazines to coincide in their determination to further the family well-being. Family quarrels should have no reason to be and in case they might occur, they are supposed to be the result of irrational behaviour of distorted minds, subversive activity by outside agitators or both. This unitary ideology gives the entrepreneurs a very comforting image of their own role. At the same time it has served to justify their paternalism in the management of labour relations and the definition of policies for 'the good' of the workers belonging to the *gran familia* in their companies -analogous to the labour relations on nineteenth-century central Mexican *haciendas* discussed by Rendón in this volume-, policies which at the same time serve as an effective mechanism of class control.[16]

The concept of private property has been sacred for the Monterrey entrepreneurs as it will be for the entrepreneurs in any economy which is primarily organized according to capitalist criteria. It found additional legitimation in the Social-Christian doctrines which I mentioned before, which emphasize the extension of private property over an ever increasing number of people *"to serve the cause of human dignity and further the life chances of the individual,"* as is stated

14. Fernando Valera, *Mitos de la burguesía* (Mexico City, 1976), offers an interesting analysis of general bourgeoisie ideology in which various of these elements are mentioned.

15. José Fuentes Mares, *Monterrey. Una ciudad creadora y sus capitanes* (Mexico City, 1976), 69.

16. Menno Vellinga, *Industrialización, burguesía y clase obrera en México: el caso Monterrey* (Mexico City, 1981). See also Rendón's essay in this volume.

*Rerum Novarum* and *Quadragesimo Anno*,[17] as opposed to the Marxian doctrine which advocated its abolition for being the cause of the exploitation of man by man. As staunch advocates of the free enterprise system, the entrepreneurs' position clashed with the way the role of the state has been defined in Mexican society. The Social-Christian doctrine parted from the principle of subordination, emphasized the primary role of private initiative and only approved of state intervention in the economy in case of obvious failure of the private sector to take care of its 'social responsibilities'. Given the clear definition the entrepreneurs had of these responsibilities within the context of paternalism, state intervention in this area for them was 'out' and had to remain limited to marginal corrections of the market mechanism.

The state, in their perspective, does have a definite role in the maintenance of the basic social and political stability which are indispensable for an unhindered development of market forces. The entrepreneurs from the beginning have been the staunchest supporters of the law and order idea. The state was to use a hard hand in maintaining a societal structure which would guarantee the basically capitalist nature of the process of development. This element from entrepreneurial ideology emerged during the period of upheaval and general instability of the Revolution. The entrepreneurs initially sided with Huerta. Subsequently several of them had to leave the country temporarily when he lost out to revolutionary forces. During the aftermath of the Revolution they never quite overcame their sense of alienation from the 'new politics' of the postrevolutionary period. In the subsequent decades their law and order stand surfaced every time reformist and pro-labour policies, in their view, set the country on a sure road towards anarchy and socialism. Especially under the presidencies of Cárdenas (1934-1940), López Mateos (1958-1964) and Echeverría (1970-1976) this ideological element was mobilised at full force.[18]

It is obvious that the development of an all powerful state in which the majority party in fact would occupy the state apparatus does conflict with the state concept shared by the entrepreneurs. Their state would be solely responsible for the creation and maintenance of the infrastructure for development while the entrepreneurs themselves would largely determine the course of the process. Since the present state began to shape up in the 1920s, the clashes between this element of entrepreneurial ideology and Mexican political practice have been numerous. The penetration of offical politics in virtually all societal spheres ran completely counter to the principle of subordination. Only recently -under the influence of the effects of the economic crisis of the 1980s- has their position on this point been more pragmatic and less ideologically prescribed. The use of national symbolism and patriotism go back to the legitimizing dimension of the Monterrey entrepreneurs' ideology. It aims to transcend the tension-ridden relationship with the state and the political regime and to affirm their loyality towards the nation. It enables them to distinguish their work for the 'common good' of all Mexico from official politics where political bickering and the defence of sectorial interests would prevent a focus on the well-being of the populace. Television spots and advertisements paid for by Monterrey industrial and financial interests invariably start with references to Mexico's glorious past and present. At the same time this patriotism has a clear economic rationale. Most of their industrial interests cater to the internal market which in its growth is heavily influenced by the appeal of the slogan *"lo hecho en México está bien hecho."*

17. See the original texts in *Socialistische documenten*, J. Barents and W. Banning, eds. (Amsterdam, 1952), 128, 116.

18. Juan M. Martínez Nava, *Conflicto estado-empresarios en los gobiernos de Cárdenas, López Mateos y Echeverría* (Mexico City, 1984).

The justifying and rationalising element in the entrepreneurial ideology in relation to its legitimizing functions with regard to the enterprise of the entrepreneurs has always been strong, often stronger than its prescriptive functions with regard to actual behaviour. At the same time it has provided a common cultural point of reference which has helped to cement the entrepreneurs into a social class.

The third point to discuss is political action. The activities of the Monterrey entrepreneurs in defence of common interests have developed within the context of a continuous tension between their strivings to build a regional economic bastion from which the central government could be challenged with regard to the objectives and means of its development policies and the insistence of this government to be counted as the supreme authority. These tendencies towards regional autonomy have a long history, going back to Latin America's patrimonial-bureaucratic regime in the colony, but they emerged clearly in the post-independence period when all over Mexico, regional *caudillos* capitalised on vague feelings of regional unity and regional identity. The rapid industrial development of Nuevo León at the end of the nineteeth century generated a strong economic base for the expression of such regionalisms and the entrepreneurs soon began to assert themselves in opposition to the central government. This led at the same time to an increasing concern with the internal political dynamics of this regional powerbase. The emphasis on accumulation through industrialisation, at the same time made the entrepreneurs competitors for the power to decide the distribution and allocation of economic surplus generated by this process. Thus, the question of control presented itself at an early stage and the entrepreneurs became preoccupied not only with the monopolisation of economic power and social prestige, but also with political power within the state of Nuevo León. This quest for political power concerned not only formal positions in the state political hierarchy but even more so the more general way in which labour was integrated in society. The unitary ideology brought an emphasis on paternalist and reformist mechanisms of integration, next of course to the straightly repressive action one may expect of the benevolent but stern fathers of the *gran familia* of company personnel.

On the surface, the paternalist policies resemble an early definition of the basic needs approach which in the 1970s made headways in the discussion on alternative development strategies in Latin America. This approach defined the ultimate goal of the development effort as the provision of all human beings with adequate alimentation, clothing, shelter, education and health care. These are seen as part of a total package with an emphasis on economic growth, full employment and greater economic equality through a redistribution of income. Its appeal to policy makers obviously resided with the possibility of its integration with a balanced and equitable growth strategy which bypasses the necessity of profound structural changes in the forces. They support and accelerate existing patterns of inequality in all spheres of social and economic life and ultimately are produced by the existing system of accumulation and distribution of capital.

The policies by the Monterrey entrepreneurs in the area of basic needs had a very practical origin and their main objectives have remained so. The objective to guarantee the reproduction of the labour force which initially had priority, was soon replaced by one emphasizing the necessity of a stable work force with reduced rates of turnover and increased skill levels and which moreover would be neutralised as a potential oppositionary force. The policies were presented as a manifestation of the social vision of the entrepreneurs in which benevolence, Christian charity and paternal responsibility struggled for prominence.[19]

This line of policy had already started during the phase of industrial take-off in 1911 with provisions in the area of housing and primary education. Forced by the food shortages arisen in the city as a result of revolutionary developments, nutrition was added to the program. In 1918 the policy was put on formal footing through the creation of councils of public and private welfare, *departamentos de bienestar* in various companies and the *Sociedad Cuauthemoc y Famosa* in the conglomerate of enterprises linked to the *Cuauthemoc* brewery. Alimentation, clothing and housing were singled out as the areas which would be covered. Education was soon narrowed down to technical training organised by individual companies and linked to their specific needs of skill. The system of credits and advances -mainly intended to stimulate the consumption of consumer durables- and recreational facilities and programs were added to the program at a later stage.

In their totality these paternalist policies in the area of basic needs indeed offered ample opportunities for control of the workers by those who manage them. Workers were totaly integrated into 'the company family' but in a situation of complete dependence almost *vis-a-vis* 'the family head' in relation to spending and other financial affairs, perspectives of occupational mobility, improvements in levels of living, and the organization of free time. Even the defence of their interests was taken care of by the *patrón*. When in the 1930s the Cárdenas-regime made a beginning with the organisation of the Mexican workers into a state controlled union movement, the entrepreneurs responded by organising a union movement themselves -the *sindicatos blancos*. In the course of time these came to organise the workers in most big Monterrey enterprises, with the exception of *Fundidora*.[20]

The situation regarding income and working conditions of the working population in the big Monterrey companies was been carefully controlled by management as much as the policies and actions of the federal government in this area allowed. The strategy has been one of taking the initiative in the area of wages and working conditions, anticipating worker demands and in case these demands are presented, the ritual was followed of 'significant concessions' 'conceded' after 'tough negotiations' with coopted union leaders. Cooptation and the distribution of small 'favors' has always been a strategy favored over straight suppressive measures. Thus in 1907 already, the Monterrey entrepreneurs decided to reduce the working day from 12 to 9 hours, presumably to prevent the worker unrest they had witnessed that year in Rio Blanco, a measure applauded by a capital newspaper as one which would *"help to prevent the victory of socialism."*[21] Betterments in working conditions and wage increases in the following decades were decided at the entrepreneurs' discretion. Federal influences in this area, which had become noticeable after the promulgation of the Federal Labour Code in 1931, were vigorously fought. Those federal regulations did not even go beyond what the Monterrey entrepreneurs were prepared to give. In particular, since the 1940s, they saw to it that the conditions of the collective wage agreements in the leading industries exceeded the normal conditions established for the region by the federal government by a small margin. However, they were determined to stay masters in their own house and to prevent any more radical claims regarding changes in the existing distribution of power, income and wealth in the region.

19. Vellinga, *Industrialización*, passim.
20. Vellinga, *Industrialización*, passim.
21. Montemayor, *Historia de Monterrey*, 291.

Until recently, the entrepreneurs' personal and direct role in organised politics has always been minimal. Political power has been wielded through their entrepreneurial organisations or through intermediaries: individual politicians, parties or movements, while the entrepreneurs themselves stayed in the background. Only in the course of the 1970s a few names of entrepreneurial families (Zambrano, Lobo, Sada, Santos) did appear among active politicians, some of them in relation with official politics, reflecting the accommodation of a segment of the Monterrey entrepreneurs with the federal government during the *sexenio* of López Portillo (1976-1982), and the need for federal support during the crisis in subsequent years. A number of prominent entrepreneurs (Garza Sada, Canales Clariond, Madero) also sided with the opposition party *Partido Acción Nacional* (*PAN*).

*Interpretation*

Above in this chapter I dealt with the presence of a *regiomontana* bourgeoisie in an objective sense. Looking at the manifestation of class consciousness at the levels of organisation, ideology and political practice, we can also establish its early presence in a subjective sense. The activities of the Monterrey entrepreneurs in the organisational field have been most pronounced. In the beginning phase integration was realised solely on a family basis, but the expansion and diversification of the entrepreneurs' interests required a common front and a more sophisticated and powerful interest representation. This necessity was the more called for in a situation where the state was trying to assert its supreme authority in matters relating to the immediate and the long term objectives of the process of national development. Time and time again the Monterrey entrepreneurs have taken the initiative in uniting the private sector and as such became also the spokesmen for these interests on a national level. Ideologically they have developed an interesting position in which social-christian ideas and nineteenth-century liberal-bourgeois elements have been fused. Their position regarding private property and the role of the state is only to be expected of entrepreneurs who in Mexico were the front runners of industrial capitalism. So is their position on law and order, defined as a firm stand against anything that would even only remotely threaten a climate in which investments and return on investment were not organised according to their criteria.

In this ample definition of order, pre-capitalist elements not only persisted in labour relations but acquired new strength and meaning. The industrial proletariat was potentially the most important local competitor for power. This potential increased in importance when the state in the 1930s stimulated their organisation in a union movement which was to function as an instrument of official politics. In that situation, the creation of a counterweight, the *sindicatos blancos*, seemed like a logical step. The additional incorporation of the workforce in the big companies through paternalist and reformist means has resulted in a highly effective system of control which seldom has to resort to open repression to prove its credibility. These big companies set the tune for labour relations in the Monterrey area, although they only effectively control part of the working population. The role of the state in the regional economy, at least up through the 1960s, has been light. In the course of the 1960s the middle class -up untill that time small and insignificant- started to acquire numerical importance. Politically it has never been a threat to the bourgeoisie. On the contrary, in times of crisis it has found in people belonging to the middle sectors a staunch ally.

The formation of the *regiomontana* bourgeoisie then, created the socio-political anchor of the regional distribution of wealth and income. Regionally it controlled the competition for power. This regional strength enabled it to influence the state in its capacity to affect the accumulation process and the distribution of income and wealth. Temporary investment freezes and capital flight towards the United States were among their favorite pressure mechanisms. During most *sexenios* they did have to resort to these mechanisms in order to have their interests respected. Especially under the presidencies of those who tried to develop reformist and pro-labour policies these confrontations emerged more clearly.

## THE *REGIOMONTANA* BOURGEOISIE AND THE STATE

The emphasis in this chapter has been on the process of class formation among the *regiomontana* entrepreneurs and the constitution and consolidation of a regional powerbloc. This process ran, at least from the 1930s on, parallel to the growth and consolidation of the new Mexican state and has been incompatible from the beginning. There is the formation of a bourgeoisie with a clear ideological position regarding the role and functions of the state in accordance with the principle of subordination, and which derives power from a strong and expansive base in the industrial-financial sector. In contrast we observe the evolution of a state which in its form and its role with regard to the economy and the society shows strong corporatist-authoritarian characteristics and which claims direct participation and control over a development process which emphasizes industrialization as the long-term priority.

During the *Porfiriato* a complete agreement existed in Nuevo León between the state and the dominant groups as to the goals and means of the development process and the role and functions of the state and the private sector, at least on the regional level. During the Huerta government, this sector (e.g. the families Calderón-Muguerza, Sada-Muguerza-Garza) tried to secure influence at the national level in exchange for financial donations from the *Cámara de Comercio de Monterrey*. They had presence in the government through Enrique Gorostieta, member of the Sada clan, and *Ministro de Hacienda*.

After Huerta's defeat and the triumph of revolutionary forces, the entrepreneurs remained far from the heart of central state power. Tensions and confrontations were bound to follow. In the years 1920-1921 a conflict emerged between the *Cuauthemoc* conglomerate and the state on the issue of tax evasion.[22] All through the 1920s the formation process of the *regiomontana* bourgeoisie on the levels of organisation and ideology ran counter to the direction taken by the new Mexican state. I mentioned the organisation of *COPARMEX* in 1929, after discussions of more than a year, in which the *Regiomontanos* played a primary role. Since then, and up till the present day, there has been a permanent undercurrent of tension and distrust between the Monterrey entrepreneurs and the state. Many times this current has surfaced and produced situations of open conflict. This has especially been the case under those *sexenios* where a reformist-minded president presented a project of development which, in its pretensions of changing the distribution of income, power and knowledge, clashed with the way the entrepreneurs had defined their interests. Gonzáles Casanova has pointed to the phenomenon of an upsurge in labour unrest, as indicated by strikes, in periods of reformist presidencies. The fact that labour anticipates presidential protection while presenting its claims obviously plays a role, but González Casanova also draws attention to manipulative action from the side of the executive where, within a si-

22. Oscar Flores Torres, "De la Edad del Acero a los tiempos revolucionarios: dos empresas industriales regiomontanas (1909-1928)," in *Monterrey, Nuevo León, El Noreste: siete estudios históricos*, Mario Cerutti, ed (Monterrey, 1987), 250.

tuation of competing claims, one sector is played off against the other. Among the entrepreneurs this phenomenon has aroused even greater suspicions with regard to the intentions of the respective regimes. The presidencies of Cárdenas, Lópéz Mateos and Echeverría are cases in point.[23]

In order to get a clearer idea of the areas of conflict I will shortly list the policy fields which the Mexican State has come to claim as belonging to its jurisdiction. These policy fields and state action on them were emerging in the 1930s and took on their definitive form in the subsequent decades.[24] They are (a) basic fields related with the internal order, continuity, and external relations of the societal system (the maintenance of internal order and territorial unity, like through the monopoly over the legitimate use of the means of violence; external relations, foreign contacts, alliances through diplomacy and semi-diplomacy; the general groundrules of society, through constitutional legislation; the bureaucratic-administrative framework of society in a technocratic sense); (b) the field of educational, technological and scientific development; (c) the field of social policies, involving levels of living, social security and social services (alimentation, housing, health), levels of income, wages and salaries, levels of employment, functioning of the labour market, the buying power of the population, the formation of the labour force; (d) the field of financial policies, involving credit (general conditions), money (emission, devaluation, exchange rates), fiscal affairs (exemptions, concessions, taxes), and, budgets, public expenditures (subsidies); (e) the field of economic policies, involving budgets, public investments (social and economic infrastructure), policies regarding the production of goods and services, policies regarding the buying and selling of goods and services (protectionism, free trade), nationalization, privatization, transnationalization; (f) the field of legal policies, involving conciliation and arbitration, legal justice (penal, civil), and, sanctions and repression; and, (g) the field of cultural and ideological legitimation.

The policies that are actually undertaken and the content that is given to them, obviously arise out of the structural imperatives and circumstances in which the Mexican state is operating, the purpose and developmental project it defines for the organisation, the influence of dominant groups and the outcome of the struggle of different groups. This struggle has been channeled to a large extent through the official organisations belonging to the *PRI*. Here representatives of each of the three basic sectors on which the party is build (the peasant, labour and the popular sector) run the party apparatus and participate in the harmonization of competing claims made by the functional interest organisations within each sector. In fact, in these sectors power has been held by one large association or combination of interest groups. The leaders of these powerblocs are closely tied to the inner circle of the party, which makes the arbitration of conflicting demands within the party 'oligarchy' possible while at the same time the decisions are taken on the integration of these demands with the developmental project. Although the entrepreneurial organisations function formally as consulting organisms of the state in matters relating to the interests of commerce and industry, the bourgeoisie has not been recognised as a full-fledged member of the official political structure. It has to lobby from outside for satisfaction of their demands with the executive. This lobbying has often involved a considerable amount of armtwisting and sable rattling as has been shown especially under the presidencies

23. Pablo González Casanova, *La democracia en México* (Mexico City, 1967), 233.

24. Pablo González Casanova and Pedro Vuskovic, "Sobre el estado, la sociedad civil y la crisis en América Latina y el Caribe" (Paper presented at the Conference on the State and International Linkages, The Hague, 1987).

of Cárdenas, López Mateos and Echeverría. The *regiomontana* bourgeoisie has often led the pack in these situations.

A permanent field of conflictive interests has been the set up of the groundrules of the state. The Constitution assignes the role of conductor of the economy to the state. This means an active participation in economic activities, the creation of the infrastructure for development and the financing, protection and promotion of such development, including for the private sector. During the beginning phase of the formation of the new state, the Mexican bourgeoisie was not yet consolidated. Consequently the state had a considerable autonomy with respect to these elements of the class structure. The various policy fields I mentioned above, developed during the Cárdenas-regime.

In the absence of a consolidated opposition on a national level, the *regiomontana* bourgeoisie emerged as the principal powerbloc against the direction concrete policies on the various fields were taking. Their main oppositions concerned the field of social and economic policies. Among the many initiatives by Cárdenas in these areas, those applying to wages and working conditions of the workers and those directed towards their organisation, generated their resistance most. The *Cuauthemoc* interests had opposed Cárdenas' election to the presidency which led to his refusal to visit the city during his political campaign. They maintained the opposition to his reformist and pro-labour policies at full force for the entire period of his administration and initially even supported covertly the *Acción Cívica Nacionalista*, a movement of fascist leanings, later disbanded by order of the president.

In 1936 the conflict between Cárdenas and the Monterrey entrepreneurs broke out into the open. This development was motivated by a dispute between labour and management, that had originated in the Vidriera glass factory, belonging to the Cuauthemoc group. Cárdenas decided to intervene personally and travelled to Monterrey. After a visit of several days, during which he met with representatives of labour and management, Cárdenas presented a plan for the settlement of the strike. At the same time he took advantage of the opportunity and defined openly and systematically his position and strategy with regard to the development of the industrial sector, the position of labour and the evolution of labour management relations. To the entrepreneurs he issued a stern warning to the effect that any attempt to shut down the factories or to alter the production process in any other way in order to frustrate the emancipation of the workers, would be met by government intervention. In the area of labour politics, Cárdenas' statement of position led to the creation of the special relationship between government and organized labour as embodied in the *CTM*. The Monterrey industrial interests, however, were in no mood to cooperate with official organized labour. All through 1938 they joined efforts in a campaign intended to stop union organizing and to destroy the nation wide organized *Confederación de Trabajadores Mexicanos* (*CTM*) as a viable union movement in the state. The *Acción Cívica Nacionalista* reappeared and attacked striking workers. This situation led to another intervention by Cárdenas. An attempt was made at a general strike which had some success in vital sectors of the Monterrey economy (public services) and eventually brought the workers some concessions.[25] In that same year the Monterrey entrepreneurs shut down their business for two days in protest against the labour policy of Cárdenas which had produced labour organisations beyond their control, had led to a mushrooming number of strikes and labour conflicts and had put personnel on the labour courts who lacked entrepreneurial approval. In

25. Joe C. Ashby, *Organized Labor and the Mexican Revolution Under Lázaro Cárdenas* (Chapell Hill, 1967), 92.

addition massive manifestations and protest marches were organised in Monterrey against *"la invasión comunista rusa."*[26] The intensity of the opposition, added to the growing problems of the economy among which capital flight -the traditional pressure mechanism of the entrepreneurs- was one, motivated Cárdenas to scale down the pace and scope of reforms during the last two years of his presidency. As his successor he chose Avila Camacho, a politician of modest and centrist reputation, but the Monterrey entrepreneurs had definitively lost their confidence. The group around the *Cuauthemoc* conglomerate supported Almazán, the conservative former military zone commander of Nuevo León and leader of the opposition party *PRUN*, the forerunner of *PAN*.

The types of conflict between the regional powerbloc from the North and the state under López Mateos (1958-1964) reflect the evolution of economy and society since Cárdenas. The state and the bourgeoisie also changed considerably in composition and strength. The state infrastructure, necessary to support its role of supreme commander of the course of national development, was consolidated, and its functions on the various policy fields expanded. The bourgeoisie equally consolidated as a more complex and powerful class, and during this period entered in alliances with foreign capital. The developmental project of the López Mateos *sexenio* had as main objectives:

- to promote import substituting industrialisation in the areas of intermediate and capital goods and including a higher percentage of locally produced inputs;
- a greater state participation in productive activities;
- an acceleration of the *mexicanización* of the industry;
- an acceleration of the pace of landreform to reduce social tensions in the countryside.

The translations of these ambitious objects into concrete policy measures obviously provoked entrepreneurial reaction.[27] But unlike the Cárdenas period, the basic conflict centered on concrete reformist projects. However, the policies in the economic and financial fields in general remained highly favorable towards private enterprise. Rather, the conflict arose in relation to the ideological discourse of the López Mateos-regime which had assumed full force after 1960, and which related to the revolutionary enthousiasm following the Cuban Revolution. The safety-valve functions of such ideological offensives in Mexican politics should be remembered. Only one year before, the strike movement of 1958-1959 had been mercilessly suppressed. In this process a sector of the labour movement -consisting of railroad workers, electrical workers and telephone workers- tried to change the internal structure of their unions and to start a more militant and independent course of action.

The fact that the rhetoric did not correspond to an actual radical change in policies and that it carefully and continuously emphasized the legacy of the Revolution and the constitution, however, did not prevent a sharp reaction from the entrepreneurial organisations. They denounced the possibility that the future course of the nation might be patterned along communist or socialist lines. The *regiomontana* bourgeoisie again was in the forefront of reaction, criticizing -through its *Centro Patronal*- the 'adventurism' of the government which -so they stated- had caused a decline in private investment and a capital flight. The nationalization of the electricity companies in september 1960, although well prepared in advance and with consent of the owners, fed rumors about other expropriations to come. The event was used to expound to a wider public their misgivings

26. Martínez Nava, *Conflicto estado-empresarios*, 98.
27. Martínez Nava, *Conflicto estado-empresarios*, 127ff.

about the growing state influence in the economy. The introduction of standard primary school textbooks in the entire republic accompanied in 1962 by one percent tax to be paid by selected segments of the population, presented an opportunity to attack the government head on about its ideological course. Action was taken through the *Centro Patronal*, but in addition mass demonstrations and publicity campaigns were supported -in coordination with the Catholic church- of the *Cruzada Regional Anticomunista* and the *Asociación Nuevoleonesa de Padres de Familia*. In subsequent years the López Mateos government softened its ideological offensive. The power position of the entrepreneurs opposite the regime found recognition in assurances and ample explanations towards them of the policies that were undertaken.[28]

Under the Echeverría-regime (1970-1976) the Monterrey entrepreneurs at one time or another clashed with the central government on virtually any issue in the fields of economic, social, financial, legal policies. There was further a total disagreement as to content of the ideological discourse which was meant to legitimise such policies. Echeverría's regime had clear developmental objectives. Economic growth with equity in the areas of employment, income distribution and levels of living, in the cities as well as in the countryside, and under conditions of a lesser dependence from the exterior in investment and technology, was to be realised though a further strengthening of the role of the state in the economy. Foreign policy was to direct itself more to Third World problems and had to intensify the contacts with the socialist countries. The official ideological discourse of the regime acquired more and more radical and nationalist overtones. At times even revolutionary phraseology was used.

The conditions under which this project had to be put into practice, at the same time determined its failure. These conditions included presence of foreign interests in the national economy, the external and internal economic crisis, the presence of a consolidated bourgeoisie, conscious of its interests and ready to defend them against a state expanding into a territory that they viewed as exclusively theirs. The *regiomontana* bourgeoisie was especially active. Their characteristics of a powerful, dynamic, cohesive and self-conscious group in recent years has left its 'enclave' in the North and diversified its interests to other areas of the republic, and has become the natural spokesmen for many Mexican business men. This leadership, accompanying their rise from regional to national prominence, was reinforced by the government's reformist project, however timid the actual reformist proposals may have been. The wide range of conflicts which emerged in the course of the *sexenio* of Echeverría meant that state and bourgeoisie now met each other on virtually every policy field. They battled:[29]

a) -basic questions of internal order (the bureaucratic grip of the state on society, the definition of foreign relations);
b) -policies in the social field: wage and price controls, redistributive policies in the urban sector (housing, etc.), expansion of social services;
c) -financial policies: taxes, questions relating to banking and credit, monetary problems (devaluation);
d) -economic policies: foreign trade, foreign investment and technology, tariffs of public services;
e) -questions of legitimation.

In particular, the ideological discourse of the Echeverría-regime not only raised charges of demagoguery on the left but also aroused the private sector's open

28. Martínez Nava, *Conflicto estado-empresarios*, 143; Marco A. Alcázar, *Las agrupaciones patronales en México* (Mexico City, 1979), 84; Soledad Loaeza, *Clases medias y política en México: La Querella Escolar 1959-1963* (Mexico City, 1988), 348ff.
29. Rosario Green, *Estado y banca transnacional en México* (Mexico City, 1981), 78ff.

hostility. Echeverría's rhetorical call for a more socially oriented economy and his criticism of the private sector's 'selfishness' and 'conservatism' were presented by the entrepreneurs as a deliberate attack on the rights of private enterprise and as the beginning of a development towards socialism.

Open conflict between the state and the *regiomontana* bourgeoisie emerged on several occasions, such as in 1971 when Nuevo León state governor Elizondo -spokesman for entrepreneurial interests- was removed; as in 1973, when Eugenio Garza Sada, the patriarch of the family behind the *Cuauthemoc* interests, was murdered by urban *guerrillas*; as in 1975 when the *Consejo Coordinador Empresarial* (*CCE*) was created after several years of preparations in which the *regiomontana* entrepreneurs played a prominent role; as in 1976 when a meeting of leading entrepreneurs from all parts of the country was organised in Chipinque near Monterrey to organise resistance against Echeverría's law of Human Settlements which was interpreted as an attack on the institution of private property. At times, efforts were made at reconciliation, as in 1974 when the Monterrey entrepreneurs together with Echeverría manifested *"their trust in the government and in the country."*[30] These efforts appeared to be little more than cosmetic operations though. It took another president to soothe the situation and to hammer out a working relationship with them: the *Alianza Para La Producción*. In this creation of López Portillo, capital and labour would cooperate in an effort to get the economy out of its decline and to put it again on a path of economic growth.

In those years the *regiomontana* entrepreneurs were at the height of their power: they controlled the presidencies of *COPARMEX* and *CONCANACO* and had a decisive influence in *CONCAMIN*, *ABM* and in the *CCE*. They played the dominant part in the *Alianza Para La Producción* and were able to dictate the terms regarding wage controls, inflation management, and industrial credit provision by the state. This situation lasted until 1982. The nationalization of the banking system in that same year, however, harmed the management of their financial affairs. The persisting economic crisis in the following years affected their interests gravely. Under these severe conditions the hegemonic powerbloc that for decades has been their trademark, began to crack. Internal political differences emerged. The defensive attitudes that automatically are acquired by those who have to weather a storm, undermined the arrogance which comes with power. Low profile became the pass word in their dealings with the state.

## CONCLUSION

In the course of its evolution the Mexican state has deviated far from the instrumentalist view of the state as a mere tool in the hands of the dominant class. It has consolidated with an economic basis in a well-developed public sector and with firm political roots in a labour and peasant movement organised in corporatist structures. This situation has given it relative autonomy *vis-a-vis* the bourgeoisie and even *vis-a-vis* certain external pressures: it has power to negotiate. The state, in fact, has been supporting a basically capitalist model of development and *has* been reproducing the bourgeois system. On the other hand, it would lose its legitimacy if it would define policies which would not serve certain interests of the working class. This situation explains the contradictory and sometimes conflicting nature of policy making within bureaucracy. The state

30. Martínez Nava, *Conflicto estado-empresarios*, 189.

experiences pressures; it gives in, negotiates and represses. She should be seen as the product, object and determinant of class conflict.

The state has a certain autonomy, I argued, with respect to the bourgeoisie of which the Monterrey entrepreneurs form a prominent and vocal part. Several authors, like Martínez Nava and Green see this autonomy declining.[31] The bourgeoisie, in their view, has been increasing to power constantly relative to the state. Green even interprets the growing foreign debt of the Mexican state in the 1970s as evidence of its impotence to negotiate successfully with the dominant sectors in the country. In the early 1980s, under changing economic conditions, these tides turned. The state suffered the effects of the economic crisis, but so did the private sector and in a more extreme way. The logic of its developmental role in Mexican society forced the state to come to the rescue of private companies which were unable to meet the payments on their foreign debts. The conflict between the bourgeoisie and the state subsided, at least in the case of the *regiomontana* entrepreneurs. In the last few years of the De La Madrid-*sexenio* (1982-1988) and under influence of the trend towards privatization of state companies in a situation where the big companies are slowly recuperating, the entrepreneurs gradually gain influence. The relationship between the state and the *regiomontana* bourgeoisie has been conditioned by the fluctuations in the strength of the economic powerbase of the *Regiomontanos*, as well as by the effect on their behavior as a social class.





31. Martínez Nava, *Conflicto estado-empresarios*; Green, *Estado y banca nacional.*

CEDLA LATIN AMERICA STUDIES (CLAS)

(JEAN STROOM, *American Studies in the Netherlands, Bibliography 1970-1987*
ISBN 90 6765 175 3 DFL. 35,00

WIL PANSTERS & ARIJ OUWENEEL, *Region, State and Capitalism in Mexico: Nineteenth and Twentieth Centuries.*
CLAS no. 54, 1989, pp. 232, English. DFL. 40,00

BENNO GALJART & PATRICIO SILVA, *Democratization and the State in the Southern Cone: Essays on South American Politics.*
CLAS no. 53, 1989, pp. 232, English. DFL. 37,50

ARIANE VAN BUREN, *The Woodfuel Market in Nicaragua: The Economics, Sociology, and Management of a Natural Energy Resource.*
CLAS no. 52, forthcoming.

HANS VAN DEN BERG, *"La tierra no da así no más": Los ritos agrícolas en la religión de los aymara-cristianos de los Andes.*
CLAS no. 51, 1989, pp. 312, Spanish. DFL. 45,00

ARIJ OUWENEEL, *Onderbroken groei in Anáhuac: de ecologische achtergrond van ontwikkeling en armoede op het platteland van Central-Mexico (1730-1810).*
CLAS no. 50, 1989, pp. 376, Dutch. DFL. 45,00

BERNARD SLICHER VAN BATH, *Hacienda Real en Hispano-américa.*
CLAS no. 49. 1989, Spanish. Forthcoming.

DAVID BROOKSHAW, *Paradise Betrayed. Brazilian Literature of the Indian.*
CLAS no. 48, 1989, pp. 260, English. DFL. 35,00

E. RENE BASTIAANS & JAN P. DE GROOT, *Agricultura Colectiva: Experiencias en la República Dominicana, Nicaragua y México.*
CLAS no. 47, 1989, pp. 192, Spanish. DFL. 32,50

E.B. ZOOMERS, *Rural Development and Survival Strategies in Central Paraguay*
CLAS no. 46, 1988, pp. 248, English. DFL. 32,50

ARIJ OUWENEEL y CRISTINA TORALES PACHECO, *Empresarios, indios y estado: Perfil de la economía mexicana (Siglo XVIII).*
CLAS no. 45, 1988, pp. 248, Spanish. DFL. 32.50

EDMUNDO MAGAÑA, *Orion y la mujer Pleyades: Simbolismo astronómico de los indios Kaliña de Surinam.* CLAS no. 44, 1988, pp. 392, Spanish. DFL. 42.50

GEERT BANCK & KEES KOONINGS, *Social Change in Contemporary Brazil.*
CLAS no. 43, 1988, pp. 228, English. DFL. 29,50

ARIE LAENEN, *Dinámica y transformación de la pequeña industria en Nicaragua.*
CLAS no. 42, 1988, pp. 424, Spanish. DFL. 49,50

J.M.G. KLEINPENNING, *Man and Land in Paraguay.*
CLAS no. 41, 1988, pp. 268, English. DFL. 29.50

ALLARD WILLEMIER WESTRA, *Axê, Kracht om te leven. Het gebruik van symbolen bij de hulpverlening in de Candomble-religie in Alagoinhas (Bahia, Brazilië).*
CLAS no. 40, 1987, pp. 290, Dutch. DFL. 29.50

ADELE G. VAN DER PLAS, *Revolution and criminal justice: the Cuban experiment, 1959-1983.* CLAS no. 39, 1987, pp. 338, English. DFL. 37.50

PATRICIO SILVA, *Estado, neoliberalismo y política agraria en Chile, 1973-1981.*
CLAS no. 38, 1987, pp. 364, Spanish. DFL. 37.50

ALFREDO A. CESAR DACHARY, *Producción colectiva y desarrollo capitalista en el agro mexicano (1970-1980).*
CLAS no. 37, 1987, pp. 335, Spanish. DFL. 37,50

LUCIO KOWARICK, *The subjugation of labour: The constitution of capitalism in Brazil.*
CLAS no. 36, 1987, pp. 126, English. DFL. 19,50

EDMUNDO MAGAÑA, *Contribuciones al estudio de la mitología y astronomía de los indios de las Guayanas.*
CLAS no. 35, 1987, pp. 306 + viii, 57 illustrations, Spanish. DFL. 35,00

EDMUNDO MAGAÑA & PETER MASON, (eds.), *Myth and the imaginary in the New World.*
CLAS no. 34, 1986, pp. 500, 64 illustrations, English/Spanish. DFL. 49,50

PETER A.G.M. DE SMET, *Ritual enemas and snuffs in the Americas.*
CLAS. no. 33, 1985, pp. 276, 72 illustrations, English. DFL. 49,50

GUILLERMO LABARCA, *Educación y sociedad: Chile 1964-1984.*
CLAS no. 32, 1985, pp. 145, Spanish. DFL. 19,50

ALEX E.FERNANDEZ JILBERTO, *Dictadura militar y oposición política en Chile (1973-1981).* CLAS no. 31, 1985, pp. 456, Spanish. DFL. 37,50

DAVID SLATER (ed.), *New social movements and the state in Latin America.*
CLAS no. 29, 1985, pp. 295, English. DFL. 30,00

Los pedidos deben dirigirse a/for information write to:

Center for Latin American Research & Documentation
Keizersgracht 395-397
1016 EK Amsterdam
The Netherlands/Países Bajos